THE TOURIST

THE TOURIST

TRAVEL IN TWENTIETH-CENTURY

NORTH AMERICA

John A. Jakle

UNIVERSITY OF NEBRASKA PRESS
LINCOLN AND LONDON

Library of Congress Cataloging in Publication Data
Jakle, John A.
    The tourist : travel in twentieth-century North
America.
    Bibliography: p.
    Includes index.
    1. Tourist trade—United States—History. I. Title.
G155.U6J33   1985   381'.45917304927   84–3698
ISBN 0-8032-2564-4

For Santa Fe, Vieux Carré, Put-in-Bay
For Mackinac and Saranac
Even Williamsburg and Gatlinburg
For Kennebunk

For Niagara-on-the-Lake and St. Andrews-by-the-Sea
For Mammoth Cave and Cades Cove
For Turkey Run and Jackson Hole
For Yellowstone

And all the other resorts large and small

CONTENTS

ILLUSTRATIONS

PREFACE

I present this book as an argument for renewed scholarly interest in tourism. Tourism is a nearly universal behavior in advanced, industrialized societies. Through firsthand observation in pleasurable circumstances, tourists explore the complexities of the world beyond everyday existence. Thus, tourism is a significant means by which modern people assess their world, defining their own sense of identity in the process. The study of tourism offers an important means of comprehending human sociability. Because tourism represents people's deliberate encounter with new places, it also provides excellent opportunity to study their cognitive relationship to landscape. Traditionally, touristic understandings have been characterized as superficial, and the real knowing of place said to lie with the natives. I argue that no widely shared human activity, irrespective of presumed superficialities, should be ignored. The role of tourism as a part of the modern world needs to be fully understood.

What follows is a description of tourists and tourism in early-twentieth-century North America. It explores a time and a place where the automobile popularized travel, spreading the advantages of tourism from society's elite to the masses. No longer did the railroads and steamship lines, and their resorts, dictate travel tastes. Motorists broke the bounds of city and town to roam the countryside in search of nature, region, and history. Across the fleeting fads and fashions of travel certain profound changes occurred. The highway and the commercial roadside, the new container for tourism, emerged as a new environmental form to influence, if not dominate, the whole of

North American life. The tourist's world became increasingly the everyday world of living and working. The same automobile that carried people on vacation also carried them to work and home again.

I argue that tourism was not merely a reflection of change. It was a precipitator of changing social values, especially as they reflected the automobile as an instrument of increased geographical mobility. Although pleasure driving was seldom espoused as the primary reason for building and improving highways, the automobile tourist, as a primary benefactor, supported highway improvement. Tourism created a favorable political environment for an expanded highway system and was a significant force behind North America's highway reorientation, the most significant environmental change to occur in the United States and Canada in this century. Thus, tourists traveled to validate the world around them: a world increasingly of their own making and a world viewed increasingly through an automobile windshield.

In this study, early chapters explore the universals of trip taking, including the manner in which motivation for travel found expression in the planning, executing, and recollecting of pleasure trips. Discussion focuses on the contrived tourist attractions as well as on the kinds of common places differentiated by tourists as work, cultural, and social displays. Emphasis is placed on the tourists' validation of place expectations, orientation to new places, and learning to play distinctive touristic roles. Subsequent chapters look at the various modes of travel available to tourists in the twentieth century and the broad categories of tourist attraction significant in North America. Travel by automobile is contrasted with travel by railroad and steamship, and by bus and airplane, although special emphasis is given to the modern highway as a new kind of travel environment. The tourists' quests for nature, region, city, and history are treated separately. The impulse toward nature spawned the continent's national parks, among other touristic landscapes. The search for regional peculiarity has always been a major generator of interest, especially in the West. Cities were also major tourist attractors, especially the metropolises. The search for the historical past pervaded tourism in all landscapes and in all places.

I offer my synthesis of a diverse literature concerned with travel in the early-twentieth-century United States and Canada. This book relies heavily on published diaries, journals, and travel books written by tourists, describing actual trips. In focusing on travelers' impressions, the following questions are asked: Who traveled and why? How and where did tourists travel? What did they see or experience? What kinds of landscapes and places did they find attractive? Since travelers' accounts constitute the basic raw material for this book, travelers speak directly to the reader through numerous quotations. It is hoped that the travelers' own words will give the reader a greater comprehension of past travel than is possible through my synthesis alone.

I have set limitations on my work. First, I do not attempt to treat all aspects of recreation. I focus on the taking of pleasure trips, where travelers are tourists, spending weeks rather than days away from home. Business trips, scientific expeditions, travel to second homes, and, indeed, the trips of sportsmen are largely ignored. Second, I take as my period of interest the years 1900–1960, although emphasis is given to the middle decades of the 1920s and 1930s. I do not pretend to describe all the changes that occurred in tourism beyond the effects of changing transportation emphasis. Tourism is discussed as only one way of knowing the world, a way substantially affected by the rise of automobile travel.

This book was written against a backdrop of declining geographical awareness in North America. There has been, in the twentieth century, a paradoxical rise of geographical ignorance when the educational establishment, not to mention the geographical profession, appeared destined to produce quite the reverse. The peculiar development of tourism is clearly implicated in this circumstance, although not alone to blame. Tourism has been transformed by speed and comfort in travel. The world seen from an automobile on a modern highway has become for many remote, standardized, uninteresting, and unrewarding in contemplation. Rather than exciting interest in landscape, tourism has tended to dull curiosity about places, a paradox indeed! This book explores the rise of modern tourism in North America in order to suggest how travel can be made more effective as an educator. It explores early-twentieth-century tourism in order to foster a comprehension of travel and an enhanced sense of place in our own time. Therein lies the purpose of this book: to make travel more effective by examining the roots of modern tourism.

CHAPTER ONE

INTRODUCTION

Travel is a vanishing act, a solitary trip down a pinched line of geography to oblivion. But a travel book is the opposite, the loner bouncing back bigger than life to tell the story of his experiment with space.

Paul Theroux, *The Old Patagonian Express*

Recreation, once merely the antithesis of work, became in the early twentieth century its necessary complement. Puritanism, writes the historian Foster Dulles, long imposed a religious sanction on work. "Idleness and play could have no place in a world where labor was the greatest good." Sociologist Max Kaplan notes that fundamentalist Christianity viewed man as serving God through work. Work was divine, whereas that which deviated from work was "imbued with human faults, frailties, and anti-religious potential." In nineteenth-century America, recreation for the masses was seen as restoring the capacity for work. It was part of that endless cycle, writes Dulles, wherein one labored to gain an opportunity to play and then played to labor more effectively. Business remained America's preoccupation, but no longer was it sport, work, pleasure, beauty, and patriotism rolled into one, as a British visitor to the United States had commented. By 1960 the American industrial workers enjoyed an additional day of leisure every week beyond the free time they had enjoyed in the 1920s, and they had twice as many hours for recreation as they had had in the 1890s. Compared to the previous century, leisure time had increased from some ten hours a week to more than seventy.[1] Increased leisure brought mass tourism in its wake.

Tourists and Tourism

Tourism is a state of mind. The pleasure trip is an act of being in the world tied to pleasurable sensations. It offers necessary relaxation from everyday routines and escape from the

1

commonplace. But tourism also connects the tourists with the highly complex world around them. It serves as a way of relating to a highly specialized, impersonal society that cannot be understood solely on the basis of everyday work and other activities. According to Kaplan, people search out other people in leisure because informality provides a psychological and emotional release from conscious normal social roles: "In a social situation with no functional or productive significance we purposely expose ourselves in terms of our 'real' selves and 'break through' others, seeing them for what they 'really are.' " The act of sightseeing draws the tourist into a relationship with the modern world as a social totality. Anthropologist Dean Mac-Cannell writes: "As a worker, the individual's relationship to his society is partial and limited, secured by a fragile 'work ethic,' and restricted to a single position among millions in the division of labor." As a tourist, the individual may step out into the "universal drama of modernity," grasp the division of labor as a "phenomenon *sui generis*," and become a moral witness of its "masterpieces of virtue and viciousness."[2]

Self-identity comes not out of isolation, but out of interaction with others, for individuality is tested among other people. It is this dimension which separates touristic from other forms of experiencing the world. Television, motion pictures, magazines, and newspapers represent a passive, distant involvement with other people in other places, as does formal schooling when restricted to classroom and library. The world is brought to us. In tourism we are freer to explore the unexpected, to face experiences directly and immediately through our senses, unedited by other minds.[3] Tourism is a vital form of social orientation embedded in a recreational or leisure aspect. Touristic understanding of oneself and one's world may be no more accurate than that obtained by other means, but it may be more significant because it appears more trustworthy. Tourism is voluntary as it is pleasurable. It cannot be coerced nor can its derived insights be coerced.[4] In tourism, seeing for oneself is believing.

Tourists have been widely accused of shallowness. The naturalist John Muir, whose distaste for the tourist in the wilder western landscapes of America led to his founding of the Sierra Club, admitted that tourism had some value. He recognized certain gains from his stagecoach trip through Yellowstone— the acquaintances made and the fresh views into human nature. The wilderness was a shrewd touchstone, even when lightly approached, and brought many a curious trait into view. "Where is the umbrella?" ' "What is the name of that blue flower over there?" "Are you sure the little bag is aboard?" "Is that hollow yonder a crater?" "How high did you say the geysers spout?" Not all travel was spontaneous and self-assured. Touring could be staid, and patently false. The author Henry Miller, commenting on fellow passengers met on trains and airplanes, wrote: "We do not talk—we bludgeon one another with facts and theories gleaned from cursory readings of newspapers, magazines, and digests."[5] Tourism, for its potential to educate, could also elicit habitual behavior stultifying to real comprehension. Tourism could produce stereotyped understanding.

The study of tourism, like the study of recreation generally, has not been recognized by most professions as a respectable field for scholarly inquiry.[6] Apart from the bias against leisure inherent in the work ethic, the supposed superficiality of touristic experience has weighed against serious study. The very words *tourist* and *tourism* carry negative connotations. The geographer Edward Relph sees tourism as an "inauthentic attitude to place," since judgments about places are nearly always preempted by generally accepted opinion. To Relph, the act or means of tourism becomes more important than the places or the people visited because tourists are too preoccupied with themselves to be objective about place. Sociologist Eric Cohen notes that tourists have been stereotyped as quaintly dressed, camera-toting strangers who are ignorant, passive, gullible, and shallow. As a visitor's guide to New Orleans warns, "A tourist is a peeker into private doings, a gawker at buildings, a person who appears thoroughly eager to be scandalized . . . a bane to civilization."[7]

The tourist's evaluation of place is usually aesthetic— and it is usually an outsider's view.[8] The tourists as strangers cannot possibly know a locality as a resident might, and thus the

3

tourists' knowledge and their capabilities may appear superficial. Nonetheless, tourists may be more appreciative of a locality's picturesque or romantic qualities than locals stuck in more utilitarian mind-sets. As seekers after novelty, tourists tend to focus on the unique qualities of place, especially scenic qualities, and they may see much that is little appreciated by locals, or not seen at all.

Although tourists are usually derided as a class, there are, in fact, many kinds of tourists. Max Kaplan differentiates between two extremes: comparative strangers and emphatic natives. Comparative strangers travel physically but never, or seldom, change familiar viewpoints. They find security wherever they go by applying their usual standards to new situations. They view, but do not understand. They do not see first and then define, but define first and then see. Emphatic natives seek by putting themselves in the place of those with whom they visit. They go native as much as possible. They seek new viewpoints and use these viewpoints to redefine themselves and their world. Most tourists fit somewhere in between Kaplan's two poles. Indeed, a tourists' behavior may swing back and forth between poles in the context of a given trip, a given day en route, or a given place visited.[9]

Eric Cohen identifies five modes of tourist experience, listed in ascending order from the most superficial to the most profound. The "recreational mode" is a quest for entertainment, and tourists act as if they are attending a performance or participating in a game. Pleasure is contingent upon their willingness to accept the make-believe, or to half-seriously delude themselves into accepting contrived situations. Landscapes seen are not part of the "real world." According to the historian Daniel Boorstin, such tourists experience places as "pseudo-events." Tourists become accomplices in the production of their own deceptions. Cohen's "diversionary mode" is escapist. Tourists travel, changing location, but they may continue acting very much as they do at home. Only the place changes, bringing with it superficial novelties. In the "experiential mode" tourists seek meaning in the lives of others by searching for experiences beyond the limits of their own everyday realms. Such experiences are lived vicariously from a distance, and for

short periods of time. In the "experimental mode" new life-
styles are adopted for short periods. In the "existential mode"
tourists cease being tourists and commit themselves to another
way of life completely external to the mainstream of their own
native society. They reject their own social reality indefinitely.
Recreational and diversionary orientations to travel may be
largely visual or scenic, whereas experiential, experimental,
and existential modes may carry stronger extrascenic dimensions. In the latter, social interaction with locals becomes increasingly important, ultimately overwhelming sightseeing as
a travel impulse.[10]

Psychologist Kenneth Craik argues for scholarly focus
on tourist role playing, including the way role expectations develop, the manner of role acquisition, and the development of
role-playing skills. He encourages emphasis on "role location,"
the cues to place that locate persons in touristic roles. Tourist
places should be understood as behavior settings, with clear
behavioral expectations attached through role playing.[11] What
are the beliefs and attitudes that different kinds of tourists
attach to different kinds of places? How are these places cued, or
symbolized, in the landscape? What are the prevailing icons of
place through which touristic meanings are communicated?

The Pleasure Trip

"A trip is an entity," wrote the novelist John Steinbeck.
"It has personality, temperament, individuality, uniqueness."
Trips are "things in themselves," he continued. The pleasure
trip lies at the heart of tourism. It is the principal process alluded
to by Kaplan and MacCannell whereby tourists differentiate
and validate the world beyond the everyday. It provides the
mechanism for touristic role playing emphasized by Craik. The
pleasure trip is a means by which individuality is forged, human nature observed, and places experienced. Pleasure trips
do not correspond to the whole of tourism. They serve only the
"recreational," "diversionary," and "experiential" modes of
travel identified by Cohen. Pleasure trips are important to Kaplan's "comparative strangers," but not to his "emphatic
natives."[12] The taking of pleasure trips, nonetheless, constitutes for most tourists the essence of tourism.

The importance of tourism is evidenced by the wide range of motivations that twentieth-century travelers assigned to traveling. As a form of recreation, travel was ego enhancing. Tourists had a sense of repairing internal mechanisms, of replenishing wells run dry. The pleasure trip provided opportunities to enrich, regenerate, recharge.[13] Almost all tourists sought rest and relaxation. Writing of her trip as "a delicious experience of sheer luxury" and "a paradise of freedom and delight," Zephine Humphrey emphasized travel's shirking of every day responsibilities. A retired couple traveling from New Hampshire to spend the winter in California, the Humphreys spent time leisurely. For Zephine there was no cooking or house cleaning; there was no telephone to answer. Most days she did not know fully where she was, nor did she care. Travel was her reward; its balm soaked into her spirit, refreshing her; it brought escape from the drudgery of place. No longer was there a sense of being bound by established scenes and routines. Tensions build between people and places, which only travel can release. Feelings of being tied to tedious tasks and of being preoccupied with basic necessities prompts travel. Steinbeck on his trip across the United States saw this impulse in the faces of people he met. It was a "burning desire to go, to move, to get under way, any place, away from any Here." People spoke to him of "how they wanted to go someday, to move about, free and unanchored, not toward something but away from something."[14]

Travel offered a change of scene, a pull as well as a push. New places promised stimulation as well as relaxation. The novelist Theodore Dreiser could think of nothing more suited to his temperament than automobiling, for it supplied just that mixture of change that satisfied him—and left him mentally poised in inquiry. Dreiser thrived on moving slowly from place to place, sampling the novelties of succeeding localities. Old routines pursued in new places also could transcend feelings of isolation or ineffectiveness at home. Personal needs unfulfilled at home could be satisfied away from home, if only temporarily.[15]

Travel could be educational. As Daniel Boorstin observed, "Travel has been the universal catalyst. It has made men think faster, imagine longer, want more passionately." The promoters of early automobile travel saw the motor car as an educational device. The automobile compelled knowledge, first of one's locality, then of one's state, and finally of one's nation, since the network of new highways was an invitation to wider and wider horizons. Travel inspired cultural nationalism by way of education. Recollecting a transcontinental auto trip, Frederic Van de Water wrote, "To us America no longer is an abstract noun, or a familiar map of patchwork, or a flag, or a great domed building in Washington. It is something clearer. . . . It is the road we traveled."[16]

There are some things best learned by traveling. "Of these one is geography," wrote David Steele, whose book *Going Abroad Overland* sought to entice Americans to "See America First." "There is a certain sense of location, a familiarity with things as they are; a feeling of identity and reality which can never come in any other way save from the seeing of them." Travel was an opportunity to validate expectations about places. Winifred Dixon set out to see whether the American West lived up to billing. She sought to see what lay behind such intriguing place names as Needles, Moab, Skull Valley, Fort Apache, Ten Sleep, Winnemucca. Was Skull Valley a desolate outpost with night riders, stampeding steers, gold seekers, cattle thieves, and painted ladies; or had it achieved virtue in a Rexall drugstore, a Fred Harvey lunchroom, a jazz parlor, a chamber of commerce, an Elks Club?[17]

Travel was the experiencing of place. With experience tourists could learn to read landscapes visited as they might read a book. Christopher Morley's way of being in the world serves to illustrate. Morley, a journalist and writer of humorous essays, focused on his native Philadelphia. He found himself able to travel extensively without leaving the city. "I am a confirmed saunterer," he wrote. "I love to be set down haphazard among unknown byways; to saunter with open eyes, watching the moods and humors of men, the shapes of their dwellings, the crisscross of their streets. It is an implanted passion that grows keener and keener. The everlasting lure of round-the-corner, how fascinating it is!" Morley made notes on what he encountered: lists of shops and names of tradesmen, or the repartees of children playing in the streets. Why? It amused him. "From now until the end of time no one else will ever see life with my eyes, and I mean to make the most of my chance."[18]

Travel has always been a call to adventure even in the most comfortable of circumstances. Irvin Cobb traveled west in Mark Twain's footsteps to write *Roughing It Deluxe*. He roughed it on the overland trains and he roughed it in the luxury hotels. "We were a daring lot and resolute; each and every one of us was brave and blithe to endure the privations." Even if tourism by 1913 buffered the traveler from real privation, travel still contained difficulties from which a fabric of adventure could be woven. Travel was a sacrifice of home, ease, and peace. Leaving home was, itself, an obstacle to be overcome, a proving of one's character. As adventure was little more than risk taking, all tourists took a chance at uprooting and going elsewhere. Once conquered, difficulties en route marked the true mettle of tourists as adventurers. Emily Post, whose early book, *By Motor to the Golden Gate,* launched her career as social commentator, noted that difficult experiences and disappointments provide a trip's remembered high spots. "Your misadventures afterwards become your most treasured memories."[19]

Some people acted out youthful fantasies through travel. Waldron Webb's trip to Isle Royale in Michigan was rooted in his childhood reading about prehistoric America with its "ancient and mysterious" copper mines. He had promised himself that someday he would go to the Lake Superior Island, and in middle age he was still fascinated by "that spot on the map," for it was still an "isle of dreams." Webb also revisited places previously important in his life to practice a kind of watchfulness, reminding him of who he was. He lingered by the river in his hometown, Bay City, Michigan. It was the river that had excited his youthful wanderlust, its water "flowing into the mysterious beyond" toward the unattainable world that lived in "entrancing, half-understood books."[20] Travel provided opportunities for withdrawing from everyday adult obligations, indulging childish or adolescent dreams, and reenacting youthful memories.

Introduction

Sociability was an enticement to tour. Companionship was an important travel motivation, and most pleasure trips involved two or more people. Experiencing new places was important, but so also was the sharing of that experience. Traveling companions needed to be carefully chosen, because, as Beatrice Massey warns in her travel book, *It Might Have Been Worse*, "If you wish to really know people, travel with them." The family was the most common touring unit. Travel could draw a family closer together. Since regular social contacts were broken, the family was thrust into an inwardly focused social world. However, broken routines and the need to modify behavior could strain family relations, even fostering feelings of restlessness and insecurity. Although many tourists systematically sought out local people in new places, typically most socializing enroute was with fellow tourists, if not with immediate traveling companions. Henry Miller, on the other hand, deliberately traveled to cultivate other people. In recollecting trips, he identified the most beautiful woman, the most masterful individual, the best adjusted person, the person happiest in his work.[21]

Quest for social status long has been a prime mover of tourists. "One goes, not so much to see but to tell afterward," observed John Steinbeck. Early in the twentieth century only an affluent, leisured class could travel extensively as tourists. Being affluent and visiting exotic places set one apart from the common herd. In 1901, Bernard McEvoy found the Banff Springs Hotel in Alberta swarming with American millionaires and their wives. "Confessing that they don't know what to do with their money now they've got it," he wrote, "they are going to every place they ever heard of, irrespective of expense or distance, and not much enjoying it either." Charles Finger encountered status seekers throughout the American West of the 1930s: "These are people, mostly the stupid rich, who, visiting a round of hotels, go about . . . seeing nothing and experiencing nothing." These people systematically excluded the unexpected and the novel by determining beforehand what they would see and do and who they would meet. "To appear, not to Be[,] is their aim," he observed.[22] With the coming of mass automobile ownership after World War I, travel was less the exclusive preserve of the well-to-do, and middle-class Americans sought to identify with exotic places also.

People's rationales for taking specific trips varied. Trips might be tied to business affairs, attending conventions, quests for health, visiting friends and relatives. The search for environmental amenities was important. Warm winters and cool summers have attracted tourist migrations seemingly always. But beneath the gloss of specific rationales lay more basic motivations equally as varied, often complimentary, and sometimes contradictory. These motivations were rooted in tourists' sense of being, their quest for distinction, and their search for fulfillment. Travel could refresh through relaxation and pleasure. It could spice life through excitement, through variety, or, at the very least, through change. Touring could be instructive and intellectually rewarding, especially when new places or new kinds of places were encountered. Touring added a degree of risk, a sense of challenge, to life. Travel tested the individual's sense of belonging to community. It enabled self-confirmation through various degrees of socialization enroute, and through a heightened sense of homecoming. Travel sparked the acting out of fantasies. No one motivation was ever predominate, since motivations always worked their magic in subtle combinations of wanderlust.

Marion Clawson divides the recreational experience into five parts: anticipation; travel to site; leisure activity; return home; and recollection.[23] Embracing the work of ethologists concerned with animal movement, I have recast Clawson's categorization into eight successive stages: predisposition to travel; trip preparation; departure; outward movement; turnabout; homeward movement; return; and trip recollection.[24] Trips thus viewed unfold in patterns of sequenced events. What is experienced in travel is, in part, a result of the trip-taking sequence.

Pleasure trips began with the recognized need to be somewhere else. Interest was aroused, and the decision made to travel, in response to a variety of stimuli, including the advice of friends, scenes glimpsed in motion pictures, and even scenes remembered from school geography lessons. Advertisements and articles in newspapers and magazines also excited the travel imagination. Emily Post conceived her 1915 transcontinental trip by reading motor car advertisements. Articles depicting the nomadic, carefree existence of automobile campers suggested to Melville Ferguson his year-long camping trip from New Jersey to California and Hawaii in 1924. Travel books promoted tourism. Emily Post's travel book prompted both Beatrice Massey and James Flagg to travel West and to write their own books that encouraged others to follow in turn.[25] In this predisposition stage, deep-seated motivations, immediate travel rationales, and an aroused interest in distant places came together in a decision to travel.

Planning the itinerary and tending to logistics could consume as much if not more time than the actual trip. One traveler wrote, "We wouldn't have missed that year of planning. The pleasure it gave us, poring over guidebooks, maps and catalogues almost equalled the pleasure of the trip itself." Emily Post telegraphed the Lincoln Highway Association in Detroit for information on western highways, but they could only refer her to another New Yorker who had driven west the previous year. She visited the Automobile Club, but they knew nothing about western roads. She bought maps of the United States, including one with four routes boldly marked, each route equally black and straight, and uninformative as shown. She wrote to friends in Nebraska who told her not to take the trip, at least by automobile. Logistical arrangements were equally important. For Beatrice Massey and her husband their trip meant leasing their house for a year, storing their household goods, closing up business matters, buying camping equipment, and servicing the car. Preparation caused anxiety as well as anticipation. Steinback commented: "In long-range planning for a trip, I think there is a private conviction that it won't happen. As the day approached, my warm bed and comfortable house grew increasingly desirable . . . I didn't want to go. Something had to happen to forbid my going, but it didn't."[26]

With friends and others looking on, departure becomes a ritual. Apart from that, it was a quiet slipping away from the safety and comfort of home into the relative unknown. Departure caused exhilaration at starting something new, at beginning an adventure. Emily Post drove up Park Avenue, her open touring car packed to overflowing. "We felt very selfimportant; it even seemed that people ought to cheer us." Ritual leavings enhanced the significance of a trip. The farewell party or the crowded railroad platform, with kissing, hugging, tears, smiles, handshaking, and good-byes, afforded a truly proper beginning. Nathan Ashe was given a farewell party. He wrote: "I had proudly exhibited my yards of ticket; women had smiled and men had been envious, and at one in the morning I had kissed everyone good-bye and had climbed into the bus."[27]

Anticipation accompanied the outwardbound trip. Travel became a process of renouncing home, and of eagerly embracing new places. At first, tourists demonstrated degrees of awkwardness as they learned new roles as travelers. They must refamiliarize themselves with the routine of railroad depots, bus stations, or airports; or, they must master again the art of long-distance driving. A degree of nervousness and uncertainty could render careless decisions. Having chosen poor accommodations her first night, Zephine Humphrey lay awake revisiting in her mind "every familiar beloved nook" at home. "Home! Why had we ever left its serene, unhaunted rooms?" At a trip's beginning, tourists tended to overindulge, to test and try novel situations of travel. Not more than forty minutes out of New York, Emily Post's party stopped to picnic. California was six thousand miles away, but out came the silver tea set, and a full-scale meal was launched upon the wayside.[28]

The outward-bound trip tended to amplify travel as an experience. Tourists sought deliberate place encounters since the freshness and novelty of travel excited heightened awareness of the passing scene. Automobile tourists, for example, might proceed more slowly at the beginning of a trip, lingering here and there, as if to satisfy at once pent-up travel anticipation. The outward-bound movement carried a sense of euphoria and exhilaration.[29] Charles Finger noted that in leaving he had "torn up roots" and "flung aside responsibilities," but rather than feeling a sense of foreboding, he knew "nothing except adventurous exhilaration." He had a felt sense of urgency. "There is a world to be seen, and, for the seeing, our days are not too many, nor too long."[30] At first, the business of touring commanded full attention, but eventually the satiated travelers lost interest. Travel was no longer novel or, seemingly, so important.

Clare Gunn, in his book on designing tourist regions, likened travel to music, where periods of prelude are followed by main themes, the tempo gradually increasing to a climax. The outward-bound movement ended when the sense of climax was reached and the sense of moving away from home became a feeling of return. Most trips were conducted as a series of sequences, from one destination to another, with one place serving as turning point. Sometimes the climax was anticipated and even planned. "I did not consider our trip really ended until we stood on the sands of the Pacific," wrote Beatrice Massey. Sometimes the point farthest from home served as a real as well as a psychological goal. Otherwise, travelers stumbled or blundered upon the "turnabout" as they tired of traveling and began to think seriously of home. Some travelers paused before their goal. "We rested up for a day, had the car cleaned and oiled, and had ourselves laundered, shampooed, and manicured, starting refreshed and full of expectation on our last lap to the Yellowstone." Some tourists lingered at the goal refreshed and not wanting fully to commit to a homeward trek. Edward Dunn's party stayed on at a South Dakota dude ranch instead of heading home. "We indulged in 'last rides' and 'last walks,' and dawdled the last morning away."[31]

For most tourists the homeward trip represented a time of diminished adventure. The excitement and exhilaration of travel slowly subsided until some recognized threshold of diminishing return loomed clear and dominant; then the pace of travel usually accelerated, resulting in a dash for home. John Steinbeck wrote: "I was driving myself, pounding out the miles because I was no longer hearing or seeing. I had passed my limit of taking in." Steinbeck's trip was over long before he reached his Long Island home. "The way was a gray, timeless, eventless tunnel." Many travelers experienced a sense of increasing discomfort both caused by and contributive to a longing for the comforts of home. As Julian Street, a widely read author of travel books, noted, his heels were running down in back, his watch needed regulating, his umbrella handle was coming loose, his razors were dull, his strop was nicked, and he had run out of the cigars he liked. His suits were spotted, baggy and worn and his travelers checks were running low.[32] Although a return trip could stand as an anticlimax, there was still a reluctance for tourists to return by their original paths. This pattern was especially true in automobile travel. Such reluctance to double back upon already trodden ground opened the way for continued adventure even in the face of travel weariness.

For the automobile tourists, the return was usually a private affair. The grime of travel, the wrinkled clothing, the disarray of baggage, the irritability, and the fatigue were potentially embarrassing. But travelers by rail, bus, or air could not enjoy anonymity. Depot or airport rituals of welcome echoed those of departure, with friends, relatives, and onlookers at hand. Many travelers indulged in ceremonies of approach and entry at home. Zephine Humphrey laid the tattered oilcloth used in camping on their dining room table. "The simple meal which we ate there had a sacramental quality," she wrote.[33] Return brought a sense of deliverance, and a confrontation with one's life undone. Returnees had to face the assumption of normal routines.

Trips live on in memory. Clawson and Knetsch speculate that many people obtain greater satisfaction from recollecting trips than from actually taking them. Such satisfaction may accrue more to people who travel in search of increased social status. Nevertheless, all tourists relive travel memories. With time, unpleasantries slake away to leave a residue of happy recollections. Here is a reservoir of thought to sustain travelers through the routine and commonplace of life. Here is a background of experience against which to anticipate the next pleasure trip. "There is a hinterland of consciousness," wrote Frederic Van de Water, "where remembered beauty dwells. It is a preserve into which the human mind may retire, to emerge heartened and sustained by the recollections harbored there."[34] Souvenirs collected sustain memories. Indeed, trips might be taken primarily to collect souvenirs: clothing, china, art, antiques. Not only were postcards mailed to friends and relatives as a means of sharing travel experiences, but when collected, they served to jog the memory of trips relived. So also did snapshots serve. Some tourists traveled primarily to photograph attractions, to capture materially places experienced.

The pleasure trip was a sequential endeavor from predisposition to trip recollection. All tourists passed through these phases. Few were fully conscious of the unwinding drama. Some tourists resisted the inevitable flow of events; others flowed with them. Perhaps, as one traveler noted, "Sightseeing comes naturally to some people, like marriage. They go at it without practice and profess to enjoy it, though without explaining why."[35] Trip sequencing influenced what was seen on a trip. More important, it influenced what was remembered. Places encountered early on a trip might seem more vivid than those encountered late. Many things are not seen or experienced at all, being encountered at an inappropriate time in the trip-taking sequence.

Successful pleasure trips required a sense of timing. Tourists not only abided the sequential phases of a trip but also had to respect the daily rhythms operative. The course of the day, with its varying light conditions, combined with growing body fatigue and recurrent hunger pangs. Sinclair Lewis described a summer day's travel across the Great Plains in his novel *Free Air*. For Claire Boltwood, Lewis' heroine:

> Driving, just the actual getting on, was her purpose in life, and the routine of driving was her order of the day: morning freshness, rolling up as many miles as possible before lunch, that she might loaf afterward. The invariable 2 P.M. discovery that her eyes ached, and the donning of huge amber glasses. . . . Toward night, the quarter-hour of level sun-glare which prevented her seeing the road. Dusk, and the discovery of how much light there was after all, once she remembered to take off her glasses. The mystic moment when night clicked tight, and the lamps made a fan of gold . . . Clare . . . settled down to plodding content, and no longer had to take the trouble of admiring the scenery![36]

Each day had its highs and lows. In the morning, travelers unlimbered, refreshed once preliminary chores were done. Frederic Van de Water wrote of camping: "One is grumpy at 6 A.M. One yearns for food at once, heartening, horizon-brightening food, followed by the soothing magic of tobacco." But first there was the tent to take down and stow away, blankets to fold, and beds to deflate. For Van de Water, morning was a grisly time filled with bungling and temper-lacerating mistakes. The early morning mists seemed to seep into his brain and clog his mentality. The period after lunch was a time of reduced vigor. "Lunch, however light, invariably made the expedition sleepy. The food and the warmth, the wind and the road sliding externally toward us, exerted an almost irresistible hypnosis." Fatigue increased with the passing day, fostering depression in most travelers. From about four o'clock each afternoon Zephine Humphrey was beset with homesickness. "The sun was sinking, night was at hand, we were tired, and had no idea where we should sleep. Experience had not encouraged a habit of complete confidence . . . [and] tomorrow looked far away."[37]

Night was a time for rest, a time to revitalize for an ensuing day. It was a time to rethink a day's adventures. Theodore Dreiser lay in a wayside hotel in rural Pennsylvania listening to the night. He could hear a train whistling and rumbling faintly far off. "I lay there thinking what a fine thing it was to motor in this haphazard fashion; how pleasant it was not to know where you were going or where you would be tomorrow." For Winifred Dixon, one day's drive over a rugged mountain road formed a part of one night's sleep. "And so to bed, and to dream I had driven the car to the third floor of our hotel. . . . I awoke to find both feet pressed hard against the footboard of the bed."[38]

Timing influenced substantially what was seen on a trip and what was remembered afterward. Morning freshness on an outward journey usually helped to make vivid place impressions. Conversely, afternoon or evening fatigue on a return journey often seemed to wipe part of the record clean. Steinbeck, who traveled with his dog, Charley, to collect impressions for a travel book, wrote of his homeward dash: "Up to Abingdon, Virginia, I can reel back the trip like film. I have almost total recall, every face is there, every hill and tree and color, and sound of speech and small scenes ready to replay themselves in my memory. After Abingdon—nothing."[39]

Travel Books as a Data Source

Like tourism, travel description has been little valued as a form of literature. Daniel Boorstin notes that twentieth-century travel books are records, not of new information, as travelers encountered new lands, but merely of personal reactions to know places. "People go to see what they already know is there. The only thing to record, the only possible source of surprise, is their own reaction." According to Boorstin, railroad and automobile travel were contrived and lacked real challenge. People moved too rapidly through localities to derive anything but superficial impressions. Tourists were passive because they expected interesting things to happen to them. They were isolated from the landscapes they traversed.[40] Boorstin may have exaggerated the differences between nineteenth- and twentieth-century travel. True, travel differed in degree of hardship and speed, but the character of the touristic experience was very much the same. Travelers once moved more slowly through landscapes, but they were also more preoccupied with the logistics of travel, and travel logistics distracted from knowing places. In addition, slow travel tended to blur differences from place to place, dulling place experience. Travel has always seemed superficial for one very important reason; place images derived through travel are always stereotyped.[41] Differences between nineteenth- and twentieth-century travel appear to be only differences of degree, and not of kind.

Nevertheless, twentieth-century travelers believed themselves inferior to their nineteenth-century counterparts. Emily Post, for example, apologized for her travel book. Only permanent residents of a place could be qualified to "present its picture." She wrote: "The observations of a transient tourist are necessarily superficial, as of one whose experiences are merely a series of instantaneous impressions; at one time colored perhaps too vividly, at another fogged." Nor could automobilists, such as herself, claim adventure in improved highways and hotels with steamheat, electric lights, and private baths.

Post could not conceive of automobile travelers in the same league with explorers and pioneers. Nevertheless, her car did disintegrate on Arizona's primitive roads, necessitating its shipment to Los Angeles by railroad. On at least one night her party slept sitting in their open car because they couldn't reach a town, let alone a hotel. [42] Her adventures were symptomatic of her times.

Authors of travel books seem obligated to self-ridicule. For example, Mark Pepys admitted to writing "merely a tally of simple happenings." His book was like a charcoal drawing "made with a few quick strokes," as opposed to a finished painting. [43] At issue was the basic fact that travelers, always outsiders, assumed themselves subordinate to local views. Tourists only sketched, but locals painted. Of course, locals do not know of the experience of travel until they themselves become travelers. Unless they do travel, for lack of true comparative base, they cannot really know their own localities. Insiders' view are not necessarily better than those of outsiders, —only different. Both views are necessary to the knowing of places because both views differ in complementary ways.

Earl Pomeroy, the historian of tourism in the American West, senses the significance of travel when he writes of travel books like Emily Post's *By Motor to the Golden Gate*. The popularity of books descriptive of auto adventuring fell off rapidly with the coming of mass automobile ownership and improved highways. "Within one short decade," Pomeroy writes, "trips that had been worth a book depreciated to the value of a newspaper item, and the dangers of the West with them." As a result, Pomeroy observes, we lose the tourist as a personality. He regrets this "decline of the tourist as witness," for the tourist "merges into the average American as the places he tours merge into the average America." To Pomeroy, the tourist's orientation was an important viewpoint lost to self-depreciation. [44]

Books on travel suffer as literature. W. H. Auden wrote: "Of all possible subjects, travel is the most difficult for an artist, as it is the easiest for a journalist." For the journalist the interesting event is the new, the extraordinary, the comic, the shocking. All the traveler, as journalist, requires is to be on the spot where and when events occur. Meaning, relationship, importance need not be his objective. The artist, on the other hand, writes Auden, is deprived of his most treasured liberty, the freedom to invent. "Successfully to extract importance from historical personal events without ever departing from them, free only to select and never to modify or to add calls for imagination of a very high order."[45] Travel, disparaged as inauthentic, the tourist depreciated as superficial, and his writings criticized as nonliterary, tourism suffers a quiet scholarly neglect.

The essayist Henry Canby identifies four prevailing modes of travel writing: the romantic, the adventurous, the anecdotal, and the informational. If arranged in a pyramid, the successive cross sections would indicate their relative numbers. At base are the "romantic" books. Here an author crams up on an area, "like an undergraduate cramming for an examination," and then "empties his notes into a manuscript." Although it may seem a harmless way to pay for a vacation trip and get published, the written results are rarely honest since the places that the author describes must have a lure and thus he sentimentalizes. Such books are often the result of the uncritical piling up of legend and fact. Mary Winn's *The Macadam Trail*, a story of a transcontinental bus trip, serves as example. Winn contrived to bus through or near areas she desired to describe. Between Dayton and Cincinnati she mused over the prehistoric past of the "Mound Builder's Land." At Vincennes, Indiana, where she stopped for lunch, she emphasized New Harmony forty miles to the south, and that town's history of communistic societies. Her trip stood as a search for romance. She confided: "For every main street, with its white lights, new pavements, machine-like uniformity, and nudity of tradition, America has a hundred obscure thoroughfares and quiet, almost unnoticed, localities where romance has flowered."[46]

Most "adventure" books are only slightly less fervid and more honest. An author, thrown into some out-of-the-way place, returns full of surprising information. Mary Hitchcock's *Two Women in the Klondike* provides an example. Leaving Seattle, Hitchcock and another woman traveled by steamer to the mouth of the Yukon River in Alaska. Four weeks later they were deposited by riverboat in the raw gold-mining town of Dawson in Yukon Territory. The book reads as a detailed description of day-to-day experiences in a male-dominated, and hence alien, place for women. With winter rapidly closing in, the two travelers continued on to Whitehorse by steamer and on foot crossed White Pass to Skagway. The book's editor commented in its preface: "The narrative of their daily life in that terrible Wonderland of the North is of itself not only a tribute to their own perseverance and determination, but to the character of intelligent and fearless Anglo-Saxon women who among all sorts and conditions of men, never fail to secure protection and respect."[47] If the natives were queer enough, the adventures surprising, and the country little known, then an adventure was worth publishing.

"Anecdotal" travel books carry a touch of the autobiographical. The traveler moves, exposing himself in the narrative as much as the places he visits. But as Canby observes, for a successful book of this type the author must have a personality that draws other personalities. The author must be able to thrust himself into situations with interesting people. Ideally, he must be also in the swirl of unusual—even sensational—events. Rarely do personalities and events adequately combine, concludes Canby, for books often dissolve into mere "ambulatory memoirs." Jonathan Daniels's book *A Southerner Discovers New England* serves to illustrate. Daniels sought to discover New England through its people, something that New England authors had been doing with the South and southerners for generations. Daniels wrote: "I not only looked and saw; I talked and listened. And the New England which makes this book is not so much mine as it is the land of those who told it to me. They were Yale professors, and solid men of [Boston's] State Street and Post Office Square, and bums and farmers and fishermen, and a fireman who had been a fisherman, even (when he was young) a whaler." Daniels's New England ran from "a filling station on the Westchester County line to Joe Guerette's beer joint just this side of the St. John River bridge in Madawaska [Maine]."[48]

According to Canby, "informational" travel books, especially travel guides, are not literary and they are unimaginative, serving only as dependable repositories for facts about places. Any relationship to the living world is usually iconographic. Writing usually dissolves into direction giving. "The facts are there," he observes, "but the facts themselves may mean nothing, else we should be content ourselves never to travel." Edward Dunn, a New York playwright, should have done better by his *Double Crossing America by Motor*, an itinerary of a trip to Hollywood in search of movie scripts to write. Of Virginia, he says, "The view approaching the Shenandoah Valley is magnificent, and the ride along the Shenandoah, after turning left at New Market, is one long to be remembered." He continues tritely, "The Hollyhock Inn at New Market is small but unusually good. The meals are excellent."[49]

Few travel books are written entirely in a single mode. The better books will have facts enough, adventure (if it happened), anecdotes (if they are relevant), and romance (if romance there was), but they will be written for none of these things alone. The good book, Canby writes, "will be an achievement, because good travel should be an achievement; it will be an exhibition of the art of geography."[50] Written travel impressions are the tourist's record of recollection. They derive from the writer's reliving of a pleasure trip so that others might share experiences. Travel books are a most important archive of travel recollection, a prime resource for comprehending travel experience. The travel literature not only exposes past travel motivations and illustrates past pleasure trips from the stage of anticipation to completion, but provides role models for future traveling. The reader, as armchair tourist, travels vicariously. Patterns of thought and action are internalized in anticipation of one's own touring. Travel as a means of experiencing the world is formulated and reformulated. Travel books contain both the fruits and the seeds of traveling.

What follows in subsequent chapters is a synthesis of the principal books published on North American travel over the first six decades of the twentieth century. I focus on the predominant images of travel, taking differences in writing style and trip-sequencing into account. I emphasize the principal kinds of place experiences recorded, placing images in the context of travel motivation. Above all, the taking of pleasure trips is treated as a kind of role playing central to tourism in its various recreational, diversionary, and experiential modes. Tourism, itself, is treated as an activity necessary to people's sense of identity in a complicated and potentially confusing modern world. Tourism is seen not only as a means of verifying the world first hand, but as a form of verification both spontaneous and mixed with pleasure in recreation: a mix that renders touristic insights trustworthy. I emphasize tourism not merely as a superficial spending of leisure time, although tourism has its superficial dimensions, but, rather, as a form of social glue that binds modern society together. Tourism is a principal means by which modern people define for themselves a sense of identity.

CHAPTER TWO
TOURISTS IN THE LANDSCAPE

> We boiled an egg in the Frying Pan Hot Spring, watched artists
> painting the Yellowstone Canyon . . . rowed on Yellowstone Lake,
> saw Old Faithful erupt three times, admired Morning Glory
> Pool . . . . We played chess and fed the sea-gulls near the mud
> geysers . . . and witnessed an eruption of the Lioness Geyser,
> which is a rare sight.
>
> Charles Finger, *Foot-Loose in the West*

Tourists are seekers after relaxation, amusement, beauty, adventure, health. Resorts and other touristic places are structured and promoted to attract and satisfy tourists, although places need not be too contrived in order to actually satisfy a tourist's needs. The entire world represents the tourists' domain, for as anthropologist Dean MacCannell writes: "Modern society makes itself its principal attraction in which other attractions are embedded."[1] Many tourists prefer places that are exaggerated for their attractiveness; places that are clearly distinctive and perceptually undemanding; places that facilitate superficial touristic role playing. More sophisticated travelers, offended by the obvious, seek subtle attractions in the everyday world. They contrive to get behind the scenes of important places, and even to participate in activities ongoing there, and they seek chance encounters with places. Although they travel to validate place expectations, like other tourists, they do so by retaining the important element of surprise. They may even seek to comprehend "personality of place" or to identify "spirit of place" as ways of communing with landscape on abstract levels.

Contrived Attractions

Contrived attractions are staged. They attract tourists, condensing for them the essence of a place so that they can consume it more readily. Contrived attractions also protect a locality from its visitors by focusing touristic activities temporally and geographically. In the early days of tourism in Lancaster

County, Pennsylvania, the Old Order Amish were plagued with visitors who, to paraphrase anthropologist Roy Buck, energetically created their own staged events.[2] The Amish men were pursued for picture-taking sessions, cows and sheep were chased by playful children, unwanted picnics were held in pastures, fences were broken down and gates left open, and the privacy of farmsteads was violated. Once established, contrived attractions in the area encouraged tourists to avoid the Amish people and to experience them from a distance. Farm displays and house museums, and even restaurants and gift shops, were presented as convenient, efficient, and authentic means of sampling the region. Although tourists consumed only packaged aspects of Amish life and culture, the Amish, for their part, were left in relative peace.

Contrived attractions are usually clustered as a means of mutual support. Clustering may involve shared promotion, transportation connecting attractions, shared interpretation, and even integrated design. In most places, like Lancaster County, Pennsylvania, contrived attractions are loosely aggregated in landscapes of only partial touristic stamp. Very popular tourist resorts contain a large number of attractions enclosed by a well-developed fabric of service establishments. In such resorts, attractions and supporting establishments fully dominate landscapes.

An attracting force, what Dean MacCannell calls a "sight," and its interpretation, what he calls a "marker," combine to form an attraction. His term *marker* refers to any piece of information about a sight: informational signs, guidebooks, slide shows, travelogues, souvenirs, and even the tourists' own comments. The development and promotion of an attraction is intended to produce stereotyped responses in visitors, what sociologist Erving Goffman calls "ritual attitudes." "Sight sacralization," the process by which the developer produces the stereotyped or ritual concensus, evolves in stages, according to MacCannell. In the "naming phase," the sight is distinguished from similar objects as worthy presentation. At the "framing and elevation" phase, an official boundary is placed around the sight to protect and enhance it; and it is opened to visitation. "Enshrinement" occurs when the "frame" itself assumes attractive power. Final phases include "mechanical reproduction" and "social reproduction." In the former stage, visual images (photographs, prints, paintings) models, or effigies of the sight are themselves valued and displayed. In the latter stage, social groups, cities, regions, and even nations use the sight as an icon of identity.[3]

An attraction's degree of contrivance is a function of both its isolation in a commonplace landscape and the extent of its structuring as a special setting for tourists. An attraction may be part of the built environment (that is, it may be man-made), or it may be natural, with its origins rooted more in nature. Anne Peck and Enid Johnson visited Virginia's Natural Bridge in the 1930s. Although a highway ran across the bridge, the gorge below was hidden from view behind billboards intended to isolate the attraction from its surroundings. Peck and Johnson approached the great arch through an entrance building containing a gift shop. Named, framed, and elevated to the scale of regional tourist attraction, the image of the Natural Bridge was spread across postcards and a wide range of other souvenirs for sale. The sight was a key sight in Virginia's tourist promotions.

Overlook near Bedford, Pennsylvania (1929). Tourism thrived where attractions were contrived. Tourists could experience place with minimum thought and difficulty.

Developers sought enshrinement for the bridge by tying visual scenery to inspirational music. To Peck and Johnson, the music of the hidden organ cheapened the beauty of the arch, even though most of the other tourists seemed to enjoy the "singing rocks."[4]

Attractions are signed as part of their development. Indeed, signs as markers can stand as attractions by themselves, or as a form of sight sacralization. Effie Gladding and her husband stopped in 1915 near Kearney, Nebraska, at the sign that marked the Lincoln Highway's halfway point between San Francisco and Boston. A picture of the marker graced the cover of their Lincoln Highway guidebook, for here was an attraction, both "enshrined" and "reproduced." A woman living nearby said almost every motor party stopped to take a photograph. For MacCannell, the act of sightseeing culminates in tourists linking a sight with markers of their own making, including the taking of photographs. Ideally, the tourists' markers indicate whether or not the sight has lived up to expectations, or whether or not the tourists have been satisfied. Verbal markers are lost on all but fellow tourists, but, as shared in casual conversation, they may be of primary importance in orienting visitors to an attraction. MacCannell continues: "Markers are passed back and forth, added and subtracted, and eventually organized in a final composition relating several markers, the tourist and the sight."[5]

Graffiti is the most blatantly obvious as well as the most destructive form of tourist marking. Irvin Cobb noted that the Grand Canyon's Bright Angel Trail was "extensively autographed" by tourists who had brought colored chalk, stencils, paints, and brushes for the occasion. He wrote that at San Diego's old mission, "There is a kind of traveler who repays . . . hospitality by defiling the walls with his inconsequential name, scratched in or scrawled on, and by toting away as a souvenir whatever portable object he can confiscate when nobody is looking." Up in the mission's bell tower the masonry was pocked where tourists had dug at it with pocket knives. One visitor showed Cobb half a brick pouched in his coat pocket.[6]

Of attractions totally man-made, none are quite so contrived as the museum. Museums, observes MacCannell, are really antihistorical, not because they destroy the past, but because in preserving the past they separate it from modernity. The museum elevates its exhibits above the contemporary world of the commonplace. Daniel Boorstin writes: "Whatever one sees in a museum is seen out of its proper surroundings. The museum visitor tours a warehouse of cultural artifacts; he does not see vital organs of a living culture." At New York City's American Museum of Natural History, the visitor of 1911 could see Peary's sledge that had reached the North Pole, the animals Theodore Roosevelt had shot in Africa, and the Tiffany collection of gems. But it was the skeleton of the dinosaur, hanging in the main hall, that attracted the most interest. Small museums, located in old houses, once the residence of some local or even nationally significant person, dominated numerically the museums of early-twentieth-century North America. Richmond's "White House of the Confederacy" was, perhaps, typical. Henry James, visiting in 1906, was admitted by an elderly woman, a lady "soft-voiced, gracious, mellifluous, perfect for her function." Inside he found "old Confederate documents, already sallow with time, framed letters, orders, autographs, extracts, tatters of paper-currency in the last stages of vitiation; together with faded portraits of faded worthies, primitive products of the camera, the crayon, the brush."[7]

Seeking Back Regions

Although most tourists are content with contrived attractions, the pretense of seeking and seeing the "real" world persists. Borrowing from Erving Goffman, Dean MacCannell differentiates between "front" and "back" touristic regions. Front regions are contrived displays where hosts and guests meet. Back regions are closed to audiences to allow for the concealment of props and activities that might discredit performances out front. In order to truly experience an attraction tourists must necessarily obtain at least a glimpse out back; they must see how the attraction itself works. MacCannell suggests six stages in a continuum of increasing sophistication by which attractions might be structured to accommodate the tourists' quests for understanding. Front regions are obvious touristic settings, what visitors attempt to overcome or get behind. Next come front regions decorated to achieve the atmosphere of a back region. At the third level, front regions totally simulate back regions, but are not real. At the fourth level, actual back regions are opened to visitors, but on a highly restricted basis, since only limited areas and activities are seen at limited times. Next come back regions altered to accommodate visitors for relatively long periods of time as the visitor becomes a regular part of the attraction's inner workings. Finally, there are back regions unaltered for tourists, which is the kind of space, Mac-Cannell notes, that "motivates touristic consciousness."[8]

In seeking to penetrate back regions, tourists are inclined no differently from anthropologists who seek to comprehend behavior as participant observers. This analogy is especially appropriate for tourist attractions built around cultural differences. With the coming of the transcontinental railroads, many Indian communities in the American West sought to sell cultural distinctiveness to tourists, and in varying degrees, they opened themselves to outsiders. As Daniel Boorstin comments, many communities embellished their ancient rites, changed, enlarged, and spectacularized their festivals, in order to satisfy the expectations of tourists. In 1920, Winifred Dixon attended the rain dance at San Ildefonso Pueblo in New Mexico. It gave her an opportunity to see inside houses with their dirt floors (on which two or three pallets were folded in neat rows or, as in the grander houses, where white enamel beds were set with lace counterpanes), with crucifixes, and with two or three portraits of saints on the walls, with rafters hung with rugs, clothing and strings of wampum and silver. But, it was the dance which interested her most. The hereditary Koshari (the clown or delight-maker) played to the tourists, even forcing Dixon to use her automobile in his ceremony. "We whirled around and around the plaza, the children shouting, dogs barking, and the fat Koshari bowing like visiting royalty to the cheering spectators, uttering shrieks in my ear . . . kicking his heels in the air, or sliding to the floor."[9]

Not only are specific attractions structured to give tourists inside views, but service establishments, such as restaurants, may also be contrived. Restaurants vary according to customer use of front and back regions. In 1913, Venice, California's, Ship Cafe was a replica of a caravel, with the inside fit with nautical furnishings and personnel dressed in sixteenth-century Spanish costumes. In 1934, Clam Allen's Restaurant in Westport, Connecticut, was a small, wooden shed on a pier where guests looked down onto the water. One intrigued visitor wrote that it was "the fishiest and most maritime restaurant" he had ever been in. The walls were decorated with models of sailing ships and the steering wheel of a motor boat. Over his head there was a gallery in which the fishing nets were stored, and just outside were the floating tanks for clams and lobsters. Beyond the tanks, gulls wailed mournfully. In Rupert Hughes's novel *The Real New York*, the "Bohemian Restaurant" of New York City was based on an actual place. When a visitor arrived, he was permitted to go into the kitchen and drink the health of the patron. He could stand by and watch his dinner cook, and if he was complimentary enough he would later be invited to have brandy to burn in his coffee.[10]

Tourists are not always able to recognize an attraction's authenticity. In differentiating between reality and tourists' ability to recognize reality, Eric Cohen finds four types of touristic situations. In the "authentic" situation, tourists encounter an attraction, penetrating to some degree its back regions. They interpret correctly what they see. With "staged authenticity" tourists encounter a front region but do not recognize it as such, whereas "denial of authenticity" involves a back region that the tourists mistake as mere facade. In the "contrived" situation tourists not only occupy a front region, but realize its pseudo character.[11]

Differentiating Common Places

As tourists are lured to sights contrived to satisfy, they are impelled to back regions to amplify experience. The same impulse also applies to common places. Indeed, it is the tourists' treatment of the everyday world that gives tourism its real significance as a social process. Tourists make distinctions about the world, validating their suspicions about life by personalizing comprehension. James Flagg discovered this aspect of travel accidently. "One of the amusing things about a long motor trip," he wrote, is that "you seem to dip into other peoples lives at odd moments, as if you opened a book at random. You gleam a chapter here—a paragraph there. It is exciting and fascinating, especially when whole chapters are missing, and you try to fill them out." Nathan Asch, on the other hand, worked hard at deliberate discovery. He stepped from Richmond, Virginia's, bus station determined to know the place. "I wanted to see Richmond; not government buildings, nor historical monuments, but the reason for the pictures that sprang in one's mind when one said the name RICHMOND. I wanted to find out what made Richmond."[12]

Differentiations of the modern world are tourist attractions. Elements of the commonplace are dislodged intellectually from their natural, historical, and cultural contexts and fitted together in tourists' minds as world views. Sightseeing, writes MacCannell, is a "ritual performed to the differentiations of society." It is, he continues, a "collective striving for a transcendence of the modern totality" through the incorporating of fragments into a "unified experience." Thus, Nathan Asch visited a Richmond cigarette factory, where he watched the deft fingers of the operators, the operators watching him in turn. He went to the tobacco worker's union, but the offices were closed. He asked about the great tobacco auctions, but it was too early in the season. "I wanted to learn about tobacco," he wrote. "How was I to begin? Whom was I to see? What was I doing here any way?"[13]

Work Displays

Tourists, as witnesses to work, gain firsthand experience with society's serious side. Comprehending economic interrelationship is the most important key to deciphering the complex modern world. To understand how work is organized, and to understand how others work is to place our own roles as workers in clearer social perspective. In order to witness work, however, we assume the role of tourist, placing ourselves temporarily above our fellows in their work settings. The worker, as tourist, writes MacCannell, is permitted to "look down" on his comrades (even those holding a higher-status position than his own in the industrial system), to offer remarks and suggestions expressive of great expertise and experience or moral superiority. Tourists may penetrate a back region to see work displayed close up. In other circumstances they are held at a distance, gaining only glimpses or seeing contrived displays organized no differently from any other tourist attraction. Nevertheless, the process of leaving our own work to view the work of others is to integrate the tourists as spectators into a "universal drama of work."[14]

Journalists carry their work with them; they seek back regions as a matter of occupation. The significance of what they write depends upon their depth of penetration. Julian Street traveled to write *Abroad at Home*. Because Europe was in the throes of World War I, and closed to American tourists, Street's purpose was to promote travel at home as a substitute for overseas touring. If Europe was play, then America was work. Street moved from one work display to another. In Buffalo he visited the grain elevators, in Cleveland the coal docks, in St. Louis the fur markets, in Chicago the stockyards. With the assistant manager at Marshall Field's he went into the back regions of a great department store by "rushing from floor to floor, poking in and out through mysterious, baffling doors." He wrote, "[As we moved], we kept taking off our hats as we went behind the scenes, and putting them on as we emerged into the public parts."[15]

Nothing was more intriguing than the inside of a mammoth automobile factory, for there was the very essence of modern industrialism. Street visited Henry Ford's Highland Park plant at Detroit. The relentless pace, the "terrible efficiency" of the factory landscape impressed him. The machine shop with its "whirling shafts and wheels, its forest of roof-support posts and flapping, flying, leather belting, its endless rows of writhing machinery, its shrieking, hammering, and clatter, its smell of oil, its autumn haze of smoke" expressed "delirium." But the assembly line was different. There he perceived the system. "No sooner had axle, frame, and wheels been joined together than the skeleton thus formed was attached, by means of a short, wooden coupling, to the rear end of a long train of embryonic automobiles, which was kept moving slowly forward toward a far-distant door. Beside this train of chassis stood a row of men, and as each succeeding chassis came abreast of him, each man did something to it, bringing it just a little further toward completion." Street obtained an interview with Henry Ford and inquired as to the secret of Ford's success. Street reported: "'It is one model!' he said. 'That's the secret of the whole doggone thing! Find out something that everybody is after and then make that one thing and nothing else.'"[16]

Like all tourists, journalists inspected work places to validate expectations about the world. In 1935, two Soviet journalists visited Ford's River Rouge plant. They had come to the United States to inspect the capitalistic system, to observe its strengths as well as its weaknesses. Work on the assembly line, they noted, proceeded at a "feverish speed." They were amazed at the "gloomy and worried" appearance of the workers. "These people seemed to be depressed in spirit, seemed to be overcome at the conveyor with a state of daily madness." Work was merely the tending of machines. "One does not see here that sense of self-esteem which is found among trained American workers with a trade. Working for Ford gives a man a livelihood, but does not raise his qualifications and does not assure his future. . . . Here is an astounding picture of the triumph of technique and the misfortune of man." The Soviet visitors met Henry Ford amid the noise and commotion of the assembly line. Ford shouted above the din: "'The farmer makes bread. We make automobiles. But between us stands Wall Street, the banks, which want to have a share of our work without doing anything themselves.'" And, amid handshakes, the interview quickly ended. "The inspection of one of the greatest sights in America—Henry Ford—came to an end."[17]

Penetrating back regions might be facilitated by well-connected friends or relatives. In the 1930s every traveling journalist seemed to know someone in Hollywood. Viewing motion picture sets "behind the scenes" was as important as viewing assembly lines. Every tourist hoped to see movies being made. One English visitor found that the large sound stages looked like airplane hangars: huge, draughty sheds full of arc lights, sliding cameras, sets of scenery, and men in shirt sleeves with cigars. The film business was just like American football, enormous periods of rest and preparation punctuated by wild bursts of furious play lasting for a few seconds.[18] Mary Winn witnessed the filming of *Moby Dick*: first a rehearsal, over and over and over again; then the actual picture taking, preceded by the mumbo jumbo of signs, lights flashing, and bells ringing, and calls of "Silence Now! Action!"[19]

Tours of various studio departments and the inspection of various movie sets were mandatory. Another English tourist, Anthony Jenkinson, saw architects, carpenters, and dress designers at work. He lingered in the research department to ask questions about the film *David Copperfield*. What uniforms did porters at Euston Station wear in 1850? What shape were the milestones in Kent in the days of Charles Dickens? He was amused to discover that the answers came from back issues of *Punch* and the *Illustrated London News*. Mary Winn questioned her guide about a scene set. How did the movie directors know what a Hudson Bay village was like? Did they send somebody up there to find out? "Naw," he said, "they don't aim to make the set look like a real Canadian street. What they try to do is make it look the way the public thinks a Canadian street looks." A drive around a studio lot from set to set was, to Jenkinson, an experience resembling "a quick, if disjointed tour of the world." At Fox Studios he passed in rapid succession from Trafalgar Square to Singapore Harbor, the Grand Canyon, a German Cathedral, and a New York subway.[20]

Tourists were not always so fortunate at getting behind the scenes. Nathan Asch wanted to spend a day in the Dodge main plant in Detroit's Hamtramck. Because he might get in the way of machinery, he was told he could only go with the daily tour, and so he accompanied a group of school teachers and several mothers with their children through the plant. They were all kept at a distance from production, and the guide knew nothing about the making of automobiles. When asked questions, the guide looked up reproachfully and said, "You know I only work here." Because he was a journalist, Asch failed completely to see the mines at Butte, Montana. The company was afraid of bad publicity. He wrote of his conversation with a mine superintendent: "'You want to see conditions, do you?' I said, 'Yes.' 'No,' he said. 'You wouldn't understand it, all you'd see is a lot of miners. Now if you were a mining engineer, I would take you down myself, because you would understand our problems.' " Nor did Ernie Pyle get far into a soap factory at Cincinnati. "They were fairly cagey, and jittery about spies—like governments. They also said part of the plant was dangerous for visitors to be in. And finally, I gathered, some of it didn't smell very nice."[21]

Tourists could watch work displays even while en route. The tour of the steamship bridge, the ride in the locomotive cab, or the visit to the airplane cockpit put tourists into back regions. On his way to Alaska, one traveler watched a ship's captain pilot by the echo of the foghorn reverberating from the shore. Another traveler rode a locomotive eastward from Missoula, Montana. The engineer apologized for not entertaining him and looked only at the track and his watch. Another traveler was invited to the cockpit as his plane landed at Los Angeles. He slipped on a pair of earphones and listened to the radio beacon. The pilot, his hands in hogskin gloves, held the wheel with nonchalant familiarity and leisurely chewed gum.[22]

Deliberately encountering different cultures is a characteristic of international travel more than of domestic touring. Nevertheless, tourists in North America can and do seek cultural differences in order to make cultural comparisons. Native Indian and Eskimo groups, ethnic communities of European, African, and Asian origin, and even distinctive regional lifeways invite exploration. Pleasure trips may embrace cultural displays as well as work displays. In Santa Fe, New Mexico, for Easter in 1920, Winifred Dixon went "Penitente Hunting." At nearby Alcade, she saw a short procession of men and boys, weak-kneed and trembling, clad only in cotton drawers and shirts bloody from self-inflicted wounds. Three men bore great crosses. Local residents treated her with great hostility, scowling and making uncomplimentary remarks in Spanish. Dixon had been warned not to take photographs or even to show her camera.[23]

Jan and Cora Gordon traveled through the Southeast, collecting folk songs in 1927. They were invited to a hymn sing at an isolated rural church in northern Georgia. They were amazed to find how much the art of the "despised Negro" had influenced these religious exercises, for both the "spiritual and the jazz" were easily discernible in the tunes. After the hymn sing there was a picnic lunch with biscuits, ham and fried chicken, and pie. The local women watched the visitors carefully, gauging their responses to each dish. The men clustered to themselves talking crops. " 'I says,' declared one member outright, 'that hawgs is the most susceptible animal there is to this here lightning.' " That was the consensus of opinion, and nothing was left of the discussion except raking up affirmatory stories.[24]

Although the whole of tourism facilitates social awareness, some situations clearly reflect on social stratification. The Gordons were invited to a rally of the Ku Klux Klan, not in the South, but in a hayfield near Plattsburgh, New York. The Klansmen, transformed from farmhands into strange anachronisms from the Middle Ages, lurched off to their duties. But no disguise could conceal the clumsy farm walk inbred by years of ponderous booting and sticky soil. A big cross was raised, not a flaming, burning cross, but an electric affair with ruby-tinted bulbs. "Shadowy Klansmen stood aloft in the night and bellowed crudities at the sea of faces which, pinkly reddened by the glow of the cross, yearned open mouthed upwards." Nathan Asch sought out Marked Tree, Arkansas, at the height of the violent tenants' strike of 1936. The town seethed with the hatred of the planters and the storekeepers. According to the merchants, "All the ills that had befallen the South were the fault of the tenants. The price of cotton was low, the cost of manufactured products high, the roads were bad, business was slow, girls couldn't get married because the tenant farmer was lazy, born lazy, improvident and shiftless; and no amount of help would do any good, would help him any, or would help the South." He visited a tenant farmer and his family near Texarkana. They lived in two rooms, sleeping in one and cooking in the other. The house was furnished with a mattress, a stove, an oil lamp, and a packing box. No one in the family had a complete change of clothes. From a nail in one wall hung a side of bacon. The place was a sieve, since light could be seen through each of the four walls and the ceiling.[25]

Luck played a part in gaining access to cultural and social displays. Cecil Roberts, an English tourist, accompanied a Chicago truck driver on a cross-country run in early 1945. The driver, of Polish descent, took Roberts through kinship and acquaintanceship networks from Grand Rapids and Detroit, through Cleveland and Youngstown, to Pittsburgh, Harrisburg, Scranton, and New York. Roberts experienced "a continental brotherhood whose tentacles stretched into every state, city, and town of the United States." He ate in restaurants run by Poles; he slept in Polish rooming houses. At Scranton he attended a costume dance at the Polish Hall. There he was pulled and bounced through Polish dances, and sometimes, in the great swinging rondos, he rode through the air. At twelve o'clock the whole company stood while the band played the Polish national anthem and then the "Star-Spangled Banner." He wrote: "I had been in 'the melting pot,' except, it seemed to me, that no real amalgam had followed the melting. The people were something new, and yet remained, even in the second and third generation, something old." From Chicago to New York he had made a journey through Poland but had never left the United States.[26]

Chance Encounters

Diligent tourists cultivate chance encounters. They flourish on surprises, even subtle surprises, and are open to the paradoxes of life, both big and small. They search for the unexpected by deliberately placing themselves in new situations, hoping for novel experiences. Surprise discoveries and their reactions to those discoveries stand as travel highlights, for chance encounters escape the stigma of contrivance, not only delighting, but appearing patently honest. Unexpected insight seems trustworthy as a candid picture of the world. Chance encounters are also highly personalized because they are the travelers' own experiences, experiences that relatively few others may have had. Chance encounters, better than any other kind, tie tourists to their world while helping them to define a sense of identity.

Anything can surprise. What surprises one may not surprise another, although being in a strange place does amplify the unexpected for all. A European recently arrived in America and emerging for the first time onto the streets of New York City may find the experience bewildering. One Englishman penned: "You never know when something utterly absurd may not follow instantly on something utterly magnificent, and *vice versa*. Round every corner there may be a Wonder of the World, or a crime, or a rather bad joke, or an ideal, or a dump of rusty tins. You cannot tell which it is going to be." For Americans in America the search for surprise presented a bigger challenge. Familiar with most codes of behavior and the structuring of landscape, Americans had only to learn regional and local variations on national themes. Lewis Gannett sought to heighten surprise on his transcontinental trip by not planning an itinerary. He picked his way through state after state, as new road maps appeared at the filling stations. He stressed, "The best will always be the unexpected."[27]

It was memorable to enter a place unexpectedly to see a daily, weekly, or seasonal event played out like ritual, or gain a sense of timing for being in a place at an unusual moment. Starting a cross-country trip on an autumn Saturday of 1928, two travelers entered Williamstown, Massachusetts, at the finish of a college football game. It was like a festival. It was a magic moment. "The whole town was celebrating. Doorways were lighted, windows twinkling, headlights swinging corners, gliding up and down the streets, groups of figures everywhere moving among the shadows, laughing, calling, singing to the clash of bells." Zephine Humphrey and her husband, caught suddenly in a traffic jam outside an Oklahoma town, found themselves at an airport dedication. The community had turned out to parade down the new runway, the parade illustrative of the history of locomation in the locality. First came Indians on foot and on horseback, and then a covered wagon drawn by rangy mules with an inscription, "Oklahoma Or Bust!" Then came a load of cotton in a wagon driven by the same woman who, in her youth, had driven the town's first cotton to the gin. Then came a Model-T, and then other cars, with each more modern in turn. And finally the airplanes, "thundering and swooping, skimming to rest on the new field, lifting away again, doing marvelous stunts in the brilliant sky."[28]

It is stimulating to be in a place when a newsworthy event occurs or to be in a place somehow associated with an occurrence. Mark Pepys was dining in a Detroit restaurant as the Joe Louis–Max Baer fight was being broadcast on the radio. "Louis leads with his left—lands. Baer counters with his right, wildly; he misses." At the conclusion of every round, a buzz of conversation filled the room. When Louis won the fight, the black waiters kept their self-control, not a flicker of feeling showing in their faces. But blacks danced outside on the sidewalks and shouted from cars, for Detroit was Louis's hometown. Back at the hotel the black elevator operator told Pepys that she was quite tired when the broadcast was over and she felt she had been "fighting every round as she heard it." The Gordons drove through Boston the night the radicals Nicola Sacco and Bartolomeo Vanzetti were executed. "Boston was as if dead. Nobody moved through the streets; a sinister silence ruled." Police barriers had been erected a mile from the prison; searchlights swept the sky. Machine guns had been mounted on the prison, or so the Gordons were told.[29]

Rare events heighten travel experience. Charles Finger and his party were idling about in one of Yellowstone's geyser basins when, with a roar, followed by an uplift of water and steam, a geyser began to erupt. They looked on, only mildly impressed, supposing it nothing but an ordinary sight, until other tourists came running and shouting. Reading the sign they discovered that they were seeing a rare sight, for that geyser, the Splendid Geyser, had not erupted for thirty-nine years. Encountering celebrities in unexpected places could highlight a trip, especially when the encounter gave special insight into human nature. Ernie Pyle looked down from his hotel window in Rapid City, South Dakota, to see a motorcade with President Franklin Roosevelt arrive. The president swung himself forward with his arms and turned, putting his legs out of the car door and locking the jointed steel braces at his knees. He straightened up. And at that moment the tension broke, and the crowd applauded, briefly and restrained. Pyle confessed: "It was the tenderest, most admiring thing, so surprising, so spontaneous. It was as though they were saying with their hand, 'We know we shouldn't, but we've got to.' When I turned from the window there was a lump in my throat." Leaving Skagway by steamship, one tourist encountered a traveler, a miner afflicted with scurvy and tuberculosis. A purse had been made up to enable him to reach his home in Toronto where he hoped to see his wife and child before he died. Tourists witness accidents and sometimes are themselves involved in accidents. Rollo Brown was aboard a train that hit and killed a small boy. The train lurched to a stop and people raced alongside the cars on foot. The boy's brother and his friends stood crying by the trackside.[30]

Most chance encounters are not profound, but they do provide the spice that gives life flavor. One early automobilist paused by a New Hampshire roadside to let the engine cool. There was an abandoned farmhouse with hewn weatherboards stained by a century of rain and sun. To have passed at twenty miles per hour, he mused, would have made "no more than a fleeting impression, like the wink of a camera shutter, the significance slighted in the crowding succession of other scenes." But the chance stopping provided an encounter of another kind. He lingered, explored, and "wondered what manner of folk had dwelt therein, and how their lives were spent." Simply moving through a landscape presented opportunities for the unexpected. Ideally, scenery was disclosed in a sequence of views, like a motion picture film slowly unwinding. When carried by railroad or steamship, the traveler could experience profound juxtapositions. After a night's sleep in a Pullman berth and a journey across hundreds of miles, the yank of a window shade invited profound juxtaposition. Julian Street, who had never seen the Great Plains, awoke one morning in Kansas. He was not surprised. He was stunned. "For a long time I lay . . . in my berth, gazing out at the appalling spread of land and sky. Even at sea the great bowl of sky had never looked so vast to me. The land was nothing to it. In the foreground there was nothing, in the middle distance nothing, in the distance nothing."[31]

Validating Expectations

All tourists travel to validate expectations. Of contrived tourist attractions, Daniel Boorstin maintains that the tourist looks for caricature and seldom likes the authentic, preferring his own "provincial expectations." Boorstin invokes the "mirror-effect law of pseudo-events." Contrived attractions become "bland and unsurprising reproductions of what the image-flooded tourists knew was there all the time." According to Boorstin, tourists' appetite for strangeness is best satisfied when the pictures in their own minds are easily verified. Earl Pomeroy echoes this view. In the nineteenth-century West, he observes, tourists sought "only what the guidebook recommended," and "according to schedule" felt the prescribed "satisfaction of having seen what 'everyone' saw." According to Pomeroy, tourists traveled assured that competent and fashionable critics of scenery had had time to "enshrine nature in words or paint, and were available to point out and interpret to him what he ought to see."[32]

Clare Gunn, in his book on designing "vacationscapes," sees a three-phase process of place validation: hypothesis, input, and check. Hypotheses are expectancies based on the accumulated confirmation of various information sources. Inputs, or the immediate stimuli of place, run the gamut of the various senses, although seeing, or the visual mode, certainly dominates. Checking relates hypotheses to perceived realities.[33] Where expectations prove to have been inflated, disappointment may prevail. When the sight exceeds expectations, a sense of exhilaration occurs. Travel is not so confined to contrived attractions as Boorstin suggests, nor so restricted to fad and fashion as Pomeroy implies. Rather, as Gunn outlines, touring is a process of validating expectations applicable to understanding both contrived attractions and the everyday world. It is a process only partly prescribed by set patterns of experiencing.

Tourists are most aware of the validating process when their expectations have been substantially exceeded or substantially invalidated. Less frequently, tourists glory in having predicted exactly what a place was like. Traveling in 1915, Louise Hale found Virginia's mountains exactly what she had expected. There were the same yellow clay roads, farm women working over big kettles outside log cabins, and tall, lank men laboring in fields and woods, just as she had imagined. She speculated that this correct mental vision came primarily from reading about mountain life, although she had a very definite mental picture of the Natural Bridge based on stereoptican views. Before going to Niagara Falls, Harrison Rhodes had encountered a whole "cataract literature." Even before he had made personal acquaintance with the place, he felt that he knew it. He was already familiar with the name and style of every hotel and its rates, and he knew in which one it was possible, by an "ingenious and agreeable contrivance of mirrors, to see the Falls even while dining."[34]

David Steele stood by the Niagara gorge listening to the comments of other tourists. One man said, "It looks like a magnified mill dam." A woman said, "Just what I expected: a great lot of water falling over a rock." Places can be too well known to produce surprise. Hypotheses about places can be too well formed. Some places, on the other hand, were structured to help tourists overcome stereotypes. Throughout the 1920s, Yellowstone featured a system of one-way roads connecting major attractions in a circuit, requiring a full day of touring by automobile. Without the one-way roads, Frederic Van de Water speculated, "Parties would come in the East Gate, drive directly to Old Faithful; see it spout and then go out the West. That is the sole thing at which many want to look. There were pictures of it in their geography books."[35]

Henry Miller loitered along the edge of the Grand Canyon, eavesdropping on tourists. At the El Tovar Hotel he overheard a woman talking who was eating ice cream while watching the sunset. Pointing to the canyon with her dripping spoon, she said, "Nothing so extraordinary about this, is there?" Evidently the sunset hadn't come up to her expectations. Miller wrote, "It wasn't all flamey gold like an omlette dripping from Heaven." But if she had looked at the ground beneath her feet she would have observed that it was flushed with a beautiful lavender color; and if she had raised her eyes to the topmost rim of rock she would have noticed that it was a rare tint of black. Irvin Cobb described his first glimpse of the Grand Canyon. "You stand there, stricken dumb, your whole being dwarfed yet transfigured; and in the glory of that moment you can even forget the gabble of the lady tourist alongside of you who, after

searching her soul for the right words, comes right out
and . . . pronounces it to be 'just perfectly lovely'!" People see
places differently according to differing degrees of ignorance
and understanding, and from having different language skills.
As Charles Finger correctly surmised, it was not what one saw
that constituted the interest, but the train of thought that came
with the seeing.[36]

Expectations built up over a lifetime tumble the hardest
and can cause the most disappointment. Cecil Roberts looked
from his railroad car at Creston, Wyoming, and saw a sign proclaiming "Divide of the Continent." What a memory of boyhood that sign evoked. Forty years before, in the course of an
early geography lesson, the teacher had drawn his ruler across
the United States and had exclaimed, "Here is the Continental
Divide!" But where was the enchantment? Roberts wrote:
"There were no towering mist-wreathed peaks, no thundering
waterfalls and giant pines, or wild buffalo-haunted uplands
rolling immense under the vivid sky." As a child, John Steinbeck was struck by the glorious sound of the words "Great Divide." It was a proper sound for the "granite backbone of a continent" because he had seen, in his mind, escarpments rising
into the clouds. But along his highway in Montana, the rise was
gradual; and if a sign hadn't informed him, he would never
have known that he had crossed the divide. The place simply
wasn't impressive enough to carry such a stupendous fact.[37]

Place Comparisons

The process of validating place expectations leads naturally to the comparing of places by tourists. How does the sight
compare with other sights? Most important, how does the place
compare with home? Home is always an intellectual, if not emotional, reference point in comparison with that other places take
meaning. Few travelers were as honest about their homing tendencies as the two Soviet journalists Ilya Ilf and Eugene Petrov.
"We had traveled over American highways, but in our thoughts
they were Soviet highways. We spent nights in American
hotels, but we thought about Soviet hotels. We examined
Ford's factories, but in our thoughts we saw ourselves in our
own automobile factories." There was not a single conversation

that did not end with a reference to the Soviet Union: "But at home it is like this; but at home it is like that; it would be well to introduce it at home."[38]

Less parochial, perhaps, are the comparisons of places visited with other places previously visited. Webb Waldron compared Minnesota's mammoth open-pit mines in the Mesabi Range with the Grand Canyon. "When one goes to the Grand Canyon," he wrote, "one is astonished but prepared by a thousand descriptions and photographs to be astonished. I was not prepared for the Mahoning Pit. It was like the Grand Canyon, yet utterly different. The Grand Canyon is ancient, immutable, complete. The Mahoning Pit is raw and in the process of making." A place could be compared to idealized or imagined landscapes, and even to models of itself. Waldron continued: "The pit dropped away at my feet, down, in shelves of earth, first yellow, then orange, then purple, down, down, down, down, down, growing smaller and smaller till the trains were toy trains, puffing toy smoke and steam, down to the lowest depths where toy steam-shovels gouged up the purple earth." It was to Waldron a surreal place. Climbing to the top of a slag pile, he looked out toward other pits, and beyond them to others still. "North, east, west, for miles and miles . . . men were scooping up the face of the world."[39]

Place-appropriate Behaviors

Places are settings for behavior. People recognize places on the basis of behavioral expectations. Every place has a location in a geographical sense, although, as Edward Relph reminds us, the "whereness" of a place may not be its most important attribute.[40] Places exist in time, both sequentially, as one point in time relates to another, and as duration. They open and close, usually on a regular schedule. Places contain various sorts of people who engage in different activities, although every place has its normative activities conducted by a regular clientele. Ongoing activities require supporting props, as in a stage set, and these props facilitate and encourage a relatively narrow range of behavior. All of these characteristics (location, timing, people, activities, and props) serve as icons that cue strangers, as outsiders, to basic place meanings. Tourists must learn to read the landscape in order to identify places. They must learn to anticipate correctly place satisfactions, and to avoid, when possible, disatisfactions.

The first problem travelers face is orientation. They must locate themselves in the landscape, tying their mental images of place to geographical reality. Henry Poor had problems when he arrived at Seward, Alaska. He felt lost. It didn't seem to be the place we had been heading for. He tried to make directions come right and to fit what he saw with his eyes into its place on the map view he carried in his mind. Poor had related easily to other places on his trip: Salt Lake City, for example, with its mountains to the east and white salt flats stretching westward. At Salt Lake City, streets met at right angles defining the compass points and, accordingly, sense of direction was easily come by and it was easy to comprehend how things fit together. But in Seward he could not get oriented. The town remained for his entire visit a "series of vivid and confused impressions like fragments of a dream."[41]

The tourist needs to learn local behavior codes. He needs to know how things are done in public places and in the private behavior settings that constitute a town, a city, a region. E. B. White commented on tourists in New York City. "To an outlander a stay in New York can be and often is a series of small embarrassments and discomforts and disappointments: not understanding the waiter, not being able to distinguish between a sucker joint and friendly saloon, riding the wrong subway, being slapped down by a bus driver for asking an innocent question." For foreigners not acquainted with American society, learning place-appropriate behavior is even more difficult. Dress, manners, and the simplest ways of doing things may be strange. Ilya Ilf and Eugene Petrov spent half an hour lighting matches and stumbling around in the dark until they discovered how to turn the lights on in their New York hotel room. A Japanese tourist learned that American women could wear hats everywhere, but men couldn't, and that men always had to stand up when introduced, but women didn't. One English visitor to the United States bought a new wardrobe in order to look like a native. He advised his fellow countrymen to discard their shirts and buy new ones when in America: red shirts with huge black checks or purple shirts with olive-green butterflies. He was confused about where to buy things. Drugstores sold drugs, but also stationery, candy, toys, fountain pens, imitation jewelery. "If you want cigarettes go to the grocer; if you want to have your shoes cleaned, go to the barber."[42]

Tourists may be excused for awkwardness in finding and using places. As strangers they may be extended courtesies and helped along by locals. But they still have a third order of problem to contend with: how to act the part of tourists. What represents an appropriate response for outsiders to a situation? As strangers, what constitutes appropriate reactions to a sight? Ernie Pyle's party was baffled by how to react to the concrete marker at the Four Corners. They got kind of silly there. First, he had to sit on top of the post. Then he leaned over the monument and had his picture taken with one foot in Utah and one in Colorado, one hand in New Mexico and one in Arizona. Dignity reigned in another tourist's party upon their seeing the Pacific Ocean. They parked as soon as they had found a suitable place from which to reach the water's edge. As the waves beat upon the beach, a minister in the party uttered a prayer recognizing the power of the Almighty Creator and invoking earnestly His blessing upon the missionary efforts in China, Japan, and the other countries on the other side of the water.[43]

Photography is an important tool in adapting to a place touristically. Camera-toting tourists photographed and were photographed as a means of entering and occupying places. Tourists were expected to take pictures. At the overlooks where David Steele stopped in Rocky Mountain National Park in 1916, he found candy boxes, but "chiefly paper covers torn from rolls of Kodak films." They littered every spot where tourists had paused and where interest had directed cameras. "These are the marks," he concluded, "of practical appreciation by those who foregathered at these points for rhapsody."[44] Professional photographers lurked at the most visited places to offer proof through picture taking of the tourists' travel success.

Tourists are always outsiders. Locals may view them as curiosities, nuisances, violaters of privacy, or destroyers of community ambience. In resorts visitors may be made to feel at home, but even there situations may be strained by the host-guest relationship. Many tourists feel out of place beyond the protection of contrived attractions. The everyday world appears potentially hostile because the tourists' roles are not carefully prescribed. One tourist observed that being in one Arkansas town was to feel the "crime of his presence." The searching eyes of the townspeople made his skin crawl. Tourists' difficulty at learning place-appropriate behaviors increased as they attempted to penetrate back regions. Behavioral codes became increasingly personalized the farther they removed from a community's public spaces into the private sanctums. In 1936 Ernie Pyle and a companion entered Teec Nos Pas, Arizona, then an isolated village in Navajo Country. Indians were loafing about the trading post. As Pyle and his friend entered the store, Indians eyed them coldly. Inside, on the floor, an old man lay flat on his back, looking at the ceiling. To break the ice Pyle and his friend bought a sack of pipe tobacco. Indians began to wander in. "They stood and stared, like so many animal eyes around a campfire. 'Well, I reckon we better shove along,' I said. Stares propelled us out the door. The rocky road away from Teec Nos Pas seemed like a ribbon of velvet."[45]

Personality of Place

Tourists, able to linger in a place, and open to even the most subtle of nuances, might capture what the travel essayist Lawrence Durrell calls "the spirit of place." It is an "invisible constant" that reflects itself in the character of landscape and people. "It is a pity indeed to travel and not get this essential sense of landscape values," Durrell writes. One does not need a sixth sense for it, because all landscapes ask the same question: "I am watching you—are you watching yourself in me?" Thus one discovers spirit of place by sitting quietly, watching a place in all of its many manifestations. One doesn't ask mental questions, one just relaxes with an empty mind, filling with impressions. Taken this way, Durrell concludes, "travel becomes a sort of science of intuitions." Durrell is not the only literary mind to suggest travel through introspection. Henry James wrote that places "disposed for human use and addressed to it,

Playing the role of tourist at Hot Springs, Arkansas (1927). Tourists were expected to act like tourists in resort settings. Obtaining photographs for souvenirs was a common rite of passage.

must have a sense of their own, a mystic meaning proper to themselves." D. H. Lawrence wrote: "Different places on the face of the earth have different vital effluence, different polarity with different stars; call it what you like. But the spirit of place is a great reality."[46]

Although few travelers border on being mystics, many are able to discover character in place, to recognize that places, like people, have personality. Julian Street wrote: "Places no less than persons, have characters and traits and habits of their own. Just as there are colorless people[,] there are colorless communities. There are communities which are strong, self-confident, aggressive; others lazy and inert." Henry Canby felt that the personality of a place was implicit in its people and their activities. Indeed, he thought that landscape as environment exerted influences of a determining nature. "The country molds the man, whatever else may be influential in his making." Tourists, according to Canby, should know that the

47

aspect of a land does mean something; that the ultimate effect of a bit of earth into which they have wandered is significant in terms of humanity as well as aesthetics. They should seek to capture its peculiar flavor and quality if they can. This quality, Canby concluded, "will prove to be like style in literature, the most imponderable quality, never to be defined and never to be neglected, which when found or felt is a new clue not merely to beauty, but to subject, significance, mood, and result."[47]

Personification helps travelers capture the essence of place. Assigning human tendencies to places helps describe and explain experiences. Julian Street wrote of Chicago: "Chicago is stupefying. It stands apart from all the cities in the world, isolated by its own individuality, an Olympian freak, a fable, an allegory, an incomprehensible phenomenon, a prodigious paradox in which youth and maturity, brute strength and soaring spirit, are harmoniously confused." Adjectives could be hurled at places like invectives. Street continued: "Call Chicago mighty, monstrous, multifarious, vital, lusty, stupendous, indomitable, intense, unnatural, aspiring, puissant, preposterous, transcendent—call it what you like—throw the dictionary at it!" Of Detroit he wrote: "She is beautiful—not with the warm, passionate beauty of San Francisco, the austere mountain beauty of Denver, nor the strange, sophisticated destroying beauty of New York, but with a sweet domestic kind of beauty, like that of a young wife, gay, strong, alert, enthusiastic; a twinkle in her eye, a laugh upon her lips."[48]

The feelings tourists have for a place reflect their own basic values as rooted in their own personalities. People experience themselves in experiencing landscapes. Basic orientations to life are reflected in responses to landscape. Henry Miller, his sense of human dignity violated, wrote from a Pittsburgh hotel room, "I am depressed beyond words. If I were to occupy this room for any length of time, I would go mad. . . . The spirit of the place, the spirit of the men who made it the hideous city it is, seeps through the walls. It suffocates me." According to psychologist Kenneth Craik, modern tourists reflect upon four principal value systems: the utilitarian, the picturesque, the romantic, and the ecological. Pittsburgh, to Miller, was too utilitarian. Certainly, he did not find the place picturesque, and it lacked romantic qualities; but, above all, it seemed to be a self-destroying habitat. Miller's view of the role of man in his environment had been violated and he felt violated, accordingly.[49]

Utilitarian values underlie the search for the useful. Clearly, utilitarianism has dominated American society in the twentieth century as it had dominated in previous centuries. It is a frontier legacy that favors action instead of meditation. Geographer David Lowenthal writes of the frontier spirit: "Action became so strong a component of the American character that landscapes were often hardly seen at all; they were only acted on. Immediate necessity made a mockery of mere contemplation." He continues: "Appreciation of the landscape itself, apart from its practical uses, was disdained as pointless and effete."[50]

Nothing better demonstrated a place's practicality then the measuring of its utility. Janette Routledge's book *How to Tour the United States in Thirty-One Days for $100* reads like a statistical compendium. In North Carolina she passed forty-three cotton mills in thirty-two miles. In Washington, D.C., she saw the $18-million Union Station. Boston Common contained 70,000 tulip bulbs, she was told. Chicago's Soldier's Field seated 150,000 people, she learned. Most guidebooks emphasized place utility through statistics. The *New York Standard Guide* of 1917 described the Park Row building as 31 stories, or 390 feet tall. The building accommodated a work force of 3,500 people in 950 separate offices; it contained 2,080 windows, 1,770 doors and 7,500 electric lights. Its ten elevators traveled 16.38 miles an hour and carried an average of 814 persons an hour, or 8,140 a day, or 48,860 a week.[51]

The search for the picturesque is a search for the scenic. It is a quest for visual delight. One traveler wrote about Colorado Springs. What spread before his vision was one of the grandest and most beautiful sights he thought the eyes of mortal man ever looked upon: "a mighty panorama" of foothills and plains with the city in the distance. Many tourists, dominated by utilitarian values, thought the quest for the picturesque required guidance. Julian Street wrote of the Garden Of The Gods: "Guides will take you through, and they will do their utmost, as guides always do, to make you imagine that you are really seeing something. They will point out inane formations in the sandstone rock, and will attempt to make you see that there are 'pictures.' " The picturesque was found everywhere, even in the works of man. One visitor to Boulder Dam found more than "a vast utilitarian device, a super-gadget." He wrote: "Enchanted by its clean functional lines[,] and at the same time awed by its colossal size, you might be tempted to call it a work of art; as if something that began with utility and civil engineering ended somewhere in the neighborhood of Beethoven's Ninth Symphony."[52]

In discovering the romantic in landscape, one finds the emotional appeal of the heroic, the mysterious, the idealized. It was often an appeal to the past unseen. One traveler in the Middle West noted that much "charm of travel" came from the "glamour with which fable and legend enshroud historic places." She wrote: "In traveling across Wisconsin one is reminded of the time when witches, devils, magicians, and manitous held sway over the Indian mind." Romance came from the obscure. Both twilight and the darkness of night invited romanticizing. Since shadows obscured vision, the world was presented in outline, thus inviting the mind to invent and imagine. A traveler wrote on approaching New York City: "How gracious the mantle of night, like a veil it hides all blemishes and permits only fair outlines to be obscured. Details are lost in vast shadows; huge buildings loom up vaguely towards the heavens, impressive masses of masonry; the bridges, outlined by rows of electric lights, are strings of pearls about the throat of the dusty river." To romance was to imagine. Ernest Peixotto wrote of the giant coastal redwoods: "It is toward evening and at night that they become positively unearthly. Dead branches, lopped off by gales and mouldering at their feet, wormeaten, moss-grown, become in the uncertain light 'the little people,' gnomes, dwarfs, hobgoblins, stunted creatures of the dark, strange freaks of nature, whose limbs stand petrified in the act of running, and whose dead arms and gaunt fingers prehensile reach out for the belated wayfarer."[53]

Naturalists contributed relatively little to twentieth-century travel literature. Ecological viewpoints were not well developed among early tourists. One tourist admits: "Nowadays we see just so much of nature as the camera sees and no more; our vision is but surface deep, our eyes are but too clear, bright lenses with nothing behind, not even a dry plate to record the impressions."[54] Twentieth-century naturalists contributed more to scholarly literature, reflective of emerging academic disciplines. Tourists continued to seek nature, but more for visual display and less for lessons in environmental interrelationship. Most tourists sought mere stimulus and not understanding of nature's underlying patterns.

Discovering the personality of place meant looking at a place from many viewpoints. Places, as they nested in landscape, had utility. They functioned. They had visual qualities, and they may even have been picturesque. Every place lent itself to romance, if only at night, or when viewed in the past tense; and places, as human constructs, were a part of the natural order. The personality of a place combined understanding of all these things. Personality of a place pervaded its location, its timing, its people and their activities, as well as the props they used to go about life. Sophisticated tourists attempted to tap this essence, to get the feel of a place for its distinctive blend. They integrated this comprehension into their behavior as appropriate to a place. Such understanding became part of their comparative frame of reference. They developed new place expectations around such awarenesses as they sought new situations which displayed a place's personality. Tourists who lacked such sophistication accepted places very much as they were presented. They accepted people and things at face value. They were satisfied with whatever comprehensions had been contrived for them, and personality of place had little meaning accordingly. Although questing the "spirit of place" often bordered more on romanticizing than on any of the other ways of valuing landscape, it too required open minds: minds open to all ways of knowing and being.

The tourists' world is a place of attractions, both those contrived especially for their benefit, and those they discern for themselves from everyday circumstances. Diligent tourists seek the extraordinary even in common places. They seek back regions, not being satisfied with outward appearances. Above all, diligent tourists are open to the surprises of chance encounters. But, few tourists are always diligent. Even the most alert frequently revert to travel by formula, relying on contrived attractions and their supporting facilities in landscapes comforting to travelers. They participate variously in their own delusions, accepting front regions as semblances of the authentic. All tourists travel to validate expectations. Places are evaluated in comparison to other places visited, and to home. Tourists constantly seek to learn local codes of behavior as they move from one new place to another, and to orient themselves geographically. These things all tourists do as they sense the essence of places visited. To varying degrees, all landscapes contain tourists. In the modern world, most landscapes are structured to accommodate tourists to some degree. Certainly, all landscapes have touristic meaning.

CHAPTER THREE

NATURE AS AN ATTRACTION

> Recreational development is a job not of building roads into lovely country, but of building receptivity into the still unlovely human mind.
>
> Aldo Leopold, "Conservation Ethic," *Bird-Love* 40 (March–April 1930): 109.

The search for natural beauty and other environmental amenities became a prime impulse in traveling in North America. Nineteenth-century resorts developed around mineral springs and scenic curiosities, or were oriented to the scenery and cooler summers of the mountains or seashore, or to the warmer winters of the South and Far West. Middle- and lower-class tourists of the early twentieth century inherited these resorts as originally developed by railroad and steamship interests for America's upper class. The evolving conservation movement and the coming of the automobile hastened the rise of national parks in the United States that were more clearly egalitarian in intention and design. In Canada, parks struck a compromise between the American national park ideal and the traditional resort. Resorts and parks in both countries represented prime destinations for railroad and automobile tourists alike, and most pleasure trips linked several attractions where aspects of nature gave excuse to pleasure taking.

Resorts

The oldest and most fashionable of the nineteenth-century resorts were the spas. Places like Saratoga Springs in New York, White Sulphur Springs in West Virginia, French Lick in Indiana, and Hot Springs in Arkansas retained some of their glamour in the twentieth century as gathering places for the well-to-do. Activity focused on the giant hotels, and on the spring houses and bathhouses where tourists drank and bathed in mineral waters. Golf, tennis, horseback riding, and polo, among other sports, augmented the traditional nineteenth-century routines described by historian Hans Huth for Saratoga: "A lady would rise, dress, go down to the spring, drink the waters to the accompaniment of music of a band, walk around the park, greet friends, chat, drink the waters again, breakfast, see who came in on the train, take a siesta, walk, and have a little small talk with groups of ladies and gentlemen."[1] Although they were much concerned with the beauties of landscape and the therapeutic benefits of spas, visitors came mainly to socialize. Most tourists were rather indifferent to natural scenery, using nature only as an excuse for a change of scene and routine.

The advantages at Saratoga Springs were listed in a 1908 advertisement, which stressed: "Absolutely free from mosquitoes and malaria! Forty natural springs of wide range from strong cathartic to alkaline table water! Grand hotels and smaller ones to accommodate all classes! Wide avenues and streets, all abundantly shaded! State automobile roads in every direction!" David Steele, a visitor in 1918, found rows of shops around, within, and under the hotels. There were barbershops and brokers' offices. Cigar stores elbowed jewelers' emporiums, and five-and-ten-cent stores elbowed trust companies. Mud-covered buggies jostled ninety-horsepower touring cars. For many the place had been cheapened by the middle and lower classes emulating the rich, and by the rich departing from traditional norms. It was a place of anomalies: a place, according to Steele, of "bankers and book-makers, of brokers and dead-brokes."[2]

No place proved more durable as a tourist resort than Niagara Falls. No visiting foreigner dreamed of missing it; no American in foreign parts would have dared call himself an American unless he could tell how he had seen his land's greatest wonder.[3] The resort was filled with many contrived attractions. David Steele seems to have favored Niagara over Saratoga because of the more varied menu of activities. He and his party roamed at leisure. They stood on Inspiration Point ("where one may count ten different rainbows in ten minutes"), they climbed out to the edge of Luna Island ("which hangs literally suspended on the torrent's brink"), and they crossed the Hurricane Bridge ("where the roar and general

Niagara Falls (1945). Scenic curiosities readily accessible to large population centers spawned thriving resorts.

tumult are deafening"). They went up the Overlook Tower and down the Inclined Railway. "There we robed in rubber coats and hats and took the boat trip, coming back happy, although drenched and blinded by torrents of vapor." Tourists might don heavy rubber boots, coats, and hats and emerge from behind the Horseshoe Falls from where, looking up, they could see water shooting outward over the precipice.[4] Tourists could also explore the power houses, walk or ride across the bridge that connected the United States and Canada, or ride the cable car suspended across the gorge.

Americans have long been attracted to the seashore. Resorts along the New Jersey coast were among the earliest of the nineteenth century: such places as Long Branch, Asbury Park, and Cape May. Atlantic City began as a real estate venture with the completion of the railroad from Philadelphia in 1852. In 1870 the first boardwalk was constructed and lined with concessions, and in 1887 the first iron pier was extended out into the surf. Most people attracted to the resort were of the middle and lower classes. Atlantic City provided only the allusion of catering to elite, although imitation of the upper class, notes historian Charles Funnel, was a primary component of the "symbolic mobility" which the resort afforded its users. The many pseudosophisticated portraits of the city offered in promotional materials were designed to impart a patrician glamour to a plebian spa. Although Atlantic City was lowbrow, it palmed itself off in high-toned terms.[5]

Atlantic City's tourism clearly illustrated economist Thorstein Veblen's principal contention regarding the American leisure class. Veblen described the elite as pursuing conspicuous consumption in order to demonstrate pecuniary standing. Leisure as a nonproductive consumption of time was thus an ideal purveyor of social status.[6] But, whereas Karl Marx had argued that each social class developed its own way of life, Veblen maintained that the lower classes emulated the upper classes. Nowhere was this more visible that at seaside resorts like Atlantic City where people with limited incomes copied the rich. The Atlantic City "rolling chair" (made famous by the 1905 song, "Why Don't You Try, or The Rolling Chair Song") was a clear example. The chair pusher, as Charles Funnell pointed out, was probably the only servant most visitors to Atlantic City had ever had. George Birmingham, a visitor in 1913, speculated: "In towns and rural districts where men and women live their ordinary lives, work, love, and ultimately die, it is the rarest thing possible to see any grown person wheeled about in a preambulator or bathchair." However, to be photographed in such a chair was exactly the thing needed to impress people back home. It was the "epitome of nouveau bourgeois."[8]

Whereas the rich might have the leisure every day to lavish expenditure on recreation, the less well-to-do restricted their free spending to vacation time. Birmingham speculated about the strange effect of places like Atlantic City on "people who are, in other places, sane enough. . . . It is the holiday spirit of the place which gets a hold on visitors. All a whole year we commonplace people, who are not millionaires, are spending our money warily on things of carefully calculated usefulness. Then comes the brief holiday, and with it the sudden loosing of all bonds of ordinary restraint. . . . It was," he concluded, "desperate reaction against the tyranny of domestic economics."[9]

Although the seashore was Atlantic City's prime excuse for being, the resort was by 1900 quite urbanized. The piers were crowded with concessions and contrived attractions, including such mechanical amusements as Ferris wheels, merry-go-rounds, and roller coasters. Hotels and boarding houses, capable of domiciling tens of thousands of people on any night, contributed to congested streets and a congested boardwalk and beach. Excitement, and even apparent disorder, prevailed on the Boardwalk. Noting the dominance of the work ethic in American society, Charles Funnel maintained that the order of the sea provided a sanctifying backdrop for the inviting disorder of the city; and the purity attributed to the sea sanctified pleasure that otherwise would have aroused guilt for breach of discipline. Discipline and pleasure could not coexist. The visitor to the city by the sea, assured that the sea conferred wholesome benefits, turned to the city for pleasure. Worship of nature was, therefore, but an Atlantic City pretense. Funnel continues: "The sentimental poetry, etchings, and prose which burbled about the sea, and the untrodden shore, the eternal ebb and flow of the ocean, the hand of the Creator in the mighty deep, and suchlike themes, conveyed a sense of order and quietude which in fact did not exist."[10] Nature, as an attraction, had no real function beyond that of cliche.

Visitors to Atlantic City emphasized its urban aspect in what they wrote. Harrison Rhodes, who visited and compared many resorts, commented: "The majestic . . . surges of the Atlantic bow in amazed admiration before gigantic piers which bear aloft 'whirlwind vaudeville,' and 'one-step' dancing, the wild music for which pulsates in the soft warm night. Theaters and 'movies' abound. Lion-tamers and snake charmers and curio-shops flourish." It was, he concluded, "a dreadful place, and yet oddly enough, it is . . . exactly what the majority of us really like."[11]

The elite withdrew to more private seaside resorts, like Bar Harbor in Maine, Newport in Rhode Island, and Palm Beach in Florida. Life was luxuriously lived: a return to nature with a mansion, a good chef, and a carriage and pair. Private yachts or private railroad cars took the gentry south or north, according to the season. Harrison Rhodes found Palm Beach "fantastically rich and idle and gay—and useless." It was a kind of "dream of blazing flower-gardens and *allées* of palms." Activities were far more refined than at Atlantic City, although there were some similarities. "Its characteristic sport is the wheel-chair—the Afro-mobile, so called from the black slave of the pedal who propels you. The golfers who languidly dot the flat green seem only to do it that they may make wheel-chair idleness the more attractive. In the same way watching the bathers from under a striped awning competes on fair terms with bathing itself." Rhodes noted the Palm Beach spell: the idea that not to be rich was a state unworthy and discreditable and thus not to be mentioned before nice people. The elite led secluded lives in private estates. Cecil Roberts found in the 1930s that Palm Beach belonged to the best people. The beach was private, from end to end, except for the public strip where the common tourists could bathe with tradesmen, footmen, chauffeurs, cooks, and parlormaids.[12]

Each Florida resort developed its own personality, rooted in the clientele it attracted. St. Petersburg catered to the lower-middle class, from the Middle West especially. Julian Street observed in 1916 that the people were identical with those one might see on market day in a country town of Ohio or Indiana. He wrote: "The park is full of contented people, most of them middle-aged or old. The women listen to the band, and the men play checkers under the palmetto thatched shelter, or toss horseshoes on the greensward." St. Petersburg was a city of rental homes as well as hotels and boarding houses. In 1925, John Van Schaick observed thousands of bungalows with their porches shaded by palm trees, covered with vines, and surrounded by flowers. "Here people sit who want to get away from the crowd. With their books and papers, their sewing and mending, and letters from home, they live normal, happy, sunny lives while the blizzards howl around their homes in the north." He concluded: "The atmosphere of the place is that of the sitter, the plain, democratic ruminative sitter, chewing the cud of contemplation." Miami Beach, on the other hand, catered to the upward-bound, upper-middle class who sought fancy hotels, good restaurants, and night clubs to enliven short stays. According to Cecil Roberts, the place accommodated the "wrench-and-screw aristocracy": the automobile executives, the designers of engines, the testers of tires, who worked in places like Detroit, but played in Florida.[13]

California also sported seashore resorts. Monterey catered to the very rich, whereas Santa Cruz, Santa Monica, Laguna, and La Jolla served the middle class. Paraphrasing a promotional brochure, one traveler described Santa Cruz: "The city is full of life and they advertise 'not a dull moment from May 20th to October 1st.' Three band concerts daily. Dance at the Casino every evening. Plunge baths, hot baths, surf bathing, fishing, boating excursions on the Bay, picnic at the 'Big Trees,' vaudeville, fireworks, electrical displays, acquatic sports— variety enough to please all people." Long Beach was the Atlantic City of the Pacific. Here one found a midway, or strand, with sideshows, chili parlors, gift shops, waffle shops, and tattoo parlors mixed in with bathhouses and hotels. Accessible by steamer from the mainland, Avalon on Santa Catalina Island was California's most unique seaside resort. The town seemed to spill down its steep hillsides to the harbor where fish and fishing were primary attractions. In a glass-bottomed boat one tourist saw "the chameleon treacheries of the devil fish" and the "breathing drift of kelp." She wrote, "Jelly-fish rise from the shell-paved bottom like lilac balloons loosed in a haze of azure."[14]

A trip to the mountains offered scenery as well as escape from summer heat. The cool air of high elevations offered relief for those suffering from respiratory ailments. Health resorts evolved at places like Asheville in North Carolina and Colorado Springs in Colorado. Emily Post found Colorado Springs a strange collage: mountains, plains, squatters' shanties, replicas of foreign palaces, cowboys, Indians, ranches, New Yorkers, Londoners. "Across the warp of western characteristics," she wrote, "is woven the woof of a cosmopolitan society." She had imagined the place as a sort of huge sanatorium with long lines of invalid chairs on semi-enclosed verandas, and even beds, as in the outdoor wards of hospitals. Instead, she found luxury hotels and extravagant private homes. She lunched on terraces, danced in gardens, and led the social life typical of any fashionable resort. The Grove Park Inn at Asheville, North Carolina, advertised: "We have pure air, common-sense, digestable food, quiet in the bedrooms at night, the finest orchestra outside of New York and Boston, a great organ, and an atmosphere where refined people . . . find comfort and a good time."[15]

Resort Hotels

At the heart of every prominent resort stood at least one mammoth resort hotel, most of them built to stimulate railroad or steamship traffic. Many hotels became major tourist attractions in and of themselves, especially for more affluent travelers who passed from one to another as if on pilgrimage. In California the Del Monte at Monterey, the Del Coronado at San Diego, the Raymond at Pasadena, and the Glenwood at Riverside were major tourist attractors. Other prominent hostelries in the United States included the Antlers and the Broadmoor at Colorado Springs and the Royal Poinciana and the Breakers at Palm Beach, to name but a few. The Canadian Pacific Railroad built large resort hotels across Canada, including the Chateau Frontenac at Quebec, the Banff Springs Hotel in the Rockies, and the

Empress Hotel in Victoria. One British traveler in America wrote: "Americans often seem to travel for the mere satisfaction of going through a new country, and staying the night in a new hotel. They add them to their collection . . . as an entomologist adds a beetle."[16]

The Del Monte was a massive structure built in the Elizabethan style, overlooking the sea south of Monterey. The famous "Seventeen-Mile Drive" gave access to one of the most picturesque coastlines in North America. One visitor wrote: "Broad sweeps of lawn, deep splashes of floral coloring, weird shapings of oak and cypress trees, all delight the artistic sense. Just to look upon that vast stretch of natural beauty, embellished by man, soothes and delights the beholder." The Glenwood at Riverside was built on the site of a Spanish mission. Incorporating part of the mission ruins, the building became a fanciful study in Spanish revival architecture. The lattice windows of one visitor's room opened onto a court filled with flowers, climbing vines, palms, and orange trees. He found it a delight to wander through the long vistas of arched arcades, listening to the murmuring of fountains and the warbling of birds, and to catch glimpses of Moorish towers with chiming vesper bells.[17]

The period between the two world wars saw very little resort hotel construction. With the completion of the Fontainbleau Hotel in Miami Beach in 1955, a new era of lavish hotel development began. Escapist themes dominated as before, and tourists were invited to engage in various fantasies rooted in past times, or in other cultures. For example, the Fontainbleau was French. Historian Horace Sutton asks: "Didn't it have the fleur-de-lis running up and down the jackets of the waiters in the Fleur-de-Lis Room? Didn't the rooms have pictures of Paris hanging on the walls? Weren't its public washrooms labeled 'messieurs' and 'dames'?"[18] Guests at the Hotel Seville could have their morning coffee in the Cafe Ole and their dinner in the Fiesta Room before moving into the Matador Room to dance.

There was a daily rhythm to life in the resort hotel. Arrival was a time of anticipation mixed with the fatigue of travel. Most hotel entrances were elaborate with welcoming rituals efficiently performed to bolster positive impressions. Theodore Dreiser wrote of his arrival at the French Lick Hotel in 1915: "At the foot of a long iron and glass awning, protecting a yellow marble staircase of exceedingly florate design, a livered flunky stood waiting to open automobile doors. Various black porters pounced on our bags like vultures. We were escorted through a marble lobby such as Arabian romances once dreamed of as rare, and to an altar like desk, where a high priest of American profit deigned to permit us to register."[19]

Hotel routine was organized around meal service. At French Lick, breakfast and lunch were served at the regularly accepted hours, but dinner was delayed until seven P.M. Dinner was a formal event and a dress affair. Dreiser went every evening to see the grand parade to the dining room, to sit in the long hall to watch "the personages go by." Guests paraded for the doubtful enjoyment of looking at each other—to see and be seen. At West Virginia's Greenbriar Hotel, the afternoon ended with the last of the riding horses led away. Wrote Louise Hale: "All day we had heard the pleasant clopping of their feet upon the asphalted circle of the court. The tennis and golf players were swinging in; even the lovers were quitting Sunset Rock for the privilege of becoming more enticing in evening dress. The hush that comes with the dusk . . . was over the house. The tea things had gone clattering to rest, the night clamour of dinner had not yet begun." It seemed to Kenneth Roberts that men took to idleness with greater difficulty than women. Businessmen, he observed, spent most of their time sitting dolefully around hotel lobbies, expecting telegrams that never came, and wondering what day of the week it was. "Is today Tuesday or Wednesday? I sort of lose track down here," went a common conversation between idlers. "I was expecting a telegram on Tuesday, and it would have had to come before Thursday. I guess it's Wednesday."[20]

Every resort and every resort hotel had a prime season, either summer or winter. The season opened and closed in at least three phases: that of expectation, of realization, and of regret. It was unpleasant during the first stage, intolerable during the second, and frequently delightful during the third, according to one traveler, who wrote: "During the first there is a period when the host and guest meet on a footing of equality; during the second he is something less than a nonentity, a humble suitor at the monarch's throne; during the third the conditions are reversed, and the guest is lord of all he is willing to survey." As hotels were closed in the South at winter's end, they were opened in the North. Julian Street wrote: "If you are in Palm Beach near the season's end, and move up to St. Augustine, or Jacksonville, or Augusta, . . . you are likely to recognize, here and there, a waiter, a bell-boy, or a chambermaid whom you tipped some weeks earlier. Next summer when you take the boat up the Hudson, or go to Boston by the Fall River Line, or drop in at a hotel in Saratoga, there he will be, like an old friend."[21]

Summer Cottages

Hotels buffered guests from nature, and the environment they promoted was basically social. Tourists came to mix with other tourists in socially sanctioned places. But summer houses or cottages provided privacy for those who wished to avoid the crowd, even the fashionable crowd. Cottages located in the relative isolation of beachfront, mountain, or woods might also orient the family back to nature. The small cottage was the middle-class version of the elite summer home at Newport or winter house at Palm Beach. "As opposed to the restless discontent of flashy summer hotels," wrote Edward Bok, editor of the *Ladies Home Journal*, "a cottage stay promised tired mothers fresh air, a vegetable garden, long walks in green fields and restful naps amid the sweet scent of clover." In cottages, families could play together in natural or arcadian settings. John Van Schaick wrote of his cottage in New York's Catskills: "At the little hill farm we bathe our souls in a delicious now. The straining forward for a better tomorrow is stopped a bit. We are able better to do what probably God intended all of us to do, live one day at a time."[22]

Colonies of cottages were sometimes clustered about resort hotels, a monotonous village of wooden houses on a grid of streets adjacent to a beach or other amenity. Life fluctuated seasonally as at the hotels. From September to June, cottages stood closed amid the weeds with shutters fastened. Then came a bustle of arrivals, chiefly women with children fresh from the restraints of school and other winter activities. Historian Earl Pomeroy writes: "The normal routine of summer set in, of afternoons on beaches and porches, of hikes to the wild berry patches, of occasional fishing and clamming expeditions, of country church-bazaars and whist-parties, of watching at the nearest dock or railroad station for weekend visitors and for fathers and grandfathers come from the city for a week or two."[23] Cottages brought informality to vacation life as cottages brought people closer to nature.

Back to Nature

The growth of cities in North America not only refashioned the physical environment but reshaped the way people viewed that environment. There evolved a "back-to-nature" movement that valued wilder places for their picturesque and romantic qualities. Historian Peter Schmitt calls it a search for "Arcadia": an urban response that valued nature's spiritual impact above its utilitarian importance. Arcadia was a kind of place, Schmitt writes, that "lay somewhere on the urban fringe, easily accessible and mildly wild, the goal of a 'nature movement' led by teachers and preachers, bird-watchers, socialites, scout leaders, city-planners, and inarticulate commuters." Tourists were no less a part of this movement. For example, Christopher Morley, the ardent man–about–Philadelphia, frequently visited Neshaminy Creek north of that city. It was his place to watch nature and capture her subtleties of mood, a place in which to become refreshed. "Along the bank, where the great bleached trunks climb out of the water, there hangs the peculiar moist, earthy pungent smell of a river that runs among the woods. Every freshwater bather must know that smell. It has in it a dim taint as of decay, a sense of rotting vegetation. Yet it is a clean odor and a cool one."[24]

Motorists found nature along the roadside. Theodore Dreiser and his traveling companions stopped frequently to explore field and wood. At a farm in western New York they struck out through waving patterns of oxeye daisies and goldenrod to a green willow grove where, stripping off their clothes, they went swimming. Dreiser wrote: "The sky, between the walls of green wood, was especially blue. The great stones about us were all slippery with a thin, green moss, and yet so clear and pretty, and the water gurgled and sipped. Lying on my back I could see robins and bluejays and catbirds in the trees about." William Saroyan wrote about a drive along Lake Michigan. In the quiet afternoon shade the smell of water blended with the smell of leaf, bark, and earth. "The world was everlasting, and unbelievable. There was nothing like the world. Being in it was beyond understanding, it was incomprehensible joy."[25]

Spiritual renewal could be found in nature's subtle places. Obviously, it also could be found in settings of grandeur. The Grand Canyon was a most suitable place for meditation and for worship. One tourist wrote: "The Divine Intelligence seems very close at Grand Canyon; it surrounds one like a consciously felt blessing."[26] Another tourist wrote about Glacier National Park's "cathedral-domed, snow-sculptured, glacier-aisled, and rock-shrined territory." "Not a place of worship exists," he observed, "save all places. There is not a sanctuary—save the million that have been builded and constructed by the creative hands of Nature's God."[27]

Experiencing nature firsthand could be physically revitalizing. Charles Finger wrote of Mesa Verde, "The joy of great heights! The happiness of clearness of sky! How the body takes on new life, and how the muscles are renewed." But only the physically fit could appreciate fully the rigors of hiking, or of otherwise getting totally away from comfortable surroundings. One tourist, having descended to the bottom of the Grand Canyon, struggled back up to the rim. "The walk back developed into a tiring, eternal struggle up an interminable staircase that had no stairs. Sometimes I half decided to rest until next day. At intervals I grasped my knees in my hands and helped to lift the heavy tired feet one above the other."[28] Such struggles built character and became the stuff from which remembered adventure was wrung.

Nature could be overwhelming. At Zion Canyon in Utah, Charles Finger felt "reduced almost to nothingness" by the vast scale of the curious landforms. "We were glad to come back to small, familiar things—the pebbled stream at our feet, and the moisture-loving ferns that grew in crannies near it. Those seemed to exist for our delight, but the tremendous sights brought a sense of anxiety." Everywhere people reduced nature to human terms. The naming of features made nature less fearsome. A group of newspapermen from Philadelphia visiting the "Big Trees" near Santa Cruz, California, found one of the giant redwoods named "Pennsylvania." They were delighted and gathered around the tree to give "hearty cheers" for Pennsylvania, for the tree, and for home. The promoters of caverns as tourist attractions were particularly apt to humanize nature. Unusual formations were named, and various displays and entertainments were devised. When Charles Finger visited Carlsbad Caverns, he saw the King's Chamber, and the Queen's Chamber, and many other chambers to which romantic names had been attached. He speculated upon the man whose skeleton was displayed and listened to a quartet sing a hymn. But even with the human touches the repetition of the visit wore on Finger and the rest of his group. The enthusiastic "Ohs!" and "Ahs!" dwindled into occasional and half-hearted exclamations. Forests of stalagmites and curtains of stalactites, still pools and vast rocks, frozen waving banners of alabaster could not, after awhile, excite the group.[29]

Nature was made human through analogy and metaphor. At Bryce Canyon, Charles Finger, saw "theatricality" in its fanciful formations that suggested pleasure domes, castles, towers, cathedrals, crooked streets, dwellings built on crags, mansions hidden in ravines, statues, monuments, mosques. To one tourist descending into the Grand Canyon, nature gave way to architecture. The precipice above threw out buttresses and battlements like the "encircling walls of a colossal fortified city." Nature had emulated art on an Olympian scale. Winifred Dixon, searching for some mental yardstick with which to measure the Grand Canyon, thought that five Singer buildings piled atop each other would not show above the rim. But another visitor speculated how all the postal cards that had been mailed away, if returned, would fill the canyon up.[30]

The "back-to-nature" movement found new values in

wilder places. Its leading proponents, like John Muir and John Burroughs, articulated sentiments that, although little understood by most tourists, could still propel tentative nature exploration.[31] Tourists could test their own reactions to nature as seen or otherwise experienced, if only for fleeting moments, and without design or purpose. Since most tourists sought to reduce nature to familiar terms, most sought contrived attractions built around scenic curiosities. Most contrived attractions humanized nature, making the little understood and potentially frightful, as well as the downright tiresome, more palpable for touristic consumption. As resorts and parks buffered the tourist from nature, so the "back-to-nature" movement, with its compromises, served up its own buffering influences. For most tourists, the quest for nature was an inclination to pleasure, and not a dedication to truly profound comprehension.

National Parks in the United States

The national parks in the United States were not born out of necessity, but out of high ideals. Beginning in 1872 with the establishment of Yellowstone as a "public park or pleasuring-ground for the benefit and enjoyment of the people," a unique philosophy of park development evolved.[32] This philosophy represents a substantial American contribution to world tourism. Shaped by the Antiquities Act of 1906 (which empowered the establishment of national monuments on public lands), the National Parks Act of 1916 (which established the National Park Service), the Reorganization Act of 1933 (which transferred national military parks, battlefields, memorials, and cemeteries to Park Service administration), and the Historic Sites Act of 1935 (which provided for the establishment of national historic sites), America's national parks, monuments, historical areas, parkways, and recreation areas form a system for recreation that has inspired replication throughout the world.[33] When Enos Mills published his book *Your National Parks* in 1917, the Park Service had already articulated much of its philosophy. Mills wrote: "A national park is an island of safety in this riotous world. Within national parks is room—glorious room—room in which to find ourselves, in which to think and hope, to dream and plan, to rest, and resolve."[34] Parks were to provide the nation with space in which to relax, recharge, renew.

The creation of America's national parks was a preemptive act. Land that might have been used by private interests toward more utilitarian ends was preempted for the public's pursuit of the picturesque, and even the romantic. It was an act of sparing places, of letting natural scenery remain relatively untouched, and of tolerating nature for nature's sake. This preempting of land and sparing of place had nationalistic and educational significance. Enos Mills continued: "The intensity of love for native land depends chiefly upon the loveliness of its landscapes—upon its scenery. We cannot love an ugly country . . . love of the land must be inspired—and inspired by the scenic loveliness of that land." As national parks stood as icons of nationhood, they could be used to bring Americans closer together. Lack of national unity was perilous, but the mingling of people of all classes from all sections of the country in places of beauty and pleasure promoted "acquaintance in the happiest of circumstances."[35] Parks were to be placed where Americans could discover communalities.

Many historians of American national parks development have emphasized the conservation ethic over the role of tourism. They have emphasized the protection of wilderness over the providing of resort environments.[36] The quest to protect nature inviolate provided much of the intellectual and emotional drive behind park development, but the tourist, as consumer, and as responsive citizen, provided the economic and political rationale needed to translate philosophy into accomplishment. Bureaucrats also saw parks in practical terms. Stephen Mather structured and promoted the parks as tourist attractions, even opening them to private enterprise through a system of commercial concessions. In 1917 the Park Service distributed 83,000 automobile guidebooks in order to promote tourist visitation.[37] The secretary of the interior encouraged Mather "in the splendid cooperation developed . . . among chambers of commerce, tourist bureaus, and automobile-highway associations for the purpose of spreading information about our parks and facilitating their use and enjoyment."[38] In

1920 nearly a million tourists visited the nation's national parks and monuments.[39]

Commercialism was encouraged for the public good. In 1917, Mather spoke out against criticism of park concessionaires. Noting that the era of elite pilgrimage to such scenic shrines as Yosemite was past, Mather argued the right of every American to visit the parks "in as great luxury as each can afford." "It is the duty of the government representing these millions to provide each one who comes as nearly as possible . . . the degree of comfort even of luxury, that he requires." It was his duty to open the parks "for the fast increasing throng of motorists, to make every spot of special beauty comfortably available by trail, and to provide all possible means for the old and the weak and the poor, as well as the young and the strong and the well-to-do, to enjoy what belongs equally to all." Mather concluded: "As Uncle Sam is not an innkeeper nor a liveryman, private enterprise must provide the means of living in and enjoying these great national playgrounds."[40]

Private corporations bid for the right to build and operate hotels and stores, and to provide public transportation in the parks. Many companies, such as those at Yellowstone, Yosemite, and the Grand Canyon, were subsidiaries of railroad corporations. Many conservationists took note of the potential for environmental spoilage. George Lorimer, editor of the *Saturday Evening Post*, warned that selling scenery was a dangerous business. How could one popularize the national parks without destroying "the very thing that we are trying to save?" According to Lorimer, the parks attracted three kinds of tourist. First were "people who had gone to the wrong place." They only wanted a change of scene and an opportunity to meet the same people and do the same things that they did at home. To them a national park without a New York City hotel and all that went with it was unthinkable. The "wind in the pines" had to be supplemented by a jazz band. They wanted to climb mountains, but on railways, and to swing across dizzy canyons snugly seated in "cars that hang from shoot-the-chute cables." The second variety of visitors were the automobile campers who searched "for something different and sometimes something worse than their daily home routine." They adventured in automobiles and tents, with most of them orderly and well-behaved, but others were despoilers of nature. The third kind of visitors were, to Lorimer, the most important so far as park development was concerned. These visitors went into wild places because they had a real love of the outdoors. "In the end," Lorimer wrote, "they shall inherit the Kingdom of Earth and defend it against the unthinking and unworthy." Lorimer concluded: "If we must jazz them up with dance halls, picture shows, funiculars, cables to all the rest of it in order to sell them to the people, why have national parks at all? Coney Island, the White City . . . and the Country Club will better answer the purpose."[41]

Conservationists were kept constantly watchful. In a society dominated by utilitarian viewpoints, it was always easier to justify development, as opposed to lack of development. The national parks owed much to conservationists, especially in the early days of park management before the general public became aware of and supportive of the benefits of place sparing. Many exploitative schemes were disapproved. In Yellowstone, for example, plans to grant long-term leases to private companies for resort development, proposals to grant rights-of-way to railroads, and plans for such contrived attractions as a proposed elevator to the foot of the Lower Falls were defeated.[42] Plans to install a cable car to Glacier Point in Yosemite, as well as a cable across the Grand Canyon, were also shelved.[43] Ski lifts, however, were built in Mount Rainier, Rocky Mountain, Sequoia, Yosemite, Lassen, and Olympic national parks. Conservationists suffered a serious defeat with the construction of the Hetch Hetchy Reservoir in Yosemite.[44]

The early development of roads in Yellowstone, Yosemite, and other parks fell to the Army Corps of Engineers. Indeed, until the establishment of the park service, park administration fell to the U.S. Army. Roads were engineered to accommodate the stage coaches that carried tourists into and through the parks from the railheads. Only at the Grand Canyon did a railroad line penetrate to the heart of a park. Automobile traffic, once encouraged, became a flood. Automobiles were admitted at Mount Rainier in 1908, at Crater Lake in 1911, at Glacier in 1912, and at Yellowstone in 1915. Mather encouraged automobile tourists since the Park Service was desperately dependent upon visitor entrance fees, not only for operating funds, but for capital improvements as well.[45] More than 55,000 automobiles entered the national parks in 1917, but by 1926 the number had reached 400,000.[46]

Roads not only attracted motorists, but served to control them as well. Roads restricted motorists to certain sections of every park, concentrating them physically in constricted areas. Historian Peter Schmitt comments: "They lived by the road, and they most enjoyed the wilderness as it was framed in their windshields. To offer scenic beauty without destroying the wilderness it was only necessary to build a limited but carefully designed road network between major park attractions."[47] Park roads were not mere routes of access, but, like the pathways of the romantic garden, they controlled the place images that tourists carried away.

Park buildings were designed to blend with nature. Structures were always intrusions into nature, irrespective of how necessary they might be for interpretation, shelter, service, transportation, or sanitation. A 1935 park service report on building design reads: "Lamentable is the fact that during the six days given over to Creation, picnic tables and fireplaces, foot bridges, toilet facilities, and many other of man's requirements even in natural surroundings, were negligently and entirely overlooked." Success in park buildings, according to the report, were measurable by the yardstick of self-restraint. The designer needed to harmonize his buildings with the natural landscape by using native materials in "rustic" designs of proper scale, avoiding rigid straight lines and oversophistication. Rustic architecture gave the feeling of having been executed by pioneer craftsmen with limited hand tools. Thus the designer needed to develop "kindred humility" toward the past. The report continues: "He becomes aware of the unvoiced claims of those long gone races and earlier generations that tracked the wilderness . . . before him. In fitting tribute he graces his encroachments by adapting to his structures such of their traditions and practices as come to his understanding."[48]

During the Depression of the 1930s, various federal

programs accelerated physical development of the national parks. The Civilian Conservation Corps (CCC) aided in reforestation and the building of fire trails, bridges, camp grounds, dams, water and sewer systems, signs, and roads. The Public Works Administration (PWA) constructed new roads in excess of 1,000 miles, as well as 294 miles of new parkway.[49] By World War II national park design had been brought to a high level of achievement. Park landscapes were not only distinctive for their natural beauty, but for the highly imaginative designs used to blend built with natural environments. Parks looked like parks for the consistency of signs, buildings, roads, and other necessary fixtures. A new place type had been developed. America's national parks were distinctive places in their design as well as in their purpose.

Before the advent of the automobile, visitors to Yellowstone Park came by stagecoach to stay at the park's hotels. Coaching was very much a sport of the well-to-do, and the coach trip became as much a part of the Yellowstone attraction as any of the park's scenic features. But in 1917 the nearly 1,400 horses in Yellowstone were replaced by motor buses, since horses and automobiles did not coexist well on the park's roads.[50] A half-dozen campgrounds, several lunch stations, and one hotel were closed since the recommended circuit of the park was reduced from six days to three.

Most early automobilists entered the park at the north gate. There army veterans in uniform collected entrance fees and warned visitors about the use of firearms. In the early 1920s traffic moved in a counterclockwise direction on the loop of roads, with automobiles required to remain fifty yards apart, and at speeds below twelve miles per hour.[51] Automobile traffic necessitated road improvement, and rights-of-way were widened and straightened, and highways paved. The many water tanks once used by the road sprinklers were thus eliminated, and the vegetation along park roads lost its covering of dust in dry weather. Telephone and power lines were removed from roadsides and screened from view. Campgrounds and hotels provided overnight accommodation. In 1915, three "permanent camp" systems were in operation, featuring tents permanently erected at set locations.[52] Spaces were also set aside for motorists to pitch their own tents. In 1923, over 138,000 visitors entered Yellowstone, with 60 percent coming by automobile. Over half of the automobilists camped.[53]

The hotel at Old Faithful was long the park's most popular hostelry. Beatrice Massey wrote: "The Old Faithful Inn is unique, it being built entirely of the park timber in the rough, hewed from the twisted trees of the forest." She was especially attracted to the huge fireplaces in the lobby that "always gave a cheery appearance" and in which "attendants pop corn for the guests." Old Faithful geyser was the hotel's principal attraction. "At regular intervals," Massey noted, "the mass of water is thrown 150 feet into the air with a roar of escaping steam that sounds like the exhaust of an ocean liner. At night an immense searchlight on the roof of the hotel plays upon it, and everyone goes to the farther side to view the water with the light showing through—a glorious sight!" Not all guests were so taken with the geyser. Thomas Wolfe, the novelist, ensconced himself in the hotel bar, as he liked to do on oceanliners. There was "more merriment here and people more prosperous, less cultured[,] and singing 'we don't give a damn for the whole state of Utah.'"[54]

Of the park's myriad attractions, none was more impressive to visitors than the Grand Canyon of the Yellowstone with its gorge of yellow rock. Beatrice Massey recorded: "With the greenish cascade of water foaming beneath us and the blue dome of the heavens above, we stood there awed by its fearful majesty and unequaled beauty. As if to make the picture more perfect, an eagle soared through the canyon, lighting on a pinnacle of jagged rock." Of Yellowstone's Inspiration Point above the canyon, Massey wrote: "You stand there in the presence of the marvelous works of God, the evidences of great convulsions of nature through the ages. You feel such an atom in the vastness, the unending space of the infinite."[55]

Wildlife was of major interest, and the bears were a prime attraction. "Living with bears," wrote Lewis Gannett in 1937, "is the major adventure of the Yellowstone. Bears are everywhere. Big black bears lie down to snooze in the middle of

Old Faithful Inn at Yellowstone National Park (1932). In the United States, national parks were created and managed so that tourists could experience nature in "wilder places," spared the usual resort intrusions. Buildings and roads were blended with the physical environment.

the automobile roads, and rise up on their hind legs to beg food when a car slows down to greet them."[56] The hotels erected platforms where each evening bears fed on garbage.

Yellowstone attracted visitors for its relative wildness. Here nature had been spared the debilitating spoilation of mine, farm, factory, and town, and even many of the influences of the traditional resort. Although "nature" was substantially influenced by human action, the sense of the primeval prevailed. Frederic Van de Water wrote: "Here is peace. Here is trust and friendliness. Here is the amazing result of fifty years truce after millenniums of slaughter. You see it and thrill to it . . . in the trust of chipmunks and squirrels and the calm benignity of bears. Here, something whispers, is one small rectangle the world where life goes on serenely, tolerantly, as the Architect planned it before Eden." But not all visitors to Yellowstone agreed. Melville Ferguson found the park a pleasure ground and not a wilderness. To him Yellowstone was laid out like a city playground. Fine broad roads swept through and circled around it, smoothing the tourists' pathway to principal attractions. These, you could see by walking but a few steps from your car. John Steinbeck found Yellowstone too artificial, with landscapes divorced from reality. Yellowstone enclosed "the unique, the spectacular, the astonishing—the greatest waterfall, the deepest canyon, the highest cliff, the most

Tourist at Yellowstone (c. 1910). Yellowstone was a domesticated place, its animals no less domesticated than its tourists.

stupendous works of man or nature." The park, in Stein-beck's view, celebrated "the freaks of our nation and of our civilization."[57]

Early tourists to Yosemite National Park also came by stagecoach. Most travelers entered from the southwest that they might approach the valley by way of the classic view at Yosemite's Inspiration Point. There, Effie Gladding wrote in 1915,

> Our stage driver took a genuine pleasure, the pleasure of the showman, in reining up his horses at the psycho-logical moment and allowing us to drink in the view that burst dramatically upon us. There was the green level floor of the Valley before us; there was El Capitan rising in massive grandeur, a sheer wall of rock, in evening greys and lavenders, above the Valley; there was the Bridal Veil—a silver thread of water falling 600 feet. And beyond were the Valley walls rising in the distance.[58]

Yosemite Valley was ceded to California during the Civil War for a state park, and the surrounding high country was later reserved by the federal government as a forest preserve. Wild-life was destroyed as the valley was cut into farms and ranches, and vegetation suffered from severe overgrazing, even in the higher elevations.[59] Land was also leased for hotels and camp-grounds. When the valley was ceded back to the federal govern-ment in 1906, the place was anything but a wilderness.

The first camp was established by D. A. Curry and his wife in 1899. They began with seven tents, a cook, and several college students to clean and help with tourist baggage.[60] Mary Bedell wrote of Camp Curry in 1923: "There are perhaps 300 permanent tents and tiny wooden bungalows all grouped around a grove of trees where is located the large dining-hall, the post office, a dancing pavilion, and a log cabin used for a writing room. . . . Almost every convenience, and every lux-ury is provided for the tourist here, such as an out-of-door swimming pool, tennis-courts, laundries and even shampoo-parlors." The evening camp fire was a Camp Curry tradition,

with its so-called "fire fall' of burning ashes dropped to the valley floor from Glacier Point some three thousand feet above.
David Steele found a "metropolis of canvas in the center of the
wilderness." There was a post office and express, telephone
and telegraph offices, as well as a general store and all kinds of
curio emporiums. The joys of camp life, he thought, commingled with "every device known to the city habitant." There
were even dancing pavilions, baseball grounds, bowling alleys,
soda fountains, and movies.[61]

Many tourists were disappointed by the extent of Yosemite's development. Lewis Gannett wrote in 1937: "When you
'camp' in a space six miles long and a mile wide, with several
thousand other 'campers,' in tents set up so close to one another
that the guy-ropes cross, you do not camp at all." To Gannett,
Yosemite Valley was an amusement park, as crowded as New
York's Central Park. Nothing in America was less wild than the
floor of Yosemite Valley. He concluded: "Once it was a wild
garden; now it is a dead museum."[62] By 1950, upwards of
30,000 tourists visited Yosemite in a single day at the peak of the
season. Nearly five hundred buildings had been erected to
handle the crowd, not counting the tent cities of canvas.[63] By
1960, the valley contained nine general stores, seven gasoline
stations, and hotels capable of accommodating 4,500 overnight
guests.[64]

The first automobile was driven into Yosemite from San
Francisco. At Camp Curry the driver ran her machine into the
midst of a circle of eastern tourists seated around the large camp
fire. The apparition of an automobile brought forth "generous
applause and hearty congratulations."[65] Automobiles in the
park were common after 1913. Mary Bedell wrote about her
approach to the valley at Inspiration Point in 1924. There she
took pictures, but what really attracted her attention was the
system for traffic control. She joined the long line of automobiles waiting to descend into the valley. On the even hours,
cars came up; on the odd hours, they went down. A ranger took
each license number to be called to a checkpoint below and
attached a bright-colored sticker to each windshield.[66]

Most tourists found Yosemite's scenery spectacular.
David Steele found it "supreme in charm and in beauty" and

"majestic and awe-inspiring." He wrote: "The awful grandeur of those rivers, rushing off precipices thousands of feet high, and the sublimity of those stupendous cliffs, springing vertically from the level valley floor, are relieved and softened by charms of rich verdure of golden sunlight. Its beauty is no less but no more notable than its majesty. It has no rival on earth for its many natural attractions. . . . Here the weary rest; but here also the poet is inspired, the artist is entranced, and the priest has a new reason for becoming pious." Charles Finger personified the park: "Yosemite's mood is one of gladness because men may see a world exquisite and fine, where joy does not depend upon excitement, but rather upon an awakened sense of wonder, at beholding so many rare sights." "Yosemite is a genial host," he continued, "full of good-nature, indulgent, happy to see his guests enjoy life on their own terms, even though enjoyment has a ring of triviality about it."[67]

The Grand Canyon was set aside as a national forest in 1893, a game preserve in 1906, a national monument in 1908, and a national park in 1919.[68] The south rim was developed before World War I as a resort by the Santa Fe Railroad. David Steele wrote of visitors between trains who "stopped, looked and listened, and marveled at the scene or complained of the cost, according to their depth of soul and past experience of travel." Tourists could take the Rim Drive to Grand View or to Hopi Point, both noted for their sunsets. Or they could descend by mule into the Grand Canyon on the Bright Angel Trail. Irvin Cobb described such an adventure:

> At the start there is always a lot of nervous chatter—
> airy persiflage flies to and fro and much laughing is
> indulged in. But it has a forced, strained sound.
> . . . Down a winding footpath moves the procession,
> with the guide in front, and behind him in single file his
> string of pilgrims—all nervous as cats and some hold-
> ing to their saddle-pommels with death grips. Just
> under the first terrace a halt is made while the official
> photographer takes a picture . . . so you can see for
> yourself just how pale and haggard and wall-eyed and
> how much like a typhoid patient you looked.

Cobb reflected on the thousands of people who had already made the trip without incidence, and it comforted him, but not much. "The trail clings to the sheer side of the dizziest, deepest chasm in the known world," he wrote. "One of your legs is scraping against the granite; the other is dangling over half a mile of fresh mountain air."[69]

The Santa Fe Railroad's Fred Harvey subsidiary operated the El Tovar and several other hotels. College students were employed as maids and waitresses and, as each trainload of tourists departed, they gathered on the hotel steps to sing farewell songs: "Till We Meet Again" and "Good Bye, Ladies," and the like. Thomas Wolfe, a close observer of such human drama, saw tears in the eyes of many of the passengers, and even in some of the girls'. Perhaps, the railroad made the Grand Canyon too accessible. James Flagg echoed the complaint of the travel sophisticates: "The inevitable drawback to this sort of place is the tourist for which the place is run." Of the news that a new highway was to be opened to the north rim, Charles Finger lamented: "There will be sign-boards, and motor-busses, and filling stations, and eating places that serve abominable meals, and cooks with dirty hands, and hitch-hikers, and absurd cold-drink stands, and well-to-do people in limousines who sleep in the day time, and other things that come with advancing civilization."[70]

Even with its margins developed for tourism, the Grand Canyon was still grand. The Soviet journalists Ilya Ilf and Eugene Petrov wrote: "The spectacle of the Grand Canyon does not have its equal anywhere on earth. It did not even resemble anything else on earth. The landscape upset all European concepts about the globe. . . . It looked like some imaginary vision, which might occur to a boy while reading fantastic romances about the moon or Mars." Above all, Ilf and Petrov were impressed with the place as a park. It was "faultlessly organized," they marvelled. "Hotels and roads, the distribution of printed and photographic publications, maps, prospectuses, guidebooks, and finally, oral presentations—all of it is here at a high standard of excellence."[71]

Wilderness

The preservation of scenery in parks did not satisfy the advocates of true wilderness, although John Muir did view the rise of the national park system as a positive first step. Muir wrote: "Thousands of tired, nerve-shaken, overcivilized people are beginning to find out that going to the mountains is going home; that wilderness is a necessity; and that mountain parks and reservations are useful not only as fountains of timber and irrigating rivers, but as fountains of life." He continued: "Even the scenery habit in its most artificial forms mixed with spectacles, silliness, and Kodaks, its devotees arrayed more gorgeously than scarlet tanagers, frightening the wild game with red umbrellas,—even this is encouraging, and may well be regarded as a hopeful sign of the times." But the United States was rapidly losing its wild aspect, a process which was accelerated by the coming of the automobile. Rationales beyond tourism and its "back to nature" impulse appeared necessary to justify preservation of wilderness. Conservationists like Aldo Leopold found such rationales in the principles of ecology. They saw the need to preserve natural systems as living organisms, and not just as visual displays.[72] At Leopold's urging in 1924, the United States Forest Service set aside the first wilderness area in the Gila National Forest of Arizona and New Mexico.

But scientific principles couldn't really carry the argument for preserving the wilderness. Advocates like Leopold constantly fell back on rationales related to tourism. They intended wilderness areas for the true outdoorsman, the sophisticated seeker after nature. Just as "canoeing in the wake of a motor launch or down a line of summer cottages" was not a canoe trip, so Leopold was sure that taking a pack train down a graded highway was "merely exercise, with about the same flavor as lifting dumbbells." Leopold called for "wild regions big enough to absorb the average man's two-week vacation without getting him tangled up in his own backtrack." To Leopold these areas needed to be "free from motor roads, summer cottages, launches or other manifestations of gasoline."[73] Conservationists wanted to keep common tourists out of wilderness preserves just as they wanted to keep out prospectors, miners, lumbermen, and ranchers.

Outdoorsmen who came unobtrusively in limited numbers were intended to be the prime beneficiaries of wilderness preservation. Nevertheless, everyone stood to benefit, because through the oudoorsmen the essence of America's pioneer spirit would be communicated to society at large. As historian Roderick Nash points out, in wilderness was total escape from civilization, a way of keeping alive the old pioneer skills and values." The American wilderness represented a distinctive American environment, an anvil upon which distinctive American society and culture had been wrought.[74] Americans could benefit from wilderness by just knowing that preserves existed. Wilderness was to be a psychological safety valve for the nation. Although various federal agencies designated "wilderness," "wild," "primitive," "roadless," "natural," "scenic," "limited," "research," and even "sacred" areas over the years, a comprehensive wilderness policy was not implemented until passage of the Wilderness Act of 1964, which established wilderness areas in various national parks and monuments, forests, wildlife refuges, and Indian reservations.[75]

National Parks in Canada

When James "Bunny" Harkin, Canada's first commissioner of national parks, assumed office in 1911, he adopted a strictly utilitarian orientation to park development. The mainstays of his park system, the Rocky Mountain parks centered at Banff, Lake Louise, Jasper, Field, Glacier, and Revelstoke in Alberta and British Columbia, had been developed as resorts oriented to the Canadian Pacific Railroad. Until 1911 much of the money for park improvement came from the railroad, and many of the buildings and roads were designed by railroad architects. The Banff Hot Springs Reservation was developed in 1885. The hotel, designed by Bruce Price, Emily Post's father, set a standard, not only for the many Canadian Pacific hotels that followed, but for Canadian park development generally. The original Banff Springs Hotel was a rustic frame building that was a cross between a Tudor hall and a Swiss chalet in design. Its replacement, built in stages between 1912 and 1928, was more a "Scottish baronial derivative of the Chateau style."[76]

Banff was established as a park, not to protect landscape so much as to serve tourists. Although the railroad used the promise of spectacular mountain scenery to attract visitors to the area, it was not above exploiting other resources even to the spoilation of that scenery. Copper and coal mines, along with their supportive towns, were established at a half-dozen locations along the line either side of Banff. Lumbering and limestone quarrying scarred large areas of mountainside. Banff became a tourist retreat and was provisioned, accordingly, with golf courses, riding stables, and all the other accoutrements of a well-rounded resort, including subdivisions leased for cottage development. As in the Yosemite Valley, wildlife was destroyed, although a small zoo was established to display wild animals. A massive tree-planting program was launched using nursery stock imported from the United States.[77] There was no intention of preserving a primeaval landscape. Banff, in fact, evolved from a frontier condition of extreme environmental exploitation. Except in the new resort, utilitarian values dominated the area.

Banff suffered many of the excesses of the traditional resort. One tourist wrote of the Banff Springs Hotel, "The only business at Banff is to enjoy one's self, to recreate, to loaf in the sunshine and worship nature. You sit at dinner in style, and eat your fried chicken *a la* Maryland to the 'March El Capitan' or a 'Fantasie From Der Freischutz' played by the Melrose Trio." Most tourists sat and watched the scenery through the hotel's big plate glass windows by which striking pictures were framed. But Banff also gave outdoorsmen a place from which to have access to the still-wild higher elevations of the surrounding mountains. Ernie Pyle rode a horse up to a mountain glacier. "We forded mountain streams—the leaping rocky kind you see in the newsreels, clear as glass and cold as ice. You could look up a quarter of a mile and see the glacier that bore the stream, or look down and see it rushing and falling away below you." Late in the afternoon, Pyle continued, "a lone rider and a white horse came out of the pass and down the trail to the lake. Their heads were low against the driving storm. The rain soaked through the rider's clothes, and ran into his shoes, and trickled coldly down his back. He had not been actually wet through from rain for many years. It made him feel kind of worth-while again."[78]

Not until the Canadian Parks Act of 1930 was policy formulated for the preservation of nature within parks.[79] As Roderick Nash surmises, Canadians have felt little need for protecting wild places. Even today, Canadians still regard themselves as a pioneering people with an overabundance of wild country. Because of the Canadian North, with its mind-boggling millions of square miles without civilization, Canadians have not been enthusiastic conservationists. Thomas Longstreth caught this prevailing sentiment as he hiked inland from a Lake Superior lumber camp. "Behind me lay six miles of climbing up from Lake Superior, before me twenty miles of the completest wilderness. I sat in a shower of solitude. In that expanse of bush were veritable wolves and moose, but no men. I was on the inside of adventure at last. Realizing this, joy spread her wings and bore me along." Of Canada's North, Longstreth concluded: "What an endless world."[80]

Tourists sought in nature physical and mental renewal. Physical exertion—drinking the waters, bathing by the shore, hiking in the woods, mountain climbing—promised good health. Whether seeking the spiritual in mountain quietude or disclosing secrets scientifically in desert wastes, intellectual exertion provided inspiration. Most tourists sought nature in extreme moderation, accepting the conveniences of the resorts with their contrived attractions, luxury hotels, and ease of access by railroad or highway. In resorts, a controlled, often domesticated, "nature" was readily consumed, and consumers, in their visibility made conspicuous in their consumption. National parks in the United States were more nature-like than the traditional resorts. But they by no means represented wilderness conditions or nature unspoiled. The national parks, as wilder places, were cultural landscapes in which place-sparing prevailed with dedication. There tourists went back to nature in landscapes where nature was respected as an attraction, and not fully exploited as a commerical resource.

CHAPTER FOUR
TRAVEL BY RAILROAD AND STEAMSHIP

> These fast through trains are really swift-moving hotels. Think of electric lights, hot and cold running water, easy chairs, a writing desk, a library, a bathroom, a barber shop, a dining-room, and spacious sleeping compartments, all whirling through the landscape at the rate of 50 miles an hour!
>
> David Steele, *Going Abroad Overland*

Travelers by railroad and steamship were relatively passive since they trusted others to move them safely and efficiently from destination to destination. Passengers could leisurely bide their time in relative comfort, either oblivious to the passing scene, or glued to window or rail as mood dictated. Landscapes passed as displays fragmented according to the traveler's span of attention and speed of movement. The train or ship was a special environment contrived for comfort. Trains and ships were also enclosed social worlds, reflecting at once idleness, expectancy, anxiety, complacency, and thrill of travel. Both technologies shared many similiarities regarding the handling of passengers and the derived structuring of travel experience. Nevertheless, the two modes of travel also provided interesting contrasts.

Railroad Travel

In 1900 railroads dominated travel in North America. Passenger service was provided on nearly all 258,000 miles of track in the United States and the 18,000 miles in Canada.[1] Most travel writers described the fast trains that connected major cities. Occasionally, journalists wandered onto isolated branch lines or rode slow local trains in search of novel experiences. Railroad service dwindled with the increased popularity of automobiles and other transportation alternatives. Whereas Pullman service in North America extended to 130,000 miles of railroad in 1930, it served only 85,068 miles in 1957.[2] Although equipment was upgraded and depots modernized, travel experience remained much the same throughout the early twentieth century. Departure, movement, and arrival defined a rhythm of travel tied to fixed routes and fixed schedules.

Accommodations varied on trains. Tourists traveling a long distance might choose to travel by coach, sitting up all night with rented pillows. More likely, they would travel by Pullman, occupying sleeping berths. Written descriptions of sleeping cars are legion. Early one morning, at Detroit, Julian Street boarded a train from New York City bound for Chicago. He found his car still arrayed for nighttime. The narrow aisle, with its shroud of long, green curtains, had been made narrower still by lines of shoes and suitcases. It was chilly, Street remembers, with "a cold which embalmed the mingling smells of sleep and sleeping car—an odor as of Russian leather and banana peel ground into a damp pulp." Street sat with his newspaper while an adjacent berth came to life, the curtains thrashing wildly. Its occupant emerged, fumbled for his shoes, and then, in his undershirt, stood up in the aisle. "His face was fat and heavy, his eyes half closed, his hair in tousled disarray. His trousers sagged dismally about his hips, and his suspenders dangled down behind him. After rolling his collar, necktie, shirt, and waistcoat into a mournful little bundle, he produced . . . a few unpleasant toilet articles, and made off down the car."[3]

Most travelers agreed that dressing and undressing within the narrow confines of a Pullman berth required great skill. One traveler thought it required the abilities of a professional acrobat. The Pullman berth, formed on the lower level by folding seats together, and on the upper level by folding down a narrow shelf, left little room for maneuver. Those who traveled in luxury, like the French journalist Andre La Fond, rented compartments or even more spacious drawing rooms. La Fond's compartment had a bed with "immaculate sheets," baggage racks, clothes hooks, an electric fan, a large mirror, a ceiling light, and electric plugs. "You push down the back of the armchair," he wrote, "and there appears a washstand with a highly-polished aluminum wash basin." But tourists like La Fond missed out on the commotion of the Pullman berths: listening to neighbors snoring, or eavesdropping on conversations inches beyond enveloping curtains. On one trip John Van Schaick lay awake as one man repeatedly asked his wife what time it was. Was she sure his pants were in a safe place? Didn't she think it was a little stuffy? And so on. Above all, compartment dwellers like La Fond missed out on the morning line-up in the public washroom. "Presently you get your turn at a sloppy washbowl," Street wrote, "after which you slip into the stale clothing of the day before, you return to the body of the car, feeling half-washed, half-dressed and half dead."[4]

Travel by train could be truly miserable. Trains were not air-conditioned until the 1940s, and then only the extra-fare "limited" trains had this luxury. Rollo Brown sweltered in a berth while traveling through Oklahoma. He stretched a sheet across the open window to keep out the cinders. It also seemed to keep out the air, although it let in noise and odor, he found. "We crashed through small towns[,] past jangling crossing-bells, and all the odors of stockpens as we swept alongside miles of freight trains that carried protesting livestock." Porters employed by the Pullman Company kept order amid the potential chaos of travel. They supplied ice water, helped to clean clothing, and soothed travelers with conversation. An English tourist commented, "There is a good deal to be said for the . . . slow, courteous, usually venerable African who polishes your shoes, brushes your clothes, and hides your hat in a brown paper bag."[5]

Travel by train involved a sequence of starts and stops with intervening periods of movement, all beyond the control of the traveler. The motion of the train and the sound of its movement created sensations unique in travel. One English visitor gloried in the "clickety click" of the car wheels on the loosely jointed tracks. Another Englishman found the "mournful" wail of the locomotive's whistle "curiously romantic," as his train swept past grade crossings. He relished the swaying coaches and his ability to move from one coach to another while the train was underway. On some railroads Western Union boys passed through the coaches collecting telegrams, or vendors swarmed aboard each time a train stopped. Trains without dining cars stopped at depots with lunchrooms. One Fred Harvey lunchroom on the Santa Fe Railroad was described as teeming with people weaving in and out. There were more people than stools, and around the big counters struggled two layers of diners, the one group leaning over the backs of the other.[6]

Many travelers were attracted to the homey atmosphere of the dining cars, which were added and subtracted from trains during the course of long trips. Rollo Brown observed how a man could spend a whole morning in a dining car if he was experienced. He could order item by item as he ate, with full pauses now and then to read a book and with other pauses for the passing landscape. "So for an hour and half," he wrote, "I sat and ate lettuce salad, and belated blueberry pie, and ice cream and read a little, and reordered coffee that was hot, and looked out." The black waiters in the dining cars provided a form of theater. The balancing of trays reminded one traveler of performers who did things on tightrope wires stretched across gorges. Dining-car food was excellent on some railroads, but bland and standardized on others. Julian Street found a single

Dining car on the Great Northern Railroad (1934). Railroad travelers tended to focus their attention inside, rather than outside, the car. Dining cars and lounge cars provided opportunities to interact with fellow passengers.

taste running through every dish he ate, as if everything had been produced from some basic substance: "The primary taste . . . is, nearly as I can hit on it, that of wet paper."[7]

Long-distance trains carried a variety of specialty cars. Lounge cars or club cars catered to those interested in socializing. There was an ebb and flow of activity as trains passed from wet into dry areas and back again, the bar opening and closing. Observation platforms placed at the rear of luxury trains offered unique views of the passing scene. One traveler asked, "Did you ever stand on the rear platform on entering . . . a tunnel and watch the receding landscape through the portal?"[8] Sometimes rear coaches, reserved as "chair cars," were provided with large, soft easy chairs that swiveled in place. Here, affluent, short-distance travelers relaxed in comfort tended by attentive porters. On long-distance trains, a restless passenger might get his hair cut. He might wander forward to the baggage car, or watch the mail being sorted in the post-office car. After World War II, as the railroads sought to meet the competition of air travel, trains were "streamlined," or modernized. Dome cars were introduced as a new way of seeing landscape, especially on transcontinental runs.

Long transcontinental train trips could prove monotonous. In order to maintain passenger interest, many railroads prepared guidebooks that described points along their lines. In traveling from Salt Lake City to San Francisco, Julian Street found that his pamphlet contained a relief map of the railroad and a paragraph or two about every station, giving the history of the place and telling its altitude, the distance from terminal points, and how it got its name. Transcontinental train travel was not a continuous experience so far as landscape traversed was concerned. Dallas Sharp realized that sleeping cars were necessary, especially on transcontinental runs, but it was "utterly violent," the spark of consciousness jumping a five-hundred-mile gap of landscape in a single night. It was fine to know that you were one thousand miles closer to California, but what about Kansas or Arizona? Wrote Sharp, "I have closed my eyes in the early dark of a winter day to a howling prairie blizzard and opened them the next morning to see cattle picking a desert breakfast from among soapweeds and prickly pears and dusty sagebrush, climatic zones and geologic aeons apart."[9]

Slow-moving local trains proved boring for most travelers. Julian Street and a companion boarded a train at Birmingham for Columbus, Mississippi, 120 miles away. They arrived five hours later, hungry and tired, but more or less resigned to their fate. When they had asked about the train's nonexistant dining car, the conductor had replied, "Where do you gentlemen reckon you're a-goin' to, anyhow?" The train contained a "Jim Crow" car jammed with blacks standing in the aisles. There followed several untidy and nearly empty coaches for whites. Webb Waldron's train in northern Michigan was a freight to which a coach had been attached. He wrote: "The stoppings, waitings, backings, switchings at every siding gave me plenty of time to explore the decayed lumber towns along the way. . . . Most of the time the other passengers and I spent picking blackberries in the adjacent woods, or slouched in our seats morosely contemplating the past and the future."[10]

Railroad travel also provided tourists with ample opportunity to observe people. Not all passengers were tourists; indeed, most railroad travelers throughout the 1950s were businessmen. Because the train was not strictly a touristic setting, one could see a cross section of the "real world." Julian Street and his companion appraised their fellow travelers. They guessed what kinds of houses they resided in, what kinds of furniture they had, what kinds of books they read, or didn't read. On one trip Rollo Brown walked to the observation car, but as every chair was taken, he only lingered for a few minutes. "Men with wide-open eyes and relaxed cheeks inclined toward each other, made sweeping gestures with hands that held half-empty tall glasses, and spoke with great positiveness." He caught only occasional words—"'General Motors'—'if I could only get him'—'New England Power'—'Tel and Tel'—'Nickel Plate.'" Another traveler observed that businessmen were usually at their best, and happiest, after dinner in a train's club car, where conditions not unlike a cocktail party prevailed. There the men with the least to say talked the loudest, the wise ones sitting in silence.[11]

A tour of the cars might reveal clear social stratification. On a train in western Ontario, Morris Longstreth walked from the chair car at the rear to the colonist car at the front. There sat migrants on their way to new farms and towns on the Canadian prairies. Wearing knickers and a hat with trout flies on the band, Longstreth wondered where he belonged. Was it with the "drowsy rustics" or the "dormant rich"? The standard sleeping cars contained well-dressed ladies with "minds unsettled by schedules." But in the tourist sleeper cars he found asylum. "Here were the elite poor, genial old ladies who made up for a lack of grammatical forms by a largess of humor, elder sons visiting the old home back East, a wave of children flowing up the aisle now and then, but clean children, and a spruce porter to maintain heaven's first law." Passengers gave a car a collective personality as a kind of place. A person could ride the same train regularly and yet find the atmosphere of each trip different. Some days the car would be full of vacationers. Another day it would be filled with delegates coming from or going to a convention. Anthony Jenkinson warned, "The greatest of all dangers that beset the traveler in American trains [is] the possibility of finding on your train a college football team."[12]

Europeans were especially amazed at how readily people on North American trains launched into conversations with each other. Cecil Roberts met affable men and women who, on the slightest encouragement, or with no encouragement at all, gave their life histories: "They narrate astonishing careers of a kaleidoscopic colour and variety possible on no other continent." There was emotional release in disclosing intimate details of their lives to strangers, and anonymity assured that disclosures would never return to haunt confessors. Bernard McEvoy was harangued with the details of one man's birth, childhood, courtship, and marriage, his wife's merits and defects, and how he was raising his children. "He said if I would excuse him he would keep on—he liked to tell the whole story—he did not always have a chance."[13]

Even landscapes that became monotonous with overexposure could excite admiration at first. George Birmingham sat on the rear platform of his train as it rolled westward across Kansas. As far back as the eye could see were the rails of the track, narrowing until they looked like a single sharp line. In every direction broad spaces of flat land reached to the horizon, and he felt "cowed" in spirit by the vastness.[14] Mountain landscapes, with their exaggerated vertical dimensions, offered views over multiple horizons. To look from the car window or the observation platform was to receive a constantly changing kaleidoscope of vision.

In mountain landscapes, the traveler's admiration shifted constantly between nature and the works of man. Of the Canadian Rockies, Bernard McEvoy wrote: "You look up and see a massive height towering in granite strength to the skies, and you say, 'what, afterall, is puny man?' Then you rattle over some daring bridge across a deep gorge, and are constrained to say that man is a very wonderful being, indeed. By and by, when you have passed through scores of miles of mountains, you transfer your admiration from man in general to the engineers who so successfully carried the great railway through." More than one traveler marveled at the spiral tunnel that carried the Canadian Pacific beneath Mount Ogden in British Columbia. The line turned a complete circle, passing under itself underground. The feature was difficult to comprehend, but fortunately there were diagrams on the covers of the menus in the railroad's dining cars that made it clear. Passengers might buy postcards showing a locomotive just emerging from the tunnel at the very time the tail end of the same train still stood above the tunnel.[15]

Railroad rights-of-way and their immediate margins constituted a substantial part of the passing scene. Everywhere, railroad passengers looked out through a tangle of telegraph lines. John Kouwenhoven wrote of a trip from St. Louis to Chicago in 1960: "Running alongside the track all the way, three tiers of shining wires dip from and rise to the crossbars on the telegraph poles—each of the three crossbars with room for ten bright insulators, some missing, leaving gaps like broken rake teeth."[16] Near large cities billboards lined the tracks.

Nothing excited more interest among passengers than the approach to a metropolis, especially if the city represented a primary destination. John Kowenhoven watched Chicago's influence grow in the rural landscape of Illinois. Almost every farmhouse had a tall, gawky television antenna, but as the train neared Chicago, the antennas grew shorter and shorter until "when you reach the suburban landscape of supermarkets, drive-ins, and rows of little square houses with little square lawns, they need be only small, solicitous bundles of branching wire rods attached to the house chimneys." The city, itself, presented a utilitarian aspect. Edward Hungerford wrote of approaching Chicago from the east in 1913. The train jolted over main-line railroads that crossed and recrossed at every conceivable angle: "To the right and to the left were long vistas with ungainly, picturesque outlines of steel mills with upturned rows of smoking stacks, of gas-holders, and of packing-houses, the vistas suddenly closed off by long trails of travel-worn freight cars, through which the traveler's train finds its way with a mighty clattering and reverberating of noisy echoes." Most travelers saw ugliness in cities viewed from the tracks. Julian Street commented about New York City: "Outside are factories, and railroad yards, and everywhere tall black chimneys, vomiting their heavy, muddy smoke. But always the train glides on like some swift, smooth river. Now the track is elevated, now depressed. You run over bridges or under them, crossing streets and other railroads. At last you dive into a tunnel and presently emerging, coast slowly beside an endless concrete platform."[17]

Restlessness preceded arrival at a major destination. The passengers had sat for many minutes in the hot car, wearing overcoats that the porter insisted be put on. Before the train stopped they were at the end of the car, lined up, eager to escape. Most big city terminals were immense. A British tourist thought the concourse of New York City's Grand Central Station rather like a cathedral. The high roof, the great windows, the hushed sound of voices, the shuffle of feet, the station porters in their red caps, all gave the impression of some Oriental mosque. Julian Street alighted from his train, emerged from the underground platform, and marvelled at the hazy light softly streaming through the concourse windows. The light, combined with the spaciousness of the place, created a paradoxical sense of being indoors and out-of-doors simultaneously: "In its

New York City's Grand Central Station (c. 1920).

stupefying size, its brilliant utilitarianism, and, most of all, in its mildly vulgar grandeur, it seems to me to express exactly the city to which it is a gate."[18]

Christopher Morely thought of Philadelphia's stations as an "unfailing source of amusement and interest." From newsstands to lunch counters, from baggage rooms to train gates, they were "rich in character study and the humors of humanity in flux." Morely found Philadelphia's Broad Street Station divided sharply into two halves. The track level was always astir with departing travelers anxiously consulting time-tables and checking luggage, or with arriving passengers greeting friends and relatives or hustling off for taxi cabs. But upstairs a quiet solemnity reigned among the long benches of the waiting room. It was like a Friends meeting where one expected momentarily to see someone rise and begin to speak. It was peaceful, but not the peace of resignation. It was the peace of exhaustion. Morley wrote: There are the "wounded who have dragged themselves painfully from the onset, stricken on the great battlefield of Travel." Every now and then a muffled, gar-

The *Noronic* at Collingwood, Ontario (c. 1925). The interface between water and land gave ship passengers a sharp sense of departing and arriving. Travel by ship offered a clear change of pace from railroads and automobile travel.

bled announcement for a train echoed through the chamber, and people did arise and stagger away loaded with suitcases and bundles.[19]

Travel by railroad in the United States and Canada afforded unique travel experiences. Travelers of various backgrounds and destinations, and with different travel rationales, mixed on the cars and in the depots. Railroad travel encouraged forms of socialization lacking in many other kinds of travel. It was a colorful world for the tourist. Anthony Jenkinson, an Englishman, summarized his travel by railroad in North America. It was a strange new world

> aglow with the rising sun on waking up in one's berth in the morning; the frenzied rushing, tearful farewells, and last-minute buying of magazines on departure, and the cheerful greetings, hasty assemblage of baggage, and fierce struggle for Red Caps on arrival; the thrill of drawing near the city of one's destination, of

seeing its mighty buildings silhouetted on the skyline, and then of crawling, twisting, and turning into its very bosom.

All these things came to have a profound significance for Jenkinson. Perhaps, they were sentimental things, but they were, nonetheless, real. For Jenkinson, they came to symbolize America more than anything else he encountered.[20]

Steamship Travel

Unlike travel by rail, which tended to be standardized throughout North America, travel by steamship varied from place to place. A steamboat trip on the Mississippi or Ohio River differed substantially from a cruise on the Great Lakes or St. Lawrence River. A trip through the Inside Passage to Alaska differed from one up the Yukon River. Steamship service augmented the railroad network of North America, thriving by linking points not served by railroads as, for example, in the far north of Canada. It also served as an alternative to rail travel—for instance, the overnight boats that ran from New York City to Albany, Boston, Baltimore, Washington, and other cities. Ships often ferried automobiles, giving motorists an alternative to highway travel. Cruise ships offered floating vacations as floating hotels.

Travel by ship was passive; as on the railroads, passengers trusted to others, tied to fixed routes and schedules. The view from the ship was distinctive. Landscapes appeared as slowly moving edges (shorelines marginal to moving ships) or as enclosures (channels of passage through which ships moved). The view was always from water level, with the traveler's ability to overview landscapes minimal. Like passenger trains, steamships also had unique sounds and unique sensations of motion. Even though a ship's motion might cause seasickness, it could also amplify the sense of being in a unique environment, and of being on a unique adventure. Voyages had definitive beginnings and endings amplified by contrasts of water and shore, and the slow movement between destinations.

Departure was a time of anticipation. To many travelers,

like William Saroyan, there was something deeply satisfying about catching a boat. It was, to him, success in its "purest, simplest, and, perhaps, supreme form." It was a "latching-onto time," and a deliberate act. He mused, "You can stand on the deck and see where you were, and you're not there any more. You can almost see yourself no longer there." Departure implied arrival—the coming back to terra firma. A voyage was clearly a linking of places across a void, and travel by ship heightened the sense of dependency since there clearly was no escape en route. Arrival was a time of expectancy, and it brought a desire to be off and about other aspects of travel. It could be a time of confusion as travelers sought to reorient to the land and its accommodations. Bernard McEvoy landed in Victoria, British Columbia, amid a babel of hotel coachmen all soliciting trade. He wrote from his hotel room: "It was the wildest, loudest, and most diversified noise you have ever heard. I am going tonight for the purpose of listening to it again."[21]

Voyaging, much like life at a resort hotel, was regulated by meal service. Between meals a ship's passengers lounged or strolled about, observing the ship and its crew at work. Most ships of any size were equipped with bars and gaming rooms for men, and lounges for women and children. Bernard McEvoy describes the interior of the *Athabasca* which provided a water linkage across Georgian Bay and Lake Superior for Canadian Pacific passengers between Toronto and Winnipeg. "One-half of the long saloon is dining-room, and the other half—well, just saloon—thickly carpeted with a crimson carpet, into which the foot slips noiselessly, besprinkled with crimson velvet sofas and easy chairs. A piano is there, too, on which some kind of amateur is sure to perform . . . pounding out harmonies that are as mechanically regular as the thud of the engine." Whereas a ship's public areas were spacious, the private spaces of its passenger cabins were compact. Efficiency ruled. McEvoy noted the *Athabasca*'s cabins for cleanliness and convenience. He observed cryptically: "There are your two berths . . . your lounge, and your washstand, your waterbottle, your bright hooks to hang things on, your little window . . . your door."[22]

River travel unfurled for passengers a continuous landscape panorama. It could also be nostalgic. Passenger travel on

96

the Mississippi, Ohio, and other inland rivers had substantially declined by the time that Bennett Abdy cast off from St. Louis aboard the *Stacker Lee* in 1918. It was night, and fog obscured stretches of the river. The boat's first landing was filled with excitement and thoughts of Mark Twain. The boat had been moving downstream, with a curiously measured sobbing sound coming from its stacks, when suddenly a searchlight cut into the darkness, followed by a jingle of bells. The engine stopped. The pilothouse window was slid back and a voice hailed the cargo deck below: "Stand by with your stage." Slowly the boat ran up to the shore, the plank was swung down, and the roustabouts scrambled ashore to secure the mooring lines. The lights of a town stood out along the top of the wooded bluff. Later, farther down river, an express train roared out of the night on a track closeby the Mississippi, its headlight momentarily blinding the passengers on the steamboat's deck. Abdy wrote: "How quiet and peaceful was our river-world, the instant the train was gone! What a chance to contrast the two modes of travel! We spoke of the old river's Romantic Yesterdays—a period more given to the graces of life and dignity of movement—a time of leisurely days and neighborly ways."[23]

Mary Hitchcock's river, the Yukon, was more primitive in 1898. However, steamboat navigation was not a relic of the past, but a symbol of modernity, a forebearer of future civilization. But Hitchcock traveled not on a ship, but on a barge placed in front of, and pushed by, a steamboat. At night Indians roamed the moored barge at will, creeping through the narrow center passageway that gave access to the tiny cabins, and crawling along the narrow ledges outside the cabin windows. Each morning passengers were awakened by the stewards dragging breakfast tables across the barge roof. The passing scene, intriguing at first, became monotonous. The constant view of the forest was interrupted only by the appearance of occasional Indian villages and trading posts. Gold was the reason for river traffic. Men moved by every conveyance conceivable to and from the Klondike. But the way up the Yukon River was slow, and the sense of adventure constantly at odds with boredom.[24]

Travel on the open water presented few surprises. But

on entering Lake Superior at Sault Sainte Marie, Bernard Mc-
Evoy obtained an exceptional view of land, lake, and sky.
Around him the gulls wheeled in a ghostly silence or gave a
faint, querulous call. He was sailing right into the sunset, and
the sunset was a glory of silver grays and lightest blues and
greens. Coastal travel usually combined long stretches of
open water with shorelines of varying interest. Ida Morris sat
wrapped in furs and heavy blankets in a deck chair enjoying
"the panorama of sea and sky" on the Inside Passage to Alaska.
Binoculars brought forth detail when the ship was close to
shore: sun-lit mountains white with the "snows of a thousand
years" and green-clad foothills covered with pines as "thick as
the weeds on a common." Occasionally the open sea revealed a
mystery. With the first whale sighted, the ship's railing
crowded with eager passengers: "O yonder he goes, a whale."
"O, see him spout." "Ah, down he goes." Then everyone questioned everyone else. "Did you see the whale?" "Did you see
our whale?"[25]

The approach to the harbor of a great city could highlight
a trip by ship. No sight in North America received more acclaim
than the approach to New York City through the Verrazano
Narrows. The distant city grew in size, lifting higher and higher
through the haze. One traveler wrote: "Gradually the bunched
appearance of the tall buildings begins to change. The group
disintegrates, certain of the taller peaks draw off and stand
alone, the lower city begins to show its profile." Color asserted
itself from the many-hued pier sheds, to the white and gold
excursion steamers, to the red and cream-colored funnels of the
docked ocean liners, to the terra cotta, brick, and stone facades
of the taller office buildings. The noise of the harbor was colorful, from the shrieks of passing steamers, to the puffing and
wheezing of tugs, and everywhere the din of escaping steam
and clanging bells. Passengers lined the rails absorbing these
most obligatory impressions.[26]

Excursion Trips

Excursion trips, whether by train or by ship, combined
the sensations of movement with the heightened impressions

of contrived attractions. The excursion of several hours' duration was specially packaged to heighten environmental impressions, although most excursionists treated their outings primarily as social events. Steamers ran from New York City's Battery Park to the New Jersey seashore resorts. They reflected the people of the city, as one traveler noted in 1929: "Ukuleles are strummed, babies coo and scream, lunch and pleasantry help while away the hours on board. The pleasures, the slang, the latest dance steps, the courtships, the rivalries of the city, are transferred to whatever playground the six million select." Some excursionists might revel in the scenery, delighting in the passing scene. Not all excursion trips by water delighted fully. Small boats and rough seas could bring seasickness. The trip to Santa Catalina Island was notorious in this respect. Harry Mac-Fadden described many of his traveling companions: "In the first stage they feared they were going to die—next they did not care whether they died or not, and at last they wanted to die."[27]

Railroad excursions were, perhaps, less trying to physical stamina. Especially popular in the early twentieth century were the incline and other vehiculars that climbed the various mountains of the East and the West: for example, Mount Washington in New Hampshire, Pikes Peak in Colorado, and Mount Lowe and Mount Tamalpais in California. Henry Mac-Fadden's group ascended Mount Lowe. As an adventure it was "a thing of terror to the timid," he wrote. An incline railway reached the Alpine Tavern three thousand feet up. From there an electric trolley line wound through gorges and along the edges of the "most precipitous cliffs." As one traveler, M. M. Shaw, noted approvingly, the railway on Mount Lowe enabled tourists to penetrate to the heart of the Sierra Madre Mountains that they might discover what an isolated mountain wilderness was like. He wrote: "It is all here and ever present, in boundless, grand profusion—mountains, wilderness, isolation—an awe-inspiring, infinite trinity of grandeur that almost makes your head swim and your heart stand still." A pathway led to the requisite "Inspiration Point" where, it was said, magnificent views could be had. But Shaw's tour group had only limited time. They hastened to the famous spring, drank its ice-cold water, and then visited the inn. A cannon was fired. Its echo rolled among the peaks, growing fainter and fainter as it gradually died away.[28]

Railroads and steamship lines set the standards for travel in early-twentieth-century North America. Travel was formal, requiring decorum appropriate to public spaces. Travel was tied to set schedules and set routes. Always travelers were at the mercy of a corporation, which could exclude, delay, and otherwise divert them from anticipated travel, although railroad and steamship travel was usually as dependable as it was efficient. Railroads and steamship lines provided a primary system for movement that catered to all kinds of travelers, tourists included. Only the excursion lines were contrived primarily for tourism, and thus beyond the pale of the commonplace. Tourists on trains and ships moved in a sort of extended back region that tied North America together through travel. Experiencing travel by train and ship enabled a view close at hand of the continent's principal geographical bindings. But the tourists' view beyond the train window or ship's deck was limited, since the landscape was framed as a series of rapidly fleeting impressions. Tourists were isolated from sights. They could not delay to explore what they saw at leisure. They remained always within a world enclosed.

CHAPTER FIVE

TOURING BY AUTOMOBILE BEFORE WORLD WAR I

> The talk was all of roads and routes and distances and interesting places thousands of miles apart, with a spice of harmless exaggeration about the performance of this car or that, its wonderful tire mileage and surpassing power and reliability. This was as natural as the elastic statements of a trout fisherman.
>
> Ralph Paine, "Discovering America By Automobile"

The automobile opened a new world of travel experience. Originally playthings of the well-to-do, motor cars spawned a new sport—automobiling. Adventure could be had in confronting the nation's primitive roads in trips across country. Long-distance endurance runs were sponsored by automobile manufacturers and other groups interested in promoting travel by motor car. In spite of the frequent breakdowns, and roads which were poorly marked and sometimes impassable, automobiling provided freedom of action, a kind of sociability, and direct contact with landscape unknown to passengers of trains and ships. What started as a sport among the rich became a recreation for the middle class. Rural roads were reborn as environments significant to American travel, for not since the early nineteenth century had so many people traveled by road.

Automobiling as a Sport

Early motor cars were not only expensive to buy, but they were expensive to operate. Before 1910 most car manufacturers produced only a few hundred vehicles a year, which sold at prices that approached several thousands of dollars. A few companies mass-produced moderately priced cars for about four hundred dollars, but even this price was well beyond the means of American workers, whose annual income averaged only $574 in 1910.[1] In addition, the expense of car upkeep and operation could run as high as $350 for a six-month's driving season.[2] The use of automobiles for recreation had clear status

Automobile tourists near Rockville, Indiana (1916). Travel by automobile placed tourists in the landscapes they previously glimpsed from train and ship. They could stop at will and meet and talk with people by the wayside.

implications as displays of pecuniary wealth. As a sport, automobiling was almost comparable to yachting or riding to hounds. Woodrow Wilson saw the automobile's class implications as dangerous. "Nothing has spread socialistic feeling in this country [more]," he wrote, "than the use of the automobile." It was to Wilson "a picture of the arrogance of wealth, with all its independence and carelessness."[3]

The superior roads of Great Britain, France, and other countries, and the survival of old inns and pubs along these highways, greatly facilitated travel by motor car in Europe. By 1910 a spate of books promoted use of automobiles in European travel.[4] But the outbreak of war and the closing of European banks stranded over 150,000 Americans in Europe in July 1914. Through a relief effort in London, ships were chartered and what were possibly the first credit cards in travel history were issued, enabling Americans to return home.[5] For the next six years Americans looked primarily to North America for travel, with automobiles, following European precedents, figuring prominently in their plans.

Automobiling brought exhilaration to landscape experience and placed drivers in an athletic relationship with their environment. Arthur Eddy, an early enthusiast, wrote in 1902: "Going 20 or 25 miles an hour on a machine . . . with 32-inch wheels and short wheel-base gives about the same exercise one gets on a horse; one is lifted from the seat and thrown from side to side, until you learn to ride the machine as you would a trotter and take the bumps accordingly." Eddy recommended automobiling for its sense of speed. No sport since Roman chariot racing afforded as much "exhilaration and danger," and required as much "nerve, dash, and daring." Mastering machinery was a challenge especially attractive to males. Keeping an automobile going for any distance required both wit and brawn because early motor cars possessed the subtle attraction of caprice. Eddy wrote: "It constantly offers something to overcome; as in golf, you start out each time to beat your record. The machine is your tricky and resourceful opponent."[6]

Automobile Touring

With increased size and improved comfort, the automobile developed, not as a plaything, but as a serious means of transportation. Compared to travel by railroad, touring by automobile offered freedom of action, closer contact with place, and novel kinds of sociability as well as the challenge of sport. Automobiles freed tourists from the "inflexible track" and the "bondage of timetables," themes repeated over and over again in the early promotional literature.[7] William Saroyan echoed this sentiment: "The thing that was best was being free, and I had known this best thing most deeply when I had been in my own car on a long drive. I had known this freedom in myself, most memorably, most unforgettably, getting into my car, going and not stopping until I felt like it." As historian Warren Belasco points out, automobile travel was a return to a simpler age of benignly individualistic travel.[8]

Flexibility of action enabled motorists to linger and see

the places through which they passed, and they could see new places off the beaten track of railroad travel. According to Theodore Dreiser, the automobile brought prospects of "new and varied roads," intimate contact with "woodland silences and grassy slopes," and the ability to change your mind and "go by this route or that according to your mood." Railroads were huge, clumsy, unwieldy affairs little suited to the temperamental needs and moods of the average human being. They were "mass carriers, freight handlers, great hurry conveniences for overburdened commercial minds. "We are seeing our own country for the first time!" exclaimed Emily Post. Train windows only gave a "whirling view" past the "back doors" of the nation, but car windshields exposed "the best avenues of the cities" and the "front entrances of farms." The motorist saw America at its best, and not through the maze of telegraph lines, billboards, and other accoutrements of industry and commerce that lined the railroads. As Warren Belasco notes, by choosing his own route, the motorist gained an insider's access to places, and thus fuller, if not more exclusive, insight. Automobiles were a key to visiting back regions only glimpsed from train windows.[9]

Automobile travel encouraged different forms of social encounter. Motorists met other motorists at the hotels, garages, and restaurants of the roadside; but, more important, they met at the mud holes, the washouts, or wherever one of their kind was stranded and in trouble. They met, not as passive passengers, but as "like-minded engineers" who could and did overcome problems with a high degree of camaraderie. Motorists were members of a great "motor fraternity."[10] Early on, the automobile was an ideal device for attracting and engaging locals in conversation. A locality could be known on a spontaneous and rather intimate basis through casual encounters. Arthur Eddy wrote: "In the presence of the machine, people everywhere become . . . childlike and naive, curious and enthusiastic; they lose the veneer of sophistication, and are approachable and companionable as children."[11]

Endurance runs promoted automobile ownership and use. The drivers who set distance and time records were championed in the press as a new breed of explorer, and as a new kind of pioneer. In August 1897, Alexander Winton drove a car of his own manufacture from Cleveland to New York City in ten days. In subsequent years, the annual automobile show encouraged much cross-country driving, with New York City as the destination. In 1901, Roy Chapin drove an Oldsmobile from Detroit to New York City in eight days by following the towpath of the Erie Canal across much of upstate New York.[12] But the transcontinental runs were the biggest attention getters. In 1898, J. M. Murdock took thirty-two days to drive from Los Angeles to New York City.[13] In 1903, three transcontinental car trips were completed between San Francisco and New York City in fifty-three, sixty-three, and seventy-three days respectively; the normal travel time by railroad was only four days.[14]

The most gruelling endurance run across North America took place in the spring of 1908 as part of a round-the-world race starting and ending at Paris. Antonio Scarfoglio, a member of the Italian team, kept a detailed diary that survives as one of the most vivid accounts of early motoring in America. In mid-February the racers left New York City in a snowstorm, arriving in Albany the next day, having fought snowdrifts throughout the night. Six days later another blizzard hit the team in western Ohio. The wind howled, vibrating telegraph lines along the road; the temperature fell to minus 13°F. They had to break the corn beef with a hammer and then cook it on the car's radiator. They removed the floorboards of the car so that they could warm their feet on the exhaust pipe, and they rubbed vaseline on various parts of the automobile to keep their hands from sticking to the cold metal. In Indiana they slept in the open when the car got stuck in a drift. Scarfoglio wrote: "We must renounce the road and take to the fields, where the snow is not so deep. With axes we beat down the slender wooden fences on which are advertised the best medicines and the best boots of South Bend." People came out in sleighs to cheer them on, and on their fifteenth day after leaving New York City, they found themselves in Chicago.[15]

With spring coming on, the roads of the Middle West turned to mud. After delaying several days in Iowa, waiting for replacement parts and making repairs, they received permission to drive to Omaha on the tracks of the Illinois Central Railroad. Most of the larger towns along their route, like Cheyenne, Rawlins, and Rock Springs, celebrated the team's arrival. The difficulties of crossing North America whetted Scarfoglio's appetite for the roads of Siberia and Russia: "The nomadic tumultuous life has entered so completely into our fibres, the need for perpetual daily motion has thrust its roots so deeply into our organism, that we have gradually ceased to regard it as an exceptional state of existence."[16]

Most early endurance runs were promotional stunts. If they did not serve to promote a certain brand of tire or make of automobile, they served the publicity-conscious driver. Alice Ramsey set out from New York City in 1909 in a touring car provided by the Maxwell–Briscoe Company. She became the first woman to drive across the continent, an act she commemorated with a book entitled *Veil, Duster, and Tire Iron*. Harriet White, owner of an anvil-and-vise factory at Trenton, New Jersey, launched a round-the-world tour with chauffeur, maid, secretary, and forty-horsepower Locomobile. They drove through Western Europe and through Egypt, India, and Japan before starting across North America from San Francisco. She was given awards and escorted by other cars in many towns. Her arrival at Rochester, New York, was heralded in the newspapers: "There arrived in Rochester last night, quietly and unannounced, a woman who had just finished accomplishing a feat that for a man would deserve universal applause, and for a member of the gentler sex almost staggers belief."[17]

Charles J. Glidden, the so-called "Globe Trotter of Automobiledom," pioneered guided auto tours. With routes carefully mapped, and meals and accommodations arranged in advance, Glidden offered motorists the safety of road competition in caravans.[18] His 1904 tour ran between New York City and the World's Fair at St. Louis. Between 1905 and 1910 his tours mainly promoted New England and the Middle Atlantic states, focusing on such resorts as Saratoga in New York and Bretton Woods in New Hampshire. The 1911 tour ran from New York City to Jacksonville, Florida. A. L. Westgard, who had mapped the route and who functioned as guide, found the trip a constant diet of dust, sandwiched as he was between the cars of the tour, itself, and the cars of enthusiastic locals turned out to escort.[19]

In 1911, the Raymond–Whitcomb Company, the agent for packaged railroad and steamship tours and owner of the Raymond Hotel at Pasadena, organized an "automobile train." A caravan of automobiles ran between New York City and Los Angeles on a thirty-day schedule at a cost of $875 one way.[20] Although the Raymond–Whitcomb idea represented the first group tour by motor vehicle (predating the use of buses by over a decade), it was the Glidden idea that proved most popular before World War I. Glidden restricted his tours to owner-driven automobiles and, in league with the American Automobile Association (AAA), gave trophies for automobile performance and driver skill. Thus, the endurance run persisted in a new form. Whereas participants traveled as tourists, many pretended to perform and, perhaps did perform, more serious functions. As a participant in the 1905 Glidden tour wrote: "The tour has proved that the automobile is now almost foolproof. It has proved that American cars are durable and efficient. It has shown the few who took part how delightful this short vacation may be, and it has strengthened our belief in the permanence of the motor car."[21]

Motoring Difficulties

Early motoring was beset with difficulties. Since the railroads handled the nation's transportation needs, no real highway system existed. Roads were poor, serving local areas only, and drivers going long distances were frequently frustrated by the lack of through connections. In the West, roads were often nonexistent, and motorists were forced to travel on the open range, or resort to using railroad rights-of-way, or even shipping cars by rail. Breakdowns and long delays occurred frequently. Dust in dry weather and mud in wet weather prolonged travel. Dirt worked its way into clothing, into luggage, and even into one's skin, for automobiling was decidedly an outdoor activity before the era of enclosed automobiles. Early automobiles frightened horses, and motorists created resentment as well as curiosity in local people. Before World War I, motoring required stamina, perserverance, and, frequently, diplomacy.

Poor or nonexistent roads alone were enough to make motoring adventuresome. In 1909, Hugo Taussig and his companion followed tire tracks across the parched Nevada landscape. Beyond Tonapah, the sparse road ended abruptly, but by opening gates and running overland they made it through to Ely. To reach Triplett, they followed stumps of old telegraph poles that not only marked the route of the nation's first transcontinental telegraph line, but also the route of the pony express. Lost near Rawlins, Wyoming, Taussig and his companion split company to search for help. A rancher on horseback led them to a road, although they had to cut through several barbed wire fences and build a bridge with lumber taken from a corral in order to regain the road.[22]

Thomas Wilby had difficulty keeping his road east of Brandon, Manitoba. He wrote: "At some indeterminate point

The National Road near Grantsville, Maryland (c. 1910). Rural roads were primitive before World War I. Even such improved highways as the National Road were relics of nineteenth-century horsepower.

Columbia River Highway in Oregon (1914). New highways brought marked improvement to automobile travel. Oregon's Columbia River Highway was built especially to attract sightseers.

we lost the main traveled highway. Then suddenly our path swerved, reeled around the back of a hut, cut through a wheat field and unceremoniously ran into a swamp." There was no road west of Swift Current, Saskatchewan, in newly settled concessions where farmers had plowed up the old trail before a new road could be established. Whilby's party picked up the railroad, lacking any other recognized route, and, by constantly opening and shutting gates, made it to Calgary. Anticipating completion of the Trans-Canada Highway by some forty years, Wilby wrote: "Canada [is] a unit only by the good-natured tolerance of the railroad, having none of the cohesion of human agglomeration which the existence of a network of continuous and perfected highways can alone impart." Although Wilby had set out to drive across Canada from Halifax to Vancouver, he was forced to ship his car by railroad both around Lake Superior and over the Rocky Mountains.[23]

Local automobile clubs had been opened throughout the United States by 1918. Many were affiliated with the AAA which, besides lobbying for sane traffic laws and improved highways, became a clearinghouse for travel information. The AAA bluebooks, with their detailed route descriptions, maps, and lists of garages and hotel accommodations, were widely distributed. An advertisement of the period read: "Taste the thrills of an explorer! Tour anywhere you wish, anywhere in the United States, with absolute confidence that you will get there and back in the best possible way and without having to ask questions en route!"[24] Most motorists sought adventure only within tolerable limits. The bluebooks reduced stress.

Organizations like the Lincoln Highway Association began to mark routes and to publish guidebooks. The National Midland Trails Association marked a route from Washington to Los Angeles. For Florissant, Colorado, the association's 1916 guidebook read: "Give Carburetor more air. Cross two bridges left with poles up long grade, past ranch house at right 40.8; 47.5, left fork and still upgrade to Pulver Divide, 48.2. Here note many old wagon ruts of what was in the early days the Leadville stage line. Fine view from this elevation over South Park. Coast on engine down long hill. Watch for prairie dog holes in road."[25] Free roadmaps, distributed by the oil companies, appeared about 1914.

Information could be obtained from locals encountered by the roadside. Theodore Dreiser advised against taking such advice. Most people didn't own cars, and many had never even ridden in one. Directions usually were given from the pedestrian's point of view. Thomas Wilby agreed. Few Canadians he met were able to judge accurately either travel time or geographical distance: "'A mile further on' would sometimes mean 'five miles,' and 'five miles,' might mean 'ten' or perhaps 'three.'" In Texas, Winifred Dixon learned the full meaning of the word "optimism." When told, "roads are splendid, ma'am. I think you'll get through," she mentally labeled it as "probably passable." But when she heard, "Pretty poor roads, ma'am; I think you'll boag," she knew positively that she would bog. Arthur Eddy thought it impractical to inquire about roads beyond a fifteen-mile radius of a place. Farmers and tradespeople in the era of railroads simply did not make long overland drives. In addition, he thought that women always gave the best advice. "A woman will reply before a man comprehends what is asked," he wrote. "A man would rather see the machine than listen."[26]

The earliest automobiles were clearly experimental. Built of wood and light metal, underpowered, with poor suspension systems, and poorly weatherized, the early machines required constant repair and maintenance. Arthur Eddy's *2,000 Miles on an Automobile* is a story fully illustrative of early motoring at its frustrating best. In 1901, Eddy drove from Chicago to Boston *on* (as he put it) a single-cylinder automobile. While distance increased in arithmetical progression, deterioration of the machine was geometrical. At Cleveland, Eddy removed and repaired the radiator, cut a link out of the drive chain to take up slack, and tightened the steering wheel. At Geneseo, New York, mud was splashed onto the exposed motor, and he had to stop every five miles or so to clean and adjust the engine's cams. At Batavia, he replaced the battery, repacked the fuel pump, and re-covered the coils. At Canandaigua, the car's differential gave out, and Eddy lost both brakes and transmission. He wrote: "The sensation of rushing down hill with power and brakes absolutely detached is peculiar and exhilarating . . . the machine is a huge projectile, a flying mass, a ton of metal rushing through space; there is a sensation of fear . . . but one becomes for the moment exceedingly alert, with instantaneous comprehension of the character of the road; every rut, stone, and curve are seen and appreciated."[27]

Tires gave motorists constant difficulty. Hugo Taussig lost ten tubes before he reached Salt Lake City on his drive from Los Angeles. At Ely, Nevada, he searched in vain for replacements, but continued on, trusting to luck, one wheel running on its rim. At Vernon, he and his companion took a train to Salt Lake City, returning the next day to resume their journey with a new supply of tubes. One touring party claimed to have suffered 172 punctures and 17 blowouts while driving two cars round trip from Cleveland to San Francisco in 1914.[28]

Poor roads not only hastened tire and motor failure, but they could bring motorists to a complete stop, their automobiles stuck in mud or hung up on a hummock. Travel diaries and journals of the period are replete with vivid descriptions of such difficulties, since such trouble was the very essence of travel adventure. It was good to have difficulty for the sake of the memory alone. Emily Post wrote: "The peaceful motorist who has no major trouble has a pleasant enough time, but after all[,] he gets the least out of it in the way of recollections." The road ordeal ratified the tourists' belief that only through motoring could they really see the country. Hardships underscored pride in having "been there." Motorists prized their road-weathered cars, not only as badges of adventure, but as partners in that adventure. Many motorists decorated their cars with banners proclaiming distant origins and destinations: "New York To San Francisco;" "Pikes Peak Or Bust;" "Ocean To Ocean." Such markers gave evidence of spiritual and physical fortitude.[29]

Trouble could occur anywhere, anytime. Thomas Wilby's machine stopped dead on a hummock south of North Bay, Ontario. He wrote of his subsequent ordeal as a gallant fight. For several hours they wrenched away like "draught horses at the block and tackle," cheered on only by the buzzing of the black flies. They jacked up the wheels one by one, filling in the hollows with stones, tree branches, and sheaves of wheat. "We practically constructed a new road," he wrote, "and having put on the anti-skid chains so as to gain more traction, we shot the car back into safety again." The episode cost them a bent drive shaft and a two-day delay at Scotia Junction waiting for repairs to be made. They sat and watched the monotonous round of arriving and departing trains and the "hungry, scrambling passengers" who trooped to the lunch counter only to vanish at the clanging bell.[30]

Help was usually readily at hand. For a price, most farmers would pull a stranded machine to safety. Many horses could perform the feat practically unattended. Effie Gladding marveled at one animal in Nevada: "It was interesting to see how the big horse threw his weight into the pulling at just the proper moment and released as he felt the machine settle on the firm ground." It was not unusual to find farmers and others deliberately sabotaging roads in order to charge exorbitant fees to rescue stranded motorists. In New Mexico, men standing by a ford motioned to Emily Post to make a wide sweep. It landed her car in soft sand up to the hubs, whereupon she was forced to negotiate the use of the several mules that stood by harnessed and waiting. Motorists were a great help to one another. Mutual aid not only solved problems but fostered that camaraderie that broke down traditional social barriers. One traveler helped a fellow motorist solve an engine problem. Soon a group assembled. Portly gentlemen stripped off their coats and wrestled with the crank case or poked about under the hood. One was a doctor from California, another a steel executive from Pittsburgh, another a retired merchant from Kalamazoo. One was a young man from Boston "who, until he took to motoring, never dreamed of speaking to any one not properly presented."[31]

Equipment

Well-outfitted motorists traveled prepared. Everett Brimmer recommended carrying a standard tool kit along with spark plug[,] socket wrench, splicing pliers, wire, tire pressure gauge, grease gun, and a sheet of cork from which to make emergency gaskets. A tire pump, a gasoline can, a collapsible canvas bucket, and several water bags were also desirable. The official guidebook of the Lincoln Highway Association recommended that the motorist carry tire chains, several jacks, extra tire casings and tubes, high- and low-tension cables, an axe, and a shovel. The tourbook of the Midland Trail Association recommended that cars be equipped with at least twenty-five feet of rope, a set of triple blocks, and a three-foot steel stake so that cars could be winched out of mud holes and ditches.[32]

Early motoring required special dress. Men wore dusters, or raincoats, wind cuffs, and caps with visors and adjustable goggles. They carried leggings and boots to slip on while

Hotel Windsor at New Baltimore, New York (c. 1910). **Automobile tourists** accepted small-town hotels and restaurants as they found them. The Windsor still advertised its stable on its sign.

working on their cars. Women also wore dusters and tied their hats on with long scarves; many women carried lap robes. The well-dressed tourist carried sport clothes for driving and more formal wear for hotel life. For her 1916 trip from North Dakota to Cape Cod, Edith Hughes packed four white suits, two dinner gowns, an evening wrap, and several kimonos. For her husband she included two gray sport suits and a white formal suit. But he insisted on wearing an old olive-drab favorite, which caused him to be taken for a chauffeur several times. Both carried rain capes, boots, and leather coats. Her luggage included an electric iron, medicine case, cosmetic case, and sewing bag. She urged her readers to follow her example and travel light.[33]

Travel Logistics

Widespread use of automobiles for travel created logistical problems along the nation's highways. Motorists required gasoline, food, and lodging, among other necessities. Garages performed a variety of functions. Automobile servicing predominated, but automobile storage was important also, many tourists preferring to store their open touring cars indoors overnight. The large petroleum corporations did not dominate gasoline retailing before World War I, and garages were locally owned and operated, usually selling the products of several competing refiners. Garages were local gathering places. Theodore Dreiser observed: "What an agency for the transmission of information and a certain kind of railway station gossip the modern garage has become." He found there the typical American "hangers-on," or "chair warmers," who gathered to pass time watching the "activity and enthusiasm of others."[34] Here locals met outsiders amid the bustle of practical activity. Garage mechanics were the ultimate problem solvers who made automobile travel, or at least locomotion, possible.

Restaurants created to serve the pedestrian or traveler by railroad served the automobilist equally well. Food was ordinary in most places, and service was often uninspired. For his novel *Free Air,* Sinclair Lewis created a typical small-town diner that he called the "Eats Garden." As Sinclair's heroine, Claire Boltwood, entered, she was stifled by a belch of smoke from the frying pan in the kitchen. The room was blocked by a huge lunch counter, and there was only one table, covered with oil cloth, decorated with venerable spots of dried egg yolk. The waiter-cook, whose apron was gravy-patterned, with a border of plain grey dirt, grumbled, "Whatyahwant?"[35] The restaurant was another place where travelers and locals met to size up one another.

At breakfast and at noon most motorists sought eating places where food could be had quickly, at reasonable prices. Cafeterias became popular after 1910, especially on the West Coast. Ruth Wood found them to be "first-aids to the hurried." She dubbed Southern California "the Cafeteria Belt." She also saw another kind of eatery, the roadside stand or early drive-in. Tea rooms also appeared on the roadside. Effie Gladding stopped at an old farmhouse near Charlottesville, Virginia. A sign proclaimed, "The Sign of the Green Tea-Pot." "It is a charming little place," she wrote, "kept by a woman of taste and arranged for parties to sup in passing." She admired the "simple, dainty furniture" and the "home-like little parlor." The views around the place were "charmingly pastoral."[36]

Traveling salesmen and other businessmen dominated most hotels, often to the embarrassment of women traveling alone and men traveling with their families. Sinclair Lewis's Claire Boltwood stopped at fictional Gopher Prairie's leading hostelry. "In the hotel[,] Claire was conscious of the ugliness of the poison-green walls and brass cuspidors and insurance calendars and bare floor of the office. Conscious of the interesting scientific fact that all air had been replaced by the essence of cigar smoke and cooking cabbage; of the stares of the traveling men lounging in bored lines; and the lack of welcome on the part of the night clerk, an oldish bleached man with whiskers instead of a collar. The bellhop led her up miles of stairs and through endless corridors to her tiny little room with its loose-jointed iron bed, its dingy bureau with a list to port, and its anaemic rocking chair." Effie Gladding stopped at such a hotel in Eureka, Nevada. The room was an old-fashioned, high-ceilinged affair with heavy walnut furniture forty years out of date. An aged ingrain carpet was on the floor, and a wreath of wax flowers of the kind her grandmother might have rejoiced in, hung set in a deep frame on the wall. At Point of Rocks, Wyoming, her hotel room was furnished with a bed, a chair without back, a tin washbasin on the chair, a pail of fresh water with a dipper, a pail for waste water, and a lamp. Few hotel rooms had private baths. James Flagg noted: "When there is a community bathroom and you would fain get into it, you stand barefooted in your rain coat, handbag firmly gripped, listening from a crack in your bedroom door for the exit of the person who is always spending his or her vacation in there."[37]

The service received in hotels and restaurants, and at garages also, often colored the tourist's impressions of a town or a locality. How could James Flagg forget Rock Springs, Wyoming? "Freight engines screamed and tooted all around the little hotel . . . all night long, as if warning the guests not to come out into the tracks in their pyjamas." Thomas Wilby remembered Trout Lake, Ontario, for the way in which the hotel was decorated: "More crowned heads cropped up in unsuspected corners; they stared at one from the dingy smoke-room and the shabby wash house, they turned up again in the diningroom, and they even crept upstairs and shot their royal looks at one from the corridors." He didn't know whether the formidable display of blue blood was to teach the advantages or the disadvantages of democracy.[38]

The costs of automobile travel varied with the extravagance of the tourist. In 1919, one traveler spent $235 on a 2,600-mile trip from Chicago to Los Angeles, two-thirds of it on meals and hotel rooms. The cost of gasoline per gallon varied between 19¢ in Illinois and 50¢ in Arkansas. Costs of operating the automobile varied by make of car also. In 1914, one group traveled 7,200 miles from Cleveland to the Pacific Coast and back. One car, a Winton, consumed 812 gallons of gasoline at a cost of $166, while the other car, a Ford, consumed 359 gallons at a cost of $59. The costs of motoring long distances were high compared with those of railroad travel. In 1906, another motorist spent $50 on gasoline alone in traveling between San Francisco and New York. The cost of a standard berth on the Union Pacific between the two cities was only $20.[39]

Automobiles as Traffic Hazards

Motor cars were an intrusion on the nation's slow-paced roads. Sprinting at speeds as high as thirty or forty miles per hour, early automobiles disrupted pedestrian and horse traffic. The machines were noisy, and horses were easily frightened. "It was no uncommon sight," wrote Arthur Eddy, "to see people jump out of their carriages or drive into fields or lanes, anywhere to get out of the way." Many horses broke their tethers to run loose for miles ahead of Eddy's car, stopping when he stopped and starting when he started. Horsemen created their own problems with automobiles when they clutched at reins, grabbed whips, and pulled and jerked until horses bolted. According to Eddy, a country plug jogging quietly along quite unterrified could be roused to unwanted capers by the person who followed behind. Farm animals fell easy victim to speeding cars on narrow roads. Julian Street wrote of Missouri's highways: "All the quadrupeds and bipeds domesticated by mankind were there upon the roads to meet us and to protest, by various antics, against the invasion of the motor car. Dogs hurled themselves at the car as though to suicide; chickens extended themselves in shrieking dives across our course. Effie Gladding found the Lincoln Highway in Iowa a trail marked by dead chickens.[40]

Various states enacted stringent traffic laws. A 1905 Michigan law required motorists to slow to ten miles per hour when approached by a horsedrawn vehicle and, if the horse was frightened, to stop at the side of the road with engine off until the animal had passed. In 1915, the maximum speed limit in Ohio was still twenty miles per hour. Emily Post complained that one must either spend days in crawling across the state or break the law. Clearly, some traffic controls were needed. One early proponent of automobiling dispaired of "autoneers who show an utter disregard for the rights and safety of others, thundering along the county roads enjoying the fright of the people they scare." But, he also thought that much of the legislation that came from the farmer- and small town-dominated legislatures was unjust and oppressive.[41] City-oriented automobile clubs organized as lobby groups to remove overbearing restrictions.

Motoring at Night

If daylight motoring had its hazards, nothing amplified the sense of adventure, the sense of romance, and even the sense of the picturesque like nighttime driving. Railroad passengers could see little after dark save train interiors. But the motorist could savor the nighttime environment as a unique experience. The narrow roads and the weak illumination of the automobile lamps presented a magic, flickering world of encompassing shadows. Thomas Wilby wrote of Quebec: "From shadowy houses, there emerged human phantoms offering, in response to the calls from the horn, half-comprehended directions in the intense gloom of narrow lanes overhung with densely-foliaged trees. Villages . . . came momentarily into the ghostly white rays of the car lamps, and then shot back into the world of unseen things." Isolated roads brought the most adventure for their lack of identifiable referents. Ernest Peixotto wrote about a California mountain road. Weird pictures succeeded each other "with the bewildering rapidity of some phantasmagoria—reversing the truths of nature, and, as in imaginative scenery, making light objects dark and dark objects light, flattening everything in their shadeless light."[42]

Theodore Dreiser gloried in night driving. Rarely did his party seek hotel accommodations before ten in the evening. He liked to ride through towns and cities at night, glancing through lit windows. In Scranton, Pennsylvania, he saw "the usual humdrum type of furniture and hangings, the inevitable lace curtains, the centre tables, the huge, junky lamps, the upright pianos or victrolas." "There are certain summer evenings when nature produces a poetic emotionalizing mood," he wrote.

> Life seems to talk to you in soft whispers of wonderful things it is doing. . . . Once we stopped the car to listen to the evening sounds, the calls of farmers after pigs, the mooing of cows, the rasping of guinea hens, and the last faint twitterings of birds and chickens. That evening hush, with a tinge of cool in the air, and the fragrant emanation of the soil and trees, was upon us. It needed only some voice singing somewhere, I thought, or the sound of a bell, to make it complete.[43]

Motoring was a form of moving vacation. It was a sporting adventure pitting the driver against his machine, and the driver and machine against the highway. It was a new way of experiencing place, of seeing things firsthand, only glimpsed from passenger trains and ships. Motoring brought tourists into direct contact with people in settings little penetrated, and under conditions little encountered in other kinds of travel. The logistical contracts of refueling, eating, and boarding overnight were important to experiencing localities. Although the costs of early motoring were high, they were more than counterbalanced by the novel travel experiences obtained. Motoring was not just a means of getting somewhere. It was, itself, the focus of trip taking. Endurance runs helped prove the new automobile technology. Despite poor roads, poor accommodations, and difficulties at pathfinding, more and more Americans and Canadians chose the automobile for trip taking. Motoring would henceforth dominate tourism in North America.

CHAPTER SIX

HIGHWAYS AND TOURISM

> The scenery is curiously different from that further back east. At first
> I was at a loss to know why it seemed so strange and unlike regular
> landscape. Then it burst upon me. There were no billboards! Unless
> you have seen it[,] you cannot imagine what a sordid[,] dull thing
> landscape is minus billboards. Just plain sky and trees, brooks, val-
> leys[,] and hills!
>
> James Flagg, *Boulevards All the Way—Maybe*

As automobile ownership increased, so did the demand
for improved highways. Although building good roads was
rationalized initially for the economic benefits, and for the contributions to national defense, recreational impulses underlay
much of the early demand for highway improvement. Automobile driving was still primarily a leisure-time activity
throughout the 1920s. Highway associations were organized to
mark and promote tourist travel on long-distance routes a decade before state highway programs in the United States, and
provincial programs in Canada, provided a numbered highway
system for North America. Only in the 1940s was an intercity
network of hard-surfaced highways brought to completion,
and only in the 1950s was a network of supplemental limited-
access freeways begun.

Traffic attracted business to the roadsides. Commercial
strips with gasoline stations, restaurants, cabin courts, and billboards represented a new kind of environment, overly utilitarian and little appreciated for its visual qualities. Experiments
with parkways sought to protect scenery as a clear incentive to
recreation. But the parkway idea gave way to turnpikes and
freeways calculated to carry a varied traffic, and not just tourists
motoring for pleasure. As North American highways became
movers of people and goods, they were little valued as visual
displays. Nevertheless, they attracted tourists as a new kind of
back region, a new kind of ordering of space. Commercial strips
were also comforting and convenient to strangers in a society
made more transient than ever before.

Highway Development

The number of private automobiles registered in the United States increased from 8,000 in 1900 to 458,000 in 1910, to 8 million in 1920, and to 23 million in 1930. By 1960, 61 million automobiles were registered, or one automobile for every 2.3 persons.[1] Canadian registration stood at 500 in 1904, and at 4 million in 1960.[2] Americans and Canadians were justifiably proud of such statistics. Automobile production reflected high living standards and the leisure time to make automobile ownership practical. As the historian Foster Dulles observes about the United States, "A car for the family to be used primarily for pleasure was accepted as a valid ambition for every member of the American democracy."[3]

Motorists demanded new highways. North America's roads were primitive after decades of neglect. Road maintenance was totally decentralized, with responsibilities vested in township and other local governments. As Thomas Wilby observed in Quebec, beggarly statute labor laws compelled personal service on roads, or accepted service in lieu of a cash tax. Thus, road commissions lacked adequate capital for road equipment, and for materials, and had little skilled labor with which to work. Local road building was an amateurish affair, lacking the expertise of trained engineers. The Quebec farmer, Wilby wrote, "does his roadwork grudgingly and badly, and as he votes the road superintendent into power, discipline is out of the question."[4] Local roads served localities, without concern for through traffic, with the result that roads connecting major cities were often little better than the most isolated of country lanes. In many areas farmers considered improved highways of value only to city motorists, and highway improvement was seen as increasing local taxes without local benefit.

Motorists, as bicyclists before them, organized and lobbied for good roads. Two-thirds of the membership of the League of American Wheelmen lived in New York and Massachusetts where, close to the cities, most rural roads had been macadamized by 1900.[5] The National League for Good Roads, meeting in convention in 1892, called successfully for the establishment of an Office of Road Inquiry in the Department of Agri-

121

U.S. 50 in Laurel Mountain in West Virginia (1932). Federal highway subsidies in the United States resulted in the development of hard-surface interstate highways connecting major cities.

culture. The office promoted good roads as a means of reducing farm transportation costs. Experiments with the free rural mail delivery at Charleston, West Virginia, in 1896 provided still another rationale for road improvement.[6] In 1910, Harwood Frost listed in his book *The Art of Roadmaking* the benefits that rural people received from new roads: improved highways decreased the cost of haulage and facilitated marketing, thus encouraging the cultivation of crops not otherwise grown; improved roads encouraged year-round marketing, thus equalizing railroad traffic across the seasons; new roads also enlarged and reinforced rural communities by promoting social intercourse, and they facilitated the consolidation of rural schools, thus improving rural education. Highway development increased rural property values generally.[7]

The manufacturers of automobiles, tires, gasoline, and paving materials actually led the fight for good roads. Early lobbying groups in the United States included the National Crushed Stone Association, the National Asphalt Pavement

Association, and the American Road Builders' Association. A 1917 advertisement for the Portland Cement Association in the *Outlook* reads: "The demand for good roads in this country is widespread and insistent. Farmers are dependent upon them; motorists must have them, and the average city dweller who does not own a motor car is beginning to realize that the high cost of living is largely due to poor road transportation." In the same magazine, Henry Joy, president of the Packard Motor Car Company and an officer in the Lincoln Highway Association, argued for "through connecting main arterial routes of travel" and a highway system that would allow "unrestricted travel in any direction from any point." Highway development was, according to Joy, "a quickening—an awakening—a national revival" that meant "a bigger, better, more prosperous and more agreeable America."[8]

In 1904 only 154,000 miles, or 7 percent, of the 2,152,000 miles of rural roads in the United States were "improved." Approximately 108,000 miles were graveled, and 39,000 were surfaced as water-bound macadam. Brick roads accounted for only 123 miles, mostly in Ohio. The remaining roads were sand, shell, or dirt.[9] In Canada, hard-surfaced roads were nonexistent outside cities and towns. North America was almost totally dependent upon the railroads for long-distance travel.

The Lincoln Highway Association brought manufacturers, road builders, and the motoring public together in a grand promotional scheme to mark and improve a transcontinental highway honoring Abraham Lincoln. Carl Fisher, founder of the Prest-O-Lite Company, initiated the project when he proposed a "Coast-to-Coast Rock Highway" to be built with funds contributed by corporations associated with the automobile and road-building industries. A road was marked from Boston to San Francisco with red, white, and blue bands painted on telephone and telegraph poles, trees, and other objects. "Seedling miles" were constructed in Illinois, Iowa, Nebraska, Wyoming, and Nevada to demonstrate to the public the benefits of hard-surfaced roads. In addition, long stretches of dirt road in Nevada and Utah were built entirely with corporate funds funneled through the association. The purpose of the association, however, was not just to build a single road, but "to procure the building of many roads by educating people." In 1913, an estimated 150 motorists drove the western portion of the highway across the Great Plains, Rockies, and Sierras; in 1924, tourist travel was estimated at 25,000 cars.[10]

The association's technical committee recommended a sixteen-foot ribbon of concrete for the highway, with broad dirt shoulders in a 110-foot right-of-way. The road was to contain no curves of less than 1,000 feet radius and to be super-elevated for speeds up to thirty-five miles per hour. It was proposed that grade crossings be eliminated, billboards be prohibited, and comfort stations and rest parks, as well as campgrounds, be located at convenient intervals. Footpaths were proposed for road margins.[11] The road was to serve as a "definite accomplishment" that would crystallize the growing interest in road improvement. It would also be a testing ground for highway-building techniques.

The Lincoln Highway was justified by its boosters as an educational device and as an encouragement to national culture. One promoter, Nelson Fuessle, wrote:

> It will lead you like no other guide, through the startling wonders of American physical geography, with all its marvels of placid lowland and tumbled mountain ranges, forest, farmland and prairie, valley and dreaming river, lake, and hill, cool seashore and savage desert. . . . Teaching patriotism, sewing up the remaining rugged edges of sectionalism, revealing and interpreting America to its people, giving swifter feet to commerce, gathering up the country's loose ends of desultory and disjointed good roads ardor and binding them into one highly organized, proficient unit of dynamic, result-getting force, electric with zeal, it is quickening American neighborliness, democracy, and civilization.[12]

The Lincoln Highway spawned many imitators: the Jefferson Highway (Winnipeg to New Orleans), the Yellowstone Highway (Plymouth, Massachusetts, to Yellowstone and Yosemite), the Pike's Peak Ocean-to-Ocean Highway (New York

City to San Francisco). The Dixie Highway was promoted by the Chattanooga Automobile Club to encourage travel through Tennessee. It incorporated bits and pieces of a host of previously marked roads including the West and East Michigan Pikes, which met at the Straits of Mackinaw. The highway was like a braided stream, with the Michigan sections joined by a Chicago branch, merging at Chattanooga to split again into separate roads in Georgia serving east and west Florida respectively.[13] Most highway associations existed only to sell advertising in their guidebooks. They oriented tourists to cross-country routes, thereby encouraging tourism, but they did not promote highway building directly. There was substantial duplication in the routes that various associations selected. One 1,500-mile stretch of road in the West carried the markers of fifteen highway groups, the telephone poles festooned with a confusing blur of colorful insignia.[14]

The numbered road system established by federal and state legislation in the United States, and by provincial legislation in Canada, replaced the named highways. The numbered roads met only limited opposition. A *New York Times* editorial read: "The traveler may shed tears as he drives the Lincoln Highway[,] or dreams dreams as he speeds over the Jefferson Highway, but how can he get a 'kick' out of 46 or 55 or 33 or 21! The roads of America would still be on paper if the pleas that were made ten years or more ago had been made in behalf of a numerical code." But the new system quickly found favor, for many more roads could be labeled without the confusion of traditional road insignias. Motorists like Frederic Van de Water found the numbers to be a "blessing to wanderers," for at every turn or crossroads they "stood affixed to a post too plainly for even the worst blunderer to miss.[15]

The federal government took the initiative for highway construction in the United States. The Federal Aid Road Act of 1916 placed $75 million in the hands of the secretary of agriculture to spend on rural road improvement over five years. The money was granted to the states on a matching basis, requiring each state to establish a highway department in order to obtain subsidy. Federal responsibilities were lodged in the Office of Public Roads and Rural Engineering, which was renamed the

Bureau of Public Roads in 1918.[16] Because money was spent as each state saw fit, the program did not establish a system of trunk highways, a shortcoming made painfully evident during World War I. The Council for National Defense created a highway transport committee with Roy Chapin, president of the Hudson Motor Car Company, as chairman. Chapin operated some 18,000 trucks between various middle western cities and eastern seaports, largely over the Lincoln Highway. The effort substantially relieved the wartime overload on the nation's railroads.

After the war, the need for an integrated system of trunk highways was justified in terms of national defense. Economic, recreational, and other road uses were subordinated to defense concerns in the successful lobbying effort. By the terms of the Federal Highway Act of 1921, each state was required to designate 7 percent of its road mileage as primary highway, and only those roads were to be eligible for federal matching grants. A 200,000-mile system of two-lane, numbered interstate highways was designed to connect every city larger than fifty thousand population. The program was financed by a federal tax on gasoline, a funding device that related highway revenue directly to highway use. The 1934 Highway Act extended federal aid to secondary roads outside the interstate highway system.[17]

During the Depression of the 1930s, relief and recovery money accounted for nearly 80 percent of all federal expenditures on roads. Between 1933 and 1942, federal relief agencies spent four billion dollars on road and street construction. In 1939, the bureau of public roads was moved to the federal works agency and renamed the public roads administration, only to be moved again in 1949 to the Department of Commerce, where it resumed its former title. The highway lobby achieved its greatest success with the enactment of the Highway Act of 1956, which established a new 41,000-mile system of defense highways, a network of divided, limited-access interstate freeways. Again, the need for an integrated system of trunk highways was justified in terms of national defense.[18]

The mileage of surfaced highways, which doubled between 1921 and 1930, doubled again between 1930 and 1940. By

1945 the mileage of improved roads in the United States had exceeded that of unimproved roads.[19] The federal government had subsidized what the historian Frederic Paxson calls "the highway frontier."[20] The automobile was accommodated completely in the establishment of a new transportation system that competed with and ultimately replaced much of the nation's railroad system. Although arguments for national defense, and not tourism, brought the federally-subsidized highway network into existence, tourists benefited immensely from the new order. Indeed, the potential for pleasure driving remained a very significant underlying current, inclining most Americans to favor highway development for whatever reason. Higher ideals than tourism prevailed in legislative language, but the recreational use of the automobile remained an unspoken impulse in support of highway funding. Tourists voted for highways by motoring. Pleasure driving increased highway use, and use increased highway revenues, thus encouraging additional highway construction.

Under the terms of the British North America Act, road construction in Canada was made primarily a provincial responsibility. Canada's most populous provinces, Ontario and Quebec, led the way. In 1896 Ontario established an "instructor of roadmaking" in the Department of Agriculture and, in 1901, allocated $1 million to aid counties in improving some 3,700 miles of rural road. Ontario completed its first concrete trunk road from Toronto to Hamilton in 1915.[21] In 1914 Quebec established Canada's first department of highways to coordinate the construction of a system of improved roads, the first section of which, Boulevard Edward VII, had been completed between Montreal and the New York state border the previous year.

The federal government in Ottawa encouraged highway construction by the passage of the Canada Highways Act of 1919. Each province was asked to develop a system of intercity trunk highways that, when combined, were intended to tie Canada together. Most provinces took as a first priority, however, the linking Canadian cities, not with one another, but with cities in the United States. Canadians were especially hopeful of attracting American tourists through north-to-south highway improvement. Quebec's Highway Act of 1928 allocated $17 million to road building with tourism primarily in mind. In the next year alone, American tourists spent $61 million in the province.[22]

The 1920s was a period of rapid highway expansion all across Canada. The registration of motor vehicles increased from 408,000 to 1,232,000. Expenditures on roads by all governments also increased threefold, to $93 million annually.[23] But, Canadians could not yet drive across Canada. In 1925, one adventurer, Edward Flinkenger, drove a Model-T Ford over 4,000 miles of road between Halifax and Vancouver, but gaps totaling 850 miles remained north of Lake Superior and in the Rockies. He fit his car with flanged wheels and drove the rails of the Canadian Pacific Railroad, which was still Canada's only binding link.

The Depression of the 1930s slowed the pace of highway development in Canada also, since most provinces took a very conservative stand on public expenditures. Money was not lavished on highway construction, as it was in the United States, to prime the economy. Quebec continued to build roads to attract American tourists. For example, the 560-mile Gaspé Highway was built. Ontario sought to improve its intercity routes. The Queen Elizabeth Way, a four-lane, divided highway between Toronto and Hamilton, was completed in 1939, to be extended to the American border at Fort Erie during World War II. Numerous military roads were built in Canada during the world war. Most notable was the Alcan Highway, later renamed the Alaska Highway. But only in 1949 did the Trans-Canada Highway Act promise to tie Canada together by roadway. The Trans-Canada Highway, connecting St. Johns, New Foundland, in the East and Victoria, British Columbia, in the West, was the longest highway in the world when completed in 1965 at a cost of nearly a billion dollars.[24]

Dirt Roads

Graded, straightened, widened, and paved, the modern highway lifted motorists out of the dust and mud of country roads. However, progress was never fast enough, especially for harried travelers whose need for good roads was always immediate. Despite the road-building activities of state and provincial highway departments, dirt roads were the typical highways of North America until the 1930s. Dirt highways provided the acid tests of motoring stamina, and tourists equipped and otherwise prepared for the worse contingencies of travel defined in terms of dust and mud.

Dust was more an irritant than a retardant. The dusters or other apparel that motorists wore in open cars could in hot weather create as much discomfort as they alleviated. Thomas Murphy described the road south of Klamath Falls, Oregon, in 1916. The road's surface was hidden by a flour-like white limestone powder up to a foot in depth in places. It hid every hole and rut, making driving a "blind chance" and enforcing a "snail's pace." Dust begrimed everything; his face, clothing, and baggage were all covered by a dirty gray film. Dust penetrated the suitcases stored in the car's trunk, even though they were wrapped in oil cloth.[25] Frederic Van de Water found dust to be motoring's greatest nuisance. It penetrated the innermost layers of his clothing. In Iowa the dry roads of loamy clay "smoked up in clouds of dust as if on fire."

Mud was often a barrier to movement. Beatrice Massey wrote of a highway in North Dakota: "Try to picture a narrow road, with deep ditches, and just one track of ruts, covered with flypaper, vaseline, wet soap, [and] molasses candy." It was a "soft, sticky, slippery, hellish mess." When she drove out of the ruts, the car acted "as if it were drunk" by sliding, zigzagging, and slithering, first for one ditch and then the other. When she mired dead in her tracks, it was nearly impossible to jack the car up and put on chains. "Your feet stuck in the gumbo so that when you pulled up one foot[,] a mass of mire as large as a market-basket stuck to it, or your shoe came off." On a wet road heavily traveled, the motorist felt close to nature if not mired in nature. Mud varied from place to place with changing soil types and the quality of road improvement. Winifred Dixon found that mud in Texas meant "gumbo, molasses, sargasso seas, broken axels, abandoned cars." Near Eagle Lake, Texas, she made a wrong choice of ruts and mired her car to the hubs in mud. She wrote: "As soon as we stopped, we were done for. We sank deeper. We got out, sinking ourselves halfway to the knees in gumbo." The situation was so hopeless that she took several photographs to mark the occasion.[26]

Dirt roads required constant maintenance. The dirt highways of Quebec, for example, were reditched every year. After every rain they were scraped and crowned by means of split-log drags drawn by horses. Many highway departments contracted farmers to do the dragging. One tourist, James Flagg, encountered a sign posted by one proud Kansas farmer, which read: "John O'Grady Drags Two Miles of this Road." In remote sections of the West, sparse population meant minimum maintenance, and roads remained barely passable for long periods. In Nevada, Flagg found a rut between the tire tracks, a trail made by hundreds of crankcases scraping the ground. Prairie dogs and woodchucks raised havoc in western roads. Effie Gladding wrote from Wyoming: "Our local guide leaflets, furnished us by garages along the route, are full of warning about 'chucks.'" Motorists often found it necessary to leave the public rights-of-way. In 1914 in western New York, Theodore Dreiser found that motorists, in the "spirit of despair," had cut out a new road, whereas the unmaintained state highway sat entirely unused. Frederic Van de Water found Iowa's highways especially bad in 1927. "Smooth and verdurous and well-tended land on either hand ran up to the roadside fences, and there all signs of care stopped abruptly. Between these fences ran a caked and rutted desolation." There were numerous detours. According to Van de Water, "A stretch of road so far gone that Iowans consider it necessary to mend it should be a masterpiece of ruin, a monument of decreptitude, a museum piece that the Federal government should take over as a national monument. We found the detours, generally, better than the highway."[27]

Paved Roads

Before World War I, so-called "improved roads" were almost certainly drained, ditched, and graded. Usually, some attempt was made to stabilize dirt surfaces with a paving material such as gravel, sometimes spread and packed with oil to produce a macadamized surface. (The term *macadam* was frequently used improperly to describe mere gravel roads, but, more appropriately, the term applied to highways where stone was tightly compacted in either a clay or oil bond. Although brick was popular immediately before and after World War I, portland cement became the principal paving material in the 1930s.

Gravel roads presented motorists with unique driving difficulties. Loose stones lodged in moving parts or shattered window glass. Gravel roads could be as dusty as dirt roads. Southern highways, Jan and Cora Gordon observed in 1927, were improved by working a little gravel into the natural earth. But, tires wore road surfaces into curious, wave-like formations called "washboarding." "Over these roads cars jiggle as though they had St. Vitus's dance." On new gravel their car progressed primarily in a "crabwise direction." "If another car appeared[,] the two were drawn together as if by an irresistable attraction, and in the loose stuff, the steering wheels had little command."[28]

Macadamizing gave way to asphalting during the 1920s. Wagon wheels and automobile tires wore ruts in macadam roads. In 1902, Arthur Eddy saw numerous signs in Massachusetts requesting drivers not to drive center road, but the incised grooves suggested that few had heeded, for narrow roads and light traffic inclined drivers towards the middle. With oncoming traffic, custom required vehicles to pass on the right using highway shoulders, although in some Canadian provinces traffic passed on the left before World War I. Bituminous concrete, or sheet asphalt, was more durable than macadam and did not develop center grooves. By 1924, some 9,700 miles of asphalt highway had been constructed in the United States.[29]

Brick and concrete offered more permanent solutions to stabilizing road surfaces. Brick highways were most popular in Ohio, where a large clay-products industry was centered. By 1924, some 4,300 miles of highway had been paved in brick, largely in that state. Theodore Dreiser wrote from Cleveland in 1916: "If anyone doubts that this is fast becoming one of the most interesting lands in the world, let him motor from Buffalo to Detroit along the shore of Lake Erie, mile after mile, over a solid, vitrified brick road fifteen feet wide at the least, and approximately 300 miles long." The road was not yet completed, and the "horrific" detour sign was constantly in evidence, but, to Dreiser, traveling over the finished sections was "something like riding in paradise.[30] Brick roads were far from perfect and presented drivers with unique challenges. They were noisy, since tires created a constant rumble, and slick in wet weather, making steering and braking difficult.

The use of portland cement came to dominate road building. Concrete surfaces were smoother, and thus quieter to drive. Tires gripped concrete pavements with greater consistency. More important, concrete ribbons and slabs were cheaper to construct by machine, as opposed to the brick pavements, which were constructed solely by hand. The first concrete highway, five miles in length, was built north of Detroit in 1909. By 1914, 2,300 miles of concrete road had been built, and 31,000 miles by 1925.[31] Brick and concrete ushered in the era of "hard roads." Hard surfaces drained easily and did not require repeated dragging to smooth out the mud, and they did not have to be dampened down to contain dust. The light highway traffic of the early years suggested that most hard roads could last indefinitely. Hard roads seemed to most Americans and Canadians to be permanent investments in the future. To hit a stretch of concrete pavement after hours of travel on dirt was like driving in a land of tomorrow.

Concrete highways also enabled drivers to relax. Near Spokane in 1924, Melville Ferguson encountered his first concrete road since leaving Minnesota. It was a "broad gray ribbon of concrete, the kind with an absolutely flat surface and a neat little binding on the sides." He lolled back in his seat, touched the steering wheel lightly with the tips of his fingers, stepped on the gas, and even looked at the scenery, which was, for a driver, a rare privilege. The 1920s and 1930s were decades of massive road construction in which detours were a constant nuisance. It seemed to Ferguson that all the highways of Oregon were being remade: "Sometimes we were diverted to a temporary trail parallel with the new grade, but several feet below it, to which we had to descend on embankments tilted at a sharp angle. There were little wooden bridges, battered to pieces by the heavy trucks of the road-builders, where planks flew up and splintered when wheels passed over them."[32]

The use of concrete for highways invited experimentation. States sought to develop width, grade, and other design specifications based on expected traffic volume, speed, and use. The Columbia River Highway, begun in 1913, was Oregon's experimental road. It was twenty-four feet wide, contained no turning radius of less than one hundred feet, and had no grade in excess of 5 percent. The highway was built especially to accommodate tourists through some of Oregon's most picturesque scenery, for in one ten-mile stretch, the road passed eleven waterfalls. An article promoting the highway read:

> Hanging in cliffs at many places, its concrete and steel bridges spanning turbulent streams that flow along hundreds of feet below, the highway reaches its greatest elevation at Crown Point, 700 feet above the river. From Observation Point the tourist may get views for thirty-five miles in an easterly or westerly direction, look down on the fish wheels taking Salmon from the stream, and spend hours in watching the changing colors of earth and sky.[33]

The Evolving Roadside

The highway was more than a smoothed and straightened surface. The highway was an array of services contrived to facilitate the motorist's passage. Well-traveled highways generated new, distinctive landscapes as commercial strips grew in urban areas, spreading cities outward into what had been countryside. Most highways were strictly utilitarian. Function and not visual quality dominated roadside planning, or lack of planning. Experiments with scenic roads and parkways designed for recreation gave way, under the press of commuter and intercity travel, to more practical concerns.

At first, commercial strips reinforced highways as arteries of travel. But in maturity, strips came to function more as trip destinations for local motorists, rather than as facilitators of through movement. Traffic was slowed by congestion. In response, a new kind of highway evolved: a highway divorced from its surroundings through limitation of access. Toll highways and freeways facilitated rapid travel as they eliminated conflicting cross currents of movement. But, high-speed travel became monotonous on the new roads divorced from their surroundings, and highway engineers were forced eventually to consider the visual properties of highway design out of safety consideration.

Motorists encountered incredible variety in roadside signage. At first, there was little consistency in official signs regulating traffic, although by World War I most states and provinces had adopted set styles for traffic signs. Standards changed as speed and volume of traffic increased. Generally, signs became simpler and larger. Maryland had posted large map boards outside large towns, each map detailing the town's main routes and major landmarks. Such signs were too detailed and required drivers to memorize information. In Massachusetts, complex signs, such as "Vehicles Using This Street Will Follow In the Direction Of The Arrow Only," were changed to read simply "One Way."[34] Each state and province began to experiment with sign wording. Messages were communicated differently in different jurisdictions, contributing subtly to a sense of state or provincial character. Signs read "Danger—Loose Cattle" in Texas, "Caution—Live Stock At Large" in Louisiana, "Watch For Cattle," in Georgia, and "Watch For Stray Cattle—No Stock Law" in North Carolina.[35]

Used to protected roadsides devoid of commerce, the Englishman Mark Pepys was disturbed by the confusion between official signs and advertisements. "Trying to pick out a 'warning' or 'stop' sign, or a road number," he complained, "is like looking for a needle in a haystack." Other European visitors disagreed. Ilya Ilf and Eugene Petrov, visiting Soviet journalists, appreciated that foreigners, even those with no command of English, could drive anywhere in North America without apprehension. Highways are carefully numbered, they wrote, "and the numbers are met so frequently that it is impossible to make a mistake of direction. The signs are placed sufficiently low above-ground so that the driver may see them on his right without taking his eyes off the road. They are never conditional and never require any decoding."[36]

Irvin Cobb believed in scenery unspoiled by commercial intrusion. He wrote: "If all the billboards which desecrate the scenic areas of America were piled one on top of another, allowing twelve inches of horizontal thickness for each billboard, the total number would form a column 114 miles high[,] and to soak them properly for burning would require 90,000 barrels of grade-A kerosene." Throughout the 1920s, billboards left the railroads and crept out onto the highways. They lined the most heavily traveled routes, especially at the fringes of cities. Most tourists considered them a blight. Kenneth Roberts wrote of Maine's U.S. 1: "The road inland from Bar Harbor to Bangor, which winds through magnificent forests, past lakes and rolling mountains and little old New England farmhouses, is decorated with steadily increasing reminders to ask for Magooslum's Maine-Made Mayonnaise, Smoke Oakum Cigars, and vote for Muddle for Sheriff, to say nothing of B. O. tobacco, visiting Fuss' Overnight Camps, buying a nice pair of four-dollar shoes from Buzzard's, picking up a Boston bag at Roorback-Skillet Company's Bangor store and attending a Lion's meeting while in the city."[37]

Large billboards were not the only commercial messengers by the roadside. Small "snipe signs" were nailed onto trees, fences, and buildings to advertise soft drinks, cigarettes, motor oil, baking powder, shaving cream. Almost all tourists found such signs of some comfort in the search for roadside services. Some tourists even welcomed them as a form of visual relief, especially on monotonous roads otherwise lacking in visual interest. One traveler wrote of a flat coastal road in South Carolina: "There was only the unending literature of the roadside to divert us: 'Gas, Beer, Coke' . . . 'Jumbo Milk Shakes' . . . 'Live Bait' . . . 'Don't Be A Litterbug' . . . 'Tiny Condon For Sheriff.'" Roadside attractions were periodically announced: "Monkey Theater," "Singing Jackass—Four Miles," "Slow Down—Wild Animals 200 Yards." Towns reached out to greet motorists with signs like "Drive Slow See Our Town. Drive Fast, See Our Judge."[38]

Beginning with the Outdoor Circle of Hawaii's effort in 1913, civic groups organized across the United States and Canada to restrict roadside advertising.[39] Legislation was passed to eliminate small signs, to move billboards back from rights-of-way, and to educate the public to the benefits of further restrictions. Thirty-two states passed laws restricting signs on fences, posts, walls, trees, and rocks. During the 1930s, Massachusetts outlawed billboards within fifty feet of rural rights-of-way, Florida within two hundred feet, and Colorado within five hundred feet.[40] Advertising interests merely increased the size of signs and moved them back the legal distances. Tourists were generally aware of, and appreciative of, landscapes uncluttered by signs. Gordon Brinley wrote of driving from Vermont into Quebec: "There is no ugliness — no ugliness anywhere we have been this morning. And now, we look upon a land expressive of peace and well-being. Harmony of flowing mountain slopes, rich surface crops and verdant forests are, thanks be to God and good citizenship, entirely free of billboards."[41]

Kenneth Roberts characterized Maine's U.S. 1 between Portland and Kittery as lined with "doggeries and crab-meateries and doughnuteries and clammeries and booths that dispense home cooking on oil cloth and inch-thick china in an aura of kerosene stoves, frying onions and stale grease." U.S. 1 was a tawdry road "rich in bad taste." Irvin Cobb described the same highway in Connecticut on a typical summer weekend. "Cars without number go skyhooting through, by day raising pillars of grit, by night tainting the air with reeks of gasoline and lubricating oils. From end to end they closely are enfiladed by filling stations, repair stations, tea-houses, road-houses, and lunch-stands."[42] By the mid-1930s, the forty-eight-mile section of U.S. 1 between the New York state line and New Haven in Connecticut was bordered by 2,900 buildings with direct access to the highway. There was an average of one gasoline station every 895 feet, and one restaurant every 1,825 feet.[43] But U.S. 1 in New Jersey between Trenton and Newark was even more intensively commercialized. Three hundred gasoline stations and 440 other business, along with 472 billboards, lined forty-seven miles of road.[44]

Commercial strips were not planned. They just grew.

Indeed, the strip resulted from a lack of planning and a lack of land-use control, such as zoning. A highway built to carry traffic could be incapacitated within a few years by urban-like growth accumulated along its margins. Four years after Romona-Garvey Avenue near Los Angeles was remodeled into a four-lane express highway, a thirty-mile ribbon development had evolved, and speed limits were dropped to twenty-five miles per hour.[45] A new order of landscape was evolving. J. B. Preistley thought it a world-wide phenomenon that had merely appeared first in North America. He wrote:

> There was rapidly coming into existence a new way of living—fast, crude, vivid—perhaps a new civilization, perhaps another barbaric age—and here were the signs of it, trivial enough in themselves, but pointing to the most profound changes, to huge bloodless revolutions. . . . There had been no planning. Some people took to moving here and there . . . to make a few dollars; that was all. Perhaps there would not be any planning for a long time, until it would be too late to plan. This new life was simply breaking through the old like a crocus through the wintry crust of earth.

Ilya Ilf and Eugene Petrov were also attracted to the strip for its larger meanings. When they shut their eyes and tried to resurrect in memory the country in which they had spent four months, they saw not Washington, D.C., with its monuments, not San Francisco with its hills and suspension bridges, nor Detroit with its automobile factories, but "the crossing of two roads and a petrol station against the background of telegraph wires and advertising billboards."[46]

As attenuated parks with roadways designed for pleasure driving, parkways offered a means by which roadside landscapes could be controlled. Boston, Kansas City, Philadelphia, and New York City, among other municipalities, experimented with scenic drives in the late-nineteenth century. New York City's suburban Westchester County constructed the first system of limited-access pleasure drives. The Bronx River Parkway was constructed between 1913 and 1925 as a means of restoring the Bronx River, long a sewer for industrial wastes. Roads forty feet wide and sixteen miles in length were constructed on both sides of the river, with rights-of-way varying from two hundred feet to one-third of a mile. Traffic was restricted to passenger cars. Eight miles of the riverbed were virtually rebuilt, and some 30,000 trees and 140,000 shrubs were planted in what was actually a multipurpose conservation effort.[47] The construction of the Bronx River Parkway set several precedents. First, it established the power of government to limit direct access to a roadway and prevent despoliation by commercial interests. Second, it established the principal of multiple public land use in highway-oriented land development. Third, it established the right of government to restrict the kinds of vehicles that used a road. By 1932, Westchester County had built 160 miles of parkway.

Robert Moses, long-time head of New York's Long Island state park commission and creator and controller of numerous public authorities in metropolitan New York City, used the parkway idea to build a bureaucratic empire. In thirty-four years he built thirty parkways, fourteen expressways, and seven major bridges, creating a system of highways unequaled in any other metropolis.[48] The Moses empire was based on park development, and highways were conceptualized and sold to the public as parkways connecting state beaches and other recreational facilities. Moses brought nature and outdoor recreation to the automobile-owning middle classes crowded into New York City. His efforts made him a folk hero.

Tourists like Cecil Roberts noted the splendid roads that sent motorists "speeding into the woods, valleys, and hills." He wrote: "The genius of Robert Moses has created a network of exit roads, all planned with the dual purpose of facility and beauty." A shopkeeper had said to him: "We guys knowses what we oweses to Mr. Moses." Moses was often unscrupulous in his quest for power, as his critic Robert Caro has established.[49] However, he knew how to turn public opinion to his ends. He used recreation and tourism as excuses to restructure geographically the nation's largest city. Moses's genius as a showman climaxed in the world's fairs, which he built and operated in New York City in 1939 and 1964.

The federal government was also involved in parkway

development. The Mount Vernon Memorial Parkway and its extension, the George Washington Memorial Parkway, were completed in the Washington, D.C., area in the early 1930s. The Skyline Drive, in what later became Shenandoah National Park, was begun with federal relief money in 1932. Of the many parkways planned, only the Blue Ridge Parkway (which extended Skyline Drive to the Great Smoky Mountains National Park), the Colonial Parkway (between Yorktown and Jamestown in Virginia), and the Natchez Trace Parkway (in Tennessee, Alabama, and Mississippi) were completed or brought near to completion in subsequent decades. The federal parkways stand in contrast to the nation's other highways built with federal funds. John Ise, a historian of national park policy, noted that speed limits were low enough so that the leisurely driver did not feel in the way. He wrote: "No billboards scream the virtues of cigarette brands or the hotel at the next junction which is 'run nice for nice people,' or the restaurant where the 'food is good'; no lumbering trucks tear up the roads.'" He concluded: "Everything is fine and artistic."[50]

Despite the promise of multipurpose planning, most highways in the United States and Canada were developed as single-purpose projects, unrelated to other public utilities in design and to other kinds of land use in their location. They were built primarily for commercial purposes. Eventually, even the urban parkways were given over to the commercial uses of intercity travel, commuting, and goods haulage. Highway planners little appreciated the aesthetic values implicit in visually interesting parkways. Instead, they focused on lane separation, grade separation, limited accessibility, and the other devices seen as speeding up travel. Increasing traffic flow, rather than improving travel experience, became an overwhelming primary goal.

Adding traffic lanes improved traffic flow. Separating on-coming traffic with a median strip and introducing rotaries and cloverleafs further speeded movement. The Du Pont Highway, built at Wilmington in the mid-1920s, was the first divided all-purpose road. At the same time, the first traffic circle was opened at Camden, New Jersey. The state of New Jersey pioneered the use of road cuts, viaducts, grade separations, and controlled exit and entrance ramps at bridge approaches out-side Philadelphia and New York City. The first cloverleaf to totally eliminate crossing maneuvers and turns against the stream of traffic was opened at Woodbridge, New Jersey, in 1928.[51] Travelers gloried when they encountered the new super highways and their innovations. One tourist wrote about leaving New York City via the Pulaski Skyway: "We bowled along the Holland Tunnel and came out, on the New Jersey side, on to the most magnificent and awe-inspiring road I have ever seen. For miles and miles it is lifted clean above the ground on a great ramp of concrete and iron, and there is room for at least six lanes of traffic!"[52]

Between 1940 and 1960, some 3,500 miles of toll highway were constructed in the United States.[53] These highways set the standards for the new interstate freeways constructed under the federal highway act of 1956. The Merritt Parkway, the first long-distance turnpike, was begun in 1938 to connect New York City and New Haven. The road featured toll gates through which the through traffic passed, local drivers entering and ex-iting at intermediate interchanges without charge.[54] Travelers were intrigued by the new highway environment, but not all were sure that they completely liked it. Jonathon Daniels was impressed by the Merritt Parkway's white lanes of concrete and miles of pretty planting that provided the motorist "every facil-itation to motion." But, he wrote, "Here is an avenue of escape from both traffic and reality." Instead of the Connecticut land-scape, he saw "mile after mile of identical right-of-way" and "mile after mile of changeless green procession." He con-cluded, "Connecticut escaped the showing. In order that the traveler may move in this land, he must give up the privilege of seeing it."[55]

Highways as Visual Displays

The turnpikes and freeways represented a new kind of travel environment in which the motorist was separated from the localities through which he passed.[56] The motorist was de-pendent primarily upon his car, the pavement, and the immedi-ate right-of-way for visual stimulation. The standardized road and roadside created boredom, presenting a safety hazard.

Slowly, highway designers came to view highways not only as a means to an end (a way of getting someplace and back), but as ends in themselves (an important kind of environmental experience).[57] Sociologists Christopher Tunnard and Boris Pushkarev write: "The highway is seen before it can be traveled upon—being seen is an integral part of its purpose. . . . The moving eye perceives the form of the highway not as an engineering problem, but as an esthetic entity, a piece of sculpture or architecture, built of earth, asphalt, concrete, steel, shrubs, and trees."[58]

Visually, highways of all kinds can be assessed according to external harmony (the relationship of the highway to the landscape) and internal harmony (the quality of the alignment of the roadway itself). External harmony has always been important to the automobile tourist, for in tourism the highway becomes a means of seeing landscapes and not just a means of moving rapidly through them. To Jan and Cora Gordon the concrete roads of the south were frankly stated without subterfuge. They wrote: "They were architectured into the country and, holding their unrelenting way across the green, green land, emphasizing the bases of the hills with their strict and positive curves, they gave a welcome contrast and brought a sense of order amongst the fluid shapes of river, field or wood." Their experience of fast driving on the smooth roads wore well. "And so in the end, we found them like poetry, like a strong serious rhythm holding down the rich riot of unhampered nature; so that what at first struck us with a sense of distaste, from its mere unfamiliarity, became the basis of a new series of observations and contrasted qualities and a source of delight."[59]

Planners John Nolen and Henry Hubbard write: "In gradient and alignment the road should lie comfortably upon the topography, appearing to occupy a miraculously favorable natural location rather than to be cruelly forced through against the 'lay of the land.'" Another planner, John Brookes, notes that buildings conceived as self-contained problems of design long have been the "bane of landscape." Designers, he feels, should consider buildings as part of the complex pattern of landscape. Highways, he writes, need this "inflection to the countryside" more than any other kind of building because they are the most pervasive of visible engineering structures, and landscapes are most often seen from highways. Tunnard and Pushkarev suggest that the following questions be asked of all highways: Does the road flow along rivers smoothly, hug slopes naturally, climb hills in convincing ways? Do they grasp mountains firmly, jump valleys decisively? Or do they, to the contrary, climb ridges needlessly, descend into valleys thoughtlessly, violate lakes brutally, cut up landscapes violently?[60]

As external harmony influences what a tourist sees in and feels about a given landscape, so also does internal harmony affect travel experience. John Nolen and Henry Hubbard comment: "There is a beauty of the alignment and curvature of the road itself. Straight should merge into curve, and one curve into another in a smooth sequented way." The driver, whose eyes watch the road almost continuously, must sense a harmonious rhythm in the road, which carries him forward gracefully.[61] Upton Sinclair, in his novel *Oil!*, described a young boy's satisfaction at accompanying his father through California's Guadalupe Pass north of Los Angeles. The road had a hypnotic effect. Sinclair wrote: "And this magic ribbon of concrete [was] laid out for you, winding here and there[,] feeling its way upward with hardly a variation of grade, taking off the shoulder of a mountain, cutting straight through the apex of another, diving on the outside corner, tilting outward on the inside curves, so that you were always balanced, always safe."[62]

The most interesting roads were those that directed the motorist's eye to scenes beyond the highway in a sequence of revelation and surprise. Straight-line roads have made sense in flat terrain where the predominant man-made landscape pattern, the road system itself, was rectilinear. But in other terrain they were aesthetically uninteresting since they were totally predictable. They became monotonous and fatiguing because the view appeared static. Straight roads encouraged excessive speeds by encouraging drivers to "get on with it" and to "get it over with." Curved roads brought the roadside more into view, showing drivers and passengers a changing panorama that aroused anticipation for what lay beyond. A curve encouraged attention and a steady hold on the steering wheel. Curving roadside provided a better optical guidance, since the landscape was seen ahead rather than peripherally.[63]

The interplay of better cars and better roads set up an endless clamor for utilitarian roadscapes. As the historian Frederick Paxson points out, "When the concrete road was built, the maker could sell a faster car; the faster car called for a road wider, safer, and more nearly straight. Every improvement by the highway engineer was matched by increased demands from users."[64] Each new pressure forced a reconsideration of highway specifications. Every year produced a new definition of what constituted an adequate highway. The aesthetics of the visual environment became increasingly unimportant. Roadside landscaping was reduced to purely utilitarian terms. Plantings were for slope control, prevention of erosion, headlight screening, reduction of fire hazard, sound dampening, ease of maintenance. The landscape architect was not called upon to relate road and roadside as landscape.[65]

Beauty for beauty's sake counted for little. In the United States, highway margins were planted in grass devoid of trees and shrubs for ease of maintenance. Wild flowers, for example, had no place. According to one highway engineer writing in 1916, "The beauty and charm of individual flowers is lost in speed . . . it would be unwise to line a whole mile with wild flowers, even if the cost could be afforded." To another engineer writing in 1936, "The proper place for the elaborate development of flowers is in the home garden, where suitable care can be given . . . [and] where they can be viewed by only those who appreciate them." Engineers made assumptions from values rooted more in cement and asphalt than in nature. Many tourists tended to think differently. They noted wild flowers by the roadside. Gordon Brinley commented on entering Quebec, "It is good to be in Canada again . . . once more under escort of purple vetch and white clover." He delighted at the sight of long stretches of roadside covered in "heavenly blue" and "feathery white." "Dame nature," he surmised, "surely knows her geography; she never puts United States borders on Canadian roads."[66]

Most Americans, intoxicated by their new-found mobility, cared little that highways were utilitarian so long as they were convenient. The rapid acceptance of the automobile in American life centered on the fact that automobiles gave owners control over movement. It was the moving that counted. The automobile was a toy when used for pleasure. Its operation on an open road heightened feelings of freedom of action as it increased the driver's sense of power. Speed exhilarated in the interplay between pleasure and fear when the bounds of highway safety were approached. Driving, for many Americans, became a testing of skill, of finding one's limits in handling the ultimate machine. Automobiling as a sport was often destinationless. The landscapes through which drivers moved meant little. Places could be taken for granted. The only environment that counted was the highway and the automobile itself.[67]

Automobiles were a status symbol and a means to personal identity. Having examined the automobile as a symbol in American literature, Cynthia Dettlebach concluded: "For the prestige and social status it symbolized, the mobility it afforded, the pleasure and power it gave its driver, the sense of place and appropriation of space it allowed, the American began to consider the car not only as a prized possession but as a necessity for his well-being." Foreign visitors quickly caught the car-ownership fever. Having dutifully criticized big city traffic and the wastefulness of automobiles generally, Ilya Ilf and Eugene Petrov bought a car. It was an ordinary Ford, without a radio, heater, ashtray, or cigarette lighter. But, they fell in love with it, treating it as a friend and partner in travel. The car took them across the United States, allowing them to experience America by highway, just as Americans experienced their country. They wrote: "Side by side with your machine pass hundreds of other machines and thousands push from behind . . . sweeping you along with them in their satanic flight. All of America speeds some somewhere, and evidently never will stop."[68]

Tourists made extensive use of North America's new highways. It mattered not that highway engineers were oblivious to the tourists' visual experience. Geographical mobility was of the essence. Getting there was the motorists' pervasive challenge in the era of primitive dirt roads. Motorists, tourists included, welcomed modern highways with their widened, straightened, and graded rights-of-way and their hard surfaces. Tourists welcomed the filling of gaps in North America's network of highways. That roads were utilitarian; that they attracted commerce in highway strip development, that they often abused landscapes through which they passed mattered little. The motoring experience was sufficiently novel that any improved highway served tourists adequately.

Tourism was, nevertheless, an important motive underlying highway development, especially in areas where tourism was a significant commercial enterprise. Highways made tourist areas accessible. The nation's first marked highways, like the Lincoln Highway, were tourist roads intended to connect tourist attractions with population centers. More important, motoring, as a recreational activity, potentially benefited every motorist. Citizens supported highway building irrespective of stated rationales because of the promise of increased geographical mobility in leisure time. The building of parkways in the 1920s and 1930s reflected recognition that tourists were important highway users. Parkways, with their land use controls, discouraged signage and other forms of commercialization. They oriented motorists visually to landscapes developed for recreational purposes. Such highways, however, were overwhelmed by the tide of geographical reorganization that came with increased dependence upon automobiles and highway technology. Thus, billboards and gasoline stations came to symbolize the tourists' view of North American highways; scenic amenities had less influence on the tourists' images of highway travel.

CHAPTER SEVEN

AUTOMOBILE TRAVEL BETWEEN THE WORLD WARS

> The result of car and holiday is: thirty-five miles an hour from day
> break to sunset, piling impression onto impression at as rapid a
> speed as possible so that in the memory nothing remains but the few
> objects of nature's facetiousness which are usually photographed in
> the tourist folders—the rock like an Indian face, the waterfall in
> seven stories, the boulder which is shaped like a frog, and so on.
>
> Jan and Cora Gordon, *On Wandering Wheels*

Inexpensive automobiles and cheap gasoline encouraged long-distance auto touring. Camping along the roadside made travel affordable to nearly all. Towns organized campgrounds partly to protect themselves against the horde of "tin can tourists," and partly to attract tourist dollars. Gasoline stations, restaurants, and motels made up a trilogy of highway services easing travel. Potentially, motoring was democratic. Tourists from all sections and from all social classes could generally mix in the campgrounds and along the roadsides. But, automobiles also served as cocoons, separating travelers from one another. Motels emphasized privacy by facilitating anonymity and catered to class consciousness by upgrading service to price out undesirables. The homogenized highway dulled the travelers' awareness of landscape as speed and distance became a North American obsession in travel. Touring by automobile became routine, with set roles acted out in set ways. A syndrome of comfortable travel was established in which the impulse to sport mixed with the old restlessness to seek new places.

The Impulse toward Constant Driving

With automobiles came speed. And with speed came the impulse toward constant driving. Even in 1902 Arthur Eddy observed that the automobile was "no respector of persons or places." It panted with impatience if brought to a stand for so much as a moment. "The throbbing, puffing, impatient machine gets the upper hand of those who are supposed to control it; we are hastened onward in spite of our better inclinations." Improved highways amplified tourists' obsessions with covering long distances quickly. Driving seemed to impose its own special momentum to keep moving. "This perpetual auto-motion," wrote James Flagg, "befitted a nation known for rocking chairs and chewing gum." The national bird, instead of being the eagle, he mused, ought to have been "the squirrel in the cage."[1] In 1916, a motorist was lucky to travel 125 miles in a day. But, distances traveled increased to an average of 170 miles in 1920, 200 miles in 1925, 300 miles in 1931, and 400 miles in 1936.[2]

Motorists became hypnotized by comfortable cars and smooth highways. Familiarity meant that tourists soon took the road for granted, and motoring emerged as a means to get somewhere rather than as an end in itself. Travel by automobile was a way of escaping the everyday. A promoter of the Lincoln Highway wrote: "Your true motorist likes to settle down behind the wheel, knowing that his motor is running smoothly, and head away over new roads amid new surroundings, away from everyday places and things that have grown hum-drum through constant association."[3] But, when highways were modernized, motoring, itself, became commonplace. Speed and not "new surroundings" became the essence of the motoring experience. An Arizona campground operator noted the average motorist's general disregard for place. The typical tourist was principally concerned with breaking his mileage record of the previous day. An auto-camp owner in Oregon told sociologist Norman Hayner that messages on the postcards he mailed for customers primarily concerned the number of miles covered for the day, or anticipated for the next day.[4]

Speed exerted a tyranny. Sociologists Christopher Tunnard and Boris Pushkarev point out the influences of speed on the motorist's powers of observation. The number of things to be seen in a landscape increases with speed. As it becomes dangerous to observe everything, concentration is fixed on the approaching ribbon of road. The driver's point of concentration recedes with increased speed. At 25 miles an hour his eyes focus some 600 feet ahead, but 1,200 feet at 45 miles an hour and 2,000 feet at 65 miles an hour. As speed increases, peripheral vision diminishes from a total horizontal angle of about 100 degrees at

45 miles an hour to a "tunnel" of 40 degrees above 65 miles an hour. Space perception is impaired. The driver is less able to estimate his car's speed or the speed of other objects. In short, the passing scene is abridged. Attention is transferred from the surrounding landscape to the car and the highway.[5]

Automobile travel involved sets of destinations connected by straight-line paths. Tourists rushed from destination to destination validating expectations. Frederic Van de Water decried those who blinded their eyes to the loveliness of the road by the "dust of their haste." At Yellowstone, he observed that most tourists saw only the major attractions as interpreted by guidebooks and signs, although he himself made a special effort to experience the subtleties of nature "past which tourists roar their cars unheeding from show place to show place." It was a sign of an inexperienced traveler to race around from sight to sight, guidebook in one hand, pockets bulging with picture postcards, and each hour of the day mapped out by stopwatch. It was also a distinctively North American travel trait. Dallas Sharp writes: "To push on from dawn to dark, and after dark, seeing nothing, resting nowhere, hailing no traveler nor station, is quite truly American."[6]

The best way to travel was to stop and linger. Of the Four Corners country around Kayenta, Arizona, Ernie Pyle wrote: "If you want to, you can drive straight through the area in two days, but if you do, you might as well stay home. The only way to feel the country is to pause in it; sit on a rock and don't worry about getting up; lie around as long as there's anybody to talk to."[7] Smart travel was slow and spontaneous.

The standard ten-day or two-week vacation, coupled with improved automobiles and highways, invited rapid travel. Less affluent Americans and Canadians, without the money to linger in resorts as the elite had done in a previous era, came to dominate tourism. The impulse toward constant driving was rooted in trip planning, whereby people with limited time and money sought to maximize distance and, thereby, maximize travel experience. Schedules often conservatively figured placed travelers constantly behind schedule, inclining them to rush through places where they should have lingered. Road maps and guidebooks were an invitation to overextension. John Steinbeck warned: "Maps are not reality at all—they can be tyrants. I know people who are so immersed in road maps that they never see the countryside they pass through, and others who, having traced a route, are held to it as though held by flanged wheels to rails."[8]

Marked highways with their guidebooks and other descriptive materials invited rapid, long-distance driving between set destinations. Nothing embodied the new travel syndrome as the National Park-to-Park Highway marked out to connect twelve western national parks in the United States in a circuit of 6,000 miles. Such promotions, subsidized by the automobile and gasoline companies, were more for keeping tourists moving than for letting them stop and look.[9] Thomas Wolfe, in company with several journalists, traveled the national park circuit in thirteen days in 1938. He wrote: "The gigantic unconscious humor of the situation . . . 'making every national park' without seeing any of them—the main thing is to 'make them'—and so on and on tomorrow."[10]

Driving Ease

Cross-country driving was no longer reserved for the doers of stunts and the questors after thrills. Anyone who owned an automobile could travel long distances with little or no special preparation. Automobiling was no longer a novelty, but an everyday occurrence. It was something that could be taken for granted.

Automobile travel fostered social cohesion. As strangers in unfamiliar territory, touring families seemed to draw together for security and companionship.[11] Trips were valued less for their adventures with strangers and more for family reinforcement through shared experience. Zephine Humphrey noted that the people they saw en route paid little or no attention to them, and that friends and relatives were completely out of touch. She wrote: "We hardly knew our location ourselves; yet, at least for the moment, we were an integral part of every mile we covered. The burden of home life was discarded, but the essence of it we had with us in the four walls of our car. Our companionship was complete."[12] As travel was stripped of its adventure and made more familiar, travelers turned to activities within their vehicles to break the monotony of travel. In-car diversions included listening to the radio, playing word games, and otherwise reducing visual and other contacts with the world that moved beyond the car. Travel became a series of social events contained within the car.

Hazardous driving did redirect travelers to the passing scene as hazard reintroduced a sense of adventure. In winter, accumulated snow could reduce highways to the most primitive of driving conditions. In 1927, Dallas Sharp followed fresh car tracks west from Winslow, Arizona. He did not follow the highway but drove overland. He frequently crossed the highway, but all that he could see of it was a smooth band of white without the mark of a single wheel. The road had been graded below the level of the desert, just deep enough to fill with snow, making driving impossible. Each driver was "free to pick his own sweet way," "steer by his own compass," and "follow the line of the trail when he could." Jan and Cora Gordon encountered a violent summer storm in Virginia. The car was blown into a skid, stopping just as a tree fell across the road, plastering their radiator, hood, and windshield with greenery.[13]

Although modern automobiles and highways promoted travel in relative comfort, motoring was not without risk. Carelessness was bred by continuous driving. Fatigue and disinterest in the passing scene dimmed attention and dulled reactions. Accidents seen in passing encouraged increased awareness and brought home the fact that even the most comfortable travel involved danger. Frederic Van de Water passed an accident scene in Nebraska. Cars were halted in a long line. Farmers in blue overalls leaned on a fence soberly watching the fire that consumed the remains of a car hit by a train. They had been a family of five, tourists returning from Colorado, but only a small infant had survived.[14]

Night driving excited interest in the passing scene for its uniqueness. Darkness obscured the landscape in romantic ways, inviting travelers to use their imaginations. Darkness also increased the sense of danger in motoring. Ilya Ilf and Eugene Petrov wrote: "It is frightful to race at night over an

American highway. Darkness to the right and to the left. But the face is struck by the lightning flashes of automobile headlights coming at you. They fly past, one after the other, like small hurricanes of light, with a curt and irate feline spit." Lines of red taillights spread out ahead of them while the headlight beams of impatient cars silhouetted them from behind. Each time a heavy truck passed, a suction rocked their small car. The big trucks were especially disconcerting at night, with their rows of green or yellow lights outlining the tops of cabs and trailers.[15]

Another way to reintroduce a sense of adventure in travel was to leave the well-traveled modern highways for back roads. Adventure could be had "off the beaten track." These roads were more difficult to drive, and there were no roadside conveniences. Tourists could not take comfort in each other's presence. Jan and Cora Gordon wrote of back roads in Pennsylvania: "This was all land of toil, no tourists loitered here, no overnight lodgings or Bide-A-Wees, none of that cheery punning . . . no Step-Inn or Dew Drop Inn." In 1928, Hoffman Birney drove to Utah's Monument Valley, feeling that he had driven where no automobile had ever gone before. Eight years later, Lewis Gannett drove to nearby Kayenta, in Arizona. The town was still the farthest post office from a railroad in the country. He did not see another automobile in twelve hours of steady driving across one hundred and fifty miles of sand and rock.[16]

Aside from recognizing risks in motoring and questing after the unique, both at night and off main-traveled roads, motorists sought to escape the ordinary through the instrument of distance. To travel long distances, even in relative comfort, was still an accomplishment requiring some stamina and some skill. One could not travel far without some small misadventure. There arose among motorists what Frederic Van de Water called "road liars": tourists whose lot in life was easy, but who needed to have others think otherwise. The road liar was a romantic at heart. He yearned to be a hard-bitten adventurer. He was immensely sensitive to thrills and practically immune to truth. Every road he traveled became, in retrospect, an ordeal safely overcome. At a campground in Iowa, Van de Water mistakenly inquired about the route ahead. The "road liars" launched into action. "They pounded at our maps. They shouted contradictions at each other. They regarded every suggestion we made with the broad tolerance of the wise in the presence of fools. [They] dragged their fingers across our maps and shouted calamity at each other."[17]

Although improved highways enabled, and even invited, long-distance travel, the long trip continued to be a badge of hardship even in the face of comfortable reality. The pretense was maintained in subtle ways. Although automobiles marked with pennants and signs were rarely seen after 1925, tourists continued to use window and bumper stickers. Mary Bedell visited five national parks to line her windshield with stickers. Even though they obscured the view, she was "justly proud of the achievement which they represented." Another traveler noted that once it was the fashion to cover suitcases with labels, but now one covered one's windshield instead. License plates also served to signify long-distance adventure. Bedell found that her New York license plate was a great curiosity in California. Her party was frequently greeted with shouts of "Hello, New York!" from passing cars.[18]

Automobile Camping

Camping was a form of social interaction. Not only was the family strengthened through mutual experience, but its members were presented with opportunities to meet strangers, breaking the inward-focused circle imposed by the automobile as mobile social container. The rationales for camping were many. Because hotel and restaurant costs were eliminated, camping was thought of as an inexpensive means of travel. Camping was seen as a leisurely way to break work routines. It offered freedom of action and it provided opportunities to get close to nature. As tens of thousands of campers took to the highways after World War I, campgrounds were organized to control and direct the crowds. More and more luxury entered the sport. Auto camps became more elaborate and equipment more extravagant. Ultimately, most automobile tourists gave up camping altogether, opting instead for the luxury and convenience of roadside motels and restaurants.

Why tourists ever gave up the comforts of hotels to camp by the roadside was a question hotly debated. The obvious

Picnic near Hot Springs, Arkansas (1927). Eating by the roadside became an American and Canadian pastime.

answer was economy. Camping was inexpensive once the costs of equipment were overlooked. Motorists who pitched tents by the side of the road and who cooked their own meals avoided room costs, meal costs, tips, parking fees, and many sundry other expenses that were part of ordinary travel. Money once spent for room and board could be spent on gasoline, thus providing opportunity for longer trips. Elon Jessup, author of books on motor camping, emphasized that there was no other method of travel where one could cover such great distances and see such variety of country in so short a time for so little money.[19] In addition, camping was often the only means of accommodation for tourists who left the main-traveled roads or wandered away from towns. Camping was especially popular in the West, where sparse populations and long distances encouraged travelers to carry bedding and cooking utensils.

Camping was not only justified as a means of breaking hectic work routines, but it was also regarded as a return to simplicity in life, a return to fundamentals. Historian Warren Belasco writes: "Slow, arduous, and close to nature, autocamping

Camping in California's Death Valley (1928). Camping was inexpensive, conducive to freedom of movement, and an opportunity for socializing.

revived what tourists imagined to be the more leisurely pace, personal independence, simplicity, and family solidarity of pre-industrial times." J. C. and J. D. Long, who together wrote several books for campers, noted: "Probably every dweller in civilization, whether of Main Street, Zenith City, or the metropolis, dreams of breaking loose some time and getting back to 'fundamentals.' He wants to get off somewhere at the end of things, near the 'jumping-off place.'" Everett Brimmer, another author and camping promoter, wrote about the annual depression and lack of interest in work that afflicted the average American in need of vacation. The world blurred "drab and irksome," food tasted "stale and insipid," and there was "a powerful craving to burst collar and conventions and become a boy again."[20] Getting "close to nature" was viewed as renewing body and soul. Leisurely pace in tune with the rhythms of nature was thought emotionally satisfying. Vigorous outdoor activity was regarded as healthy. A return to primitive conditions was a return to beginnings, like returning to one's youth.

Eldon Jessup reminded his readers that camping beside a trickling trout stream, smoking one's pipe before a peaceful camp fire, and rolling in for the night to the music of the stream and woods was a "privilege of no small importance." Campers' diaries were full of romantic descriptions to that effect. Although campers wrote favorably of their hardships in communing with nature in isolated places, most were actually quite content in the comfortable confines of campsites near or along highways or in towns. As Warren Belasco notes, campers embraced a "soft primitivism." Its model was not the Spartan camp, but the Garden of Eden, where men lived effortlessly. In addition to their cars, typical campers brought tents, cots and mattresses, stoves, portable ice boxes, cooking utensils, and a wide array of other paraphernalia designed to buffer them from nature. As Winifred Dixon wrote, "With a sense of elation we looked at the circling stars through our tent windows, and heard the wind rise in gusts through the bare branches. The world becomes less fearsome with a roof over one's head."[21]

For tourists used to the comforts of middle-class homes, camping, even under the best of conditions, could bring discomfort. Hardship was a relative thing. Melville Ferguson warned that tourists had to make adjustments when they camped: for example, to learn that it was not fatal to have wet feet, that pneumonia did not always follow undressing in shivering haste, that a bath in a bucketful of tepid water was sometimes a luxury. Limited hardships gave meaning to travel. Discomfort overcome was the essence of adventure in an otherwise overly modernized and standardized environment of highway travel. Camping, Belasco maintains, was an "antimodernist sport."[22]

Camping, it was claimed, enabled tourists to get close to the real America, and the real Canada. "You cannot comprehend America unless you go to see it," wrote Frederic Van de Water. "You can not see it with the intimacy, the closeness that only a motor-camping trip affords without returning to your home . . . a broader, more confident, immensely heartened person." Camping enabled tourists to get "behind the scenes," to see "back regions." Melville Ferguson camped in Hawaii. He pitied the tourists who had come on cruise ships. These folks were hustled into automobiles at the dock, driven around Honolulu, given fleeting glimpses here and there, and told that they had "done" the Hawaiian archipelago. Ferguson, on the other hand, camped with his family on isolated beaches, near active volcanos, on pineapple plantations, and wherever curiosity took him. As Van de Water reminded readers, "One of the advantages of motor camping is that the art is self-teaching, leading you on from discovery to discovery and emphasizing each with discomfort or humiliation so that it is not easily forgotten."[23] Seeing, however, was not a function of living in a tent. Camping only provided novel opportunities to see.

Promoters claimed that camping gave tourists freedom of action. According to Elon Jessup, "Time and space are at your beck and call, your freedom is complete." At Yellowstone, Frederic Van de Water observed that the dust-covered, tanned camper with a pile of sun-bleached dunnage in his car had innumerable privileges of flexibility over visitors to the great hotels who were rushed from point to point in the sightseeing buses.[24] In reality, camping, especially at national parks, often placed as many restrictions on the campers as the railroad timetables and hotel reservations placed on other tourists. Campgrounds filled early, and campers had to be prompt to secure valued spots. Campers were burdened with daily routines of tending camp. Camping could offer freedom in theory, but not always in actuality.

Camping provided opportunities to socialize with fellow travelers, to break the closed social circle of one's automobile.

Frederic Van de Water appreciated the "warming friendliness of neighbors." He wrote of one campground: "By grace of the fact that they were all there, the campers regarded each other as acquaintances. They squatted together in the shade and debated many things. They compared equipments. They sought information regarding the road ahead. The camp was filled with lazy, pleasant talk all day long." Above all, he concluded, "The tale of men who, weary and worn out by office work, had taken to the road was almost endless." Men and women often neighbored separately. Women talked of recipes, places visited, life at home. Men talked of weather, cars, sports. Again, "road liars" came to the fore. "Yes, sir. I drove three days and two nights without stopping except for gas and oil." Or, "If he hadn't drawn aside I'd a' taken the fenders off him. He was just trying to hog all of it jus' because he'd got a new Cadillac an' I got an old Ford."[25]

Friendliness prevailed, but anonymity reigned. Most campers were careful not to overstep acquaintanceships. You could tell a stranger virtually anything about yourself, except your name. In the campground everything normally private and personal became impersonally public. Frederick Van de Water, for example, stayed at the municipal campground at Lyons, Iowa. In the morning he found himself shaving within six feet of Main Street in plain view of the townspeople. In many towns where Van de Water stopped, locals considered the auto camp a sort of zoo. They walked the rows of cars and tents to see the strange specimens that had collected. "Hey, Ed! Look here. Gosh, this feller's all the way from New York!" Campers viewed one another from a distance as a kind of entertainment. Melville Ferguson's party gave nicknames to people: "the Dutchman," "the Old Gent," "the Woman with the Green Sweater," "the Busybody," "the Old Hen," "the Fat Man from Kansas City."[26]

The mixing of different kinds of people from different areas suggested that camping was "democratic." As Jan and Cora Gordon wrote of their southern trip, "Easy, good natured democracy ruled the camp. The possession of a car was enough to frank you into camp society." Everett Brimmer expressed a typical view when he wrote: "There is a great free masonry and democratic fraternity in autocamping." The friendly mixing of people from different states seemed to break down regional differences. One tourist sat in a Michigan campground watching Missouri, Kansas, Nebraska, and Oklahoma cars drive past the parched plains seeking cool northern lakes. He wondered what "this breakdown of state boundaries" was going to do to America. The prospects were not all bright. Would this mixing of people intensify the deadly uniformity and standardization of life and thought? But to Frederic Van de Water motor camping did nothing less than drive out the evils of sectionalism to "knit the American people into a more cohesive, more sympathetic union." Thus, strangers could not sit around a camp fire and talk without "achieving something of national worth."[27]

At first, motorists camped along the roadsides, often intruding onto private property. Abuse of the roadside grew alarmingly, especially in the West. Effie Gladding thought the Lincoln Highway across Nevada was marked as effectively by discarded tin cans, cheese rinds, whiskey bottles, and the other remains of careless camping as by any other signs. According to George Lorimer, writing in the *Saturday Evening Post*, American highways were becoming "trails of trash and swill." Campers searched for spots where trees and flowers were most enticing, only to foul them up by hacking and trampling, and by leaving behind their greasy papers and other filth. Then, nature lovers that they were, they pushed on to find fresh beauty to despoil elsewhere.[28]

In 1920, Waterloo, Wisconsin, became the first community to establish a free municipal campground.[29] Soon, nearly every locality, especially in the West, had established campgrounds to contain geographically the problems campers brought. The campgrounds were also a means of capturing tourist dollars, for camping promised to be big business. Elon Jessup estimated that nine million Americans would go camping in 1921. J. C. and J. D. Long estimated that some five million cars would be used in camping in 1922, or one out of every two cars on the road. Everett Brimmer estimated that the average camping party spent five dollars every day.[30] Such figures were highly unreliable, being extrapolations of bits and pieces of information gleaned from state and local government surveys. For example, Coeur d'Alene, Idaho, reported that 1,382 people in 439 cars had camped in the town during the 1920 summer season, while Denver estimated 20,000 campers for the same year.[31] In 1923, Colorado reported 247 campgrounds in the state with some 643,000 campers.[32]

During the 1920s, the typical small-town camp, usually located at the edge of town in a field, offered potable water, privies, electric lights, wood- or gas-burning stoves in a central kitchen, a lounge, cold showers, and laundry tubs.[33] If located on a main highway, the camp could expect fifty to sixty cars a day in season.[34] Anthropologist Oscar Lewis described the typical campground from the point of view of the tourist. It is past the middle of the afternoon when the tourist sees the first of the signs the town fathers have erected along the highway: "Municipal Free Auto Camp. Free Water. Free Lights." As he continues on, the signs grow more frequent, cunningly revealing attractions hitherto unmentioned: "Free Shower Baths. Social Hall." If the campground is not too awful, if it is not another barren field swept by clouds of dust, he pulls in to find a place. The car is unloaded, the tent erected, the fire started, and preparations for the meal begun. Lewis wrote: "The rolls of baggage have been removed from running-board and rear luggage carrier and the equipment of a complete camp drawn magician-like from them. The khaki tent is stretched with ceaseless tension on its umbrella pole, the thrown-back flap revealing blankets folded with precision on camp cots. Blackened vessels simmer above the fire and the mellow aroma of coffee fills the air."[35]

The largest campgrounds were built near cities. Denver's Overland Park Campground covered 160 acres on what had been a country club golf course. The former clubhouse contained a grocery store, meat market, restaurant, dance hall, billiard parlor, and barbershop in addition to the standard conveniences. Eight hundred camp sites, each twenty-five feet by thirty-five feet, were marked by posts driven in the ground and numbered. The camp also had a gasoline station and auto-repair shop as well as a moving-picture theater.[36] The East Potomac Campground at Washington, D. C., handled up to one thousand automobiles. Paved streets with boulevard lights made the place, like Denver's Overland Park, a virtual city under canvas.[37] Los Angeles's large campground at Alhambra

was shaded by eucalyptus trees. Its laundry room had a concrete floor, hot-and-cold running water, sewage system, a large
new electric washer with wringer, and ironing boards. There
was also a wash rack for hosing down automobiles.[38] Tampa,
Florida's, campground had a school where children could
attend at a cost of fifty cents a week.[39]

The free campgrounds had all but disappeared by 1930.
Towns and cities imposed fees, registration requirements, time
limits, and police supervision at their camps in order to discour-
age "undesirables." Most municipalities sought to keep out
poor people who spent little money locally. Although campgrounds had been championed for their democratic character,
whereby people of all social ranks mixed freely, in reality people
of disparate backgrounds rarely mixed well. Middle-class tourists were alienated by migrant laborers and other transients
who sought the campgrounds to avoid the squalor and tyranny
of farm camps and the high cost of boardinghouses. Many were
clearly vagrants drifting aimlessly from place to place in junk
automobiles. They were a reminder of economic dislocation. As
Warren Belasco concluded, their dilapidated Fords mocked the
studied shabbiness of regular autocampers, since their shabbiness was real. Frederic Van de Water saw drifters everywhere in
the West. They had learned they could earn or beg or pilfer
enough to live on, and so drifted along. Gradually the virus of a
nomadic life infected them and they became "motor hoboes."
Middle-class moralists, Belasco noted, worried about lower-
class restlessness. There was something indecent and dangerous about poor people enjoying what had so recently been the
prerogative of the upper and upper-middle classes.[40]

Camping fees invited private businessmen to enter the
campground field, bringing to an end in most towns governmental involvement in the camping business. There was a
marked shift, recorded in American Automobile Association
campground directories, from public to private camps. For example, in 1925 only nine of Colorado's sixty-four listed camps
were privately operated; but by 1928, sixty-five were private
and twenty public.[41] Most private camps were small. Many
were connected with gasoline stations or roadside refreshment
stands. As one tourist wrote: "Alas for romance! It is generally

the gas station that provides the camper with a safe, watered, lighted, and convenient place to set up a tent for the night."[42]

For those who tenaciously sought to camp by the roadside, rural school yards made good camping sites. They were quasi-public places and usually had drinking water, toilets, and shade. But one camper found nearly every school yard he passed posted with signs reading, "Tourists Keep Out." In many cases, the signs were reinforced by strands of barbed wire and locks on the gates.[43]

Although camping was promoted for its "back to fundamentals," discomfort did not long remain a necessary condition. Manufacturers of collapsible beds, portable ice boxes, and other equipment introduced degrees of comfort. And campers, far from rejecting these innovations, embraced them out of fad and fashion, if not from necessity. One tourist, a noncamper amazed by what he saw in Florida campgrounds, marvelled over folding chairs, accordion mattresses, knock-down tents,

Royal Gorge near Canon City, Colorado (1932). New highways stimulated the development of new tourist attractions and the reinterpretation of old ones. Before the suspension bridge was built, tourists knew the Royal Gorge by looking up from passenger trains 1,200 feet below the canyon's rim.

come-apart stoves, and telescopic dishwashers, as well as "dinner-sets, tin cups, water-buckets and toilet articles that fold-up into one another and look like a bushel of scrap-tin." The burden of camping fell hardest on the women, who generally did the cooking. Dehydrated foods, ready mixes, and other innovations were adopted to ease women's work. Jan and Cora Gordon encountered one immigrant woman in a New England campground who stated the situation succinctly: "Dot kemping. Dot ain't no holidays for us vomans. It's yoost vash and cook yoost like de vay ve do it at home. Yoost de same."[44]

Dedicated campers began to customize cars and trucks, introducing elaborate labor-saving devices. At Yellowstone in 1924, Melville Ferguson encountered what seemed to him a small house mounted on a truck chassis. He wrote: "It was filled with windows, electric lights, and a running water supply. A comfortable full-width bed, a wood stove for cooking, a kitchen table, a cupboard for dishes, a clothes closet, and a couple of rocking chairs furnished the interior." When the proprietor wished to make camp, he let down the back steps and the thing was done. Manufacturers began to produce truck and car bodies specially fitted for camping. For example, front and back seats were made to hinge down to form beds. To Dallas Sharp, ideal motor travel involved such "pullmanized autos." At the first call of the whippoorwill, or at the first faint wash of dusk, one could turn into a pasture beside a stream, or into an arroyo, unlimber the bed, and be in one's sleeping bag "before the coyotes began to howl."[45]

The first house trailer, a homemade affair, was pulled from Florida to California in 1929.[46] Trailer owners expropriated the title "tin-can tourist." First applied to vacationers who camped by the roads to eat out of tin cans, and then to campers who drove "tin-Lizzies" and other cheap automobiles, the term ultimately described the tourist who pulled a small, metal roofed trailer.[47] J. N. Darling coaxed a trailer from Iowa to Florida in 1936 expressly to write a book, *The Cruise of the Bouncing Betsy*. His home on wheels contained two wicker deck chairs, a gasoline stove, a charcoal heater, a davenport that folded out into a bed, washbowl, a kitchen sink, an icebox, and a toilet. In

Georgia, Darling began to see trailers almost everywhere. It was like joining a fraternity. He wrote: "Our new brothers and sisters hailed us as we passed, came over to call the minute we paused at the side of the road or pulled up for gas." He found trailer folk to be a good natured lot: mostly middle-aged people who were having a fling at freedom from work for the first time. Except in Florida, trailer courts were few and far between. But, in Florida, nearly every town had its elaborate trailer camp that looked to Darling "like a huge herd of blue, pink, and green elephants lying down, closely packed."[48]

Motels, Roadside Restaurants, and Gasoline Stations

Middle-class tourists might seek simplicity, sociability, and a sense of getting back to fundamentals in camping, but as modern consumers they valued comfort even more. Realizing this, campgrounds, especially the small private camps, began to provide additional luxuries. Permanent tents were erected on wooden platforms, and small cabins were built. Tourists could rent mattresses, pillows, sheets, and blankets, thus reducing the need for carrying bulky camping equipment, and cutting down the work of camping routine. Cabins also appeared around small resort hotels in the West and, in the East, around tourist homes. The first record of a cabin camp opening was in Douglas, Arizona, in 1913.[49] But it was not until the early 1920s that the idea caught on in the West, later to spread east.

In 1926, Frederic Van de Water noted cabins in auto campgrounds throughout California and Oregon. Cabins rented for fifty cents or seventy-five cents a night over and above the fifty-cent camp fee. Melville Ferguson encountered his first cabin camp at Los Angeles. It contained some three hundred one- and two-room rough framed "shacks," arranged in rows on long streets, and spaced just far enough apart to permit the parking of one car. Along one side of the camp ran a smelly and unsanitary creek, an open sewer for the public toilets. Most cabin camps were primitive. Jan and Cora Gordon wrote: "Few were inviting aesthetically; they were merely pieces of open flat field with a row of cabins like hen houses at the back, a toilet and perhaps a store which might serve primitive sandwich meals and rank coffee." They were hopelessly unattractive places, with names like "Rainbow Camp" or "Rosebud Camp."[50]

The cabin camp represented a transition between the auto campground and the luxury motel. As cabin camps became more substantial, the word "cottage" crept into their naming, implying winterized construction and private toilets and running water. Everett Brimmer stayed at a cottage court at El Paso. Built of concrete in Spanish-mission style, the "bungalettes" were arranged around a central courtyard. Each building contained two apartments with a living room and kitchenette, bedroom, and bath. A recreation hall (a beer garden before Prohibition), laundry, grocery, and gasoline station completed the complex. Norman Hayner described a typical cottage in his 1930 study of motels in the Pacific Northwest: "The main room was equipped with a good bed (bedding could be rented for 50¢ if desired), chairs, mirror, and clothes closet. The kitchen was a separate room with an excellent wood cook stove, running hot

Gasoline station and cabin court at Platteville, Wisconsin (c. 1930). Highway travel fostered roadside commerce in the form of gasoline stations, motels, and restaurants.

Cabin court at Manistique, Michigan. The comfort of motels replaced the adventure of camping for motorists.

and cold water, sink, cupboards, table, chairs, dishes, cutlery, cooking utensils, and even a line for hanging up dish towels. The bath was also a separate room and included a flush toilet, wash bowl, mirror, hot and cold shower. The walls were plastered, the windows attractively curtained, and there was linoleum on the floor."[51]

    The cabin camps and cottage courts attracted not only travelers who had previously camped, but many who otherwise stopped only at hotels. Hotels in cities and towns continued to dominate the lodging industry, but most hotels were oriented geographically to railroads and public transit, and few were convenient for automobile travelers. Hotel design emphasized the public spaces: large entrance lobbies, lounges, dining rooms, coffee shops, bars, ballrooms, and meeting rooms. Private spaces were cramped, the standard bedroom consisting of a bed, a chair, a desk, and enough space to reach a tiny closet and small bathroom. Modern motels, however, offered relatively spacious rooms placed in parklike settings. Motels were readily accessible at the edges of towns, and tourists did not have to fight rush-hour traffic at the end of a long day's drive. In addition, informality reigned. Tourists did not have to face hotel dress codes, and they could come and go without constant scrutiny. Motel patrons parked adjacent to their rooms, loaded and unloaded their own cars, and thus avoided tip-hungry bell-hops. Finally, motels were cheaper than hotels.[52]

The term *tourist court*, or *motor court*, tended to describe motels that integrated individual units under a single roof, often organized around a courtyard. Even the largest motels, representing substantial capital investments, still sought to maintain a homelike atmosphere. Zephine Humphrey, like most tourists, praised this homey ambience. Her first tourist court was a "notable experience," not unlike the "joy of home-coming." She wrote: "The place was a real little home. Every-thing was in perfect order. There were fresh curtains at the windows and clean rugs on the floor." For $1.50, she and her husband bought "sixteen hours of home."[53] Motels, for their comfort, convenience, and informality, became a roadside in-stitution. By 1935 some 9,800 tourist courts had been built, and by 1939 the number had grown to 13,500.[54]

As motel rooms supplanted tents, so restaurant food supplanted picnic lunches and camp dinners. At first, motorists used main-street and downtown cafes for lunch and dinner, but by 1930 tea rooms, roadside stands, and new, "drive-in" res-taurants provided other options. The first drive-in restaurant with "curb service" was opened by the Pig Stands Company of Dallas in 1924.[55] Eating and automobiles were integrally linked, and roadside food was usually as bland as it was standardized. Foreigners commented on North America's tasteless food. Ilya Ilf and Eugene Petrov wrote: "Americans are used to it. They eat fast, without wasting a single extra minute at the table. They do not eat[,] they fill up on food, just as an automobile is filled with petrol." But roadside food was typically American. William Saroyan commented: "A true hamburger is America. Eating it is participating in a food rite."[56]

Drive-in restaurants epitomized the tourist's search for simplicity and informality. According to Cecil Roberts, they might be elaborate pseudo-Spanish buildings with aluminum soda fountains, or mere shanties with wooden counters. But, more important, one did not need to get out of the car. "You draw into the curb, sound your horn, and a white-jacketed, sailor-capped youngster brings you your lunch on a tray that he clamps to the door of the car."[57] Elaborate drive-ins appeared in large cities, featuring gaudy neon signs, blaring loudspeakers, and female carhops.

As the landscape historian J. B. Jackson noted, the roadside restaurant not only had to catch the attention of the passing motorist, but it had to suggest pleasure and good times. The restaurant avoided suggestion of the workaday world or any hint of the severely practical, the economical, or the common or the plain. On the contrary, an atmosphere of luxury, gaiety, and the unusual or the unreal prevailed. According to Jackson, a new public taste had emerged reflecting the involvement of the lower classes in leisure-time activities. Previously, leisure activities were essentially imitations of a superior elite—the so-called leisure class. Jackson wrote: "We went to hotels which resembled at a dozen removes the palace of a prince, to movie houses which resembled court operas, to restaurants and bars adorned with mahogany and crystal and gold." Touristic places were designed and decorated to suggest a sumptuous way of life. But the wage-earning class with leisure time and money sought not superior social worlds, but worlds remote in terms of time and space. Roadside restaurants adopted escapist themes rooted in historical and regional stereotypes or adopted the trappings of the future by emphasizing things big, electric, shiny, and modern.[58]

Restaurants served as places for entertainment and socializing. Ilf and Petrov marveled at the ubiquitous pinball tables. "You drop a nickel in the proper slot; automatically a cue is liberated by a spring, and the pleasure-seeker, having decided to spend the evening in revelry, can shoot a steel ball five times." Upton Sinclair captured the spirit of the roadside eatery in his novel *Oil!* The father liked to "josh" the waitresses in such places. "He knew all kinds of comic things to say, funny names for things to eat. He would order his eggs 'sunny side up,' or 'with their eyes open, please.' " He would chat with the farmer at his side, learning about the wheat crop or the price of oranges or walnuts. When one went into such places, one found "the spirit of jollity rampaging on the walls." The boy read one sign which said, "In God We Trust, All Others Pay Cash."[59] Restaurant counters and tables offered sociability, in contrast to the relative isolation of automobiles and motel rooms.

Clearly, a good meal in an interesting restaurant could fix a town firmly in a tourist's memory. Winifred Dixon wrote from Texas: "The flakiness of the biscuits, the fragrance of the wild honey, and the melting deliciousness of the river fish, caught fresh in the Rio Grande an hour before, caused us to see Del Rio with happy eyes." Lewis Gannett wrote of Amarillo: "We shall not soon forget the melting T-bone steak that went with a 35¢ three course lunch at a cafe opposite the Ford Garage."[60] Although basic foods, such as hamburgers and ham and eggs, were served everywhere, some dishes did vary regionally: hot dogs and baked beans could be had in New England, barbecue and grits in the South, and tacos and enchiladas from Texas to California.

Refueling was a constant necessity in automobile travel. By 1920 gasoline was available at gasoline stations organized as chains of near look-alike establishments by the petroleum companies.[61] By the 1930s the various competing companies had brought service to a high order, especially in the Middle West and the West, where competition was most keen. Hoffman Birney wrote: "No one knows what a real SERVICE station is until he crosses the Mississippi River. Your tank is filled, your oil checked, your tires tested, your radiator filled, and your windshield polished without a word of instruction on your part." Mark Pepys found the same high quality of service whether he was in a big city or on a rural highway. At one station in the Panhandle of Texas, two uniformed men sprang to the car. While one filled the tank, the other brushed out the inside of the car, and on paying the bill, Pepys was presented with a free road map.[62] Gasoline was cheap. As the price of gasoline could not be cut, service sold a company's products. In 1920, the cost per gallon of gasoline averaged twenty-nine cents across the United States. By 1927, it had dropped to twenty-one cents despite an average three-cent gasoline tax.[63]

Travel Costs

Beatrice Massey and her husband kept a detailed record of their 4,100-mile trip from New York City to San Francisco in 1919. Although on the road seven weeks, only thirty-three days were actually spent in driving. In that time their car consumed thirty-four gallons of gasoline at a cost of $100. Oil, repair, storage, and cleaning added another $106. Hotels and tips cost $256 and $50, respectively. Food not included on hotel tabs, laundry, postcards, postage, and other miscellaneous expenses totalled $51. The fare for overnight service on a Detroit-to-Cleveland steamship was $15. Thus, two people traveled coast to coast in luxury for about $18 a day. In 1929, Paul Vernon's party spent $7.25 per person per day in covering 9,300 miles in forty-two days between New York City and San Francisco and return. The party relied primarily on inexpensive hotels for overnight accommodation. In 1931, Charles Finger's party spent $5 apiece per day in covering 12,000 miles round trip between Denver and Los Angeles. They cut costs by camping. In 1940, Janette Routledge calculated daily expenses for a thirty-one-day, 8,400-mile round trip between Los Angeles and Boston at just over $5 per day. She stayed at tourist homes and cabin courts.[64]

Although railroad travel was still cheaper than travel by automobile, railroad traffic declined 22 percent between 1921 and 1941, whereas passenger car travel increased sixfold.[65] In 1935, 85 percent of all vacation travel was by automobile, accounting for over half of all expenditures for recreational purposes—$1,788 million out of $3,316 million. In 1935, Americans spent almost 5 percent of their total income on vacations.[66] The automobile was a possession, a thing to own and to have; it was also a toy, an especially useful plaything during vacation time. The relative high costs of automobile travel could be partially ignored as an investment in the family car. Conversely, vacation travel gave clear rationale to a family's automobile ownership. So also was the purchase of camping equipment not only a vacation expense, but an investment in life-style. Railroad travel was direct, as it was efficient, but it did not carry with it the extras of property ownership. Touring by rail could not provide the sense of increased mobility, both geographical and social, that automobile touring and ownership could.

The period between the two world wars was one of transition for North American tourism. Tourists preferred to travel primarily by automobile, rather than on the railroads. Once the sport of the well-to-do, automobiling was embraced by and dominated by the masses, the middle classes joined by lower-income groups as well. Camping became a fad and a fashion, necessary at first for many travelers' long-distance travel. But camping proved to be more a means to an end than an end in itself, for as comfort became available at reasonable prices in motels and roadside restaurants, most travelers abandoned their tents and their picnic lunches. Traveling long distances between stops was another way of stretching travel dollars, although the impulse toward constant driving may have been as much psychological as economic, related as it was to standardized automobile and highway environments. The seeds of modern automobile travel were laid in the 1920s and 1930s, flowering after World War II.

CHAPTER EIGHT

TRAVEL BY BUS AND AIR

> The chic sport of the moment was to go out at midnight to the flying field and watch for the overland mail that came gliding down out of the stars on schedule every night between rows of dazzling electric lights.
>
> James Flagg, *Boulevards All the Way—Maybe*

Relatively few people traveled by bus or by air before World War II. The vast majority of tourists used private automobiles in their trip taking, or rode trains. Buses appealed primarily to low-income travelers, especially those who did not own cars. Tourists sought out buses to reach places not served by rail, as a diversion from other forms of travel, or for short sight-seeing trips. Air travel appealed to the well-to-do, especially businessmen in a hurry. Few air travelers flew for pleasure before World War II except for the prestige of having flown. After the war, both bus and air travel came to the fore as mass movers of people, playing roles traditionally reserved for the railroads. Intercity buses were a natural outgrowth of improved highways subsidized by the federal government. So also was air travel federally supported through air mail contracts, airport improvement, and the provision of air navigation aids.

Travel by Bus

The first intercity bus service was initiated in 1912, between Hibbing and South Hibbing, Minnesota. Crudely fashioned passenger bodies were affixed to truck chassis and used to carry workers to jobs in the iron mines.[1] By 1925, 6,500 bus companies operated over 7,800 different routes in the United States, the vast majority of the companies operating only one or two buses.[2] In 1927, bus service extended to 650,000 miles of highway in the country, or to approximately two-and-one-half times the railroad passenger routes.[3] Between 1926 and 1941 railroad passenger routes decreased 18 percent while bus passenger mileage increased 212 percent.[4]

The New York, New Haven, and Hartford Railroad established in 1925 a bus subsidiary, enabling the company to drop passenger service on unprofitable branch lines.[5] In the next decade railroads promoted bus travel vigorously. In 1935, sixty-two railroads were operating buses, either directly or through subsidiaries, thus producing substantial cooperation in the scheduling and interchange of bus and train passengers. The Pickwick Corporation, a subsidiary of the Southern Pacific Railroad, scheduled the first long-distance bus service in 1925, between Portland, Oregon, and El Paso by way of San Francisco, Los Angeles, and San Diego. Pickwick formed the westernmost portion of the Greyhound system when, in 1935, the railroads were forced by the federal government to divest themselves of long-distance bus operations. Greyhound grouped the bus subsidiaries of the New Haven, Pennsylvania, New York Central, Union Pacific, Northern Pacific, and Southern Pacific railroads into a single transcontinental bus system. Continental Trailways, a rival, was formed out of Santa Fe and Burlington railroad subsidiaries.[6] By 1940, Greyhound and Continental Trailways had cut the cost of one-way bus fares from New York City to Los Angeles to $42.50.[7]

Bus depots were established in cities, but ticket agents operated out of cafes, gasoline stations, or hotels in small towns. Bus depots were far from impressive. Mary Winn, who traveled by bus coast-to-coast in 1930 to write a travel book of her experience, described New York City's Greyhound terminal near Pennsylvania Station. Along one side of a large paved lot, enclosed by a board fence, stood a small, one-story brick building with a long, low porch. She thought it very much like any railroad depot in rural America. "The groups that stand under the low portico, waiting for arriving and departing coaches, have the leisured, friendly informality of a village gathering waiting for the 6:15." Lord Kinross, an English aristocrat, traveled by bus south from Richmond, Virginia, in order to meet a class of Americans he would not have otherwise encountered. He studied the bus depots as a kind of theater. At Charleston, a voice, nearly incomprehensible, announced each arrival and departure: "Waterboro, Yemassee, Pocotaligo, Savannah, Brunswick, Jacksonville." Lord Kinross wrote: "The amplified voice, like that of a disembodied pastor reciting a litany, droned on, on its single note, dropping mournfully at the end of each line." At New Orleans, he was taken with a slot machine that promised relief from nervous and muscular tensions. "Step Up for a Pick-Up, for New Pep and Energy," the sign read. Putting in a dime, he received a mild shaking.[8]

Departure could be a slow adventure, with the bus tied up in city traffic. Mary Winn, primed for impressions, observed, "Getting out of New York City is a tedious business, since the stage, unlike the train, has to dispute almost every inch of the way with taxis, private autos, street-cars, trucks scuttling pedestrians, push-cart vendors, and wheeled racks of ladies' dresses." For passengers new to bus travel, departure excited curiosity about the driver and the bus itself. Nathan Asch wrote about departing from Salt Lake City:

> We lay on our white seat rests, waiting; saw the driver climb into the bus, look at us, count us, watched him shut the door, slide into the seat behind the wheel, twist little knobs and push buttons that produced little colored lights on the instrument board; turn off lights in the bus so that before us in the aisle only tiny spots of red and yellow could be seen; heard the motor turn over, start, be warmed for a while; and then the gear shifted into low, the bus slowly crossing the sidewalk and turned into the street.[9]

Bus technology improved rapidly. Mary Winn described her "night coach" trip from St. Louis to Kansas City. The bus had sleeping accommodations for twenty-six people, with two dressing rooms and a small kitchen or galley. "Ranged along a central aisle were thirteen state rooms on two levels, each room containing two berths about the size of those in a Pullman." The ticket agent had declared humorously that each roomette had "almost enough room to swing a cat." Each space was fitted with a shelf to hold toilet articles, reading-lights, ashtrays, a thermos bottle of cracked ice, and a basin with hot and cold running water. She looked around for the Gideon Bible and the radio and felt a vague disappointment that they had been over-looked in this hotel on wheels. In a high, glass-enclosed space over the engine sat the captain in a gray uniform. The passengers waited amid a "wharf-like bustle of departure"—friends saying good-bye, a conductor scanning yard-long tickets, and a white-coated steward staggering under piles of luggage.[10]

The advantages and disadvantages of bus travel were debated, pro and con. Like automobiles, buses put travelers close to everyday landscapes, but without freedom of individual action. Except on the night coaches, where passengers were isolated from one another, buses did encourage sociability. Rows of tightly spaced seats separated by a narrow center aisle made buses crowded, and, according to Nathan Asch, passengers quickly became acquainted. "One said something banal; one was answered with a banality; one offered a cigarette; with words one searched the neighbor. Talk continued and time passed; one began to see in the man nearby the beginning of a personality." Thus travelers began to let personal details of their lives slip out. Of one conversation, Asch wrote, "Yes, he said, in his life he had done many things. He had skinned mules and laid pipelines and washed dishes and been a plumber and worked on a dredge boat and been on a section gang."[11]

Conversations on buses seemed to be different from those on trains. Undoubtedly, that related to the different kinds of people normally found on buses. Trains were more formal. As Nathan Asch observed, he reserved a seat and put on his best clothes. When he got to talking to a stranger, he was not himself but was apt to put on airs. Mary Winn found a spirit of camaraderie on a bus such as one seldom found on a train. People in the little, self-contained unit were within sight and hearing of each other; all bumped through the same mud hole at the same time, swallowed the same cloud of dust from a passing car, looked out simultaneously to thrill and exclaim over the same view. At rest stops almost everyone got out together to stretch their legs and to "stand round the huge vehicle like a flock of chickens round a mother hen, smoking, gossiping, and munching chocolate bars."[12]

On the negative side, however, buses were often very

uncomfortable; and they were disruptive to bodily routines. Mary Winn gained ten pounds, nibbling from coast-to-coast in lieu of regular meals at regular hours. She succumbed to the popcorn, orangeade, peanuts, ice cream, chewing gum, Coca-Cola, lifesavers, and hot dogs found in every bus depot and at every intervening stop. Rough roads meant rough riding. Nathan Asch wrote: "Everything the huge wheels meet upon the road is transferred, is applied to the sitting body, and you vibrate and shake; and at night[,] when there is not distracting scenery[,] you sit and try to doze; and you feel the road." Cramped, lurching buses might encourage passengers to socialize, but the sedentary state imposed could also tire. There was no getting up and changing one's position in a bus since there was no steadiness of motion as on a train. Ventilation was often a problem. Early buses were heated by using the hot air of the exhaust manifold. One transcontinental traveler saw several people partially overcome by fumes, and between Chicago and St. Louis, two women had to be revived by the pulmotors of a small-town fire department.[13]

Bus travel was more popular in the West than elsewhere. West of the Mississippi River a greater variety of people rode buses, and bus travel there did not carry the stigma of lower-class association. Even basic descriptors varied from region to region. In the East buses were called "motor buses," but "motor coaches" in the Middle West, and "stages" in the West. Nathan Asch wrote: "The people in the East rode a bus as if it were a shame. They hid their faces, or they always began the conversation by saying this was the first time they had ever used such a cheap transportation." In the South, Asch observed, most bus passengers were black. Clearly, bus travel represented cheap transportation and, as such, it attracted lower-income, less-educated people than other modes of travel. Lord Kinross's image of American bus passengers was crystalized by a young soldier who sprawled across several seats reading a pile of magazines. Looking over the boy's shoulder, Lord Kinross read the headlines: "Your Mysterious Sex Glands." "The Truth About Paris Prostitutes." "How to Join a Nudist Camp." "Why I Strip for a Living."[14]

Middle- and upper-middle-class tourists avoided bus

travel, although trips on sightseeing buses represented one significant exception. Trips with tour groups represented another. Mary Winn sampled the latter in California. A tour guide hurled "little tidbits of information" through a megaphone at passengers. They were fascinating little facts, like the exact moment when the highway crossed a county line, or the gross annual income from sardines caught in Monterey Bay.[15] Greyhound conducted its first personally conducted tours, the "Western Wonder Tours," in 1935 with six passengers.[16] Most of the tour business, however, was handled by small carriers who specialized in "packaged tours." Tourists left from their hometowns on set itineraries that took them from attraction to attraction, lodging and meals all prearranged.

Travel by Air

Whereas intercity buses initially served commuters and business travelers, the first scheduled passenger service by air catered to tourists. In 1914 the first passenger airline was established. It ferried, in "flying boats," Florida vacationers between Tampa and St. Petersburg. In 1919, Aero Limited began service between New York City and Atlantic City. Its successor, Aeromarine, also flew tourists in the winter between Miami and Nassau and Key West and Havana, and between Detroit and Cleveland in the summer.[17] The public thought seaplanes safer than other aircraft since they could land on the water when in trouble. Pilots rarely flew higher than a few hundred feet over water, further reinforcing the sense of security.[18] Coastal locations were ideal for the first experiments in air travel since seaplanes did not require expensive runways and airport buildings. Tourists in seaside resorts represented a ready market for the novelty of flying, and air trips became another resort attraction.

During the 1920s air passenger service and federal airmail contracts became integrally tied. Airline profits lay in carrying the mail, with passenger revenues becoming supplementary. In 1925, Ford Air Transport, operating between Detroit and Chicago and Detroit and Cleveland, became the first line to combine airmail routes with passenger service on a year-round schedule. In 1927, Colonial Air Transport began the first night passenger service on its route connecting New York City and

Boston.[19] Throughout the early 1930s, most commercial flights were made at night, not only to accommodate the mail, but to provide businessmen with fast intercity connections after business hours. An early Colonial advertisement read: "Cut corners to your destination! There is less time in travel, more for pleasure and business—complete absence of dust, dirt, or 'traffic jams' . . . swift, safe travel with no stops."[20] The airline maintained a ticket office in the Pennsylvania Hotel in New York City. Special buses conveyed passengers to the airport in Newark. James Reddig, an Eastman Kodak executive, went directly to the airport on his own. The field was a sea of mud. The airline agent slogged out to meet him, shook his hand, seized his bag, and led him to a small shed. He shoved a mass of dirty engine parts along a bench to make room for a battered typewriter retrieved from the floor, finger-picked the ticket following a sample tacked on the wall, took Reddig's $25, and carried his bag to the airplane.[21]

Herbert Hoover's postmaster general, Walter Brown, envisioned a system of competitive, transcontinental airlines intersected by an extensive network of feeder lines. By manipulating airmail contracts he coerced numerous airline mergers, bringing into existence the companies which would dominate air travel in the United States in subsequent decades: American, Trans-World, and United Airlines.[22] One of TWA's predecessors, Trans-America Air Transport, or TAT, initiated the first coast-to-coast air flights in 1929, in cooperation with the Pennsylvania and Santa Fe Railroads. Passengers alternately rode the trains and flew, arriving in Los Angeles forty-eight hours after departing from New York City.[23] Service was erratic because of the weather, and critics of the service referred to TAT derisively as the "Take-A-Train" airline. Passengers departing Los Angeles left from the Ambassador Hotel by "Aero Car," a Studebaker coupe pulling a three-wheeled trailer. On arrival at the airport, baggage was weighed using a fish scale, and passengers were put on board a wrinkle-skinned Ford tri-motor.[24] The tri-motor, called affectionately the "Tin Goose," carried ten passengers and cruised at slightly over one hundred miles per hour. The cost of the trip was $352 one way.[25] In 1930, TWA introduced the first transcontinental air service without train

DC-3 downed at Moline, Illinois (1953). Fear rode the empty seats on airline flights.

travel. At first, travelers could fly coast-to-coast in thirty-six hours with ten stops and an overnight rest at Kansas City. In 1932, night flying was added, cutting the time to twenty-four hours.[26] The federal govenment subsidized emergency landing fields every twenty miles along the route, and revolving beacons every ten miles to guide pilots.

Flying in daylight was very different from flying at night. Night flights turned the traveler inward on himself. It was not really travel at all; it was merely being sent in an enclosed capsule substantially divorced from outside reality. The historian Bernard De Voto writes of his flight after dark: "An airliner at night is one of the most beautiful, most peaceful, most comforting places. Only the focused cones of reading lights break the darkness; one sinks deep into oneself. The dark has brought a sense of the plane's speed and power that cannot be felt by daylight; it is a sense too of serenity, and the enclosed snugness is a subtle assuagement of some longing never quite conscious." In the empty areas of the West, only the flashing acetylene beacons gave a sense of landscape below. According to Mark

Pepys, each revolving beacon shot out a brilliant "pencil of light," describing the full 360 degrees like clockwork: the red back of its lamp alternately swinging into view "wih so sharp a flick that one felt it should be audible." Viewed from above, the circumference traced by each beacon seemed just to overlap that of the next.[27]

The principal benefits of air travel were speed and the view. To publicize speed, the airlines promoted various stunts. For example, a descendant of George Washington flew in a single day in 1932 over all the routes which Washington had traveled in the course of a lifetime.[28] An early advertisement for American Airlines emphasized, "Be there in a matter of hours, not days. You'll arrive refreshed, rested, and ready to put to good use all those extra days you've saved." But, the ad also continued, "You'll have the time of your life viewing the gorgeous scenery from the air."[29] Anne Peck and Enid Johnson flew from Newark to Washington, D.C. in 1932. As the aircraft gained altitude on take-off, the earth flattened out into a fascinating pattern of "checkerboard fields," "toy houses," and "curving ribbons of rivers." The small, nonpressurized planes of the early 1930s flew low, often with windows open in warm weather. At Washington, their plane flew directly over the dome of the capitol and "skimmed so close to the tall Washington Monument that it looked as if we might graze it with a wing."[30]

Of all the journals kept by air travelers in the 1930s, the most detailed, and thus the most insightful, is that of Mark Pepys. Pepys, an Englishman, came to the United States to mix business with pleasure. He drove from New York City to Los Angeles and, after a short stay, flew by scheduled airline back over the route he had just driven. Looking down, the earth looked like a relief map. "The desert below," he wrote, "might have been modelled in plasticine, its general tone drab, its sole variations the tortured volcanic outcroppings." As the airplane approached the Grand Canyon, he became especially watchful. "I sought for, and traced, the road by which I had approached its brink a month before and stared into its mile of depth. But from the air the highway now looked like a thin, yellow ribbon laid straight and flat as a ruler upon the face of the desert." As the airplane descended to the airport at Albuquerque, the pines reached up from the mountain peaks; snow was sheltered in the hollows. And then abruptly the mountains fell away, and the plane shot out over flat wasteland. Pepys concluded: "Only travel by air can provide such striking contrasts."[31]

When clouds closed in, one could not always get a view. Bernard De Voto thought that overcast skies changed flying from the most exciting to the dullest mode of travel: "You must be in touch with geography, you must be able to see the earth, or boredom will come upon you." Even when visibility was good many travelers got very little from the view. Travelers who flew frequently were used to the experience of viewing life in miniature below. But more often, the lack of seeing was a function of ignorance. Travelers simply did not appreciate what lay below. Most tourists described their air trips in short, cryptic generalizations. For example, one traveler described the scenery from San Francisco to Los Angeles as follows: "We flew at about 8,000 feet over mountain and valleys, treeless for the most part, encountering a dust storm on the way which made the air look quite brown." De Voto had little patience with the average tourist's lack of comprehension from the air: "As a professed geographer, I am especially irked and mortified by ignorance of the terrain and lack of orientation with it."[32]

Diarists were more concerned with describing the logistics of flight than the scenery. Take-offs and landings or meals attracted much comment. At Los Angeles, Mark Pepys's airplane taxied to the end of the runway and turned into the wind, the pilot revving up the motors against the wheel brakes before taking off. At first the passengers made a great show of reading their evening newspapers, but with the first signs of bumpiness they switched out their reading lamps, and settled down to feign sleep.[33] The first stewardesses, eight registered nurses, were hired in 1930 by Boeing Air Transport (later part of the United Airlines).[34] For several years the copilots on other airlines continued to serve meals and otherwise tend to passenger comfort. Dinner on Pepys flight included an assortment of cold meats, rolls, and biscuits wrapped in cellophane envelopes. Grapefruit salad came in a carton, coffee in a thermos. Even in the 1950s, airline food was usually cold, although otherwise intended. De Voto wrote: "The American know-how we read about breaks down on the problem of keeping food hot, and though I hear of flights that serve fine trout or steak, my lot always turn out to be antique chicken or dismayed veal just off the ice, and I have insufficient know-how to keep the coffee from splashing across the tray."[35]

Traveling by air had its disadvantages. Early airliners were not pressurized, which caused much discomfort at high altitudes. One tourist wrote of flying with a bad cold. When his ears began to ache, the stewardess used doses of oil and phenol to ease the pain. Mark Pepys's airplane flew at 12,000 feet for well over an hour, but he found it "not unpleasant" when no exertion was demanded. A cigarette cured the dryness in his throat. On landing he checked his suitcase carefully to see if the lids had stayed on the hair-lotion bottles. Air turbulence often made flights bumpy. Pepys's plane fell several thousand feet, pitching and yawing. He wrote: "Men with hunched shoulders moved restlessly in their seats, looked out first one side and then the other, glanced across the cabin and glued their noses again to the window next to them. They made praiseworthy efforts to appear unconcerned, to read their newspapers. Others openly clung to the arms of their chairs and put the best face on it that they could."[36] Some types of aircraft handled turbulence so poorly that they regularly had to be hosed out upon landing.[37]

Fear of flying was a great detriment to air travel, for it was fear that rode the empty seats. In 1932, one of every 2,200 air passengers was involved in a flying accident, and one in every 20,000 was killed. A $5,000 insurance policy for an airplane trip cost $2, but only 25¢ for a train trip.[38] In the mid-1930s, the Actuarial Society of America calculated travel by Pullman car to be fifty-three times as dangerous as flying by commercial airline, but, although there were fewer airplane crashes than train wrecks, air crashes almost always resulted in fatalities.[39] Even the look of the early airplanes contributed to the lack of confidence. Not until the Ford "Tin-Goose" appeared, with its cantilevered wings sheathed in metal (lacking as it did bracing wires), did an airliner suggest great strength. This plane was made entirely of metal, suggesting dependability, and there was also a sense of reassurance in its extra motor.[40] Before World War II, most tourists viewed flying as a kind of stunt. John Van Schaick made a new will before he took off. Although he found the experience rewarding, he was very happy to be back on the ground.[41]

Aircraft improved rapidly. The Douglas DC-2 (a sleeper transport) and the DC-3 (the more popular day-coach version) revolutionized air travel. By 1938 the planes had cut flying time across the country to fifteen hours eastbound (with prevailing westerly winds) and seventeen hours westbound. The DC-3 was the first practical airliner. Capable of carrying fourteen passengers at 175 miles per hour, the aircraft produced profits on passengers alone. Mail contracts were no longer vital to successful air routes.[42] The DC-3 also caused a rapid reduction in the number of airplanes needed by airlines in North America. By 1941, 80 percent of the 358 passenger planes in service in the United States were DC-3s. The late 1930s brought other innovations, including the Boeing 314 Clipper, known as the "Flying Boat." It carried eighty-nine passengers in the luxury of fashionable staterooms. In 1954, the first giant airliner appeared, the Boeing 707, which carried 189 passengers at 600 miles per hour. Its speed and its range of 6,000 miles made the Clippers, and, indeed, all sleeper transports obsolete.[43]

Herbert Hoover, as secretary of commerce, had drawn a parallel between air commerce and waterborne commerce. As the federal government had lit, marked, and chartered water channels, improved harbors, and inspected ships and those who manned them, so it would also aid air travel.[44] Given federal backing, airports improved rapidly during the 1930s, with improvement accelerating during World War II. In 1941, 72 airfields in the United States were capable of handling the largest aircraft, but by 1945 the number had climbed to 655.[45]

Mark Pepys spent several hours inspecting the airport at Los Angeles. He toured the steel and concrete hangars with their thick glass doors hinged at the top. The passenger terminal, built in Spanish style, contained ticket windows, waiting room, rest rooms, a restaurant, and a barber shop. A single covered gangway led to the runway apron where planes arrived and departed, one by one, taking turns in sequence. A balcony on top of the building gave visitors a clear view of the field. Pepys inspected the room where weather maps were drawn, with its row of teletype machines sprouting ribbons of paper tape.[46] Airports were great tourist attractions. Spotlights were used to illuminate airplanes as they took off and landed at night.

Airports could be frustrating to passengers. Missed connections or delayed flights placed even the most exciting airports in a poor light. Bernard De Voto claimed that passengers were treated like nonentities on the ground: "Once in the air, you are surrounded with luxury above your station and treated with a deference elsewhere reserved for movie actors. Until you are airborne, however, you are just an annoyance, to be chivied by announcers, ignored by everyone else, and given as little information as possible."[47] Big airports were also frustrating to get to, being located well beyond a city's edge. As new airports replaced old, problems of accessibility became increasingly acute. Chicago's new airport of the 1950s was located twenty-three miles from downtown; Detroit's airport was thirty-one miles out.

Flying was an experience. It was a package of thrills, apart from the getting from place to place. In quite no other way could the traveler feel as close to danger as in the air thousands of feet above the ground. His safety was entrusted solely to others. Flying offered a unique way of seeing landscape. The view from above was usually spectacular: the earth below reduced to miniature scale. One could embrace immense territories at a single glance. Mark Pepys calculated that he had viewed 605,812 square miles of scenery from his airplane, or 20 percent of the entire United States. Of course, his view, a very distant one, was highly generalized. In this regard, air travel removed and isolated tourists from passing landscapes even more completely than had rail travel. "To see a country properly," Pepys wrote, "we must fly over it." But he admitted that seeing was not necessarily experiencing landscape in any meaningful sense. He continued: "To pass comfortably through it we can take a train. But to know it in passing, we need a car. And really to live in it, we still ride horses or walk, according to our fancy."[48]

Buses provided cheap transportation for people who

could not afford to travel otherwise. They connected places not served by other modes of public transport. Airplanes provided rapid transportation for those who could afford the luxury of traveling fast. Both modes represented alternatives to travel by railroad and automobile. Indeed, most tourists who traveled by bus and by air tended to do so in combination with railroad or automobile trips. Most Americans opted to tour by automobile. Glamour in travel belonged to the airplane as sophisticated technology, but the automobile, which provided freedom of action and a sense of self-sufficiency, and which was affordable to the many, proved to be the most popular mode of trip taking. Economy in travel belonged to bus riders, although most tourists were willing to give up economy for the increased geographical mobility of motor cars.

CHAPTER NINE

THE AUTOMOBILE AND TOURISM AFTER WORLD WAR II

> The more we move about, the more difficult it becomes not to remain in the same place.
>
> Daniel Boorstin, *The Image: A Guide to Pseudo-Events in America*

Pent-up buying power and increased leisure time after World War II served to flood North American highways with vacationers. Tourism, a substantial economic enterprise before the war, had an impact on the North American landscape as never before. Highway improvement accelerated commercialization of American and Canadian roadsides. By 1960 the commercial strip had become so commonplace that it was a dominant new place-type in the North American travel experience. Touring by automobile offered less adventure and fewer surprises than ever as the smooth highways and encapsulating services of the roadside standardized travel. A sense of the commonplace greeted the tourist almost everywhere as cities, towns, and rural areas were remade in the universal highway order.

Tourism in a Postwar Economy

Travel for recreation fell off sharply during World War II. Gas rationing cut substantially into the use of automobiles, and many resorts closed for the duration of hostilities. After 1945, the accumulated savings of war-time employment were funneled into tourism as a kind of delayed expenditure, just as money was spent on automobiles and other goods and services generally. Resorts reopened and roadside commerce boomed. Tourism after the war was an even more lucrative economic enterprise than before. Not only had the economic depression been ended, with most people back at work, but workers enjoyed shorter work weeks and longer vacation periods. In 1940,

185

the average work week was 44 hours, but by 1950 it had fallen to 40 hours, and by 1960 to 37.5 hours.[1] Americans turned to their automobiles to escape work routines and to put their leisure time to use away from home.

Statistics began to appear that were descriptive of tourism as a growth industry. In 1949, a Department of Commerce survey reported that 62 percent of all Americans took vacation trips. The average number of trips per family per year stood at 1.8. The average trip lasted 10.5 days and involved 2.2 persons. The report estimated that 23 million families had taken 43 million vacation trips.[2] In 1963, the Bureau of the Census reported that 43 percent of all American families took long vacation trips annually. Such trips averaged 600 miles in length and, taken in the aggregate, accounted for 5 percent of all automobile travel. Short weekend trips of less than thirty miles accounted for another 16 percent of all automobile use.[3]

Affluence increased a family's propensity to travel. A 1954 survey of 2,000 households by John Lansing and Ernest Lilienstein found that 83 percent of all families earning over $10,000 a year took a vacation trip. Only 47 percent of the families earning under $4,000 traveled for pleasure. Thirty-nine percent of all households did not travel at all. Seven percent of the adults interviewed had never taken a pleasure trip of more than one hundred miles from home. Principal reasons given for not traveling included lack of money, lack of time, and poor health. Affluence also meant that families could travel long distances beyond their home state. A survey of 1,500 out-of-state tourists registered at Wisconsin resorts and state parks on July 16, 1949, disclosed that 48 percent were owners or managers of businesses, or professional people; 18 percent were categorized as sales or clerical people; and 15 percent as skilled craftsmen. Less than 7 percent were blue-collar workers.[4]

Automobiles assumed ever-increasing importance in travel plans. A 1950 survey by the *Saturday Evening Post* showed that 80 percent of all long-distance pleasure trips in the United States were by automobile. In 1953, the Bureau of Public Roads set the figure at 83 percent, while reporting that the automobile trips also accounted for 93 percent of all trips for outdoor recreation. The U.S. Bureau of Public Roads estimated that some 13 percent of all trips were by train, 11 percent by bus, 4 percent by air, and 2 percent by ship. Use varied seasonally across modes, with railroad, bus, and air travel doubling in importance during the winter and spring. Air trips tended to be the longest. In 1953 trips by car averaged 1,108 miles, but 6,521 miles by air. Affluent families were more likely to travel by air. The Lansing and Lilienstein survey in 1954 showed that 45 percent of the professionals and business managers had traveled by airplane, but only 22 percent of the blue-collar workers.[5]

Various surveys sought to establish why people traveled. Apparent discrepancies from survey to survey reflected different definitions of pleasure travel. In 1954, sociologists Lansing and Lilienstein found 19 percent of their respondents traveling for business, 25 percent to visit friends and relatives, 39 percent for vacation, and 17 percent for other personal reasons. The Bureau of the Census agreed in 1957 that 19 percent of all trips were for business, but set the figures for visits to friends and relatives, pleasure travel, and other trips at 46 percent, 27 percent, and 8 percent, respectively.[6] By combining vacation trips and visits with friends and relatives, however, well over two-thirds of all travel reported in the two surveys can be calculated as pleasure related.

State tourist bureaus were especially interested in the tourists' uses of leisure time. A survey of 1,600 tourists in Michigan in 1952 disclosed that 70 percent came for sightseeing, 55 percent to fish, 40 percent for the beaches, and 13 percent to camp. Of major state attractions, scenery was mentioned by 62 percent of the respondents, climate by 32 percent, friends and relatives by 26 percent, historic sites by 24 percent, and museums by 6 percent. A 1953 survey of 2,600 tourists in Colorado gave similar, although more detailed, results. Ninety-four percent expressed interest in general sightseeing, 77 percent in taking pictures, 72 percent in "taking it easy," 62 percent in visiting historic sites, 60 percent in picnicing, 49 percent in shopping, and approximately 40 percent in fishing, camping, and hiking. Clearly, tourism had an outdoor orientation. Nevertheless, the more passive involvements were the most widely sought; looking, sitting, eating, strolling, visiting, and obtaining souvenirs were the behaviors implicit in the leading activities reported.[7]

Many surveys estimated tourist-dollar expenditures. For 1949, the U.S. Department of Commerce reported that Americans spent $43 billion on food and beverages, $16 billion on clothing, $13 billion on household furnishings, and $8 billion on automobiles. Americans were estimated to have spent $7 billion on vacation travel.[8] Expenditures varied from region to region, and from state to state. An estimated three million tourists, for example, spent $457 million in Southern California in 1949, with the average tourist dollar breaking down as follows: 23¢ for food, 79¢ for lodging, 12¢ for automobile transportation, and 13¢ for clothing.[9] Tourism was Southern California's second largest source of income, exceeded only by aircraft manufacturing. In income generated, tourism was followed by petroleum, motion pictures, apparel, and citrus. Tourism ranked as either the first or second income generator in Vermont, New Jersey, Michigan, Florida, and Oregon, among other states.[10]

State and local tourist bureaus sought to identify trade hinterlands. In general, tourist numbers decreased in proportion to increased distance away from an attraction, and with the population size of the originating place.[11] Victor Lanning's study of out-of-state tourists in Wisconsin revealed that 53 percent came from metropolitan Chicago and 20 percent from downstate Illinois, but only 5 percent from Indiana and 3 percent from Ohio. A study of Ocean City, New Jersey, one of the first studies to suggest the relationship between distance and size of place in origin of tourists, found that the five nearest states supplied over 95 percent of the resort's vacationers, with 35 percent of the total coming from Philadelphia. International travel also varied according to distance. In 1949, Americans made an estimated two million trips outside the United States, or approximately 5 percent of all trips taken. Canada was the destination for 73 percent of these trips. Mexico accounted for 9 percent and Cuba for 5 percent; but all of the Western European countries combined accounted for only 6 percent. In 1960, Americans spent $370 million in Canada. Canadians, on the other hand, spent $469 million in the United States. Throughout the 1950s, Canada was the only country to have a consistent travel deficit with the United States.[12]

Not only was pleasure travel focused close to home, but much of it was habitual. Sociologists Eva Mueller and Gerald Gunn found that 53 percent of those who traveled for pleasure preferred to return annually to the same place for vacations.[13] Much of this habitual trip taking involved second home ownership. During the 1960s, an estimated 1.7 million households in the United States owned vacation cottages.[14] Pleasure travel was also concentrated seasonally. Travel in the fall accounted for an estimated 26 percent of all trip taking, while travel in the winter and in the spring accounted for 11 percent and 13 percent, respectively. Fifty percent of all trips were taken during the summer months.[15]

Highway Environments

Highway development was accelerated after World War II. By 1949, 55 percent of the rural roads in the United States had been improved, although slightly less than 200,000 miles had been hard surfaced in concrete or asphalt.[16] By 1951, the total mileage of improved roads in Canada, including gravel roads, stood at 173,000 miles.[17] The quality of main roads changed rapidly in both countries. Highways were made wider and straighter, enabling motorists to achieve even higher speeds over longer distances. Toll roads were completed in the United States: first in the Northeast (Maine, Massachusetts, Connecticut, New York, New Jersey, and Pennsylvania) and then in the Middle West (Ohio, Indiana, and Illinois). Ontario opened sections of the MacDonald–Cartier Freeway, which ultimately connected Windsor in the West with Montreal in the East. The first sections of the new American interstate freeway network were also completed. By 1960, it was possible for motorists to drive one-third of the distance across North America on limited-access, four-lane highways.

As before the war, tourists were both delighted and chagrined by the new toll roads and freeways. John Steinbeck found them wonderful for moving goods and people rapidly, but terrible for the tourist's inspection of the countryside: "You are bound to the wheel and your eyes to the car ahead and the rear view mirror for the car behind and the side mirror for the car or truck about to pass, and at the same time you must read all the signs for fear you may miss some instruction or orders." Roadside commerce had been eliminated from the freeways and concentrated around interchanges. The activities and sense of life accumulated along the margins of the old roads were absent. The new roads cut boldly across the established grain of things, and there was little to see on a freeway except the monotony of the road itself. Steinbeck predicted: "When we get thruways across the whole country, as we will and must, it will be possible to drive from New York to California without seeing a single thing."[18]

The new freeways were built to satisfy the needs of faster travel and higher traffic volume. No one seemed to care where such change was ultimately to take society, as more and more landscapes were re-engineered to fit the new technology. Americans stopped building roads as human places, as critic John Jerome maintains, and began building roads solely for automobiles. Formerly, the old roads served to tie travelers and localities. Life built up along the highway edges. What appeared on an engineer's plan as a connecting line through space was, in fact, a living interface, a method of human social organization. The high-speed road was not only an interconnection, but it was a division, one side of the road divided from the other. To Jerome, adaptability has allowed mankind to gradually tolerate the movement and disruption along the dividing lines as traffic has accelerated not only in density but also in speed—three miles per hour, ten, thirty, fifty. As speeds have increased, the dividing widths have necessarily grown larger, both physically and psychically. He writes: "The attendant resculpturing of the earth grows more dramatic. The division gets more massive as the mobility through it grows swifter. Finally the division must be protected from man himself; one finds the ultimate absurdity of the stilted, concrete-encased, landscaped, fenced-off freeway, a total barrier."[19]

Tourists, isolated by their own speed and by the structure of the new road built to accommodate that speed, turned increasingly in upon themselves. As William Saroyan wrote about motoring on Michigan's new highways, he was mainly in his car and "only incidentally in Michigan." John Steinbeck found that all his reactions in driving became automatic on the new roads; nearly all his driving technique was deeply buried in a machine-like unconsciousness; and his conscious mind was left free for daydreaming. He planned houses he would never build, made gardens he would never plant, and wrote detailed letters he would never put on paper. When the radio was on, music stimulated his memory of past times and places.[20]

Radios had become all-but-standard equipment in American and Canadian automobiles. Radios helped pass the time, and, inadvertently, they diverted attention from the road-side, although on the new freeways many drivers found them vital to breaking the sense of monotony that the lack of visual interest imposed. John Updike captures the radio's importance in his novel *Rabbit Run*. Rabbit Angstrom fleeing from his wife and marriage, drives westward from Philadelphia into the twilight of West Virginia. On the radio he hears "No Other Arms, No Other Lips," "Stager Lee," an advertisement for Raiko Clear Plastic Seat Covers, "If I Didn't Care," a commercial for radio-controlled garage door openers, and "I Ran All the Way Home Just To Say I'm Sorry." After nine o'clock the music changed. "The rock and roll for kids cools into old standards and show tunes and comforting songs from the Forties. Rabbit pictures married couples driving home to babysitters after a meal out and a movie. Then those melodies turn to ice as real night music takes over, pianos and vibes erecting clusters in the high brittle octaves and a clarinet wandering across like a crack on a pond."[21] Radio was more than background noise. It was a new sonic environment for travel, largely divorced from the visual landscape.

Commercial Strips

Commercial strips thrived as never before. Beyond the freeways they lined the older roads in city suburbs and at the edges of small towns. The small businessman, who had dominated roadside commerce before World War II, now competed with large corporations that not only controlled gasoline retailing, but controlled the new roadside motels and restaurants as well. With the corporation came a sameness in layout, architectural design, and signage of roadside businesses. Thus, not only were highways standardized, but their margins were standardized also. It was a world new and shiny and modern, without a sense of past. It was a place intended to make travelers feel at home, and yet it was a place unlike any home previously known. It was a standardized world thousands of miles long, which constantly intersected itself. At every point travelers found the same cigarettes, the same breakfast foods, the same radio and television programs, the same topics of conversation.

Geographer Edward Relph has coined the phrase "placelessness," in part to describe the new order of the roadside. Placelessness, Relph maintains, involves a casual eradication of distinctive places and the making of standardized landscapes.[22] But Relph's concept is poorly labeled. Placelessness, as planner Asa Briggs suggests, results when one's conceptualization of a place is confused. According to Briggs, "If our image or perception of a specific environmental order is

REST HAVEN
MOTOR COURT
SPRINGFIELD, MO.

MAY PHOTO CO.
Springfield, Mo.

Motel at Springfield, Missouri (1948). Motels and other highway facilities became luxurious in keeping with the preeminence of motoring as a travel mode.

confused or unclear, then there is no place." What Relph alludes to might best be called "commonplaceness." Roadsides are not confusing; indeed, their surprise and mystery have been stripped away by the totally expected. Roadsides are predictable: the new universal order is too well known. Relph sees tourism as a homogenizing influence that destroys local and regional landscapes, replacing them with "conventional tourist architecture and synthetic landscapes and pseudo-places."[23] Tourism, in other words, brings the conventional, or commonplace, in its wake.

Commonplaceness was seen everywhere that mass consumption dominated. It was the result of mass marketing, the businessman's search for common denominators in retailing. Upton Sinclair wrote of a California town:

> This was the United States, and the things on sale were the things you would have seen in store-windows on any other Main Street, the things known as "nationally advertised products." The ranchman drove to town in a nationally advertised auto, pressing the accelerator with a nationally advertised shoe; in front of the drugstore he found a display of nationally advertised magazines, containing all the nationally advertised articles he would take back to the ranch.

National brands, and the life-styles they promoted, were reflected in landscapes everywhere. Julian Street had noted early that American cities had "a general family resemblance. . . . Houses and office buildings in one city are likely to resemble those of corresponding grade in another; the men who live in the houses and go daily to the offices are also similar; so are the trolley cars in which they journey to and fro; still more so the Fords."[24]

But never before had the sense of commonplaceness been so profound as in the commercial strips that had sprung up along the highways of North America. These were landscapes uncomplicated in the extreme, which, according to Edward Relph, declared themselves far too openly. There were none of the ambiguities, contradictions, and complexities that made landscapes interesting. They were simple landscapes, ordered in such a way that behavior was totally anticipated. They were "unifunctional landscapes": one building serving one purpose, one planning zone serving one objective. They were "univalent landscapes": each element having its own significance and identity unrelated to any higher unity except through proximity. There was a leveling of experiences: everything pitched at a common level of emotional and intellectual involvement. Finally, roadsides lacked historical dimension. They were ever new, always reflecting the present in anticipation of the future.[25]

Asa Briggs saw commonplaceness rooted not only in the national corporate economy of mass merchandising, but also in local planning responses to corporate initiatives. Local planning was limited not only by a lack of imagination, but by the increasing power of central government, often expressed bureaucratically in terms of building standards defined with quantitative formulas. Standards, once adopted, turned into norms, smoothing down the built environment into a set of commonplace solutions to simplistically defined problems. Planners searched for *general* solutions, as distinct from *specific* solutions that started with particular places. Thus, richly varied places were being rapidly obliterated under a monotonous fabric of standardized building.[26]

Some critics thought of the new commercial strips as inherently ugly. Sociologists Christopher Tunnard and Boris Pushkarev not only found commercial strips visually offensive, but they were disturbed that American society did not count the cost of such visual offense. City living was made obsolete by the complete acceptance of the automobile, and new suburban environments were accepted for their newness as superior to the traditional city. They wrote: "Familiarity with the mediocre, dull, or downright ugly in our travel may in the future be as detrimental to the American spirit as the in-city slums which we are now all committed to remove." To some, ugliness, expressed in the roadside, was a necessary correlate of progress as organized around automobile technology. Ugliness was to be decried, but not prevented. Charles Finger predicted: "Hideous advertisements will deface the landscape, and, when the boosters have had their will and cars throng the highways, no more shall men move as we moved, in untroubled happiness."[27]

Roadside Services

By 1960, a full range of retail services could be found along most commercial strips, although provisioning the traveler retained primary importance. Motels, restaurants, and gasoline stations remained the dominant types of businesses and increased in number. Throughout the 1950s, large corporations mostly took over the motel and restaurant business, just as they had long dominated gasoline retailing. Place-product packaging came to the fore across the trilogy of vital traveler services. Place-product packaging was a "total design" idea, involving the coordination of building design, building decor, product design, service routine, and signage. Corporations operated chains of look-alike establishments contrived to elicit ready customer recognition and maintain customer loyalty through standardized products and services. Establishments were carefully engineered as behavior settings where customer expectations could be profitably anticipated. Place-product packaging lay behind much of the visual homogenization so apparent along North America's highways.

After World War II, motels were larger and more luxuriant as the motel industry sought more affluent travelers. By 1948, there were over 26,000 motels in the United States, twice the number recorded in 1939; by 1961 there were 62,000. Tourists in increasing number used motels. One survey in 1950 determined that 33 percent stayed primarily at motels en route to principal destinations, while 30 percent depended on hotels, 20 percent stayed with friends and relatives, 10 percent used tourist homes, and 3 percent camped. The same survey disclosed that at final destinations, 43 percent stayed with friends and relatives, 24 percent stayed at resort hotels, 16 percent at vacation cottages, 9 percent in motels, and 4 percent in tourist homes. Another 4 percent camped. Motels functioned primarily as overnight stops for transients headed elsewhere. Their use varied regionally. In Colorado, 55 percent of tourists surveyed stayed at motels; in Michigan 47 percent used motels.[28]

Motels continued to excite description in tourists' diaries. John Steinbeck marveled at the way motels were furnished, with everything standardized within and without. His motel at Bangor, Maine, was immaculate: "Everything was done in plastics—the floors, the curtain, table tops of stainless burnless plastic, lamp shades of plastic. Only the bedding and the towels were a natural material." In the bathroom the water glasses were all sealed in cellophane with the words: "These glasses are sterilized for your protection." Across the toilet seat a strip of paper bore the message: "This seat has been sterilized with ultraviolet light for your protection." He mused: "Everyone was protecting me and it was horrible. I tore the glasses from their covers. I violated the toilet-seat seal with my foot." Whenever he wanted ice at a motel, there was sure to be a machine near the office. "I got my own ice, my own papers. Other guests came and went silently. If one confronted them with 'Good evening,' they looked a little confused and then responded, 'Good evening.' It seemed to me that they looked at me for a place to insert a coin."[29]

Motor inns appeared in the 1950s. They were substantially larger and more luxurious than motor courts, often consisting of a complex of two-story buildings organized around a courtyard with swimming pool. They also featured expanded public spaces indoors: a coffee shop, a dining room, a cocktail lounge, and even banquet and meeting rooms. A small lobby contained the registration desk. Motels took on many traditional hotel characteristics, but guest rooms remained large: the typical room containing two double beds, a nightstand, dresser, baggage rack, lounge chairs and table, as well as dressing and bathing areas with sink and vanity separated from shower and toilet. Rooms were air-conditioned, and no decor was complete without a television set and telephone.[30]

Entrepreneurs like Howard Johnson brought the chain restaurant to the roadside. Johnson combined the soda fountain with the dining room to create the highway-oriented "coffee shop." His buildings (as those of his numerous imitators) were designed for high visibility, instant recognition, and brand identity. By 1950 several hundred orange-roofed Howard Johnson restaurants had been opened across the United

States. To the soda, shake, and sundae concoctions based on his twenty-eight flavors of ice cream, Johnson added hot dogs, hamburgers, chicken, steaks, and clams. As in the new chain motels, Johnson offered a standardized product along with standardized decor and service. Motorists knew what to expect, and although there were sometimes disappointments, there were few surprises.[31]

Roadside restaurants also continued to be described in travel diaries. Lord Kinross wrote:

> I had grown familiar with these places, each one so like the other, with its warm smell, compounded of hamburger and hot milk and cardboard and central heating; its armoury [*sic*] of intimidating machines, steaming for coffee or freezing for ice-cream; the bright but time-worn plastic "leather" of its bar stools and booths; its slot machines . . . its counters stacked with candy and souvenirs and ten-cent cigars, and it racks with such enticing magazines as *Uncensored Confessions* and *Daring Romances*; and, to accompany all, the monotonous muted psalmody of the juke box, canned and unchanging from coast to coast.

John Steinbeck wrote about the new restaurants at freeway interchanges:

> At intervals are places of rest and recreation, food, fuel and oil, postcards, steam-table food, picnic tables, garbage cans all fresh and newly painted, rest rooms and lavatories so spotless, so incensed with deodorants and detergents that it takes time to get your sense of smell back. . . . Everything that can be captured and held down is sealed in clear plastic. The food is oven-fresh, spotless and tasteless; untouched by human hands.

Food in such places was clean, Steinbeck thought, but it was also "tasteless, colorless, and of a complete sameness."[32]

Standardization was the earmark of the maturing age of automobile travel. New kinds of motels and restaurants evolved, sustained by the large corporations which sought the benefits of place-product packaging that had earlier been used in gasoline retailing. Uniformity characterized commercial strips from one part of North America to another. Universal standards were also applied to the highways themselves. Commerce was banned from the margins of the new freeways, creating an isolated world for motoring. Smoother, wider, straighter roads of all kinds increased speed in travel, isolating the motorist from the passing scene. Increasingly, tourists were ensconced in a comfortable, commonplace world incompatible with tourism as a search for unique place experience. The adventures of motoring had been replaced by monotony, and even boredom in travel. Modern highway travel did not alert tourists to distinctiveness in landscape and place so much as it hid distinctiveness from view.

A new kind of travel was emerging, perhaps captured in fiction by Jack Kerouac's *On the Road* and Vladimir Nabokov's *Lolita*. In *On the Road*, Kerouac's characters drive a car at high speed on the open road, performing the "essential and quintessential American trip." Kerouac's Sal Paradise crosses the continent numerous times with a sense of joy, exhilaration, and freedom. His travel is a never-ending, life-affirming process. But, he never seems to arrive at any distinctive place. Landscapes are incidental to his travel since being in motion is the thing. The road is all-important. The same restlessness appears in Vladimir Nabokov's characters. The highway and its margins loom as containers for self-centeredness. Nabokov's Humbert Humbert summarizes his travels with Lolita: "We had been everywhere. We had seen nothing."[33]

CHAPTER TEN
THE REGION AS AN ATTRACTION

> There were nothing but isolated images. . . . I had thought that one
> part of the country would explain another part; cities would explain
> farming communities; individuals would become symbols for many
> people; city, country, farms and mines, and forests and mills, would
> all stand in my mind and glowing in my imagination would fuse,
> synthesize into a clarifying whole
>
> Nathan Asch, *The Road in Search of America*

The region, as a concept, provided tourists with a means of organizing the diversity of sights encountered in travel. Different kinds of people, economies, and physical environments produced different kinds of landscapes from one part of North America to another. Thus, the North was stereotyped in one way, the South, East, and the West in other ways. An important purpose in travel was to verify these stereotypes firsthand, and to make one's own regional discoveries. Travel by air obscured regional differences except in the broadest outlines of scenery as glimpsed from above. Although travel by train disclosed more of the landscape, often juxtapositioning the patterns of different areas quickly, travelers by railroad were relatively isolated from scenes glimpsed through train windows. At first, travel by automobile thrust tourists directly into landscapes, and the sampling of regional differences was close and immediate. But, with improved highways and the rise of roadside commerce, regional differences were obscured beneath a veneer of roadside homogeneity.

Speed and comfort of modern motoring required constant vigil from travelers lest clues to regional variation be ignored. For tourists who remained alert to the changes in landscape en route, regions remained travel attractions. Tourists sought to identify the elements of landscape that differentiated one region from one another. Kinds of people seen, prevailing activities rooted in local economy, or distinctive architecture contributed to the sense of regional place. Astute travelers overcame the pervasive standardization of the roadside when they played the regionalization game. Where did a region begin? Where did it end? Where was a region's core? How was it defined? Could the largest regions or sections be further subdivided? If so, how?

Regional boundaries were elusive. Nothing overtly marked the North from the South, or the East from the West. Only at state or provincial boundaries, or at the national boundary between the United States and Canada, were most travelers reminded that differences might be seen. The majority of travelers sought the obvious, ignoring the subtleties of place. They looked for traditional stereotypes rooted in sectional history and were often wont to overlook modernization in its distinctive regional forms. In comparing regions, most tourists sought to deal with extreme differences, overlooking shades of divergence. Tourists' images were often isolated, with no happy synthesis emerging. Quests for regional understanding often raised more questions than they answered.

Overcoming the Commonplace

Authors of travel books usually sought to orient their readers to regional peculiarities. American journalists assumed that their readers would consider such differences essential to interpreting the Continent. Jonathon Daniels confidently asserted: "All people are regionalists."[1] Foreign journalists, however, emphasized not the differences but the similarities of North American locales. They doubted even their own abilities of discovering regional variation. These writers appreciated the extent to which modern communications had obscured peculiarities from place to place, and they emphasized the landscape as seen through utilitarian eyes, discounting or ignoring the romantic and the picturesque. They tended to see North America more as a unity, as being a cohesive, functioning whole.

Lord Kinross, in traveling across the United States, thought small towns everywhere were much the same, having no identity of their own except in relation to the automobile. Towns consisted primarily of garages, parking lots, gas stations, car dealers, motels, restaurants. Soviet journalists Ilya Ilf and Eugene Petrov wrote:

An American small town acquires its character not from its buildings, but from its automobiles and everything that is connected with them—petrol stations, repair stations, Ford stores. . . . You may drive a thousand miles, two thousand, three thousand, natural phenomena will change and the climate, the watch will have to be moved ahead, but the little town in which you stop for the night will be exactly the same as the one which you had seen somewhere two weeks before.[2]

Even in backwater places, where local peculiarities persisted, it was the modern trends that attracted the writers' attention. Those who sought nostalgia did so from a clear understanding that a new, modern world would soon replace the old. An artist in search of material for his paintings, and hopeful of renewing his familiarity with life-styles rapidly disappearing, Thomas Hart Benton visited isolated Arkansas Ozark farms and towns in 1934. He wrote: "Towns, even those on the main arteries of travel, where the garage, the filling station and soda fountain have found their place, are yet full of the rustic and frequently dilapidated spirit of America's yesterday. But the automobile has come, and with it passable roads, and an influx from the modern world bringing its load of new ways, beliefs and habits." Old ways were mixed up with the new. The traveler had to sort diligently to find out what places were like before "mass production, the movie, the radio and the paved road started . . . [the] present chartless journey."[3]

Travelers looked for regional identities in relics, survivals from the past. When Thomas Benton stopped at a farmhouse to request a room for the night, a woman said, "I reckon if ye kin stand we'uns, we kin stand ye." Benton was appreciative of such linquistic forms "running back into the times of Elizabeth." John Steinbeck was a collector of dialects. "One of my purposes was to listen, to hear speech, accent, speech rhythms, overtones and emphasis." But, regional speech was in the process of disappearing. Concluded Steinbeck: "Forty years of radio and twenty years of television must have this impact. Communications must destroy localness, by a slow, inevitable process. The idioms, the figures of speech that make language rich and full of poetry of place and time must go. And in their place will be a natural speech, wrapped and packaged, standard and tasteless. Localness is not gone but is going."[4] So also were other cultural forms disappearing: types of houses, kinds of barns, kinds of crops and crop combinations, food preferences, religious beliefs, music, games and sports, dress, manners. But the careful observer, knowledgeable and watchful, could still discover regional peculiarities.

Cultural traits previously unnoticed might become remarkably apparent once a state or provincial boundary had been passed. Henry James wrote about entering Massachusetts from New York: "To be on the lookout for differences was, not unnaturally, to begin to meet them just over the border and see them increase and multiply." Winifred Dixon considered the crossing of state lines adventurous. Even with no apparent difference of landscape there seems inevitably a change, if only "the slight psychological variance of knowing the people think themselves different." Crossing from Texas into New Mexico, she sensed a "new wilderness" with "a hint of lawlessness, a decade nearer the frontier" and a "touch of Old Spain enameled on." The sign that greeted Lord Kinross as he entered New Mexico read: "Welcome to New Mexico, The Land of Enchantment." The cafe at the state line was called "El Corral"; its hamburgers were Mexican burgers and were served with a hot chili sauce. John Steinbeck was amused by the changes in highway signs from state to state; each state had its individual prose style: "The Northeast states use a terse form of instruction, a tight-lipped, laconic style sheet, wasting no words and few letters. New York shouts at you the whole time. Do this. Do that. Squeeze left. Squeeze right. In Ohio the signs are more benign. They offer friendly advice, and are more like suggestions."[5]

Tourist Regions in Canada

Crossing the border between Canada and the United States increased the expectations of tourists seeking regional peculiarities. Indeed, many travelers expected to see the substantial differences tourists might expect when crossing political frontiers in Europe. Lack of startling changes brought disappointment; subtle differences suggested sameness, and not variation. Many Americans crossing into Ontario or into the Prairie Provinces assumed that Canada was little more than an extension of the United States. Arthur Eddy wrote: "Canada is an anachronism. Within the lifetime of men now living, the Dominion will become a part of the United States; this is fate not politics, evolution not revolution, destiny not design." Although Canadians were "exceedingly patriotic," with close ties to Great Britain, the American population in 1900 was growing at twice the Canadian rate. It was merely a matter of time, Eddy thought, before Americans would overwhelm Canada, absorbing her culturally as well as economically.[6]

If English-speaking Canada seemed to many tourists an extension of the United States, it could be admitted, at least, that it was a very new extension. Therein lay Canada's most significant difference. Newness was a pervasive theme. Canada seemed less than a generation removed from a state of wilderness, a kind of northern frontier equivalent to, but different from, the western frontier. Canada also seemed different from the U.S. in that its rural population was more closely akin to European peasantry in economy and cultural tradition. Thomas Wilby wrote about the New Brunswick of 1914. The people he met on the road were mostly Scots cutting hay with great scythes. "They spoke eloquently of hopes and struggles, and of the hard fight with the soil to win a foothold in what had once been an inhospitable, but always picturesque wilderness." In Ontario, Mark Pepys found "an air of considerable freshness and charm." Small homesteads promised self-containment and security. Here was opportunity like that found in the United States. Here was spaciousness, an answer to overcrowded Great Britain and Europe.[7]

It was only in French-speaking Canada that generalizations comparing Canada to the American frontier or to England broke down. Quebec seemed old to tourists, not new, and it seemed crowded, and the people dependent upon authority. Clearly, Quebec was not America extended; it was not even Britain extended. It was France in the New World. Thomas Wilby found himself "surrounded with French faces, French farms, and French language, French customs, French peasants, French churches." Another traveler wrote: "There are interminable, indefinable French touches everywhere: in architecture, clothing, manners, religion, everything. All signs are in French and only the very official ones are repeated in English underneath. French flags fly everywhere."[8]

The Roman Catholic church dominated the villages and hamlets everywhere. Thomas Wilby, an English-speaking Canadian and probably a Protestant, found the churches, with their immense spires and high-pitched roofs of burnished metal "startlingly out of proportion and keeping with their settings." Everywhere the church seemed to have "swallowed all the glory, all the importance of locality. . . . It was noble, while the hamlet was ignoble. It soared while the hovels grovelled. It spoke of things Eternal—the people of things inconsequential and temporal. It spoke of wealth, the people of poverty. It embodied privilege and the people submission." Wilby found religion "the dominant and insistent note of the highway" since crosses marked the roadsides at frequent intervals. "The crown of thorns, the hammer and nails, the pincers, the ladder, the Roman soldier's spear and the sponge—all the dread material symbols of Christ's vicarious sacrifice—were there." Even the American, who was perhaps less biased, Jonathan Daniels, thought the churches and shrines looked as if they might be "a load as well as a light for the people."[9]

Typically, the Quebec countryside was organized in narrow strip farms, the farm houses strung out along the highways one after another. Again, Thomas Wilby wrote: "The villages were generally long and straggling. They began with the name of one saint and and ended with another, showing that in the course of the years two remote parishes had caught up with one another and decided to make common cause."[10] Away from the roads stretched the long, narrow river farms. Beginning at the water's edge, these farms undulated over hill and vale and across the highways far back into the countryside. The houses looked peculiar to Wilby, with their extended corbeled eaves. The barns were different: low, double-decked structures with sloping runways and huge wooden threshing wheels. But above all, Wilby found the people different from elsewhere in

North America. Here the populace appeared to be peasantry, as, indeed, they were, for in 1914 they still suffered under land tenure and governmental arrangements almost feudal in nature. Quebec seemed backward, progress delayed. Quebec was strangely European: a peaceful island in a continent otherwise given up to the turmoil of change.

The Canadian travel industry seized on Quebec as a regional attraction. A 1926 advertisement headlined: "Explore! North America's Normandy!" It asked: "Did you know that Normandy is just overnight from New York and that the Seventeenth Century still lives in Quebec? The language, the very look of things, are all of Old World Europe. There are medieval moats and battlements. Lovely old shrines, churches, and monasteries. Historic names to thrill you—Champlain, Wolfe, Montcalm, Montgomery." The ad also assured visitors of "curved-roofed cottages and peasants Millet would have loved to paint." Above all, tourists would find "good roads in a romantic country."[11] Gordon Brinley and his wife were enticed to Quebec in 1936. The trip left vivid memories. White houses with sky-blue shutters trimmed in red lacquer lined the roads. He remembered highways made attractive by the mingled colors of goldenrod, purple vetch, yarrow, and fireweed. There were cows being driven into a field by a boy, and vegetable gardens, pigs, and calves. He wrote: "Ahead I see a silvery spire and roofs of metal, which seem to say 'Canada'!"

Most tourists thought of Canada as divided into east, west, and north. In the East were the Maritime Provinces, joined in 1949 by Newfoundland. Eastern also were Quebec and Ontario, although the latter was sometimes likened to the American Middle West. To the west were the Prairie Provinces and British Columbia, considered by many tourists as extensions of the American West. The North Country spread across the whole of Canada, from Labrador to the Yukon, and from Lake Superior to the Arctic Ocean, Alaska being an American extension.

Tourist Regions in the United States

In the United States, most tourists vaguely identified the "East" or "Northeast" as centered in New England and adjacent New York, New Jersey, and Pennsylvania. The Northeast, when combined with the Middle West, formed the economic core of the nation, what southerners referred to as the "North." Here the majority of North Americans lived, and here the continent's industrial power was concentrated. The South, from Virginia to Louisiana, remained depressed economically, the effects of the Civil War and Reconstruction lingering until World War II. Only in Texas and Oklahoma had the discovery of oil brought economic boom. Of all the regions, the American West was the most attractive to tourists. The West, embracing the Great Plains and the Rocky, Sierra Nevada, and Cascade mountains, as well as the Pacific Slope, was the quintessential American region. This section epitomized the American frontier experience, and it was an accessible area of outstanding scenic beauty.

The Northeast was an urbanized, industrial area, to Rollo Brown, quite simply, "a region of smoke."[12] It was an area easily symbolized by city skylines with soaring skyscrapers, but it was also an area characterized by city slums. For Zephine Humphrey, the small coal towns of Pennsylvania said it best. She wrote: "Not only ugliness but misery was apparent in the black blasted realms through which we traveled. The wretched hovels, filthy with grime; the poorly clad people; the general air of hopeless endurance cast over our spirits a heavier pale than the dust and smoke cast over the sky." Jan and Cora Gordon drove back roads through the coal district around Scranton. At one coal camp, comprised by a few stores and blocks of cottages "built in progressive stages of standardization," they saw women sitting on the stoops, "with much of the European left in them," and "a tendency to bunchiness and blousiness." Here and there they passed miners, their clothes polished with damp, grease, coal, and sweat, and their faces studies in black and white.

Irvin Cobb thought New Jersey epitomized the industrial Northeast. Once, the state must have been a land of smooth, bare beaches, of salten meadows alive with waterfowl, of staid contented villages, of placid roads wandering from farm to farm. "But just look at the blamed thing now!" he wrote. "Coal tipples and garbage dumps and freight tracks and smelters and refineries invade the marshes, and the birds are mostly fled away, and for wild life the mosquitoes are left." He continued: "The elm-shaded towns[,] where once upon a time future statesmen were born and patriots grew up and writers ripened their art, have become clamorous, cindered, smoky, factory places. . . . Stack and flume, hoisting crane and slack-pile, belching chimney and coughing 'scape-pipe, and coal heap—these rise thickly, as grave-markers for the tombs of a vanished peacefulness, murdered and gone forevermore."[13]

Beyond the factories, where farming still thrived, small towns suggested pastoral peace and tranquility. Writing of Gettysburg in southeastern Pennsylvania, Clifton Johnson observed, "All the streets are lined with trees, which, with their suggestion of cooling shade in the heat of summer, give the place a touch of the idyllic." The houses were snug to the uneven brick walks, elbowing each other quite closely. Porches, porticoes, and steps promoted comfort and sociability. He wrote: "Little alleys branched off from the main streets, and appealed agreeably to the eye with their whitewashed walls and fences contrasting with vines and flowers and foliage that overhung them." Some towns thrived as appendages to city life: as suburbs or satellites to nearby metropolises. Irvin Cobb wrote of Princeton, New Jersey: "There is calm in Princeton—calmness and gentility and an ordered beauty still unwrecked, with stately old homes abounding, and noble halls, where coltish youth and ripened scholarship somehow blend into an harmonious intellectual current."[14]

Most tourists included New England in the Northeast, but often treated it as a place apart. Metropolitan influences might bind the Northeast as a single region, but Yankee culture, no matter the immigrant dilution, preserved a persistent identity. The New England landscape retained a sense of the past critical to perceived regional character. New England was a place of industrial cities and towns. In Berlin, New Hampshire, Jonathon Daniels passed a cluster of mills at one end of town, and at the other end the ski jump of the first skiing club in the United States. There was a Carnegie library. Westerns and Tarzan pictures were playing at the movie theater. There were signs in French, but the names of the merchants were Russian,

Southwest Harbor, Maine (1936). Every region had its distinctive look in landscape. New England's rockbound coast was a readily recognized icon.

Polish, and Italian. "It seemed a sad town," he wrote, "quick-grown with people from all over the earth, but uncertain of its future." Even the old farming towns were dominated by recent immigrants. Daniels continued: "Old Connecticut was good to see: the stone walls, the white houses with the green blinds, the churches and their spires, and the common and the town hall. The familiar picture of New England was a real picture on a real road." But the characters were different from what he had anticipated. Italians and Irish were at home in this Yankee scene. Another tourist found Portuguese people in the gasoline stations and Greeks in the restaurants. But the picture-postcard towns were there. Henry James wrote: "These communities stray so little from the type, that you often ask yourself by what sign or difference you know one from the other. The goodly elms, on either side of the large straight street, rise from their grassy margin in double, ever and anon in triple, file; the white paint, on wooden walls, amid open dooryards, reaffirms itself eternally behind them."[15]

Rural New England was a place of abandonment. According to Henry James, the countryside presented "scenes of old, hard New England effort, defeated by the soil and the climate and reclaimed by nature and time—the crumbled, lonely chimney-stack, the overgrown thresholds, the dried-up well, the cart-track vague and lost." In the reclaiming forests lay the record of agricultural failure and defeat. But out of failure had come enlightenment. Jonathon Daniels, a southerner in search of the New England spirit, wrote: "I suspect that the greatness of New England grew less directly from the high morals of the Puritans than from the inhospitality of the land to which they came. Time and winter dramatically pointed the need for energy. My back still aches from the stones they pulled out of the fields. The long shut-in winters turned the man to the tool and the book." The forest was a dominant landscape element, especially in northern New England. Daniels wrote: "Factories in New England, after an old fashion, still huddle close together in groups upon a stream. Even the farms seem tight and small. But the forests go everywhere."[16]

In many areas, tourism as an industry had replaced farming. Poverty had given way to the resort. Hotels and cottages stood by the sea, where harbors were too shallow for ships, and inland, where soils were thin and hills too steep for the plow. Daniels drove through the White Mountains where landscapes attracted sightseers and campers in the summer, and skiers in the winter. He wrote: "My own Southern Mountains rise by cove and cabin and hound dog's bark nearer to the sun. But these were mountains made almost articulate by innkeeper and poet, philosophers and passenger agents[,] while other American mountains were merely rising to the sky." Tourism was focused on the highways, as Irvin Cobb wrote of Maine: "We were in tourist land of summer hotels, of balsam pillows and souvenir postcards and filling stations; a land where venerable farmsteads fought a losing battle against the invading vacationists from New York and Boston. Some had succumbed, becoming boarding-houses or tea-houses, mostly called Ye Olde Something or Other. Others stood forth, defiant and angular and four-square . . . the homes of a stalwart, humorous, self-reliant race, with the barns built smack up against the houses and joined to them by covered passageways." Cobb found the "smell of the garage and the asphalt" commingled with the "savors of earth and woods and waters."[17]

Although the Middle West had cities and industry, the region also carried strong agrarian connotations, images of rural fertility and productivity. As David Steele summarized, "On from Ohio, out through Kansas maybe, before the real West begins, there lies that portion, flat, corn-planted, red-barned, and barb-wired, wind-milled, siloed, and soil-sunburned. There[,] things are symbolic of that land without a soul but with a belly full of fat things; short of learning but as long of sentiment—of a camp-meeting sort. Dull, flat it is, and with a populace short-sleeved, suspendered, tooth-pick eating, hand-shaking, back-slapping, and whistling." Theodore Dreiser, returning to his childhood haunts in Indiana, was, at first, struck by the region's dreariness: the small farmhouses set in endless spaces of flat land with nothing but scrubby trees, wire fences, and, occasionally, white frame churches to vary the landscape. But, beyond Napoleon, Ohio, the party stopped. They tossed a ball back and forth in a field opposite a grove of trees as a lone buzzard soared in the sky overhead. Dreiser wrote: "Truly this is my own native land. . . . I have rejoiced in hundreds of days just like this. All the Middle West is like it—this dry, these clear skies, this sleepy baking atmosphere. For hundreds of miles, in my mind's eye, I could see people idling on their porches or under trees, making the best of it."[18]

The Middle West had a wholesome, hometown image. It was the nation's cultural heartland, rooted in the soil. A farming impulse from New England and the remainder of the Northeast, and even from the Upper South, had been transplanted here to thrive. Theodore Dreiser commented: "It is a region of smooth and fertile soils, small, but comfortable homes, large[,] grey or red barns, the American type of windmill, the American silo, the American motor car—a happy land of churches, Sunday schools, public schools and a general faith in God and humanity as laid down by the Presbyterian or the Baptist or the Methodist church and the ten commandments."[19]

Main Street at Watertown, South Dakota (c. 1925). The Middle West was a region of prosperous small-town "main streets."

Dallas Sharp drove slowly across Iowa looking at the farms. The barns glowed a pale red in the sunset, the gabled peaks and ridge poles and weathervanes ablaze in the twilight. Below, in the gray-blue shadows were the ricks and stacks and sheds and cribs amid the clutter of the farmyards. He wrote: "Nowhere in the world have I felt a more perfect harmony between earth and man than among the farms of Iowa, nor more comfortable space and spiritual freedom between man and man." A college professor, Sharp admired farm life, but from a distance. It was agriculture's aesthetic side that entranced him, and not its everyday utilitarian aspect. He wrote: "I thrill at a furrow. I love a fistful of soil, fecund, arable, habitable loam; subsoiled, sifted, fined, and mellow. A plough thrills me. So does a drill, a harrow, and a hoe. There is romance for me in a string of red drain tiles across a soggy sour field."[20]

Many travelers found the flat landscapes of the Middle West dull. Bernard De Voto looked down from his airplane to write: "The Middle West is a monotonous landscape. . . . There is little for the mind to focus on and it sinks into reverie. How open, how uncluttered it is!" From the air, the landscape appeared clearly divided into a vast grid by roads running along the section lines. At ground level, the sense of a far horizon and the immense bowl of sky, with its ever-changing weather made boldly visible, was vividly impressive. But mile after mile of driving on straight highways could also be boring. Mark Pepys wrote of a rainy Illinois road that went "grimly ahead with a boring insistence on being straight for too long. . . . In the mood of depression induced by such driving conditions, the endless lines of telegraph poles started to annoy me. We heard only a continued swish—the noise of our own wheels in the wet, swollen from time to time by the like sound of cars we met or overtook."[21]

The small towns of the Middle West displayed a high degree of uniformity. Theodore Dreiser, traveling by auto-mobile in 1916, wrote: "Assemble 400 or 500 frame or brick houses of slightly varying size and architecture and roominess, surround them with trees and pleasing grass plots, provide the town a Main Street and one cross street of stores, place one or two red brick school houses at varying points in them, add one white sandstone court house in a public square, and a railroad station, and four or five red brick churches, and there you have them all. Give one town a lake, another a stream, another a mill—it makes little difference." The historian John Kowenhoven, traveling by train in 1961, wrote: "Most of the towns you go through are small and irregularly square, with streets at right angles to the railroad, many of which do not cross the track but stop short at earth mounds partly covered with grass. Each town has a corrugated sheet-metal grain elevator . . . near the wooden station. The houses are wood, with fruit trees blooming in their board-fenced yards. But there are almost no people in sight, just a few cars moving in the streets or parked at the curbs. And in less than a minute you are out on the prairie again.[22]

Tourists coming from the East were struck by the friend-liness they encountered in the Middle West. John Steinbeck wrote: "Almost on crossing the Ohio line it seemed to me that people were more open and more outgoing. The waitress in a

212

roadside stand said good morning before I had a chance to, discussed breakfast as though she liked the idea, spoke with enthusiasm about the weather . . . even offered me some information about herself without my delving. Strangers talked freely to one another without caution." In the Middle West the promise of the frontier had been fulfilled. Said Steinbeck, "I had forgotten how rich and beautiful is the countryside. . . . It seemed to me that the earth was generous and outgoing here in the heartland, and perhaps the people took a cue from it."[23]

A sense of a region required a certain state of mind. As Jonathon Daniels wrote of his native south, the land called "South" was "no realm for geographers." It had no spatial boundaries, no exact location. It was only a general location in the minds of men. The South had been given political expression in a great civil conflict, the scars of which had not yet healed. The South was as much a sentiment as a place, for the memories of prewar glories made southerners backward-looking. Conversations with southerners constantly turned on some mention of the Civil War. To northerners, the Civil War had taken its place along with the American Revolution as something to be studied at school, but to southerners it was history that still lived. Mary Winn wrote in 1931: "Everywhere one gets the visual impression that the Civil War and its ravages was a thing of only yesterday. . . . At intervals on the road one passes a group of magnificent live-oaks, in the middle of which rises a tall chimney, all that is left of the 'great house' that was once the center of a feudal property."[24]

Time had stood still in the South. Jonathon Daniels wrote in 1921: "If anywhere in America there has been an uninterrupted continuity, it is the South. Only now is the machine intervening to supplement labor of white and black hands. No tide of immigration has changed racial patterns since the first white and black striping. In no real sense did the Civil War alter the South. Indeed, in the South generally, America, under a thin surface of modernity, goes on as it began." The "most profoundly disturbing agitators" in the region, Daniels claimed, besides the union organizers, were the salesmen of Chevrolets and radios, gaudy machine-stitched dresses, and "other shining gadgets and gewgaws." But spindle and automobile had just arrived. The region's backwardness was still reflected in its landscape as, for example, in the lack of roadside services. Jan and Cora Gordon observed: "Perhaps a surer sign of poverty was the almost entire absence of advertisement; even the ubiquitous Coca-Cola and chewing tobacco signs no longer brightened the tree trunks; these people were not worth advertising for. Supreme expression of commercial contempt!" Instead, spiritual messages appeared: "Prepare To Meet Thy God" and "Jesus Is Waiting for You Round the Corner."[25]

Tourists were alert to symbols of southern identity. Louise Hale stopped to photograph the sign that marked the Mason and Dixon Line between Pennsylvania and Maryland. Its yellow paint and black lettering stood for "the soft warm things of life." It spoke to her of jasmine and mocking birds, slaves, old mahogany, and ruffled shirt fronts." Edward Hungerford rode the train south from Philadelphia. Southern accents grew more pronounced, the very air seemed softer, the Negroes more prevalent, the porter of his car continually more deferential, more polite. "Charleston, sah," the porter said. He had been a "haughty creature" in Philadelphia and "ebon dignity" in Baltimore and Washington, but in Charleston he was "docility itself."[26]

To most northerners, the strict separation of blacks and whites set the South apart as a region. Travelers encountered segregation in every public place. Clifton Johnson wrote in 1904: "You now find the interior of the better railway carriages placarded with the word WHITE, and the poorer ones with the word COLORED, and the negroes must keep entirely to the latter whether they wish to or not. What you see on the railroad is characteristic of the whole social structure of the southern states. . . . The negro occupies a position of servility and inferiority, and he is constantly reminded of the fact by restrictions when traveling, by discriminating laws, and by the habitual attitude of his white neighbors." Akira Oto, a visitor from Japan, was perplexed to know which waiting rooms to use and where to sit on the buses as he traveled through the South. He wrote that at Winston-Salem, "It seems that I belong to the whites, for the bus driver shoved me forward to a front seat when I took a back seat."[27]

Most tourists looked at the southern caste system superficially, abiding by its tenets. Walter Citrine "amused" himself
at New Orleans by watching blacks. He wrote: "I could not discern any serious discriminating against the negroes. Certainly I
never saw one get off the pavement to let a white walk by. On
the other hand, I never once saw a white walk in company with a
negro. I saw negroes buying in the stores, although in some
drug stores . . . where 'soft drinks' and meals are served, negroes were evidently not permitted inside." Some tourists
looked critically at the system. George Birmingham tried unsuc-
cessfully to understand segregation from the prevailing white
point of view. He wrote: "The 'Man and Brother' theory has
broken down hopelessly, and the line drawn between the white
and coloured parts of the population in the South is as well defined and distinct as any line can be. The stranger is told horrible
tales of negro doings, and is convinced that the white men believe them by the precautions they take for the protection of
women." Birmingham viewed segregation as a white man's
problem. The victimizers, themselves, were the victims of their
own social system. The South, he thought, sought to hold
blacks in servitude: not in slavery, but in modified forms of slavery. Prejudicial treatment of blacks contributed directly to the
region's economic backwardness. It also cast whites in unethi-
cal if not immoral roles.[28]

Jan and Cora Gordon thought blacks were themselves
partly to blame for the indignities they suffered. It seemed to
them that too many blacks were too deferential too much of the
time. In collecting folk music, they visited black churches and
even attended a black vaudeville show in Atlanta. At the door of
the theater a sign read: "Positively no white people admitted."
In the performance, blacks made fun of themselves, elaborating
all the prejudicial stereotypes. The Gordons wrote: "The shiftless, lazy, drunken coward, with a loose and easy tongue,
sneaking out of difficulties by means of a verbal twist of talk
drew volleys of applause. . . . The more he showed himself to
be the contemptible nigger, the better they like him." Edward
Hungerford found at Charleston that black men always
touched their hats when they passed him and, when eye contact was made, they always stepped into the gutter to let him

pass. The Gordons saw the same thing with blacks driving on the highways in cars. As they passed whites, even at high speeds, they nodded politely.[29]

During the 1950s, travelers encountered civil rights agitation as blacks attempted to throw off the yoke of segregation. John Steinbeck visited New Orleans to witness school desegregation. A crowd of whites in an ugly mood had assembled before a school to jeer students as they entered for the first day of classes. First, a little black girl arrived, escorted by federal marshals. But the crowd was waiting for any white man who dared to bring his child to school. Steinbeck wrote: "And here he came along the guarded walk, a tall man dressed in light gray, leading his frightened child by the hand. His body was tensed as a strong leaf spring drawn to the breaking strain; his face was grave and gray, and his eyes were on the ground immediately ahead of him. The muscles of his cheeks stood out from clenched jaws, a man afraid who by his will held his fears in check as a great rider directs a panicked horse."[30]

The South also meant to tourists cotton, tobacco, rice, and sugar since agriculture there had a sub-tropical emphasis. Zephine Humphrey wrote of Virginia: "When we came to our first cotton gin, we stopped and got out to inspect it. For some miles we had been notified by its approach by the wagon loads of cotton moving along the road." Drawn by mules and followed by mongrel dogs, the loads were held in place by whole families, some black and some white, mounted on top and going to town. Mary Winn wrote about Louisiana. Suddenly her driver stopped the bus, jumped out, pulled a knife from his pocket, and slashed off and trimmed a stalk of cane. For the rest of the afternoon she chewed pieces of cane like a southerner.[31]

Common house styles in the South differed from those up north. Clifton Johnson thought of the South as the "land of cabins." One saw them scattered in groups, or singly, over the face of the country and at the edges of towns and cities, shabby and unpainted. Jonathon Daniels was taken by the "shotgun" cabins of the Arkansas Delta country: two- and three-room houses, unpainted, and lifted above the ground on low pilings. Half-naked and pot-bellied children played in the dirt before them, "careful as if from birth not to trample the little cotton plants which came almost to the door."[32] Log cabins were numerous, especially in the mountains.

Although progress seemed retarded in the South, modernization was advancing rapidly. Irvin Cobb wrote about the "Old South" that was disappearing. It was to him a rutted dirt road winding aimlessly through the piney woods; to one side a clearing with a slab cabin, unpainted, forlorn, dismal. The fields were runneled with gulleys and grown up in sassafras sprouts. Around each house wandered scrub cows and razorback hogs, and everywhere were the multiplying signs of slackness and untidiness and indifference. But the "New South" was a "smartened, new-looking cottage of the bungalow sort; a concrete highway, broad and smooth; a modern model brick district school-building just over yonder; looping away across the valley the great cables which, on tall steel towers, are carrying . . . captured waterpower." The "New South" was a housewife "who has learned the spiritual and material value of trim hedges and posy beds and green lawns and shade trees," and a husband "who has a car of his own in the garage and a savings account in the bank." Jan and Cora Gordon wrote: "The new image of the South is one where the cotton mill and the fertilizer plant have brought radios and second-hand Fords to the poor whites who have acquired at least the humble ambition of working as hard as the next man in order to keep a wife socially content."[33]

New highways promised prosperity; they also brought tourists. Jonathon Daniels stopped at a gasoline station in northern Georgia. The owner shrugged as he related his town's misfortunes. But there was no resignation in the boy who filled the tank. "When they finish this road," he said, "it'll be the through road from Kentucky to Atlanta. People will come through on the way to Florida from Chicago. "It'll be a good place to stop." Mountain highways attracted tourists for the sights. Daniels wrote of the highway north from Greenville: "All along the turning, rising road the dogwood, the mountain magnolia, the azalea and the tiny nameless wild flowers bloomed in profusion on the May highway. From making textiles the country turns abruptly to taking tourists for a living. And at Caesar's Head, fenced off, is the eminence from which tourist or traveler might look back upon the green South Carolina lands below: Adults 25¢ — Children 10¢."[34]

The tourist trade had a greater impact on Florida than on any other portion of the American South. Kenneth Roberts described the typical visitor: "He is a sun-hunter. He is sick of four months of snow and ice. He is heartily tired of cold feet, numb ears, red flannel underwear, rheumatism, stiff necks, coal bills, coughs, colds, influenza, draughts, mittens, ear-tabs, snow shovels, shaking down the furnace, carrying out ashes." Florida seemed different from the remainder of the South, not only because of its tropical vegetation, but because of the works of men. South of Jacksonville, Cecil Roberts looked out of his train window. The unusual, to his northern eyes, had already begun. Grey-green jungles lined the rivers. Then the land was flat, with palmetto and scrub oak. Here and there the train passed clearings with houses of pink plaster and concrete. Everywhere in Florida one was conscious of palm trees. The palm was the symbol of the sun by which Florida flourished.[35]

Florida architecture was exotic, especially in the resorts. Cecil Roberts wrote: "Just as drab tourists from a grey northern clime blossom forth into riotous garments and become strange objects in a foreign landscape, encouraged by the holiday spirit and the brilliant sun, so here, one felt, people on holiday from all over the earth had let themselves go, and played at building houses." It was an "amazing architectural jazz spirit." Spanish haciendas mixed with Italian palazzi and French châteaus. Roberts wrote: "Spanish baroque and German gothic sit cheek by jowl with Italian Renaissance and English Tudor, with old excrescences of Turkish, Egyptian, and Moroccan inspiration peering from palm-grit retreats." Flowers abounded. "We passed a house with a scarlet hibiscus hedge; an avenue of royal poincianna trees opened before us. There was a blaze of azaleas and vistas of bougainvillea. Giant magnolias lifted their creamy cups to the sky, a bank of poinsettias shone in the shadow of a giant eucalyptus tree. And everywhere the houses vied with the flowers, houses that seemed to have come from the French Riviera, the Italian lakes, the Adriatic shore."[36]

But not all of Florida was a garden. Civilization seemed to dissolve along the highways into vast tracks of pine land and cyprus scrub. Occasionally the motorist driving south along the Atlantic Coast caught a glimpse of the ocean across the railroad tracks, through the telegraph wires. Julian Street wrote of travel by train: "The ride through Florida is tedious. The miles of palmettoes, with leaves glittering like racks of bared cutlasses in the sun, the miles of dark swamp, in which the cypresses seem to wade . . . the miles of live-oak strung with their sad tattered curtains of Spanish moss, the miles of sandy waste, of pineapple and orange groves, of pines with feathery palm-like tops, above all the sifting of fine Florida dust, which covers everything inside the car as with a coat of flour — these make you wish that you were north again."[37]

The 1920s was a time of real estate boom in Florida. John Van Schaick wrote: "Everywhere there were developments, new real estate tracts being opened up, roads and sidewalks where there was not a sign of a habitation, street signs where there was nothing but swamp and jungle, cities with three houses and a real estate office." But the boom bubble burst in the 1930s. Florida's highways were left lined with the decaying gates of failed residential speculations. Cecil Roberts, visiting "Alcantara Heights" to check an investment, wrote: "A triumphal arch which had collapsed, beaten down by wind, lay all splintered and dusty, under the fierce sun. There were vestiges of concrete which had marked the corners of branching avenues. And that was all. Nothing but the coarse sun-dried grass, and a few scrubby bushes met the eye." He remembered the sales office in London and its window display of baskets of fruit and the sign that had said: "Grow these in your garden at Alcantara Heights."[38]

North to Alaska

Tourists to Alaska sailed from Seattle or Vancouver or, after the opening of the Alaska Highway, drove north from Edmonton. Herbert Lanks, a journalist, was one of the first to drive the new highway. As he made his way north through Alberta, the endless wheat fields of the prairie gave way to flat bush country, broken occasionally by fields of timothy and clover niched into the wilderness. Log structures with sod roofs predominated, with a few frame buildings occasionally marking a crossroads center. Whitehorse, once a boomtown during the gold rush, retained much of its pioneer picturesqueness. Lanks made his way about the uneven sidewalks, past low, one-story buildings of peeling logs. Old steamboats sat rotting on the river bank. On first approach, Dawson seemed to be a deserted city since buildings on the outskirts were empty, with gaping holes for windows and doors, many settled in the permafrost at crazy angles. Only the center of town was inhabited.[39]

Nature ruled the North Country. The forests and the tundra and the lakes and mountains were the prime attractions. Herbert Varnum, an artist employed as a wartime correspondent, made his way to Alaska by ship along the Inside Passage. Day after day the ship ran through "pale, unearthly, luminous mists." There was no horizon, and scarcely any difference between water and air since the water had substance only where broken by the ship's bow, or churned by its propeller. "Held down by this low ceiling of cloud and mist, the land odors, the

Alaskan coast (c. 1920). The Canadian North and Alaska formed a cold frontier inhabited by fishermen, hunters, miners, and lumbermen. Except along the Alaskan coast and inland up the Yukon River, the Far North was inaccessible to tourists.

nostalgic scent of the evergreens, the musty smell of moss and lichens, the strange indescribable dryish and brimstone smell that comes from rocks—these odors, after the mingled oil and salt smell of the ship which had been in our noses for a week, carried in them the very essence of northern lands."[40]

Throwing gear right and left, one of Henry Poor's cabin mates fumbled for a movie camera. Everyone swarmed out on deck, staring. Icebergs were at hand, and a walrus, too. Small whales were blowing and plunging, and parrot-billed puffins flew by, along with flocks of brown ducks. Mary Hitchcock was also intrigued by the ice floes through which her ship moved. There was great excitement as passengers crowded the ship's decks. A sailor went aloft to indicate a passage. She wrote: "It was difficult to describe the solemn stillness which pervades this vast region, dotted with ice-floes speeding noiselessly to destruction; the silence unbroken by a single sound save the throbbing of the steamer as it advanced slowly through this wilderness of space."[41]

Alaskan towns were crude, rough-built accumulations of log and of frame constructions, mixtures of Eskimo, Indian, Russian, and American concoctions. One traveler described St. Petersburg as typical, with its cannery, sawmill, and flocks of herring gulls. Old totem poles stood guard, worn almost smooth by the elements. Along the Arctic coast, towns were little more than overgrown camps. Henry Poor described Point Barrow as the "jumping-off place—the top of our northern world." He wrote: "It looked the part. It had all the shabbiness, all the ugliness of the refuse of our civilization. Discarded oil and gas drums were scattered everywhere. . . . On the highest swell of the low tundra was a long boardwalk raised some two feet over the ground and leading along past a school, a parsonage, a white church . . . a hospital, and ending at the yellow frame buildings of the government radio station and weather bureau."[42]

Anchorage was especially affected by wartime activity. Henry Poor found the bars and lunch counters lined with soldiers. "Seemingly crowded out of the stores, the natives of the town stood on corners. They were unmistakably Alaskan, many with high laced boots, checked wool shirts, and heavy windbreakers with big collars, caps, or old felt hats—all like a weathered battered collection from the Montgomery Ward pages of hunters' equipment. . . . Mixed into the group of old-timers were young men who, though perhaps only in their teens, were bent upon becoming old timers as quickly as possible and seemed subtly to imitate in their young faces and their postures all the qualities that had been stamped upon the others by many long winters, much brooding, and the recreation of long hours hunched over a bar." He concluded: "I realized that the sourdoughs would never be a thing of the past, that no matter how 'modern' Alaska might become, how much laced with highways and covered by airplane, so long as empty places exist, at least one type of the world's misfits will drift, hunting for the unknown and the undiscovered. They are the incurable romantics of our pioneer heritage."[43]

World War II enabled travelers to see Eskimo and Indian cultures that were relatively unchanged by American ways, although the intrusion of the war would forever change native lifeways. Henry Poor was invited into a sod igloo by an elderly woman. The entryway was full of meats, skins of seal oil, pans of salmon heads and eggs and various offal of recent killing. The room into which they crawled was surprisingly large, light entering through a skylight made of transparent membrane taken from the stomach of a walrus. As he squatted on the floor, the woman dumped the contents of a little bag before him. A dozen neighbors drifted in, men and women and children and babies. He wrote: "I took a few little broken shafts of bone and ivory and gave them chocolate bars and packages of lifesavers and a few packs of cigarettes and everybody was happy and amused. . . . The whole village was a village of bones—clean, bleached, gleaming bones—shining now in the misty sun that played over the point and over the gray water on each side. The big uprights of the drying racks by each home were bone. Up and down the village the gleaming white of these great bones shone out from the soft gray and green and brown of the tundra."[44]

Poor was invited to a dance, an extraordinary opportunity to see behind the scenes of Eskimo life. Previously, he had been to the Indian festivals in New Mexico, but they had been contrived spectacles that had not drawn him in as a participant. Here an elderly man stood up to dance. He wore an old gray shirt and worn trousers. Movement started with his knees and flowed up through his body, rippling out through his flexible shoulders into his arms to pass into the air through the cotton gloves with their wide, square fingers. It was a pantomine of seal hunting. First came the slow looking, under a cupped hand, off over the endless wastes of ice. Then came the stalking, the sudden freezing of movement, the waiting, followed by "the sudden electric and fierce rush of the kill and its exaltation." Then he journeyed to a friendly igloo, entered, and greeted his friends, ate and drank, and departed. Poor wrote: "Through that little man the whole of Eskimo life passed like a pageant, and we couldn't see enough of it. It was incredibly graphic, and we were all caught up in excitement and would not let him go."[45]

Flying was, perhaps, the best way to see landscape in Alaska. Ernie Pyle accompanied a mail plane outward from Anchorage in search of back regions. The pilot wore hipboots and overalls, a leather jacket, and a common hat around which was draped a mosquito net. Hooked onto the cabin walls were a rifle and an oar. Pyle observed: "One seat had been taken out to make room for sacks of mail, boxes tied with rope, boots, bed rolls, a coil of cable, and other paraphernalia of the frontier. The floor was covered with dried mud." They flew across the Alaska Range, dog-legging between peaks with snow-capped mountains to either side. He saw so many moose and so many bears that he lost count. But, the seaplane was damaged while landing at their destination, and he was forced to hold over for several days in total isolation. He fought mosquitoes the whole time. He wrote: "Inside the cabin, you dashed around like a fool with the spray gun. Outside, you didn't dare lift your face net or take off your gloves. And cold—we were chilled to the bone. And there was nothing to do."[46]

The search for regional diversity in landscape remained a significant motive for touristing, despite the standardization and homogeneity brought in part by the tourist industry. The

Northeast, especially New England, the Middle West, the South, the West, and the North displayed distinctive characteristics visible in landscapes. Many differences were subtle, requiring tourists to leave the railroads and main highways, to search off the beaten paths of travel. Concern with the subtleties of place invited tourists to overcome the commonplace: to seek diversity where it survived, usually in relics of the past. But other icons spoke boldly of sectional character and were very much a part of modern economy and contemporary society. Each section had its distinctive places: church-spired villages in Quebec, red-bricked mill towns in Massachusetts, bustling main streets in Indiana, sun-baked cotton plantations in Georgia, mist-shrouded fishing ports in Alaska. Regional differences underlay the very essence of travel in the search for place experience.

CHAPTER ELEVEN
THE AMERICAN WEST AS A REGION

> It is true that the Old West of the stories is almost gone; that Billings,
> Miles City, Bismarck, are more given to Doric banks than to gam-
> bling hells. But still are there hints of frontier days. Still trudge the
> prairie schooners; cowpunchers in chaps still stand at the doors of
> log cabins—when they are tired of playing the automatic piano; and
> blanket Indians, Blackfeet and Crows, stare at five-story buildings—
> when they are not driving modern reapers on their farms.
>
> Sinclair Lewis, *Free Air*

The West drew more attention from tourists than any
other region. The West epitomized the very things that Americans thought their country to be, and Canadians also gloried in
the myths that spilled northward across the border. The West
was a place of unmatched natural beauty, a land of the picturesque. The West was a spacious place where the frontier had but
recently languished, but where seemingly unlimited resources
still promised bright futures. Cowboy individuality flourished,
and the West's unique history of Indian and Spanish beginnings also spoke of romance. Above all the West was accessible.
First the railroads had come, and then automobiles, buses, and
airplanes. One couldn't know North America without traveling
west.

Differences East and West

Tourists searched for particular western features. Sometimes the cues were obvious and fit popular stereotypes, but
sometimes they were subtle. In western Kansas, Julian Street
saw his first adobe house and his first sage brush and tum-
bleweed. At the "verge" of the West, Frederic Van de Water
pocketed his first silver dollar. Dead jackrabbits lined highways; prairie dogs and magpies were seen frequently. In Nebraska, the Lincoln Highway carried Van de Water alongside
the Union Pacific Railroad. The terrain looked flat, but a higher
elevation marked on each station sign told of a constant incline
in the land. Gradually, moisture seemed to vanish from the air.
He wrote: "Distant prospects no longer appeared soft, vague,

blue. They became sharply outlined, amazingly distinct, deceptively near." To Lewis Gannett, in the West the grass became sparser, and patches of prickly pear appeared. The sweet smell of the wheat fields and of the corn fields gave way to the dry aroma of parched grazing land.[1]

Differences could be observed in people, too. Out beyond St. Paul or Omaha, according to David Steele, women began to look modest, and young men were in charge of "large affairs." One began to whiff the mental, moral, and economic, as well as physical, ozone of this "rarer region." One English tourist wrote: "The grading process between the highly strung men of the East and the leisurely-moving men of the prairies was slow, but it was sure." Another tourist sensed a feeling of neighborhood in the West. There was a general confidence in the decency of life. He met "effortless generosity" and "instinctive helpfulness." To Lewis Gannett the West began where the garage men greeted travelers with warm smiles and sent them off with such winning invitations as, "Come see us again soon."[2]

Differences could be observed in railroad travel. Beyond the Mississippi River, David Steele found that parlor cars bore numbers, thus giving up the pretenses of long, fancy names. Railroads were all single track, and freight trains bore unmixed cargoes of corn or lumber or wheat or cattle. Julian Street wrote: "Railroad travel in the West does not seem so machine-like as in the East. West of Chicago you do not feel that your train is sandwiched in between two other trains, one just ahead, the other just behind. You run for a long time without passing another train, and when you do pass one, it is something in the nature of an event, like passing another ship at sea." Train crews were friendly. Street adds: "You feel that the conductor is a human being, and that the dining-car conductor is distinctly a nice fellow." The modern passenger train was in many ways an eastern intrusion into the West. It buffered travelers in eastern comfort, suddenly thrusting them into western discomfort. One English traveler thought his train a "slice out of one of the eastern cities set boldly in the midst of a perfect wilderness."[3]

Differences could be observed in highway travel. "Barbecue" gave way to 'Chili con carne" and "hot tamale" inducements. The names of motels reflected regional roots. A 1946 guide to Highway 66 listed the Deluxe, Mack's, the Ozark, the Rock Village, the Snow White, and Otto's motor courts for Springfield, Missouri. But for Albuquerque it listed the El Dorado, the Rodeo Court, the Coronado, the Aztec, and the Pueblo Bonito Court, along with the Silver King and the El Rancho. The brands of gasoline were different. Beatrice Massey wrote: "We saw no Socony gas after leaving Chicago; the Red Crown gas had taken its place. There were a dozen other makes—Union, Iroquois, Shell, Associated, etc." Except along the Pacific Coast, tourist accommodations tended to be more primitive in the West. Luxury was less frequently encountered. James Flagg wrote from western Kansas: "It is getting more storybook western now; comfort is setting, stark necessity is rising in its place!"[4]

Although all travelers saw gradual changes from east to west, a few persisted in identifying a precise boundary at which the West began. Such discoveries were often more imagined than real. John Steinbeck found his division point at Bismarck, North Dakota. He wrote: "Here is the boundary between East and West. On the Bismarck side it is eastern landscape, eastern grass, with the look and smell of eastern America. Across the Missouri, on the Mandan side, it is pure West, with brown grass and water scorings and small outcrops." The return trip offered fresh opportunity to contrast east and west. Winifred Dixon wrote: "We saw the West fade, and give place to the East. The easy-going, slap-dash, restless, generous, tolerant, gossipy, plastic, helpful, jealous West was departing, not to reappear even sporadically. In its place we began to encounter caution, neatness, method, the feeling for property and the fear of strangers that we were brought up with. We were clicking back into the groove of precedent and established order." She identified Fargo, North Dakota, as the "pivotal town" where the transition was complete. Julian Street returned east by train. He wrote: "The farms, flying past, are small, and are divided into little fields which looked cramped after the great open areas of the West. Towns and cities flash by one after another, in quick succession, as the floors flash by an express elevator, shooting down its shaft in a skyscraper; and where there are no towns

227

there are barns painted with advertisements, and great advertising signboards disfiguring the landscape." As another tourist, James Flagg, reported, there wasn't the same high spirit of
adventure coming east. The feeling of romance was gone.[5]

Western Scenery

Western landscapes were of a vast scale often deceptive
to eastern eyes. Every part of the country had its own native
scale: a proportion that landscape features seemed to preserve
toward each other, and according to which they seemed either
normal or abnormal. The mind needed to adjust when transported from region to region. Irvin Cobb had to multiply what
he thought he saw by two or three or four in order to reconcile
his visual concepts with actual realities. J. B. Priestley thought
the dry western air acted like a powerful stereoscopic lens. Everything far away was magically colored and brought closer. As
Ernest Peixotto commented from New Mexico: "The landscape
is built upon the vastest scale, but the extraordinary purity of
the rarefied air renders the sense of distance extremely
deceptive."[6]

Eastern travelers first encountered vast stretches of flat
plain. Driving from Omaha to Cheyenne gave Emily Post a clear
impression of the "lavish immensity" of the United States. She
wrote: "Think of driving on and on and yet the scene scarcely
changing, the flat road stretching as endlessly in front of you as
behind." Thomas Wilby drove west across Canada's prairies.
The road maintained an undeviating straightness, ornamented
on either side by wolf willow, huckleberry, and badger weed. A
sense of "dreariness" and "disenchanting isolation" had set in
with his first contact with the prairie, but with time its subtleties
had begun to charm. The sky commanded attention: a vast bowl
of cloud marked off by flat, distant horizons. The distance was
pinkish purple, the sky blue, the horizon steel and indigo. The
world was silent, but majestic, in its hush, and in the "sense of
arrested motion." Zephine Humphrey and her husband found
Oklahoma's sky commanding. It was tremendous. It was a
"mighty immensity" that all but enveloped them with a sense of
vastness and lonely simplicity.[7]

The western mountains were taller and more rugged

than anything in the East. They thrust up sharply when approached across the plains. Emily Post wrote about the Rocky Mountains of Colorado. "Steep your sight for days of flatness, until you think the whole width of the world had melted into a never-ending sea of land, and then see what the drawing close to those most sublime of mountains does to you!" Dallas Sharp commented on New Mexico's Raton Pass. "Where in Kansas, hill crowded hill, bumped up against the zenith, and shouldered back the circling horizon for infinite bare terrain, here over New Mexico, space seemed vertical as well as horizontal, concaved and deeply vaulted, earth as remote and almost as purple as heaven, serene, and just as fair." Mountains needed the contrast of adjacent plain to show to advantage. Thomas Wolfe wrote of facing Mount Rainier: "We stood trying to get its scale, and this was impossible because there was nothing but mountain—a universe of mountain, a continent of mountain—and nothing else but mountain itself to compare mountain to."[8]

Desert and mountain provided contrast. J. B. Priestley wrote about Death Valley as a land "entranced and bewildered

Highway south of Lake Louise in Alberta (1922). The West was a region of vast scale: endless plains, vast deserts, and, especially, spectacular mountains.

by mirages." "First the mountains would blur and then change their outlines; great bastions would dissolve; peaks would fade like smoke; whole ranges would waver and drift; as if Doomsday had quickly dawned." Then the desert would quiver in the strong sunlight, and stretches would glassily darken as lakes appeared; and then the next moment all would be gone, and then there was nothing but the desert quivering and winking again. The northern Arizona desert reminded Winifred Dixon of the sea: glittering in the sun, sands often ribbed as if by waves, sky and horizon often meeting in unbroken monotony, and mesas seemingly floating like islands. "We made for great promontories looming up in a sea of sand; tacked and veered to the next landmark; skirted reefs of rock; and looked for windmills, arroyos, and buttes to guide us as a mariner does for lighthouses and buoys."[9]

Deserts were notoriously hot. Edward Dunn apologized for stating the obvious. It was trite to say that the hot wind caused by the movement of the car gave one the sensation of leaning close to a fire or of opening the door of a blast furnace, but there was no other comparison to give. Another traveler in New Mexico felt he was wandering in some infernal region. No shade was to be found, not a stick or a stone underneath which one could crawl for relief from a "relentless sun." Not all travelers liked the western deserts. Beatrice Massey found them "utterly desolate and God-forsaken." In the silence she found a "deathlike stillness." But Zephine Humphrey was intrigued: "Space. Silence. Serenity. An enormous sky. A horizon line blurred and trembling with heat. The desert!"[10]

Desert driving was best done at night. Hoffman Birney left the Grand Canyon in the late afternoon, ate a midnight dinner at the Fred Harvey Hotel at Needles, and made it across the Mohave Desert before sun-up. The dry, cool air made the night sky vivid. As J. B. Priestley observed, the desert was "geology by day and astronomy at night." Dry air made sunrises and sunsets spectacular. Effie Gladding wrote of Nevada: "Nowhere else have I seen such wonderful sunsets; glorious in crimsons, purples, violets, rose lavenders, ashes of roses, and finally soft greys. Nowhere have I seen lovelier dawns, the air so crystal clear, the morning light so full of rose and lavender mysteries." Winifred Dixon apologized: "If I tint these pages with too many sunsets, it is not from unawareness of my weakness, but because without them a description of Arizona does not describe." Drought in the 1920s precipitated numerous forest and prairie fires that filled the air with smoke, Dust storms were common throughout the 1930s. Melville Ferguson wrote: "Great yellow clouds were banked directly in front of us, like the smoke of some tremendous conflagration, and as we entered them the sun was blotted out in an instant." For three hours he crawled through the "opaque pall," reaching Albuquerque full of grit. Ernie Pyle found it hard to drive as dust settled on the inside of his windshield in a film and sand blew across the highway like a "horizontal waterfall." He drove in darkness, it being impossible to see from one telephone pole to the next. The car was light on its wheels in the buffeting wind, and he could not hear the motor.[11]

Extremes of topography, weather, and climate aside, the primitive character of western landscapes proved a principal attraction. As Irvin Cobb noted, it was still possible to come to a mountain, or a lake, or desert, or geyser, or glacier, or chasm— and find it more or less "just as the Good Lord made it." Compared to the East, few bad restaurants were scattered about. Booths for the sale of souvenirs and postcards were few and far between. There were few importuning guides, vociferous cab drivers, or greedy custodians waiting to be tipped. He wrote: "There is . . . nothing except majesty and solitude, and a great soothing peacefulness of the soul and restfulness of the spirit."[12]

Western Genre

As tourists approached the High Plains from the east, nothing gave them the sense of being in the West as much as signs of ranching. The open range, with the cattle and the cowboys who tended them, spoke of freedom and individuality. In western Kansas, James Flagg noticed that the cows had changed from "sleek deer-faced Jerseys" to "sad-eyed, tragic, rough-coated animals." Where farther back east they fed contentedly on lush grass tended by friendly countrymen, here they stood motionless—seemingly sullen, hopeless—or stumble aimlessly down one side of a dry gulley and up the other, watched like convicts in the desert prison by hard-mugged horsemen." Beatrice Massey found ranch hands disappointing. On the big cattle ranches she saw only "near" cowboys— boys in their teens herding cattle, and some ordinary, dirty-looking men on horses. She had hoped to see cowboys in the Hollywood mold, "real" cowboys of the William S. Hart type.[13]

Other travelers were not so disappointed. At Magdelene, New Mexico, in 1919, Caroline Poole found the streets full of carts and wagons and the ever-present Fords. Cowboys galloped by on horses or stood in groups, bridles over their arms. She wrote: "There he goes, riding always at a gallop, swinging his lariat by way of exercise. He has his chaps on, or high slender heeled black boots, or both together." Even the red bandana handkerchiefs were there and the broad belts studded with silver buckles. Lacings of leather thongs or woven horse-hair bands ringed the sombreros so jauntily worn. In 1922, Vernon McGill found Springerville, Arizona, a very "wild and wooly" western town. "Picturesque groups of cowboys galloped down the Main Street, disturbing the Sunday quiet with an occasional yell of 'EE-YOW!' " He attended a dance where some of the men carried guns in their hip pockets, or slung them on belts in front. They strutted the foxtrot with a "defiant, devil-may-care attitude." East of El Paso, Mary Winn's bus was stopped by a man waving a revolver. He stepped on the bus to shout how he wasn't going to hurt anyone. "I been ridin' round this country for two weeks, and I got so damned lonesome I couldn't stand it. I said to myself . . . that I just couldn't go another day without I kissed a pretty gal."[14]

Dude ranches were contrived settings where tourists could get close to the cowboys' lifestyle. Edward Dunn and his family spent a month at the Cross-Triangle Ranch in Arizona. They were given menial jobs to do when they weren't riding horses for pleasure or lounging in their cabins. Dunn wrote: "Everyone dressed in western costumes from sombreros to high-heeled boots, and there was much talk of 'wrangling,' 'roping,' and 'rounding up,' despite the fact that there was not a sign of any cattle within fifty miles." Tourists glimpsed ranch life when they stopped at ranches for meals or boarded over night. Melville Ferguson found one ranch house east of Yellowstone especially symbolic of western lifeways. The walls were adorned with mounted heads of big game. A massive center table was covered with pelts; a rack in one corner was filled with rifles; a rack in another corner was filled with fishing gear. Heavy, upholstered chairs sat before a large, open fireplace.[15]

"Wild West" shows provided a means of celebrating western life, and attracting tourists. Early in the twentieth century the railroads staged western extravaganzas in order to stimulate passenger traffic. In 1905, Harry MacFadden rode one of the special trains to Bliss, Oklahoma, where some 75,000 people had gathered to witness a show. It began with a parade led by various Indian chiefs. Geronimo, escorted from prison for the day, created a sensation. Then came prairie schooners drawn by oxen and farm machinery drawn by giant steam tractors. Then followed strings of automobiles, with marching bands scattered throughout. MacFadden wrote: "One of the most realistic events of the day was the attacking of the emigrant train by the Indians and their subsequent burning of the wagons."[16] The West had become conscious of itself and sought through spectacle to present a face attractive to easterners. But the Old West lived only in caricature.[17] In the 1930s, Tombstone, Arizona, created "Heldorado," a week-long celebration of the vanished frontier. The program listed a stage hold-up, the lynching of a bandit, open games of cards, dice, and roulette, and continuous performances, in the Bird Cage Theatre, of the play "The Girl and the Gambler." Most festivals were built around rodeos.[18]

Western life-styles were reflected in the ways people dressed. In 1914, Julian Street observed that collars became lower beyond the Mississippi River, with string ties predominating. Western watch chains were apt to be massive, with western buttonholes sure to show the insignia of a fraternal order. Coats were cut loose. Broad-brimmed black, tan, and putty-colored hats began to show up at Kansas City. A year later, Effie Gladding noted: "Many customs of the West strike the eye of the

Easterner with astonishment. This custom which permits men to be at ease in public places and in the presence of ladies without coat or waist-coat in hot weather; the custom which permits ladies to sit in church without their hats; these and others which belong to the free West, the Easterner has to become accustomed to and to take kindly." Beatrice Massey thought women in the West most unattractive. They often wore khaki breeches and matching blouses, and hats like sunbonnets or like cowboy sombreros. But most tourists accepted and conformed to western ways by wearing western dress themselves. In the 1930s, Anne Peck and Enid Johnson reported that tourists in New Mexico fairly clanked with the heavy silver concha-belts and squash-blossom necklaces made by the Indians. "Men from the East swagger about in the loudest of checkered woolen shirts and biggest of ten-gallon Stetson hats, outdoing the cowboys of the movies."[19]

Western informality was reflected in speech as well as in dress. Englishman Anthony Jenkinson found westerners good-natured, happy-go-lucky, and impulsively generous. When he drove into a gasoline station he was always greeted with a smile. When he bought an ice-cream soda he was always asked if it was OK. People responded to his requests with the ubiquitous "You bet." Irvin Cobb called the West "Youbetcherland," a region that geographers had somehow overlooked. "It sums up the undimmed and undimmable optimism of the individual western American. You hear it a dozen times a day; a hundred times a day, some days. You ask the homesteader if he can put you up for the night in his one-room shack on the desert, and without a moment's hesitation he replies, 'Youbetcher!' With the ticket agent at the railroad station it is a favorite response, and the lunch-stand girl says it so often she almost has forgotten the word 'yes.' " Such turns of phrase marked an underlying friendliness. Priestley observed that one was not a stranger long in the West. To Priestley westerners lived in a world of first names and nicknames: "Jack and Smoky," "Shorty and Hank," "Bud and Tex."[20]

So far as the Indians resembled ancient peoples of the Old World they evoked admiration from nearly everyone. The Harveycar Motor Cruises of Santa Fe advertised: "Is this really

234

the New World? Two thousand years before Columbus . . . civilization flourished in our own Southwest. Here in our own country Americans have a treasure of romance, archaeology and history such as many have supposed existed only abroad." One journalist, walking through a pueblo, looked at the swarthy, strangely dressed men and women busy about the streets or moving silhouetted against the sky on housetops. "Is this really the United States?" he asked. "Or is it Egypt, or a dream?" Lewis Gannett wrote: "The East is the new country; the West is old. In the East, history begins with Columbus. . . . In the West, time reaches back indefinitely and continuously."[21]

A visit to a pueblo promised glimpses of Indian back regions. J. B. Priestley's party arrived at a pueblo and had the embarassment of "wandering like mad sheep through other people's homes." "Our guides, all smiles and enthusiasm," he wrote, "explained how these Indians lived a happy communal life, almost entirely free from crime; and we representatives of the roaring, racketeering world outside stared at the plump mahogany women and children." The Indian women made a living by selling trinkets to tourists, and thus their homes were constantly on view. They belonged to a dispossessed society; and yet Priestley thought they looked deeply content, unlike the female tourists, most elderly, who stared at them. Priestley added: "I could still see the two sets of faces—the white women, rather bony, arid, worried, and anxious, looking as if they were nervously scratching the surface of life; and the Indian women, with their sleepy fat smiles, sunk deep into an instinctive life as rich and satisfying as butter." But, Priestley concluded, American ways of life had superseded those of the Indians, and the Indian ways of life seemed to be reduced to sideshow status, without real future.[22]

On the Navajo Reservation in Arizona, Hoffman Birney blundered in upon the birth of a child. The mother lay clothed only in a shirt, on a pile of sheepskins and ragged blankets on the dirt floor of a hogan. A lariat was loped around her middle, the free end over a log rafter. "When the spasmodic pains seized her, two old women gripped her firmly by the shoulder, pinning her to the ground, while another woman and a man hauled

lustily on the rope." Indians understandably protected their
privacy. Front regions were contrived to contain visitors. Many
Indian communities forbade tourists to use cameras. At one
New Mexican pueblo, the appearance of Melville Ferguson's
camera was greeted by a shower of rocks, at another he watched
Indians overturn the car of one tourist caught photographing.[23]

Many tourists saw Indians only where souvenirs were
sold at railroad stations or along highways. Emily Post was intrigued by the railroad depot at Albuquerque. "You have always on picture postcards seen it filled with Indians. There is
not one in sight. Wait though until ten minutes before the California Limited is due. Out of nowhere appear dozens of vividly
costumed Navajos and Hopis; their blankets and long braids
woven with red cloth, their headbands and beads and silver
ornaments fill the platform with color like a flower display."
The Santa Fe Railroad had arranged an exhibit room where passengers were entertained briefly by Indian dancers. Post continued: "The typical step is a sort of a shuffling hop; a little like
the first step or two of a clog dancer . . . or else just a bent kneed
limp and stamp accompanied either by a droning chant or merely a series of sounds not unlike grunts."[24] Such brief glimpses of
Indian culture rarely prompted much admiration. Most tourists
were either repelled by or just indifferent to these stereotypes of
Indian society.

A Touch of the Mediterranean

During World War I the railroads promoted the West as
an alternative to traveling in Europe. Trains were likened to passenger liners, the crossing of the Great Plains to the crossing of
the Atlantic. New Mexico, Arizona, and especially California
were compared to Europe itself. Crossing the Rocky Mountains
and the Sierra Nevada was made an Alpine simile, while Indian
antiquities were compared to Old World relics. As analogies
were extended to climate and to modern society, many tourists
came to see portions of the West as the North American
Mediterranean, the touristic equivalent of Italy and Spain.[25]
Winifred Dixon meandered through San Antonio's "Cabbage
Patch," steering around "tin cans, Mexican babies, and goats."
She wrote: "Mexicans hung [around] outside their little shops,

whose festoons of onions and peppers painted Italy into the landscape." Edward Dunn found the pueblos of New Mexico and Arizona, built upwards in progressive stories, calling to mind the fortified hill towns of Italy. Ernest Peixotto devoted a chapter of his book *Romantic California* to "Italy in California." He wrote of the soft breezes, "fanning the face like a caress," of "limpid air—the *cielo sereno* dear to every Italian heart," of the scent of orange blossoms, and of "shimmering olives backed by dark oaks."[26]

World's fairs at San Diego, San Francisco, and Portland were built in Spanish-mission style. The old California missions themselves were promoted as tourist attractions, with most variously restored. Tourists visited the missions as they visited cathedrals in England. But it was in New Mexico that the Spanish connection seemed best established. The colonial past still lived in Spanish-speaking barrios, and in the Indian pueblos in which Indian and Mexican ways had become mixed. Most tourists were pleasantly surprised. Caroline Poole found Concha, her first town in New Mexico, "a most picturesque little village of adobe houses rich in color effects and unconscious charm." "The window frames and doors were painted in bright striking colors crudely pink, blue, and green. The low roofs[,] at this season heaped high with yellow squashes, gay gourds and pumpkins, string upon string of gorgeous scarlet peppers hanging from the roof-beams, painted a picture both unusual and artistic." In a deepening twilight, Winifred Dixon drove north to Albuquerque along the Rio Grande River. "It was under the deep-blue night sky that we saw our first pueblo town. Solitary meadows with bands of horses grazing upon them, a gleam of light from an adobe inn at a crossroad, a stretch of darkness, strange to our desert-accustomed senses because of the damp breath from the river . . . then the barking and yelping of many mongrel dogs, and we were precipitated into the winding, barnyard-cluttered alleys."[27] Such landscapes were rooted in human experience quietly accumulated through time.

Other tourists found the Hispanic landscapes of New Mexico squalid and alien. Anglo-Saxon biases came to the fore. Guy Austin wrote of Santa Fe: "Mexicans, dirty and greasy,

237

lolled in the streets, sat on the edge of the sidewalks, or jostled through the crowds on the narrow streets, endeavouring to pass themselves off as good American citizens with the aid of light business suits, sombreros and chewing gum." He continued: "Mexicans, thousands of acres of nothing but desert and sagebrush and boulders, all hemmed in by the everlasting mountains and still more mountains, were beginning to get on my wife's nerves. So we took a walk along the gaily lighted streets of Albuquerque among civilized beings again in a civilized town just to remind ourselves that such things as towns and white people and lights and life as we know it still existed."[28]

Artists were attracted to the natural and cultural diversity in New Mexico. Santa Fe and nearby Taos became artist colonies. Anne Peck and Enid Johnson found Taos a strange mixture of Spanish settlement and the curio shops, studios, and picture galleries. The plaza with its bandstand was filled with woolly ponies and teams of mules and automobiles. American ranchers in "rough clothes and great curly-brimmed hats" mixed with "brown faced" Mexican farmers and Indians "swathed in pale blankets." Sightseeing buses disgorged tourists into the swale.[29]

A Touch of the Frontier

Movie makers in Hollywood used the West to advantage, elaborating on the myths of the frontier to produce a national fantasy. For many tourists, merely to be in western landscapes was to evoke Hollywood stereotypes. In Nevada in 1925, James Flagg drove through rocky gorges along snaky precipitous trails "such as you see in the movies where devil-may-care bandits ride," and then across sagebrush mesas for hours at a stretch toward rocky mountain ranges "where desperate rustlers hide in screenland." He wrote: "I was rather astonished that a Wells Fargo express coach didn't come rattling over the hills with the hero holding the heroine with one arm and shooting pursuing road agents out of their saddles with blank cartridges. It was great!" But in 1910 Harriet White did see a stagecoach near Tonapah. The intoxicated driver had dropped the mail sack, which White and her party retrieved. Throughout the 1920s, tourists could still see covered wagons hauling migrants or caravans of freight wagons. Caroline Poole was astonished to see immigrant trains "so completely did they hark back to supposedly by-gone days." They symbolized, she wrote, "a sturdy, dauntless and intrepid spirit not altogether gone from our land."[30]

The frontier could be seen in the look of towns, especially those in areas still opening to settlement, as in the Dakotas, or across Canada's Prairie Provinces. In 1901, Bernard McEvoy saw towns in various stages of development as he rode the Canadian Pacific from Calgary to Edmonton. "The unit, the primal cell—the germ," he wrote, "is the store." Stores were little more than "magnified packing-boxes." But the spirit of competition soon attracted other merchants who duplicated the architectural poor taste, thus "desecrating a beautiful landscape with the most detestably ugly buildings that can possibly be erected." By the 1920s, the rough packing-box look had begun to disappear from more prosperous towns. James Flagg wrote of Bend, Oregon: "True, a good deal of the straggling old village was still in evidence, but the fine new buildings in course of construction made it clear that such structures would soon elbow the ragged old wooden shacks out of existence." Beatrice Massey found the larger towns of Montana provided with modern hotels, wide, paved streets, fine churches, office buildings, and theaters. There were plenty of electric fans. She wrote: "These cities were equipped with every modern device and invention. They claimed your admiration and deserved your unstinted praise. It was almost impossible to believe that the next morning, ten minutes after you left the pavements, you would again be out on the prairies and perhaps meet no one for hours."[31] The frontier was not only something to be romanticized in Hollywood movies, but it stood as a baseline against which to measure progress in a real world.

California

California was a special part of the West. For many tourists it was the ultimate goal of western travel. As one traveler said, "There is something of magic in the words, 'going to California.' For the Eastern man they mean much the same as 'going to Europe.' . . . It costs money. It takes time. It is 3,000 miles away." Most tourists thought of California as primarily a coastal manifestation. They spoke about traveling to "the coast." Guy Austin pictured California as an Eden surrounded by a wilderness of mountain and desert. Instead of sagebrush and cactus, he found orange groves and vineyards. Instead of shacks and wooden hotels and narrow, dust-ridden roads, he found gorgeous stucco homes, magnificent buildings, and wide, clean boulevards. Instead of cowboys and Indians, there were fashionable people and cars and life. California was something approached through a mountain pass, where suddenly one obtained a different world. John Van Schaick wrote of the approach to Los Angeles by train: "It is but one step from the desert to a smiling, fruitful country. The tall yucca in bloom gave the signal, a field where a man was turning hay followed, and then suddenly we began to go by beautiful orange and lemon groves, nut trees and groves of avocado."[32]

Pastoral images dominated. Effie Gladding wrote: "Leaving San Jose, we were more and more charmed with the valleys as we drove along through orderly orchards and past tasteful bungalows. This was the California of laden orchards, of roses and climbing geraniums, of green hills rising beyond the valleys, of which we had read." To Gladding, California was "an immense garden." "Orchards, towns, grassy spaces with a silver river winding through them, all give me that sense ever present in California, of happiness." In 1916, Emily Post thought of California as happy: "Where giantism, self-inflation, or personal ambition plays a prominent part in the characteristics of other states, the Californians are merely happy— happy about everything—happy all the time." To Dallas Sharp, California was a "dreamland" shaded by eucalyptus trees and tropical palms. His highway west of San Bernardino was lined by hedges of roses, heliotrope, and geraniums. Oranges could be had by the bucket, by the bushel. There were "honey, and ecstasy, and transport, and wonderment—all the way to Claremont!"[33]

California's pastoralism was rooted in its mild climate. A 1907 advertisement read: "California[,] where flowers bloom all winter and where you can enjoy boating, bathing, fishing, driv-

ing, golfing, automobiling every day of the year." According to
Lewis Gannett, Californians suffered from "weather patriotism." They were "climate mad." He was constantly expected to
make "prayerful appreciation of the sunshine," and everyone
asked if he did not like the climate, and if he was not planning to
stay and buy a house and settle permanently. California's climate was not perfect. Ruth Wood, who found it cold in January,
despite chamber-of-commerce promises, wrote: "At noon,
summer reigns—if the sun shines. Swimmers laugh in the surf,
golfers throw off their jackets. By three or four o'clock[,] those
who are sensible put them on again." She continued: "In a
country where climate is capitalized by the hotel-keeper and the
land agent no less than it is immortalized by the poet, the vaga-
ries of dustwinds, bleak 'trades' and white fogs are suppressed
by the loyal citizens, or, if admitted at all to the stranger, are
attributed to a rival town—never to his own."[34]

California was a cosmopolitan place. To Winifred Dixon
it was the West "dehorned," for it possessed "climate, boulevards, and conveniences." To another tourist, California was
"cosmopolitanism of the western slope, half pine woods and
half Paris." California's cities were seen as modern suburbias
where nature was brought successfully into urban stability.
Guy Austin wrote: "Stately royal palms lined the shopping
thoroughfares. Colour seems the predominant feature of
Southern California cities, with fine homes everywhere, and
every one of them architectured in perfect harmony with the
beauty that lies all around. Even the smallest homes were ablaze
with colour—windows, tiled roofs, awnings, gardens." California's modern highways enhanced the progressive image.
Thomas Murphy wrote: "California is easily the motorist's paradise over all other places on this mundane sphere. It has more
cars to the population—twice over—and they are in use a
greater portion of the year." Nowhere but in California were
roads as good, and gasoline as cheap.[35]

Stereotyping Other Western States

Tourists stereotyped each western state, attaching a
cluster of beliefs and attitudes to elements of landscape for each.
These icons symbolized places in a kind of shorthand fashion.

People of each state were thought of as having certain attributes in common. For example, John Van Schaick could write of Oregon and Washington: "These people up here take no back seat for Californians. They hold up their heads and proudly boast of water as something as vital as sunshine—water in rain, in lakes, in waterfalls, in salt sea sounds, in canals. They want their sunshine a bit filtered through the clouds; they dislike the bright white glare of Southern California; they do not believe that life is meant to be lived where it is so hot. They consider pines and spruces as beautiful as olive trees and lemons, the making of cedar shingles as honorable as keeping boarders."[36]

Texas evoked much curiosity. After a miserable night on a train, one traveler went to the observation car to examine the Texas of romance—"the Texas of the Rangers, of the cattle trails, of incredible feats with pistol and lasso, of skirmishes with Indians." He wrote: "But what I saw was a Texas of a thousand oil-derricks, sticking uglily above the horizon, a Texas of pipelines running under glorious autumned leaves, of heavy, oily palls of smoke lowering blackly on to the ranges, of railroad sidings cutting their ways in all directions, crossing and criss-crossing, and twisting and turning, a Texas of square oil-tanks waiting to be filled, of acres of derelict machinery . . . of litter and tins and garbage and dirt." John Steinbeck found Texas to be many kinds of "country, contour, climate, and conformation. . . . There is no physical or geographical unity in Texas," he wrote. "Its unity lies in the mind." According to Steinbeck, stereotypes about areas were often confused and sometimes contradictory. Usually they were overly simplistic ideas of places with which travelers validated or invalidated place expectations as circumstances warranted. According to Steinbeck: "There's no question that this Texas-of-the-mind fable is often synthetic, sometimes untruthful, and frequently romantic, but that in no way diminishes its strength as a symbol." There were places where fable, myth, preconception, love, longing, or prejudice stepped in and so distorted cool, clear appraisal that a "kind of high-colored magical confusion" took permanent hold. Texas was such a place.[37]

Utah was another. Driving north toward Salt Lake City, Thomas Wolfe found dusty little Mormon villages, blazing and

blistering in the hot dry heat. Forlorn little houses, many looking like cramped and warped wooden boxes, all unpainted,
were hidden under merciful screenings of dense trees. There
was just a touch of strangeness in a set of eaves here, the placing
of a porch there, or the turning of a gable to the street "temple-
wise." He thought of the architecture as denuded and as
curiously sterile as the religion. But the fields, rimmed by
windbreaks of poplar and cottonwood, burgeoned in green fertility. It was a landscape, he wrote, "with the cruelty of Mormon
in it, but with a quality [of] its own that grips and holds you."
Ernie Pyle, however, took time to linger and talk to the people.
"I found to my surprise that Mormons were people. I had in-
nocently assumed that they were a strange race you couldn't
talk with—cold, bluenosed, mystic, and belligerent."[38]

Tourists were an integral part of the stereotypes about
Nevada. A state with little to attract tourists, Nevada remedied
the situation with liberal laws governing gambling, divorce,
and prostitution, among other established vices. J. B. Priestley
wrote: "A road there seems to lead endlessly from nothing to
nothing. A solitary filling station soon gives the Nevada traveler
a sense of bustling urban life. When they do achieve a town
there, they throw it wide open, probably feeling that any restric-
tion would be intolerable at the end of such trails." David Steele
wrote of Reno in 1916 as a place of prize-fighting, horse-racing,
open gambling, and easy divorces. "Here is a spic-and-span
city, up-to-date, progressive, modern, concrete-paved, elec-
tric-lighted, full of stores and shops with goods of quality. Not a
vehicle in the whole city is not gasoline driven or electrically
propelled. It is populous and prosperous, yet the center of a
population of pickpockets and procurers. It raises its revenue
from race-track and from prize-ring, open gambling halls and
Sunday baseball. It is truly a place, not of liberty, but of license."
Divorce dominated the Reno that Mary Winn saw. "Sex appeal,
often thwarted, walks the streets; it coquettes in the smart little
shops . . . spends hours of patient effort at the many beauty
parlors; and keeps the courthouse . . . aflutter with well-
dressed men, good-looking women, brisk lawyers, curious
reporters, congratulations, flowers." Gambling dominated
Hoffman Birney's Reno. Virtually every cigar store ran a $5

change-in-table-stakes poker game. In gambling clubs you could get any kind of action—faro, craps, blackjack, poker, roulette, chuck-a-luck.[39] The first big hotels appeared in Las Vegas in the early 1940s: the El Rancho, the Last Frontier, the Western Horseshoe, the Pioneer, the Golden Nugget. In the 1950s, exotic themes dominated hotel contrivance: the Desert Inn, the Sahara, the Tropicana, the El Morocco, the Dunes.[40]

The West surprised, amazed, disturbed, and disappointed tourists. It was many things to many people. However, whatever the images, the West was always attractive to tourists. It was the region that popular sentiment said was most worth visiting. Travelers first had to find it. Where did the West begin? Where did it end? Then they had to ascertain its true character. Expectations were validated, or invalidated. Although the West changed throughout the early twentieth century, the prevailing touristic images remained remarkably consistent. The West was vast. Its scenery was superlative. Its cities were progressive. Its people were unhurried, friendly, happy. The West was a place both of opportunity and of contentment. The West was not as refined as the East, since frontier conditions lingered there, but the future belonged to the West. The West was North America's promised land.

CHAPTER TWELVE

THE TOURIST IN THE CITY

> When you have . . . seen the layout of the town and caught a view
> of the lake or the river from every imaginable point of view, and you
> have heard of all the things that have been done and are going to be
> done, and may or may not be done, and ought to be done . . . when
> you have it demonstrated to you in incontrovertible facts and figures
> what the town stands for, exists for and means to live for . . . then
> you begin to see this aggregation of busy humanity in a new and
> altogether fascinating light.
>
> Thomas Wilby, *A Motor Tour through Canada*

North American cities grew both in substance and in stature during the early twentieth century.[1] American and Canadian economic growth, as well as cultural life, was centered in urban places. Never before had so many people lived and worked so densely packed over such large areas. Every variety of human function, every experiment in human association, all technical processes, as well as modes of architecture and planning, were centered in cities.[2] Tourists were attracted to urban places, for only there could modern life be seen in its most abundant flowering. In the cities, fads and fashions bloomed. Cities were vast gardens of visual delight. Christopher Morley likened his Philadelphia to a forest. He wrote: "Who can describe the endless fascination, allurement and magic of the city? It is like a great forest, full of enchantment for the eye and ear. What groves and aisles and vistas there are for wandering, what thickets and underbrush to explore!"[3]

Cities were promoted through pamphlets, books, and newspapers designed to attract and to hold tourists' admiration. Guided tours oriented visitors to positive viewpoints, and to positive points of view. Many cities organized exhibitions and fairs to enhance images of success and progress. Whether attracted by a world's fair or by the ordinary life of a city, city visitors were customers, clients to be entertained and sold city wares, if only those of the resort or vacation variety. Cities provided pleasure grounds for rest and relaxation, and they opened up back regions of commerce and industry, or created front regions catering to tourists' curiosity. Tourism was a part of every urban place.

Tourists approached cities with definite expectations. Often a city's tourist facilities, especially its hotels and restaurants, dominated place images. Sometimes it was the city's nightlife or other forms of entertainment that formed a tourist's impressions, or sometimes it might be a city's illicit side. As strangers enjoying relative anonymity, unhindered by the normal social ties of home, tourists were relatively free to engage in licentious behavior. Cities were places of freedom, if not license, and they were places of adventure. Most tourists formed their impressions of cities from a wide variety of everyday sights and sounds, and social experiences. The variety and density of activity and its rapid pace set cities apart as peculiar touristic attractions.

First Impressions

A new city was something to be approached deliberately. The typical tourist was awake to sensations, forming impressions as soon as his train or car approached a city's suburbs. The traveler by steamship, anxiously waiting on deck, surveyed the approaching waterfront; the air passenger studied the ground below, nose pressed to the window of his airplane. First impressions often set the tone for an entire visit. Exceedingly positive or negative impressions were rarely overcome by subsequent experience. Impressions of the first hours always had the value of their intensity, and they were vivid for their newness. Julian Street wrote: "What a curious thing it is, that mental process by which a first impression of a city is summed up. A railway station, a taxicab, swift glimpses through a dirty window of streets, buildings, people, blurred together, incoherently, like moving pictures out of focus; then a quick unconscious adding of infinitesimal details and the total: 'I like this city,' or: 'I do not like it.'"[4]

Comparisons were made with other places. On arriving at Winnipeg, Bernard McEvoy set out on a walk "to get impressions with a fresh eye." At first, he thought things looked like London, especially in the vicinity of the railroad station, which had the marks "of an everlasting crowd coming through it" and

Business district in Winnipeg (1919). First impressions of cities often set the tone of visits. The traveler was, or was not, impressed by his first glimpse of city streets, buildings, people.

a "begrimed and much used aspect." But the station platform was made of plank, as were the adjacent sidewalks, and he gave up the notion of London and thought instead of Chicago, especially as he spotted a dozen dollar-a-day hotels upon leaving the depot. Around the corner he found a "touch of Liverpool and a dash of the east end of Toronto" in the telegraph poles and wires and wide roadway. The buildings became larger and more important, and he could count as many banks as previously he had counted hotels. The Union Jack flew over city hall, with its war monument and bust of Queen Victoria in front.[5]

Foreign tourists were often overwhelmed by the strangeness of American cities since it was hard for them to draw convenient parallels with other places. At first, Lord Kinross found only confusion on the streets of New York City. He was unable to comprehend the whole, having eyes only for details. He wrote: "Its so unlike Europe in the sense that there's so little to look at. Little pleasure for the eyes, as you pace the streets. No graceful buildings, no trees, no people—at least they haven't yet become people to me. And are they people to each other, this hurrying heedless mass?" Anthony Jenkinson found himself preoccupied with petty things: "Corner news stands where the morning papers were sold at seven o'clock on the previous evening, the infinite number of soda fountains, the hot-dog stands, the spurts of steam coming up from unexpected places in the streets, and the traffic signals, mile upon mile of them, all changing color together."[6]

No city was more impressive than New York City when approached by ship, for its harbor approach stood in a class by itself and did not need comparisons. In 1908, John Van Dyke stood at his ship's rail, the distant skyline lifting higher and higher as the ship neared its pier. The deck buzzed with excited passengers. Ships moved in the harbor, whistles shrieking and bells ringing. The city's waterfront glowed in the evening half-light. Soon he was in the pier shed, getting bags and boxes together for the customs inspection, the crowd moving, gesturing, calling, perspiring. Then into a cab and away to the hotel. He wrote: "West Street is crowded with trucks, drays, carts, cabs, cars, trolleys that tangle into knots and bunches and then somehow untangle; the pavement is broken by car tracks and an occasional hole into which wheels drop with a thud and come out with a jerk; the dingy battered-looking buildings that line the east side of the street, the cheap and gaudy signs, the barrel skids across the sidewalks, the lampless lamp posts, the garbage cans, the stained awnings, are all somewhat disturbing. Dull-looking women sit on the low stoops and survey the street in which dirty children are playing among the standing drays or ash barrels or coal heaps." After a flourish of the whip, his cab driver deposited him at an ornate Fifth Avenue hotel. "Carriages in plush and velvet, ladies in silk and satins, flunkies and footmen in lacings and facings, pages in gloves and buttons, blend in a gorgeous confusion about the entrances. Within there are glimpses of marble and gilding, oriental rugs and hurrying porters, telegraph boys, call boys."[7]

Orienting to the City

Tourists were aided in their exploration of cities by guidebooks and pamphlets. Boosters revelled in the use of statistics to impress visitors with a city's size and underlying economic strength, and, more important, a city's potential for continued growth and increased commercial power. Julian Street found himself regaled everywhere with "inspiring statistics concerning the population of 'our city,' the seating capacity of the auditorium, the number of banks, the amount of their clearings, and the quantity of belt buckles annually manufactured." He was amazed by the variety of things cities could be first in. "It is a miserable city, indeed, which is first in nothing at all," he observed. Detroit in 1914, for example, was first in the manufacture of overalls, stoves, varnish, salt, adding machines, pharmaceuticals, aluminum castings, and, above all, automobiles. Webb Waldron learned that Milwaukee of 1922 was the greatest machinery manufacturing city in the world, and most of the machinery used on the Panama Canal was made there. The city was also the nation's leading producer of enamelware and tinware, toilet soaps, silk hosiery, and wheelbarrows.[8]

Promotional literature focused on city parks, museums, and other manifestations of cultural prowess and the good life. Milwaukee was said to have more miles of public bathing beach than Atlantic City. Kansas City was proud of its boulevards connecting its many parks, and in 1935, especially proud of its civic auditorium and its art museum. The chamber of commerce bulletin that Anthony Jenkinson read claimed: "Kansas City today is a homey and hospitable place for the resident, visitor, or convention delegate. It truthfully can be said of Kansas City that it blends the culture of the East, the vision of the West, the energy of the North, and the hospitality of the South."[9]

Much of the promotion was oriented to the future. Claims were made for cities not as they were, but as they were going to be. Julian Street read that "practically the whole front of Chicago along Lake Michigan will be occupied by parks and lagoons, and that Chicago expects . . . to have the finest waterfront of any city in the world." In Kansas City, Street's attention was continually called to the new construction, and he was clearly infected with the city's sense of progress. He wrote: "All over Kansas City old buildings are coming down to make place for new ones. Hills of clay are being gouged away and foundations dug; steel frames are shooting up. It seemed to me that I

could feel expansion in the very ground beneath my feet." But
J. B. Priestley was not so easily swayed. He thought that copy-
writers in the publicity departments of local chambers of commerce showered their adjectives on places like gushing oil
wells. "These professional enthusiasts are ruining travel for us.
No reality can hope to compete with their purple eruptions.
What is this real world after those shiny folders?"[10]

Journalists who intended to publish their observations
usually sought out personal guides at the local chamber of commerce. Guides cut short the journalist's need to research a city.
But local boosters were seldom unbiased, and many were totally taken in by their own rhetoric in a partially if not completely
unreal world. Webb Waldron took a tour of Ashland, Wisconsin, in 1922. The car traveled out an avenue that had a muddy
parkway down its center, on out past the last staked-out street
and street sign, and into open farm land. Most of the houses and
barns were built of log, having been constructed by Finns and
Scandinavians. His guide exclaimed: "Room for a city! Look at
it! Look! Miles and miles! Did you ever see anything like it?
Room for a hundred thousand? Five hundred thousand! Look
at that sweep of land!" Waldron wrote: "We squinted our eyes,
and thought hard, trying to see rows of ornamented lamp-posts
instead of telegraph-poles, cement sidewalks instead of ditches, apartment hotels . . . instead of log houses, limousines instead of tractors."[11]

Tourists could also become oriented to cities by what
they read. Before going to Chicago, George Birmingham read
Upton Sinclairs' account of the slaughter of pigs, and he read
Frank Norris's account of wheat trading. He wrote: "I had a
vague idea that Chicago was both better and worse than other
places, that God and the devil had joined battle there more definitely than elsewhere." Friends and acquaintances passed on
information and impressions. When Birmingham announced
his intention to go to Atlantic City, some of his friends had said:
"You won't enjoy *that* place." Other friends varied the emphasis in a way flattering to his sense of cultivated gentility. They
said: "*You* won't enjoy that place." Foreign visitors were especially struck by the American and Canadian willingness to aid

travelers in their sightseeing. Ilya Ilf and Eugene Petrov found hospitality everywhere to be "limitless." It far outstripped "everything possible or conceivable of its kind" in the Soviet Union. They wrote: "New friends were filled with one desire: to show us everything that we would want to see, to go with us wherever we'd like to go, to explain everything to us that we did not understand."[12]

Commercial sightseeing tours were available in all the major cities. Edward Hungerford encountered a barker near the White House calling, "See'n Washington! A brilliant trip of two hours through the homes of wealth an' fashion, with a lecture explainin' every point of interest an' fame." Hungerford mounted the open-air streetcar and was soon passing along Washington's streets as the guide rattled off through his megaphone: "Site of first p'lice station in Washington, oldest hotel in Washington, Washington's Chinatown." Hungerford wrote: "You sit back complacently in your seat and smack your mental lips at the sight of the mansion of the man who owns three banks; of him who, the lecturer solemnly affirms, is the president of the Whiskey Trust; at a third where dwells 'the richest minister in the United States.' A little schoolteacher from Hartford, Connecticut, makes profuse notes in a neat leather-covered book." Gordon Brinley and his wife rode the sightseeing trolley in Quebec City. From the motorman's level the seats of the open car rose step by step like bleachers, affording everyone an unobstructed view. The car swung through the narrow streets, children racing alongside acclaiming the car's entry into their neighborhood and cheering them on to the next.[13]

Sightseeing buses were first introduced in New York City at the turn of the century. The Royal Blue Line advertised nine electric buses for "Seeing New York—Uptown, Downtown, and over the great bridges to Brooklyn." In many cities tourists could tour by boat. Sightseeing yachts, like the *Halcyon* and *Tourist*, sailed from New York City's Battery Park. A 1917 advertisement read: "All around New York Harbor and Manhattan Island in about 2½ hours. All points of interest explained by lecturer. Up the East River, under all bridges, past the Navy

Yard, Blackwell's Island, Hell Gate, through Harlem Ship Canal, and down the Hudson past Palisades, Grant's Tomb, skyscrapers of New York, ocean steamers, warships, emigrant station, Statue of Liberty."[14]

In Pursuit of Personal Memories

Tourists returning to cities previously visited or to cities previously lived in had personal reminiscences to direct their explorations. The view was not forward to a golden future so much as it was backward to a golden past, with a sense of loss felt for places changed. The sense of loss was especially acute among travelers returning to childhood places where progress had played havoc with landmarks cherished in memory. Henry James returned to New York City and wrote: "One's extremest youth had been full of New York, and one was absurdly finding it again, meeting it at every turn, in sights, sounds, smells, even in the chaos of confusion and change; a process under which, verily, recognition became more difficult." Julian Street found "signs of a sad, indefinite decay" on Chicago's southside where he had grown up. He wrote: "Strange sensations, those which come to a man when he visits, after a lapse of years, the places he knew best in childhood. The changes. The things which are unchanged. The familiar unfamiliarity. The vivid recollections which loom suddenly, like silent ships, from out of the fog of things forgotten."[15]

Expositions

Cities promoted themselves by creating fairs and expositions. Not only were tourists attracted to spend vacation dollars, but they returned home full of a city's sights, and, presumably, admiration for its accomplishments. World's fairs were held at St. Louis in 1904, Portland, Oregon, in 1905, Seattle in 1909, San Francisco and San Diego in 1915, Chicago in 1933, and New York City in 1939. Harry MacFadden described the Lewis and Clark Exposition at Portland: "There were ten large exhibition palaces on the grounds, erected in the mission style of architecture, and treated in a beautiful and harmonious scheme of color. With the large expanse of water, artistic bridges, extensive lawns and multitudinous flower beds, with 20,000 rose bushes in full bloom, the grounds in daylight presented a very pretty sight, and at night thousands of glowing fountains, flowers, trees, terraces, lakes, lagoons and massive picturesque buildings."[16]

Every fair had a midway of gaudy attractions blatantly advertised by billboards and electric signs. At Portland it was called "the Trail," at Seattle "the Pike," and at San Diego "the Prado." Each fair had a theme. Seattle honored its connections with Alaska and the Yukon. San Francisco and San Diego celebrated the opening of the Panama Canal. Chicago and New York City celebrated the future. Lewis Gannett was disappointed by Chicago's display. He found the much discussed "modernism" a sham. The sharp right angles copied from books on modernism were laid onto the buildings and were not integral expressions of function. "Everywhere," he wrote, "the straining for effect was obvious." Anthony Jenkinson found other contrivances excessive. He saw the world's largest thermometer, standing 227 feet high, and the world's largest foun-

Hotel Sherman in Chicago (1934). The hotel was the tourist's "home away from home" in the city. By 1934 the Hotel Sherman had added a parking garage to attract automobile tourists.

tain, shooting 68,000 gallons of water seventy-five feet into the air every minute. He saw the world's largest sky ride suspended 210 feet in the air between two 628 foot towers, 1,850 feet apart. At night he saw the world's largest searchlight. Clearly, the fair was "the world's largest display of the world's largest things." At the Western Union building, visitors to the Chicago Fair could send one of several "special greetings": "The Century of Progress is the thrill of the age. Love to all." Or, "Entire family enjoying visit. Starting back tomorrow—tired but satisfied." Or, "Wish you were here. Don't miss Century of Progress."[17]

City Sojourns

Formality governed the tone of city visits. Tourists abided by hotel dress codes and organized their days by hotel schedules for meals and housekeeping. The hotel room was at once a place from which to learn about a new city, and a buffer from the city's uncertainties. The longer Lord Kinross stayed in his New York City hotel room the more isolated he became. Acquaintanceships forged in the hotel bar proved superficial and unrewarding. New York City, he found, was a city of the "lonely crowd." Society was not cohesive, but broken up into an infinite number of social fragments based primarily on people's work, the "fraternity of the job." A chance encounter and an invitation to share an apartment in a quiet residential neighborhood changed everything. Kinross wrote of his visit: "It was draining the life out of me. But now I have friends and back it flows. Intimacy, I suppose because of the inherent loneliness of the place, comes quickly if it does come. Hearts are worn on the sleeve. And the city itself falls into perspective. You belong." New York City came quickly into focus, developing a coherent personality in terms of neighborhood life. "It was a relief now to dress casually in sweater and slacks—staying far from the maddening skyscrapers for days at a time, enjoying that sense of ease and human proportions which broad streets and low buildings afforded."[18]

For most tourists, however, hotels remained their only home in the city. On short visits, the hotel symbolized the city. Emily Post wrote: "You arrive at night and leave early in the morning and all you see is one street driving in, and another going out, and a lobby, dining-room and a bedroom or two at the hotel." At Des Moines she learned nothing more about the city than what she read in the morning newspaper. "Des Moines is ever going forward!" the newspaper said. "With our new thirteen-story building and the new gilded dome of the Capitol, Des Moines towers above the other cities of the State like a lone cottonwood on the prairies." A decently appointed and well-serviced hotel was a city's best advertisement. Irvin Cobb commented: "The stranger may forget your proposed civic center or plans for a Great White Way, but if at your leading hotel he badly was bedded and poorly baited he will remember your town forever after as a spot to be cursed and avoided."[19]

Staying at Terre Haute in Indiana, Theodore Dreiser enumerated the requirements of a truly fine hostelry:

> There must be (1) a group of flamboyantly uniformed hall boys and porters, all braids and buttons, whose chief, if not sole duty, is to exact gratuities from the unwilling and yet ecstatic visitor; (2) an hotel clerk, or three or five, who will make him feel that he is a mere upstart or intruder, and that it is only by the generosity of a watchful and yet kindly management . . . that he is permitted to enter at all; (3) maids, manicuresses, and newstand salesladies, who are present solely to make him understand what he has missed by marrying, and how little his wife knows about dress, or taste, or life; (4) a lobby, lounging room, shoeshining parlor and barber shop, done entirely in imitation onyx; (5) a dining room in imitation of one of the principal chambers of the Palace of Vairsigh [*sic*]; (6) a grill or men's restaurant, made to look exactly like a western architect's dream of a Burgundian baronial hall; (7) a head waiter who can be friends only with millionaires of their equivalent, the local richest men.[20]

But to Charles Finger, the typical hotel was a fancy lobby with loungers and polite deadbeats who lived elsewhere and ate at cheap restaurants, but who used hotel stationery. It was a desk clerk with a plaster-of-paris smile, and a bellhop who did unnecessary things and stood around expectantly, waiting for a

Lobby of New Rosslyn Hotel in Los Angeles (c. 1920). Hotels emphasized the public spaces of lobbies, dining rooms, and cocktail lounges over the private spaces of the guest rooms, which were often cramped.

tip. It was stiff and angular bedroom furniture and insufficient cakes of soap.[21]

Foreign visitors appreciated North American hotels more. Frenchman Paul Morand thought the big American hotels were like small towns; they met all his requirements. "You can get your railway-tickets there, theatre-tickets, Turkish bath, medical advice; you can be massaged, you can hire the services of a secretary or a shorthand typist, and give your broker orders to a stock exchange." Soviet visitors Ilya Ilf and Eugene Petrov were delighted to find private bathrooms with hot and cold water wherever they went. Stationery, telegraph blanks, postcards with views of the hotel, laundry bags, printed laundry blanks, and a shoe-shining cloth were valued novelties. The Gideon bibles elicited comment, their tables of content directing readers to various passages for "allaying spiritual doubts," for "family troubles," for "financial troubles," for "success in business." This latter page was always greasy with frequent use.[22]

City hotels were primarily male habitats until World War II. Hotel services catered primarily to masculine needs: barber shops, meeting rooms, clerical help. Hotel food tended toward the masculine in taste: red meat, starch, and heavy seasoning. What hotel dining rooms lost on food they made up on liquor.[23] Women were given separate entrances and separate waiting rooms. As late as 1950, the Statler hotel chain estimated that four-fifths of its guests were men, with three quarters traveling on business: 25 percent salesmen, 20 percent business executives, and 19 percent professional people.[24] Emily Post stayed mainly at hotels of the "saloon-front and ladies' entrance-in-the-back" variety. She writes of "traveling men to the right of us and traveling men to the left of us, with hats on the backs of their heads and cigars . . . tilted in the corners of their mouths. . . . Traveling men standing and leaning, traveling men leaning and sitting, but always men in cigar smoke, talking and lounging and taking their rest in the lobbies." Thomas Wilby saw the hotel lobby as a man's world of smoke and loungers. Women absented themselves "because of the smoke, spittoon,

Guest room at the Warwick Hotel in Toronto (1954).

and the all-pervading, monopolizing masculinity which had forgotten its best manners."[25] With prohibition, city hotels began to cater more to women. Coffee shops and tea rooms were introduced to stimulate the luncheon trade; beauty shops and dress shops appeared. Women were encouraged to use front entrances.

Travelers seldom went more than a few nights without experiencing some discomfort. In New Orleans, Walter Citrine slept badly every night. The streetcars rattled and banged under his window. The sirens of police cars and fire trucks screamed constantly. Of Des Moines, Emily Post wrote: "When I went to bed the electric lights would not turn on, and as no one answered the bell I gave up ringing and went to bed in the dark. The thermometer was about 95; everything felt gritty, and in front of my eyes blinked mockingly an intermittent electric sign which in letters six feet high flashed all through the night about a snow-white laundry!"[26] Air conditioners, introduced in the 1950s, did much to reduce outside noise and glare, and keep room temperatures cool. But no hotel room, no matter how luxuriously appointed, could replace home comforts completely.

Hotels provided tourists with opportunities to see and know one another, although discerning travelers, like Lord Kinross, might have found hotel encounters superficial. Harrison Rhodes sat in his Atlantic City hotel observing people. He wrote: "You overhear the gentlemen at the next table to yours . . . say to the pretty woman who is lunching with him, 'I'm going to buy my wife a new string of pearls.' You catch no more, but you feel sure that this is the least that he can—and ought to—do." In Chicago, John Steinbeck was given his room before it had been cleaned. Steinbeck began to investigate the previous occupant in the bits and pieces left behind. He knew where he lived from the laundry strips from several shirts, and that he was married from the letter in the wastebasket that he had started to his wife: "Darling—Everything is going O.K. Tried to call your aunt but no answer. I wish you were here with me. This is a lonesome town." He had had a visitor: a woman who wore very pale lipstick and who left an ashtray full of cigarette butts. They had drunk Jack Daniels, a whole bottle. Steinbeck concluded: "A human occupying a room for one night prints his character, his biography, his recent history, and sometimes his future plans and hopes."[27]

A tourist could also express his personality in what he took with him. Hotels inadvertently provided tourists with souvenirs—perhaps the most significant souvenirs a city could yield, given the amount of time most tourists spent in their hotel rooms. William Saroyan wrote from London, Ontario: "Before leaving the room, I gathered together the usual souvenirs—stationery, ashtray, a small towel, and the *Don't Disturb* sign."[28] Such theft was epidemic. For example, in 1936, New York City's Hotel Pennsylvania reported 2,000 face towels and 300 bath towels stolen each month.[29]

Eating in restaurants not only provided sustenance, but provided opportunities to be entertained. One could interact socially with friends and acquaintances or merely observe other people. Restaurants varied from the swank and expensive to the utilitarian and inexpensive, since literally any taste could be accommodated in a large city. Hotels depended upon their restaurants for a substantial proportion of their income. Typically, only half of a hotel's profits came from room rentals.[30] But to really know a city, one had to venture beyond one's hotel to sample the delights of a variety of eating places, restaurants known not only for their food, but for their decor as well. In New York City in 1910, there was Rector's, with its mosaics of stained glass, its paintings, and its marbles half hidden in a forest of green palms. There was Canfield's Bronze Door, famous for its carved mahogany railing of dancing nymphs, sweeping up the staircase. There was Murray's with its colored lights reflecting through rooms filled with mirrors. And there was Delmonicos with its subdued hum of soft laughter mingled with the tinkle of silver and crystal.[31]

Edward Hungerford frequented New York City's less expensive restaurants. He wrote: "There are little restaurants that cast a glamour over their poor food by thrusting out hints of a magic folk named Bohemians who dine night after night at their dirty tables. There are others who with a Persian name seek to allure the ill-informed, some stout German places giving the substantial cheer of the Fatherland, beyond them restaurants phrasing themselves in the national dishes and the cooking of every land in the world, save our own." Inexpensive food could be had in a multitude of cafes, grills, or chop houses. Paul Morand was astonished by their number. "Thousands of beings are sitting side by side, hat on head, in a single row as in a stable, putting down food. . . . They stoop over their plates of meat balls; and behind them others stand waiting their turn." Of the typical customer, he wrote: "He orders coffee at the same time as his soup, and gulps down the electrically cooked meal which is thrust before him. . . . So you find all Americans dyspeptic at forty," Morand continued, "as the thousands of medicines proclaimed in the newspapers bear witness."[32]

Some cities were noted for their fine food, especially cities with large ethnic populations. Ruth Wood wrote of San Francisco: "Down on Broadway are Italian basements and the mellifluous menus which afford a good meal for 50 cents. One climbs the clean stairs of rebuilt Chinatown to drink tea brewed in glazed bowls, to crush the bossed shell of lichee nut and prod with a two-tined fork sugared roots and the rind of melon." But New Orleans was the most celebrated city in North America for its food, mixing as it did Creole, Cajun, southern, and certain European eating traditions. Restaurants, open fronted with big ceiling fans, served sheepshead and red snapper, terrapin, snapping turtle, crabs, shrimps, grouse, and wild turkey, along with such special New Orleans delicacies as bouillabaisses and gumbos. At such celebrated eateries as Antoine's, Arnaud's, Broussard's, La Louisiane, Kolb's, and Tujacque's, one could eat huitres en coquille a la Rockefeller or pompano en papillote or crayfish bisque or red beans and rice or sauerkraut and wiener-schnitzel.[33]

Seeking the Illicit

Prohibition proved disasterous to America's quality restaurant trade. Alcohol could not be served openly, leading to the popularity of "speakeasys" and "nightclubs" that siphoned away restaurant business. The first nightclub in New York City, Club Deauville, opened on East 59th Street in 1921, and by the end of the year some 5,000 clubs had opened, mostly in midtown Manhattan. By 1930 an estimated 32,000 clubs had been established.[34] As Paul Morand observed, most were situated in basements and were identifiable by the large numbers of empty cars standing outside. Doors were opened only after visitors had been scrutinized through a door-catch or a peephole. He wrote: "There is a truly New York atmosphere of humbug in the whole thing. The interior is that of a criminal house; shutters are closed in full daylight. . . . Italians with a too familiar manner, or plump, blue pseudo-bullfighters, carrying bunches of monastic keys guide you through the deserted rooms." Andre LaFond was telephoned by a bootlegger in his hotel room. The man was systematically working his way through the passenger list of the recently arrived *Ile de France*.[34]

Throughout the 1930s, the most popular nightclubs in New York City included places like the Cotton Club, Small's Paradise, and Connie's Inn up in Harlem. Tourists not only imbibed in the illegalities of drink, but flirted with the color line as well. Europeans were especially attracted by America's black subculture. Morand found Harlem "a place of exotic gaiety, of picturesque human confusion." "They shatter the mechanical rhythm of America," he wrote of Harlem's blacks. But the contrived nightclubs hardly presented the white visitor with Harlem's real face. A. G. MacDonnell paid the "customary visit of ceremony to Harlem." Every British traveler had always been to Harlem, and so every British traveler would always continue to go to Harlem. It was one of the things that was "done," for when he returned, the first, and often the only, question that would be put to him was, "Did you go to Harlem?" If he faltered, stammered a little, and replied, "Well, not exactly," there would be a painful silence and then a change of conversation. He went in the small hours of the morning to a club "run entirely to attract strangers" and saw as much of the real Harlem as a tourist "sees of the African jungle sitting in a cocktail bar in Cape Town." He found the club a "loathsome place" in which "the visitor does not dislike and despise the negro singers and dancers quite so heartily as the negroes themselves dislike and despise the visitors."[35]

Prostitution was a vice universal to all cities. Reformer Samuel Wilson estimated the number of houses of prostitution in Chicago at six hundred in 1910. He wrote: "Prostitution is an appalling evil in Chicago. One can scarcely look in any direction without seeing some evidence of it. Street walkers parade the most prominent thoroughfares, dance houses and low concert halls flaunt their gaudy signs in public, and houses of ill-fame are conducted with a boldness unequalled anywhere in the world." Periodically, a city would close its houses in a burst of municipal reform, or undertake to control prostitution by restricting it geographically to set locations or districts. Nathan Ashe wrote of Butte, Montana in 1936: "Right in back of the town's main street and half a block from police headquarters was Mercury Alley, a passageway wide enough for a car to drive through, and along one side of it were show windows with indirect stage lighting. And whores sat in these windows, a whore to each window, dressed up and painted and lighted up to please, and on top of each window was the name of the whore: Gloria, Maria, Rose, Violet."[36]

Tourists were attracted to cities, for only there could modern society be observed in its complete range of tradition and experiment. In cities the best and the worse of human inclination found ready outlet. Although tourists might deviate little from normal routines and activities while in the city, an urban sojourn left the impression that extraordinary opportunities, whether seized or not, had been available for the taking. The potential for excitement and adventure was high. For most tourists such potential was adequate enough reward. Contented with the novelty of a change of scene, most tourists thrived in the buffering comfort of the hotel room, the restaurant, and other city attractions, including fairs and expositions, contrived for visitor comfort and safety. The semblance of adventure was enough. Subdued excitement was sufficient. As often as not, a tourist's first impressions or past memories, mixed with the stock promotions of guides and guidebooks, sufficed to give a city meaning. Fun and relaxation in the experiencing of a city was more important than the sense of full comprehension based on real exploration.

CHAPTER THIRTEEN

THE METROPOLIS AS AN ATTRACTION

> As one walks and speculates among all this visible panorama, beat-
> ing one's brains to catch some passing snapshots of it, watching,
> listening, imagining, the whole hullabaloo becomes extraordinarily
> precious. The great faulty hodgepodge of the city, its very pave-
> ments and house-corners, becomes vividly clear. One longs to clutch
> the whole meaning in some sudden embrace—to utter some testa-
> ment of affection that will speak plain truth.
>
> Christopher Morley, *Travels In Philadelphia*

Tourists sought to explain cities by using broad generalizations.[1] Stereotyping involved images sustained by beliefs
and attitudes variously attached to elements in cityscapes that
stood as icons to symbolize the whole. Landscape elements that
served as icons included: skylines, bird's-eye views, major
streets and nodal points, unusual interior spaces, highly visible
landmarks, and clearly recognized districts. In addition, every
city was known by its prevailing urban fabric: the manner by
which the city blended together as a vernacular form.

Some cities were more imageable than others. Writing in
1917, Julian Street thought only six North American cities were
truly distinctive. New York City was important as the largest
city in the world, combining "the wonder, the beauty, the sor-
didness, and the shame of a great metropolis." San Francisco
was a visual delight: "so vivid, so alive, so golden." Washington was a "clean, white splendor," and the "embodiment of a
national dream." Quebec City was "like some fortified town in
France," more European than North American. Charleston
was a "sweet and aristocratic city," and a "museum of tradition
and elegance." Finally, New Orleans was a "most perfectly
foreign little tract of land," distinctive for successive cultures
residual in its landscape.[2] Each traveler saw each city in his own
way according to his own personality and interests. Nonetheless, certain images in every city were widely shared.

Some urbanscapes were positive in their charge, while
other places carried neutral or even negative valences. One

tourist wrote of Los Angeles: "Los Angeles is a white city. It gives the effect of an exposition, a world's fair placed against the background of the mountains. There is about it the impression of a beautiful mirage, likely to fade into unreality." St. Louis, on the other hand, held little mystique. There was little of the picturesque and the romantic in the look of the city; even its utilitarian face showed poorly. Julian Street wrote: "St. Louis leads the world in shoes, stoves, and tobacco. It is the world's greatest market for hardware, lumber, and raw furs. . . . it makes more woodenware, more native chemicals, more beer. But what it does not do is *look* as though it led. Its streets are, for the most part, lacking in distinction. There is no center at which a visitor might stop, knowing by instinct that he was at the city's heart."[3]

Skylines

Skylines offered a quick and easy way to size up a city. Skylines spoke of what a city had been, and what it was intending to become. Low skylines were indicative of slow growth and an adherence to tradition. Tall buildings silhouetted boldly against the sky spoke of power and a quest for new ways. Skylines were ideal instruments for generalization, being necessarily viewed from a distance, since distance obscured minutae and only broad outlines remained for the seeing. North American skylines spoke of worshipful success. Tall office towers were evidence of business enterprise-turned-religion. Theodore Dreiser wrote: "Skyscrapers—these inevitable evidences of America's local mercantile ambitions, [are] quite like the cathedrals religionists of the twelfth and thirteenth centuries loved to build." John Kouwenhoven found all urban skylines paradoxical. They didn't make any sense in human terms. They resulted from "insane politics, greed, competitive ostentation, megalomania, the worship of false gods" and their by-products were traffic jams, bad ventilation, and noise, among other ills. But the net result was, illogically enough, "one of the most exaltedly beautiful things man had ever made." The total effect was made of innumerable buildings, each in competition (for height, or glamor, or efficiency, or respectability) with all the others. He wrote: "Each goes its own way, as it were, in a carnival of rugged architectural individualism. And yet—as witness

Manhattan skyline, New York City (c. 1935). Tourists used icons or sets of icons to generalize cities as visual displays and to stereotype their meaning as places. Skylines were prime among the symbols of a city's worth.

the universal feeling of exaltation and aspiration which the skyline as a whole evokes—out of this irrational, unpleasant, and often infuriating chaos, an unforeseen unity has evolved."[4]

Travelers reacted to skylines by comparing them and evaluating their visual impact.[5] Some sought a sense of harmonious fit, reacting negatively when individual buildings failed to blend. Henry James, writing in 1907, found New York City's "multitudinous skyscrapers" standing up to the view from the water, like "extravagant pins in a cushion already overplanted, and stuck in as in the dark, anywhere and anyhow." Some travelers appreciated the sense of punctuation which buildings made against the sky. John Van Dyke found New York City more striking, more impressive, than any other city anywhere. "It looms with a feeling of tremendous bulk and power. The mass of it made one realize the energy back of it. It excited wonder as to its fashioning, and overawed with its possibilities."[6]

Other travelers mused about the sense of layering. The most impressive skylines rose by levels to a climax of high towers at the center. Will Irwin wrote of lower Manhattan in 1927: "At the foot stands the classic Custom House. . . . Above that, roofs and pillared balconies rise tier on tier as though they cling to the hillside; and finally at the summit upsprings that temple which is the wings and towers of the Standard Oil Building." Lower Manhattan appeared to Irwin a sophisticated and glorified version of the traditional Indian pueblo of the Southwest. Many tourists delighted in the abstract form and giant scale of buildings taken individually and in combination. One tourist marveled at "the 'giant bird-cage skyscrapers' whose interstices were filled with stone and concrete." They depended for their effect, not upon ornament, which appeared trivial and inapposite, but upon their mass. The vast masses that loomed over Wall Street and Broadway in Manhattan appeared to him austere, like the pyramids. They seemed the work of giants, and not of men.[7]

Skylines of skyscrapers not only symbolized individual cities, providing visual stimulus in the process, but they signified America as the land of modernity and progress. Stuart Mais, an English visitor, wrote of New York City's towers: "They are more than beautiful. They symbolize the whole spirit of this nation; its forthrightness, its love of experiment, adventure, and extremes; its sublime faith in human endeavor." Mark Pepys, another Englishman, thought New York City's skyline "symbolical of the age of crowded progress."[8]

Bird's-eye Views

The view from above offered memorable means of knowing a city. Again, removal to a distant point generalized urbanscapes, removing trivial detail and emphasizing broad patterns. In San Francisco, Rollo Brown climbed Telegraph Hill to glimpse the city. His appetite whetted, he walked downtown to the tallest building, obtained the key to the roof, and stepped out into a world of grand panorama. "I felt as if I had the key to the city—and I had. The door opened out to a view not to be matched in America: plenty of well-kept city covering many hills, gigantic bridges suspended over vast expanses of clean water."[9]

But it was New York City where bird's-eye views were

obligatory. Paul Morand visited in 1929 the Woolworth Building's fifty-sixth floor. The wind tore at his clothing, a young
couple embraced, Japanese tourists laughed and took pictures,
German tourists bought postcards. He wrote: "How can one
describe from such a height this miniature metropolis? Below,
these flat planes and chessboards are not streets, but the terraces of the highest buildings, topped with towers like the risers
of staircases." Smoke or steam swirled in the cold air like
plumes on helmets. He continued: "From up here the plan of
New York is easily read in all the simplicity of its enormous grill,
with its sunny avenues and its cross-streets filled with blue
shadows." Then it was time to go. The elevator fell floor by floor
causing his ears to sing. He was back in the crowd that flooded
Broadway. He wrote: "Lifting my head, I try to fix the spot
where I stood a moment before, but I see nothing but oblique
monuments sliding and toppling backwards."[10]

Hulbert Footner went to the top of the Empire State
Building. There he found "one of the great sights of earth." It
was a "panorama of power and beauty and terror such as the
world never offered before." It gave a quite ordinary man

Bird's-eye view of lower Manhattan (c. 1930). Bird's-eye views helped tourists
orient to cities as places.

"some god-like moments." No sound came up from below, but a low growl: distance generalizing sound as well as sight. Footner continued: "Seen from this height the city becomes something that you can encompass in a glance. The printed map you have been familiar with since schooldays, comes true. Below you lies an animated model town with toy ships moving on the rivers, miniature trains crawling along the elevated tracks, microscopic motor cars in the streets and pinpoint humans."[11]

Ilya Ilf and Eugene Petrov marvelled at the view from their hotel room high above Lexington Avenue. The city spread out on several planes. On the upper level were the tops of skyscrapers taller than the hotel. They were capped with spires of glass or gold gleaming in the sun, or with towers with large clocks. Below was a level of chimney stacks and skylights, and of roof gardens with their skimpy trees, little brick paths, and small fountains. And then came the fundamental plane of the street, which required leaning out of the window to see. "There, as in reversed binoculars, one could see a tiny crossing with tiny automobiles, pedestrians, newspapers strewn on the pavement, and even two rows of shining buttons attached to the lanes where pedestrians are allowed to cross the street." Lord Kinross looked at Manhattan's skyscrapers from his hotel. "No longer a pigmy on the pavement, I now saw them on a less intimidating scale, as a large mountain is seen from the top of a small one." It was a "truly vertical landscape receding in perspective and rising to a diversity of levels bewildering to one familiar only with the horizontal world."[12]

Paths through the City

Tourists knew cities according to the ways by which they moved about; as Kevin Lynch has established, people know a city from the paths they follow.[13] Life and vitality made streets vivid. Streets, like skylines and bird's-eye views, could fix a city firmly in memory. Every city had its show streets where important businesses and other institutions elbowed one another in competitive display. Broadway and Fifth Avenue dominated in New York City. In Chicago it was State Street and Michigan Avenue. In Atlanta it was Peachtree Street, in San Francisco Market Street, in Vancouver Georgia Street.

The Italian Antonio Scarfoglio spent a day wandering about downtown Chicago "with nose to the wind and eyes to heaven." Streets did not tie together as they did in Italy; they appeared to be "a consequence and not a determining cause." They existed only because buildings could not stand in isolation. In Italy streets were not only useful, but beautiful. Scarfoglio wrote: "A man is complete and perfect as a citizen in so far as he loves the street and takes pleasure therein. This is not so in America. It is merely a means of communication and traffic." North American cities seemed to lack street life rooted in locality. People moved briskly, always seeming to pass through to some other place, and never seeming to fully belong anywhere.[14]

Automobiles increased the alien nature of North American city streets. Pedestrians were pushed aside by the rapid flow of motor vehicles. Lord Kinross walked New York City's streets obediently stopping before the signs that blinked "Don't Walk." He wrote: "The cars pouring past us were all vividly parti-coloured—yellow and violet and crimson and turquoise—like dodgem cars in a fairground." He continued: "The traffic moves in a series of convulsive jerks, worrying to the nerves, from one set of lights to the next." To Kinross the streets appeared to go on unendingly, with never a curve or an oblique angle to add interest. "But," he concluded, "they're chaotic in height and in proportions, each building for itself, regardless of its neighbour and of the street below." The buildings were all out of scale with the people, even with most of the people ensconced in automobiles.[15]

Broadway was New York City's main thoroughfare during much of the early twentieth century. Many of the city's prominent landmarks could be seen along its route. As one visitor noted, the Broadway streetcar "plowed its way through scenes varied and appealing." It passed the Washington Arch in Greenwich Village, and Union Square, with its statues of Washington, La Fayette, and Lincoln, and Madison Square, with the clock in the Metropolitan Tower looming overhead. It passed the Flatiron Building and gave a fleeting glimpse to the many columned portico of the Pennsylvania Station several blocks away before entering Times Square. Another visitor

Herald Square, New York City (c. 1900). Major streets and squares were used to stereotype cityscapes. Elevated railroads were important "paths" by which tourists came to know cities.

writes: "A skyscraper stands side by side with a theatre built in the classic style with columns, capitals, and pediment, and . . . next door may be a one-story wooden candy store, four feet by six. If New York is a miniature world, Broadway is a miniature New York. All the rushing haste is there."[16]

Broadway was best seen at night. To Rupert Hughes, writing in 1904, Broadway was one long canyon of light. Even the shops that were closed displayed brilliantly illuminated windows. From most of the buildings hung great living letters. Some of these winked out and flashed up again at regular intervals. "The hunt was always for something new, something different, something that caught the eye by its super-ingenuity, its hyper-phosphorescence among all the other radiances." He exclaimed: "Broadway, the most brilliant street in all the world, was aglow, agleam, ablaze!" Paul Morand, writing in 1929, found light that was not only white, but yellow, red, green, mauve, blue; lights that were not only fixed, but moving, tumbling, running, turning, zigzagging, rolling, dancing, epileptic." He concluded: "The electric lamp is no longer a lighting device, it is a machine for fascinating, a machine for obliterating. Electricity bedizens this weary throng, determined not to go home, determined to spend its money, determined to blind itself with false daylight."[17] Centered on Times Square, Broadway's "Great White Way" improved with each passing decade.

Fifth Avenue in Midtown Manhattan, once the residential street of millionaires, became New York City's principal retail street. Paul Morand wrote: "The American women makes herself supreme on Fifth Avenue pavements with overwhelming assurance, happiness and superiority. She goes shopping before lunching at the Ritz or the Colony Club. All the furred fauna of the creation seem to have been butchered to clothe these women—sable, badger, gray squirrel, Persian lamb." Here the luxury hotels were located: the Plaza, the Savoy-Plaza, the Sherry Netherland. Morand stopped to look at the rare books at Dutton's, to glance in the windows at Kohler's, with its fancy bathroom fixtures, and to browse the window at Thomas Cook's travel bureau for even more exotic places to visit.[18]

Not all New York streets were glamorous, especially those under the elevated railroads where property values were depressed. A. G. MacDonnell found the elevated lines "weird contraptions" that lacked the qualities America yearned for most. They were neither the "swift silent efficiency of modernity" nor the "quiet dignity of age." Their noise, he thought, could drown a fair-sized artillery bombardment. But in 1934 a nickel took the tourist everywhere on the system, offering him, at a range of some twelve feet, fleeting glimpses into about ten thousand domestic interiors as he sped along.[19] Elevated railroads were important paths along which people, including tourists, came to know the city.

Nodal Points

In every city, life seemed to focus at certain key intersections or at plazas and squares central to the business district. Movement focused at railroad and rapid transit terminals. Nodes were places of interchange within a city where people came and went their various rounds. In New York City, Times, Madison, and Union Squares were important nodes, as were the Pennsylvania and Grand Central depots. In New Orleans, Jackson and LaFayette Squares served. In Detroit, it was Cadillac Square. In Montreal, it was Place d'Armes or Victoria Square or Dominion Square. Tourists oriented to cities from such focal points, often starting and ending sightseeing tours there. Cities were less imageable for the lack of clear nodes. One tourist wrote of Los Angeles: "Fifth Avenue is New York. Market Street is San Francisco. Paris is the Champs. Peking is the Forbidden City. But there isn't any place that is Los Angeles."[20]

On another scale, a city's entire central business district was a node. There the city's streets, railroads, and transit lines focused. Downtowns enjoyed maximum accessibility to places both within and without cities. Many tourists characterized the cities they visited exclusively in central business district terms. There was the city's ceremonial heart: the city in a ritual sense. There it appeared that its economy, politics, and society were focused. In some cities the lines of transportation defined the center clearly, even inscribing it boldly in the landscape. In Chicago, a loop of elevated railroads defined the city's heart both structurally and functionally, giving a name to the district: the "Loop."

Interior Spaces

Ceremonial enclosures of interior space made cities imageable. Paul Morand wandered in and out of buildings in New York City. He entered the marble lobby of the Cunard Building on Lower Broadway to gaze at the mosaics, each representing the voyage of a famous explorer, and the huge painted maps, each with vivid blue oceans. At the public library he found a vast reading room. A "close silence" filled the marble-floored room; the clicking of his hard-soled shoes reverberated in the quiet. Many tourists visited the New York Stock Exchange to verify expectations of turmoil and confusion. "Within this splendid temple one finds very little calm to match the gracious exterior," wrote one tourist. "About the trading posts, set like lighthouses in a sea of churning, roaring humanity, the brokers assemble, waving papers, watching the annunciator boards for a summons to the telephone, shouting, gyrating, moving in a patter that is never still."[21]

272

Landmarks

Landmarks stood out in contrast to their surroundings: buildings, monuments, or other features easily seen and thus easily remembered. They made good visual cues by which tourists could measure their movements about a city. Tourists did not move through but, rather, moved past landmarks, noting their peculiarities in passing. Landmarks stood as obvious icons. The Golden Gate Bridge symbolized San Francisco in the popular eye. The Chateau Frontenac Hotel atop Cape Diamond represented Quebec City. Cities without universally recognized landmarks suffered for lack of imageability. Webb Waldron wrote of Milwaukee: "We set out to explore. The downtown streets of Milwaukee have nothing distinctive in lay-out or architecture. There are no striking buildings or vistas. This might be the downtown of any one of a dozen unindividualized Middle-Western cities."[22]

New York City abounded with landmarks. The city was a

St. James Street in Montreal (c. 1905). Prominent landmarks, such as a city's post office or its prominent bank buildings, served as icons of places.

273

place of contrasts. John Van Dyke wrote: "If an office building soars twenty stories into the air, a bank near it will more than likely stop at a story and a half. If one lifts upward in terra-cotta, the other will flatten out in white marble." Skyscrapers made good landmarks for their visibility from a distance. They also made distinctive architectural statements unto themselves, romantic aspects of the city being on the summits of towering buildings where the architects burst into reminiscences of Ur of the Chaldees, the Hanging Gardens of Babylon, the Campaniles, domes and porticoes of Italy, and here and there the mosques and minarets of the East." One was always looking up to a sky filled with fantasy. Relatively few landmarks were old. North American cities lacked symbols of permanence. In New York City, only the churches seemed to symbolize changelessness. Once church spires dominated Manhattan's skyline, but in the twentieth century churches served more to tie tall office buildings back to earth as anchors in a restless sea. Their small scale offered counterpoints, relating the massive office towers to human forms on the street. Perhaps, Trinity Church was the most striking. As one visitor noted, "Trinity Church has a singularly suggestive position, right opposite the end of Wall Street—God in protest against mammon."[23]

Districts

Central business districts, as special zones of concentration within cities, were themselves characterized by areas of specialization. In New York City, Wall Street was the traditional financial center, midtown Fifth Avenue the exclusive retail area, and Broadway at Times Square the principal entertainment district. Such concentration of economic function usually produced clearly identifiable townscapes: localities characterized by distinctive kinds of people and activities. Metropolises were also differentiated socially. Extremes of wealth and poverty created their own peculiar landscapes: districts of privilege and poverty. The more diligent tourists sought evidences of social diversity in cityscapes, especially evidences of ethnic and racial diversity. They were not satisfied solely with the institutional attractions of central business districts, which served as ceremonial front regions. They sought understanding of how people lived. They sought the back regions of city neighborhoods.

Boosters pointed to a city's elite as personifying a city's drive and ambition. Every city had its gentry class that forged the look of downtown through its business investments and political influences, and that retreated to exclusive residential streets and private clubs to display its wealth and power in extravagant architecture. To Julian Street, writing in 1917, the urban gentry class seemed divided three ways. There was the "affluent group" who kept butlers and several automobiles and who traveled extensively. The ladies gave much time to societies founded on ancestry. This group shouldered social responsibility when not pursuing personal gain. The "fast group" considered themselves "unconventional" by frequenting night clubs, drinking too much, and making too much noise. The "young marrieds" went to private clubs, especially country clubs, to eat lukewarm suppers that tasted like papier-mâché and to dance themselves into "wiltedness." These women worked violently for suffrage and talked incessantly of "birth control, social hygiene, and sex attraction."[24]

Journalists who wrote travel books invariably sought contacts with a city's elite to get a sense of being behind the scenes. Those journalists who came from gentry backgrounds moved naturally through the acquaintance linkages of their class. Julian Street sought out the elite club wherever he went. "Every large city had at least one solid dignified club, occupying a solid, dignified old building on a corner near the busy part of town. It suggested "a fine cuisine, an excellent wine cellar, and a great variety of good cigars in prime condition." He wrote: "You know that there is a big, high-ceilinged room, at the front, dark in color and containing spacious leather chairs, which should (and often do) contain aristocratic gentlemen who have attained years of discretion and positions of importance."[25]

Tourists who didn't or couldn't penetrate elite social settings might at least inspect the domiciles of the rich vicariously. Elite residential streets, contrived for display, made ideal tourist attractions. Sightseeing tours regularly swept through elite neighborhoods in most large cities. Beverly Hills in Los Angeles was especially popular because of the movie celebrities that lived there. Lord Kinross noted that each star displayed his own architectural fancy—Rosalind Russell for the French style, Hedy Lamar for Queen Anne, Jimmy Durante for Spanish, James Stewart for Jacobean, Tab Hunter for contemporary." Jonathon Daniels rode through Atlanta's prestigious suburb along Paces Ferry Road, viewing the "palaces of the new masters of Dixie." He wondered what kind of folk these rich were behind the hedges and the fences, all artfully designed to conceal and display at once. It seemed a pity that some case worker could not go into the gates and ask such questions as were commonly put to the poor."[26]

Elite districts were not impermeable to change. Indeed, large houses on large lots close to downtown made ideal properties for commercial development. Visitors to a city often confronted a deteriorating elite neighborhood downtown and a newly evolving gentry district at the city's edge. In 1913, Edward Hungerford found on Cleveland's Euclid Avenue old houses with great lawns, but the grime of the city's industry has made them seem doubly old and decadent, while commerce had pushed stores and offices out among them. Cleveland's elite families were moving to suburbs like Shaker Heights. To Julian Street the automobile had offered the residents of Euclid Avenue a swift and agreeable means of transportation to a pleasanter environment. Then, having lured them away, it had proceeded to seize upon their former lands for showrooms, garages, and automobile accessory shops.[27] But such change was not inevitable. In some cities, the traditional show streets continued to thrive: Delaware Avenue in Buffalo, St. Charles Street in New Orleans, Sherbrooke Avenue in Montreal.

Many tourists, especially foreign visitors, were struck by the extremes of wealth and poverty displayed in the North American metropolises. David Steele thought Chicago's Lake Shore Drive was the finest in America, but it was like the lobby of a country-town hotel, introductory to overcrowded, underclean rooms and to civic backyards as atrociously unkempt. Ilya Ilf and Eugene Petrov wrote: "Scarcely anywhere else in the world have heaven and hell intertwined so intimately as in Chicago. Side by side with the marble and granite facing of sky-scrapers on Michigan Avenue are the disgusting alleys, dirty and stinking. In the centre of the city factory chimneys jut out and trains pass, enveloping the houses in steam and smoke. Some of the poor streets look as they would after an earthquake: broken fences, twisted roofs of boarded kennels, wires askew, piles of rusty metal trash, broken chamber-pots, and half-rotted soles, filthy children in rags. Yet only a few blocks away—fine broad streets lined with trees, filled with beautiful private residences with . . . Packards and Cadillacs at their entrances." Indeed, the contrasts between the lovely country houses standing among the wooded-ravine suburbs like Lake Forest on the northside, and the doleful tumble-down shanties, built by the unemployed on the refuse dumps of the southside, was pretty grim.[28]

Theodore Dreiser was astounded by New York City's areas of "poverty and beggary." He sought moral lessons. Contrasts in wealth reflected differences between the dull and shrewd, the strong and the weak, the wise and the ignorant. But there was "glory" in variety. The "creatures" at the lower end of the social ladder, "far from having brains or executive ability, or wealth or fame," he wrote, have "nothing save a weird astonishing individuality." Dreiser was intrigued by the poorest people on the streets: their hats with holes in them, the hair protruding. He wrote: "The hats, the coats, the shoes, the motions! The bodies! What misfortune or accident or condition of birth or mind had worked out the sad or grim spectacle of a human being so distorted, a veritable caricature of womanhood or manhood." For those at the top there was the brilliancy of Fifth or Park Avenue apartments, and the delights of intelligence and freedom. For those at the bottom, there were the dark rooms, the hanging smoke, the pallor, and the fowl odors of a wretched home, or life without a home on the streets.[29]

Most Americans, especially tourists, seemed hardly to notice the down and out. Writing in 1937, Nathan Ashe noted that Americans had no tradition of suffering. If the American slogan, everyone is born equal, and with an equal chance, has so often proven to be a misleading slogan, still for all its falseness it was better than no slogan at all. It was better than the knowledge so many people had abroad, that what they were born for was to die someday. He wrote: "It's what makes it possible to travel in this country, looking at places dispossessed, and see much want and hear of many troubles, and still feel there is hope, there is a chance, there is a future. It's what makes it possible to be happy while traveling in America."[30] Foreigners traveled expecting to find in America the land of opportunity fulfilled. Americans traveled definitely knowing America to be a land of fulfillment.

The United States was a culturally heterogeneous country, although a "melting pot" of sorts did seem to work. Canada was divided between English- and French-speaking people with most English Canadians assuming ultimate superiority for their language and ways. American and Canadian tourists tended to ignore cultural diversity in landscapes much as they ignored poverty. Cultural diversity was not part of the North American self-view. Foreign visitors, however, found ethnicity even in unexpected places. Frenchman Andre La Fond observed: "One can obtain an idea of the various elements of which the population is composed by making a visit to a building under construction. The excavators and masons are Italians, the steelworkers are Anglo-saxons, the metal-workers are Czechoslovakians and Hungarians, the electricians are Germans, and the interior decorators are for the most part French."[31]

Ethnic neighborhoods evolved when minority people voluntarily sought mutual support through proximity. Strangers in a strange land buffered themselves in communities patterned along Old World lines. But, ethnic neighborhoods also resulted from prejudice when people were involuntarily restricted to ghettos. Every city had its ethnic communities: Italians in Boston and Philadelphia, Poles in Chicago and Detroit, Ukranians in Cleveland and Winnipeg, Chinese in Vancouver and San Francisco.

New York City's ethnic neighborhoods were probably the most widely visited. It was possible, within the confines of Manhattan Island, to make a tour of almost all the nations of the world as Konrad Bercovici's book *Around the World in New York* demonstrated. But, New York City's Semitic "Lower East Side" and Harlem always stood out in journalistic descriptions. Henry James considered the Lower East Side to be "a great swarming." The swarming thickened the closer he got to Rutgers Street, the traditional heart of the Jewish section. He wrote: "The children swarmed above all—here was multiplication with a vengeance; and the number of very old persons, of either sex, was almost equally remarkable; the very old persons being in equal vague occupation of the doorstep, pavement, curbstone, gutter, roadway, and every one alike using the street for overflow." Rutgers Street rewarded the eye with its complexity of fire escapes with which each house front bristled. The analogy with cages at the zoo was all too obvious. Nearby Mulberry Street also swarmed. Those who were not in the street or in the sidewalk were hanging from the windows and calling to one another from the fire escapes. Pushcarts were jammed and tangled everywhere. Theodore Dreiser was especially taken by the pushcart men. He liked to see them trundling their two-wheeled vehicles about the city, vendors of fruit, vegetables, chestnuts. On the East Side, however, they even sold dry goods, hardware, and groceries.[32]

Paul Morand visited Harlem both at night and during the day. In the daylight he found the sidewalks of Lennox Avenue swarming with children. He wrote: "Young Negresses, precociously mature, dash wildly along, swinging their bodies harmoniously, on atrociously noisy rollerskates, with an animal swiftness, a warlike zest, something savage and triumphant." Adults crowded doorsteps arguing and bickering and "flirting with ornate words and simple eyes." Harlem was the intellectual center of black America. Konrad Bercovici was quick to point out that the giant Abyssianian Baptist Church on 138th Street was designed by a black architect, built by a black contractor with black labor, and financed by black banks. But segregation also had bred immorality, criminality, and disease with its increased mortality. "One twelfth of the population of the city," Bercovici wrote, "can not harmlessly be restricted to live in one fortieth of its area, and be excluded from most means of earning a livelihood." Thus prostitution, bootlegging, and gambling were "rampant on every corner." By the 1950s most white tourists considered Harlem too dangerous to visit. The evening trek of whites to the black nightclubs ceased.[33]

San Francisco's Chinatown was a major tourist attraction. Harry MacFadden's tour group set out "to explore the haunts of the wily Oriental." He had heard of the opium dens and of "genuine wickedness and depravity" hidden in the quarter. He seemed to have been instantly transported and set down in a picturesque corner of Asia. "The dim, soft, quavering light shimmering from the many-colored and queer-shaped lanterns, the grotesque signs, with their spider-like hieroglyphics, the quaint and flitting forms, with their flowering costumes, the clattering of the sandaled feet, their dark almond-shaped eyes, all tended to increase the feeling of strangeness, mystery and the foreign air of it all." But he found not a single opium den or "other evil place." He did see a Chinese theater, a temple, and a myriad of shops all selling souvenirs.[34] Tourists found Chinatown's opium dens open, but run only as museums.

Prevailing Urban Fabric

North American cities shared an overall form. A central business district sat near a river or lakefront where railroads and streets with their mass transit lines were focused. Outward from the business district along certain of the railroad radials were warehouses and light and heavy industry, with working class housing intermixed. Major thoroughfares were lined with businesses. Toward the city edge, in certain sectors, upper class and middle class housing predominated. There suburban expansion was most vigorous. The North American city was a spread-out affair, especially in the new sections oriented exclusively to automobile travel. Cities expanded, one much like another, as the middle classes fled deteriorating inner cities for pastoral-like suburbs.

Most tourists recognized these patterns as they rode trains or drove or walked through cities visited. In 1913, Edward Hungerford walked into Philadelphia from beyond the city's outskirts. Between the Quaker meeting houses he passed immaculate, whitewashed farmhouses with broad sweeping lawns. At Chestnut Hill, numbered houses began city-fashion, and the yellow trolley cars multiplied, the highway becoming a city street. Then came Germantown, a village absorbed by the city with tightly packed houses and stores interrupted by the large estates of the well-to-do. Then came Philadelphia proper with its railroad yards and industry, and row upon row of narrow streets lined with small houses. The monotony of the housing was only accentuated by the occasional church spire. In the distance loomed the tall buildings of the downtown.[35]

The basic residential pattern of each city was repeated over and over again. In Philadelphia, Hungerford noted mile after mile of the flat roofed, red-brick row houses flush with the sidewalks. They seemingly must have been made at some mill, in great quantities and from a limited variety of patterns. They were almost all alike, with their two or three stories of narrow windows and doors and their steps and lintels and cornices of white marble. Only the details of architectural decoration varied across neighborhoods built at different periods. As Hungerford observed in St. Louis: "You can trace the varying fads in American house architecture in layers as you go back street by street in the new St. Louis—Norman, Italian Renaissance, American Colonial, Elizabethan—all like the slices of a fat layer-cake."[36]

The urge to attain middle class respectability showed in the look of twentieth-century suburbs. Lord Kinross was surprised by the perseverance of traditional colonial architecture in suburban New York City. Mile after mile he passed new houses with Georgian windows and fanlights and weatherboarded fronts. He was amazed by the lack of privacy which the open lawns afforded, lacking as they did hedges and fences. He noted that each suburb was carefully graded between one income group and another: middle here, upper-middle there, and so forth. Suburbs seemed to be interchangeable from one city to the next, every suburb having its counterpart elsewhere. Suburbs of a given income level displayed a high degree of homogeneity. Although many Americans and Canadians prided themselves as individualists, firmly believing in individual rights and freedoms of action, most foreign visitors saw conformity instead. J. B. Priestley wrote of the 1930s: "The ordinary American citizen does not want to be odd, critical, detached, whimsical, rebellious; he wants to be solidly fixed into the community, a regular fellow. In short, his outlook is not strongly individualistic."[37] Americans attached themselves to their communities through visual display of house and garden. The well-trimmed lawn and the car in the driveway spoke of security and contentment.

The expanding suburbs placed the older inner-city neighborhoods in jeopardy. Around Seattle, John Steinbeck saw "frantic" growth. Bulldozers rolled up the green forests and heaped the resulting trash for burning. When a city began to grow and spread outward, he noted, the center, which was once its glory, was "abandoned to time." Then the buildings grew dark and a kind of decay set in. Poorer people moved in and small fringe businesses took the place of once flowering establishments. The district was still too good to tear down, too outmoded to be desirable. All the energy had flowed out to the new developments." The North American city was like a huge robot adding to itself at the fringe, and subtracting from itself around the center. Jan and Cora Gordon wrote: "Skyscrapers march across the land; business men breed to keep them filled; immigrants and first generation Americans swarm in the slums; clerks and mechanics fill the suburbs and are preyed upon by the realtors. Such is a modern city."[38]

City Stereotypes

As tourists grappled with city details, attempting to simplify city complexities into broad generalizations, certain images always stood out. As often as not elements of landscape stood as icons signifying discovered truths. New York to Paul Morand was "the great image of towndom, and the supreme expression of city rush." "New York is what all towns will be tomorrow—geometric. It is the simplification of line, of ideas, of feelings, the reign of directness." To each city certain adjectives seemed to be attached over and over again. Emily Post found New York City "omnipotent" in contrast to "ambitious" Chicago. Between New York and Chicago was strung a chain of cities that had many qualities, like mixed sample of these two terminal points. But beyond Chicago, no trace of New York remained. There every city was "spunky and busy, ambitious and sometimes self-laudatory." Henry Miller wrote of southern cities: "The new Atlanta, sprung from the ashes of the old, is a hideous nondescript city combining the evil ugly traits of both North and South. The new Richmond is lifeless and character-less. New Orleans lives only in its tiny French Quarter and even that is being rapidly demolished. Charleston is a beautiful memory, a corpse whose lower limbs have been resuscitated."[39]

The idea of constant change seemed to characterize most North American cities. Henry James noted New York City's "perpetual passionate pecuniary purpose which plays with all forms, which derides and devours them." Personifying the city's movers, he wrote: "I build you up to tear you down, for if I were to let sentiment and sincerity once take root, were to let any tenderness of association once accumulate, or any 'love of the old' once pass unsnubbed, what would become of *us*, who have our hands on the whip stock please?" Change was univer-sal. It was the profound constant, the thing always seen. The only way to be comfortable in a city like New York was to accept transition as its ruling characteristic; neither to mourn the de-struction of old landmarks, nor to rail against new unsightli-ness. New York City was a place "where things break, pall, and are forgotten with staggering brevity." Not only did nothing last, but nothing was intended to last. The city was the architect's and builder's "experiment station."[40]

Urban change was an attraction in itself. Many tourists, returning to New York City after years of absence, thought the transformations prodigious. But one common city noise re-mained: the roar and tremor of dynamite blasting. Kinross wrote: "All around me the air was thick with the dust of falling masonry and loud with the roar of the bulldozer and the drill . . . as regiments of demons, wearing yellow asbestos skull-caps and overalls like space-suits, tore buildings down or built them up. Hypnotized into silence, groups of people stood watching them from observation platforms." Every generation knew a different New York City. "A succession of Rip Van Winkles awakening from twenty-years' sleep," wrote Vernon Bailey and Arthur Maurice, "would stare with astonishment at the spectacle of the city changed."[41]

City stereotypes gave tourists something to take away for easy mental reference. They gave tourists a sense of having experienced the city with some real understanding. Stereotypes were necessarily superficial, but to insist on anything approaching definitive understanding was to seek the impossible in short visits. Most tourists arrived in cities with set expectations. Some left with their preconceptions very much intact. Others added new impressions or found old notions diminished in importance or eliminated altogether. Successful travel involved a constant juggling of impressions for interpretation. Synthesizing ideas was critical in viewing the city as an attraction. Without simplification the city did not attract; it alienated in its confusion. Without simplification cities could be fearsome.

The most attractive cities were the most imageable places: cities where belief and attitude attached readily to elements of landscape. Impressive skylines and bird's-eye views, unusual streets and nodal points, unusual interior spaces and landmarks, and easily defined districts, all contributed as icons to making cities legible and memorable. Where landscapes were vivid, tourists oriented easily, and remembered where they had been. The more legible a city, the more positive the tourists' reactions. Lack of legibility led to confusion and a diminished sense of attraction, although tourists did thrive in cities where landscapes contained elements of limited surprise. When expectations regarding scale, juxtaposition, or sequence were violated within an overall sense of plan, tourists were visually pleased. The juxtaposition of big and small or rich and poor in a city was stimulating, and discovery of the unusual in a walk or drive through a city was exciting.

Cities were the most important tourist attractions in North America. More tourists traveled to see cities than any other kind of place. Nonetheless, no city was deliberately designed either to attract or to hold a tourist trade. World's fairs and other expositions came the closest to achieving such ends. But ordinarily, cities in the early twentieth century made little effort to accommodate tourists as a special class beyond the provisionings of hotels and restaurants. Contrived attractions in cities were few. The city itself was the attraction. The city as a concentration of people, activities, and opportunities was by itself the attractor. Tourists came to do what city residents themselves might do in their leisure time. Tourists also came to see city residents at work: to see how the metropolis worked as the supreme expression of modern economy. Tourists sought the city to get a sense of modern civilization: the metropolis stood as the ultimate expression of advanced society and culture.

CHAPTER FOURTEEN
HISTORY AS AN ATTRACTION

> An elderly woman . . . with bobbed hair, seemed in a state of great
> enthusiasm about everything, but by some unlucky trick of the
> memory, she had Buffalo Bill mixed in her mind with Theodore
> Roosevelt. "I remember, honey," she said to a little girl who accom-
> panied her, "when he organized an army called the Rough Riders,
> so they elected him president. She added, . . . "History is a wonder-
> ful thing."
>
> Charles Finger, *Foot-Loose in the West*

Although the tourist's sense of history was often inaccu-
rate, it was usually a well-developed preoccupation in travel. A
large proportion of the contrived attractions in North America
celebrated the past. Most museums, for example, were historical museums. Contrivance ran the gamut from monuments and
shrines to house museums and outdoor villages to restorations
of whole towns. Celebrating the past was important to a sense
of nationhood, statehood, and locality. It was educational as a
means of orientation to one's cultural heritage, but above all,
visiting historical attractions could be entertaining and relax-
ing. Historical sites offered a sense of permanence in an ever-
evolving world of new, highly standardized landscapes. Historical flavor served as a counterpoint to modernity.

History and Its Uses

History tended to be packaged as contrived attractions.
As geographer David Lowenthal points out, the past became
The past. It became historical heritage and not an integral part of
the contemporary scene; it was not an equal partner with the
future. Historical features in landscape tended to be fenced off
in a preserve called History.[1] The treating of history as special
reflected the dominance of other values. The past was merely
prologue since the present day, as it anticipated the future, was
all important. Americans and Canadians looked forward and
not backward in time.

To be utilitarian in one's orientation to place was also to
be future oriented. Landscape had utility according to its future

286

worth. To engage the past was to be impractically romantic, or to dwell on the anachronistic as picturesque. John Van Dyke's discussion of New York City skyscrapers in 1909 is instructive. Skyscrapers meant tearing down the old city, and some people, Van Dyke realized, would protest. Not that there was any great value, aesthetic or otherwise, to the old, but it had become familiar and had pleasant associations attached. This protest, he observed, had always been made and had always gone unheeded, and the world went right on tearing down and building up anew. The city was a shop and not a historical museum since the past history of a city was wholly insignificant when compared with its present and future commercial importance. Old landmarks could be tolerated until their space was needed for new construction. He found New York City's Old Trinity "pleasing to the eye and calming to the brain." Thousands of "worried and harried" people "pushed and surged" past its iron fence and were "helped by the peace and quiet of it." Nonetheless, the church's days seemed numbered. It was already "out of place" in an area dominated by banks and offices. He writes: "Everyone will be sorry to see it go, for it has been for many years a lovely spot of brown and green upon gray." In North America, most old buildings, like Trinity Church, weren't really antique. Van Dyke concludes: "American antiquity has, at best, some very positive limitations. Most of the things we call 'old' are within the memory of men still living." Thus nothing could really be historically significant that wasn't very, very old.[2]

With the emphasis on newness, antiquity was often hard to find, and when found, was easily submerged by the modern unless special effort was taken. Henry James visited the House of Seven Gables at Salem, Massachusetts, to write: "I took the neighborhood, at all events, for the small original Hawthornesque world, keeping the other, the smoky modernism, at a distance." He forced himself to think of the place "in the rural light of the past." To Stuart Mais, Boston missed a tremendous opportunity to "trade on its great and glorious past," since all the oldest buildings were "hidden away" in Italian, Chinese, or other quarters.[3] Thus, what was not destroyed of the past was neglected in isolation. Only through neglect or near abandonment could whole townscapes escape redevelopment and thus present a historical face. Yet, what was isolated from society at large tended also to be isolated from tourists. The past required as much searching out in the landscape as poverty and minority cultures, since, indeed, the three were often intertwined geographically.

Once found, oldness and historical significance could be romanticized. Meanings could be attached that the modern contemporary scene did not warrant. Romance was always in the past tense. Things and places acquired romantic value after they had all but vanished. Only after an era was gone, and relics relegated to isolation, did feelings of longing for the past emerge. Romance did not attach while things were coming to pass. A sense of history was required. Irvin Cobb wrote: "No doubt our children and our children's children will read in the textbooks that the first decade of the twentieth century was distinguished as the age when the auto and tango came into use, and people learned to fly, and grown men wore bracelet watches and carried their handkerchiefs up their cuffs; and they will repine because they, too, did not live in those stirring times." Age and antiquity gave an added value to everything except eggs, Cobb concluded.[4]

The uses of a romanticized past were many. Historical significance attached to places associated with significant persons, events, or activities of the past. Especially significant were attachments of national importance. These sites served to create a sense of national identity, to bind the tourist closer to the national body politic. Such sites were called "historic" rather than "historical" in order to signify their special importance. Christopher Morley wrote of Valley Forge: "A curious magic moves in the air of Valley Forge. There is the same subtle plucking at heart and nerves that one feels when, coming home from abroad, passing up some salty harbor on a ship, he sees his own flag rippling from a home staff. It is a sudden inner vision of meaning of America. It is a realization of the continuity of history, a sense of the imperishable quality of human virtue."[5] In the United States, George Washington's Mount Vernon, Jefferson's Monticello, the Gettysburg Battlefield, and Lincoln's

Tomb all served as icons of nationhood; in Canada, these icons included the Plains of Abraham, the Lundy's Lane Battlefield, and Rideau Hall.

Historical attractions are as much a product of present-day values and needs as a product of past history. David Lowenthal asserts that memory not only conserves the past, but adjusts recall to current need. Instead of remembering exactly what was, the past is made intelligible in the light of present circumstances. Historical attractions are contrived accordingly, often destroying authenticity. Agnes Rothery visited Mount Vernon. The shrine suffered from hackneyed description. School children and tourists were unceasingly herded through the grounds and corridors, and only one thing lifted it from the ruck of commonplaceness—its own sheer loveliness. Mount Vernon served as a pedagogical device to teach about the founding of a nation. But its very use for this purpose diminished its value as a setting of historical significance. It was not a piece of the past frozen in time, since the lines of tourists largely destroyed the sense of historical ambience. What was left was a place of "loveliness" where tourists could enjoy themselves as in a pleasure ground. The past could be fun as well as inspirational and educational.[6]

Monuments and Markers

The lack of historically authentic landmarks plagued the celebration of the past everywhere in North America. Tourists in cities had an especially hard time visualizing the past in landscapes that constantly changed with new construction. But judiciously placed monuments and markers partially remedied the deficit. Indeed, surrogates to authentic structures were in many ways superior to real relics. Messages about a heroic past could be communicated without mundane counterevidence clouding issues. Thus Frank Kelley in his 1913 *Historical Guide to the City of New York* was content to lead the tourist from one bronze tablet to another. As Helen Henderson wrote of New York City: "If historic landmarks are few, a plentiful distribution of tablets, diligently erected by the various societies interested in colonial relics, marks most of the important sites."[7]

A heroic monument substantiated a heroic past. Enshrinement also served to protect relic features. Jonathon Daniels visited Plymouth, Massachusetts. He found Plymouth Rock sitting after some pilgrimaging of its own, cemented and safe in a sort of bear pit in a temple that guarded it against those patriots who might come with hammers to knock off pieces for souvenirs. Whole landscapes could be converted into monument gardens. Jamestown, Virginia, was such a place. When Clifton Johnson visited the site in 1904 he found the old church tower, the only visible remnant of the colonial settlement, surrounded by a wire-mesh fence, suggesting at first glance "some vernal hen-yard." The floor of the church was strewn with grave markers much weathered by stress of time and broken by vandal sightseers. A custodian admitted visitors and answered questions, and volunteered such information as occurred to him. For example, he noted the location where the first black slaves were auctioned in 1619.[8]

A parklike setting suggested hallowed ground. Clara Whiteside had a "feeling of reverence" on approaching the Old North Bridge at Concord, Massachusetts. On one side of the bridge stood a granite shaft, marking where the British gathered. On the other side was Daniel Chester's Minute Man statue, marking where the "embattled farmers stood." But Arthur Eddy was disappointed with the marking of the site and town. Monuments and tablets had been erected in great numbers, but the original roads had been relocated and renamed, and a glossary was required for interpretation. The markers and the park development had all but "obliterated the localities of those great days."[9]

Battlefield parks and cemeteries commemorated the heroism of the American Civil War. At Gettysburg, Louise Hale drove about among "the 5,000 memorial shafts and the 1,000 tablets" that marked the battlefield. A photographer had stationed himself at the Devil's Den, and visitors could have postcards made of themselves "where the dead were once piled thick." At Antietam, however, the monuments and markers and souvenir sellers intruded less. She wrote: "We secured at Antietam what we missed at Gettysburg: the vision of a battle. It did not come from government roads, nor acres of land turned into park. . . . It came from the fields of grain serving as they had served in war time, fulfilling their mission as the soldier fulfilled his." Ilya Ilf and Eugene Petrov were taken with the ubiquitous civil war monuments that graced small town squares and cemeteries in the United States. Little soldiers stood idly leaning on rifles, haversacks on their backs. "They were quite alike," they wrote. "They do not differ from one another any more than a standard model of one Ford differs from the next."[10]

Shrines

Homes of patriots, sites of famous "firsts," and prominent battlefields served as shrines in a patriotic sense. Monuments enshrined sites when they became as important as the historical events or persons celebrated. Important also were places of religious pilgrimage where the memorializing structures were equal to if not more important than the history remembered. Religious shrines were especially important to Roman Catholics in Canada. The Basilica of Sainte Anne de Beaupre near Quebec City, Saint Joseph's Oratory at Montreal, and the Martyr's Shrine at Midland, Ontario, displayed piles of canes and crutches marking marvelous cures among past pilgrims. The Church of the Latter–Day Saints enshrined Salt Lake City's Temple Square. A. G. MacDonnell did the accepted round of the temple, listened to the perfervid description of Mormonism, and examined, "with an alarm that almost verged on terror," the statues of Joseph Smith and Hiram Smith. Shrines as icons tended to elicit extreme responses in tourists. Believers were captivated in proportion to the strength of their beliefs. Nonbelievers frequently verged on the caustic. Some, like Thomas Wolfe, were repelled by what they considered unnecessary superstition. Wolfe found the Salt Lake City temple sacrosanct and ugly, grim, grotesque. He found Temple Square filled with "pomposities of bronze rhetoric."[11]

North American tourists thronged to literary shrines. Authors captured past times and places in their works, and were historically significant persons in their own right for having done so. Jonathon Daniels searched the cemetery at Concord, Massachusetts, for Author's Ridge where Hawthorne,

Thoreau, Emerson, and Alcott lay. At Salem, Massachusetts, Mary Winn knew that Hawthorne had disclaimed the House of Seven Gables. In Hawthorne's day it did not even have seven gables. But she went anyway. Edith Hughes was completely taken in. She climbed the smuggler's chimney. Everyone laughed when she mistook a brass warming pan, hanging by the fireplace, for a corn-popper! Ilya Ilf and Eugene Petrov visited Samuel Clemens's boyhood home at Hannibal, Missouri. The guide pointed to a chair and said, "In this chair, Aunt Polly always sat, and it was through this window that the cat Peter jumped out after Tom Sawyer gave him castor oil." She had Mark Twain and his literary works completely intertwined. She concluded by offering postcards for sale.[12]

Museums

Local historical societies flourished, many operating museums in the former residences of local notables. If not the historical society, then the Society of Colonial Dames or the Daughters of the Confederacy served as preservation agents, soliciting contributions of china, old glass, samplers, and furniture to display. Most museums emphasized elite society, presenting the past as a place of happiness and contentment. Jonathon Daniels also visited the museum at Concord. To him it reflected a richly upholstered past, since there was little that represented plain living. Its displays of china and mahogany ran back to the earliest settlers "through a procession of loveliness and luxury." Daniels thought the past, even in Concord, would be more clearly presented by the junk as well as the beautifully carved, by the clutter as well as the costly and the chaste. The heirlooms served the pride of the heirs better than they preserved the picture of the ancestors. Obviously, there had been poor people in Concord, and he wondered how much truth there was in the dictum that they always loved and honored the rich.[13]

Historical museums often truncated the past by over-emphasizing some historical periods and totally neglecting others. And, as museums preserved selectively according to social class and period, they also isolated past from present. The

The Betsy Ross House in Philadelphia (1910 and 1938). Historical house museums dominated numerically North America's contrived tourist attractions. Style and authenticity at any given site could change appreciably over time.

past languished under glass. It was roped off from the everyday world and presented as something dead, as something divorced from the future. Perhaps, as David Lowenthal maintains, Americans prefer history parceled out in tidy segments because it is easy to describe, thematic, and represents no threat to the present. Isolated history became an object for reverence and pleasure. Cecil Roberts visited the whaling museum at Sag Harbor, New York. "You enter the building under the arch formed by the jawbones of a whale. In the junk-cluttered, dusty, daguerrotype-haunted rooms of the museum the dead come out of their past in the faded spidery penmanship of their journals, or are evoked by bits of carved whalebone, pieces of old lace, costumes, bonnets, shoes, walking sticks—all that once paraded, sustained by warm blood, in Main Street."[14]

293

The great houses of great men attracted much attention from antiquarians. Julian Street visited Charles Carroll's home in Baltimore. It was a treasure house of ancient portraits and furniture and silver. The beautifully proportioned dining room, the wide hall which passed through the house from the front portico to another overlooking the terraces and gardens at the back, the old shadowy library with its tree-calf bindings, the sunny breakfast room, the bedchambers with their four-posters and chintzes all impressed. Perhaps, the greatest great house museum was built by Henry Du Pont at Winterthur near Wilmington. There house interiors were assembled from across North America to create hundreds of period rooms for the display of Du Pont's extensive furniture collection. When Lord Kinross visited the museum he encountered bus loads of ladies, flower-hatted and tight-skirted and bespectacled. Each was ticketed to show who, what, and whence she came: Home makers of Baltimore, Garden Lovers of Pittsburgh, Parents Educational of Norfolk. Occasionally, a male or two followed in their wake.[15]

Kitchen of the Wayside Inn at South Sudbury, Massachusetts (c. 1930). In museums, the past was made distinct from the everyday world.

Museum preservation saved many valuable artifacts and buildings. In 1901, Arthur Eddy visited the Wayside Inn at South Sudbury, Massachusetts. The inn sign creaked mournfully as it swung in the wind. Entering, he found the place still functioning as a hostelry. But, already the proprietor was struggling with the problem of what to do with automobiles, and what to do for those who drove them. He was vainly endeavoring to reconcile the machines with horses, and to house them under one roof.[16] But when Clara Whiteside visited the inn in 1925, Henry Ford was the owner. He had undertaken to return the inn to its eighteenth-century condition, asking Thomas Edison to design a lighting system to simulate candlelight. She approved, since so many colonial buildings were being torn down and sold piecemeal, the bricks going in one direction, the doors and window frames in another, and the paneling going to art museums or to antique dealers.

At Dearborn outside Detroit, Henry Ford carried the traditional historical museum to its ultimate expression. Ford, cognizant of the fact that automobiles and highways spelled vast change for America's future, began to collect farm, industrial, and domestic artifacts reminiscent of life as it had been. The massive hall of Ford's Edison Institute covered twenty acres, its entrance a replica of Philadelphia's Independence Hall. Giant machines in working order were set in brick foundations. Entire railroad trains were displayed, and hundreds of automobiles were on view. Ilya Ilf and Eugene Petrov found wooden ploughs, harrows, wooden spinning wheels, the first sewing machines, the first typewriters, ancient gramophones, engines, locomotives. Ford maintained the Edison cult. He celebrated his former employer and friend by moving and restoring Edison's Menlo Park laboratory, placing it in Greenfield Village, an outdoor museum of industrial and farm buildings. There Ilf and Petrov found one of Edison's early assistants who guided them through the maze of equipment to show them the world's first electric lamp. He demonstrated, by means of impersonations, how it's development had occurred, how they all had sat around the little lamp awaiting the results. Although Ford honored Edison, Ford also honored himself. As Ilf and

Petrov noted, Ford was a man of Edison's generation who also "brought the machine to life and gave it to the masses."[17]

Henry Ford spent nearly $30 million on his museum at Dearborn.[18] But John D. Rockefeller, for a like investment, substantially improved on Ford's sense of history. Rockefeller undertook to subsidize restoration of an entire town: Williamsburg in Virginia. Williamsburg was not to be a museum in the traditional sense. It was to be a living landscape brought back to the image of the eighteenth century. Unlike Ford, who served as his own expert, Rockefeller acted in consultation with many professionals. Williamsburg was not to be eclectic, reflecting one man's hobby, but as authentic a display of the past as archeological and historical expertise could make it. Consulting architects and landscape architects rendered the plans, rather than engineers borrowed from a corporate drafting room.

During the 1930s visitors to Williamsburg noted the restoration work. Anne Peck and Enid Johnson looked forward to the time when visitors would see "how a colonial village really looked." The streets were to be arranged "as in the old days" and the houses were to be "perfect down to the smallest detail." Jonathon Daniels wrote of the town in 1938: "It is all near perfect, perhaps even a little more than perfect. The historical sometimes looks a little like tomorrow morning." Another visitor noted a disconcerting newness about the antiquity that suggested the "snowy glitter of grandpa's false teeth." Already tourism was well established. Daniels appreciated the new hotel that preserved "the best of the present and past together, with shining plumbing and covers to the beds turned back, air-conditioning and black pages to bring soda water and ice." Scores of tourist homes had been opened. Antique shops had invaded. Daniels saw one sign that read: "Antiques: Curb Service." Lord Kinross visited in 1958. The place was in effect a stage, and the people tripping out of their neat, white, weatherboarded houses, through Jacobean cottage gardens, were merely players—ladies in farthingales, gentlemen in ruffles and breeches and hose—for the diversion of an audience. Dawdling and chattering through the past, visitors bought bread at the bakery and gazed upon the blacksmith in his shop. The milliner supplied them with handkerchiefs and toilet waters, and fine French perfumes, fans, and boudoir caps. They were photographed with their heads in the pillory and they were served at the King's Arms Tavern with foods "prepared by the Oldeft and moft approved Recipes." According to Kenneth Chorley, president of Colonial Williamsburg, the project was "proof that history could be sold." It was no longer true that tourists would buy only "sun, sex, and sports."[19]

Historical Places

Sections of some cities seemed, and were, clearly rooted in past time. They had changed relatively little. In the South, economic depression following the Civil War had made museumscapes of many urban areas. In the North, geographical isolation contributed to the fossilization of whole landscapes where economic enterprise had simply shifted elsewhere. Some cities were overly conservative, changing little through choice and tradition rather than allowing progress to take the upper hand. In some cities, historical districts were protected as icons reflecting and perpetuating desired life-styles: the preservation and restoration of old buildings encouraged through zoning ordinances and neighborhood associations. In other places pilgrimages and festivals promoted awareness of and respect for the past in landscape.

Every city had its old areas, but some cities seemed old everywhere: Quebec City and Victoria in Canada, and Boston and New Orleans in the United States. Boston seemed to change slowly, giving an impression of greater antiquity than was actually merited. Boston was also a state of mind. Conservatism attached readily to its prominent landmarks made famous in history textbooks. One tourist wrote of Boston: "You turn a corner, and know not what will confront you; you drive down a side street, and are uncertain into what century you will be thrust. And everywhere is the diversity which comes of growth, and which proves that time is a better contriver of effects than the most skillful architect." Irvin Cobb wrote of New Orleans: "There were doorways for painters to rave over, and balconies that were floating dreams of cobwebby ironwork, and marvelous, moldly old inner patios opening through crumbling arches, and a hundred happy tricks and quirks of accidental architecture such as are to be found nowhere else on American soil."[20]

New Orleans was a pioneer in the art of preserving architecture and neighborhoods with the establishment in 1925 of the Vieux Carré Commission to oversee the French Quarter. Charleston was another pioneer with historic district zoning adopted in 1929. Since 1946, Historic Charleston Foundation has used revolving funds and other financial devices to restore and recycle old buildings.[21] In Charleston and New Orleans the past was not ignored, but made an integral part of urban redevelopment. Although benefits were intended primarily for property owners, surviving landscapes proved attractive to tourists, and tourism became a leading industry in each city. Jonathon Daniels compared Charleston to Williamsburg. Charleston was what it was. Its houses were the old houses, and their occupants often enough were the descendants of the old occupants. So it was differentiated from Williamsburg, which was archaeology, but only archaeology. Williamsburg was a reproduction and would be so labeled in any honest Charleston shop."[22]

In Natchez, Mississippi, garden tours and house pilgrimages saved the city's elite architecture. Each spring, tourists followed custumed ladies through the double doors at Gloucester, under the six high, fluted columns at D'Evereux, and through the garden of boxwood, azaleas, and japonicas at Arlington. Jonathon Daniels wrote: "Poverty is a wonderful preservative of the past. It may let restoration wait as it ought not to wait, but it will keep old things as they are because it can not afford to change them in accordance with style or preferences. In Natchez the living occupy the past." Poverty also reigned at Nantucket, Massachusetts. Daniels thought the town a better museum than the formal hall where they kept on show the souvenirs of whaling. "Down in the poor South, Mr. Rockefeller had built a brand new Williamsburg to show an old one; but in rich New England poverty had prevailed over progress and had done . . . a better job. Without benefit of archeologists, the fishing town is truer in persistance than the Colonial Capitol of restoration."[23]

Santa Fe, New Mexico, was a place fast becoming what it should have been: a place that would be what it never was. New buildings were required to conform to old adobe ideals. To James Flagg writing in 1925, Santa Fe was "un-American" to the eye. It had a lazy romantic air about it and a lack of up-to-date vulgarity. But the town also seemed to be overdone, and a little too insistent on its special favor to be a "real place." Ernie Pyle, who visited in 1936, disagreed. "I would not allow even a dog-house to be put up in any other style," he wrote, "and in fifty years we'd have the most charming city on the continent." Lewis Gannett found Santa Fe a "tourist's paradise." Every other shop about the plaza was filled with trinkets and curios, and the outlying sections were quaint with imitations of primitive adobe houses built by sophisticated exiles from the East.[24]

The West also offered ghost towns. A. G. MacDonnell thought the sensation strange to walk the grassy streets of the dead Marysville in Montana. Names were still faintly legible on some of the shops. Here was an advertisement for caps, $8 each, and there a notice on a saloon of some passing troupe of entertainers. Faded lettering and figures announced that the Masonic Hall was built in 1884. The old West seemed to live on feebly. Charles Finger found Tombstone, Arizona, languishing in "sunshine and silence." Two men sat in rockers under a verandah, smoking cigars. A donkey, hitched to a post, slept. Two boys and a man on horseback watched a painter working on a cold drinks sign while a cowboy leaned against the drugstore wall eating an ice-cream cone.[25]

Beyond the intrigue of old places with their attractions historical and historic, a sense of past was vital to tourists. Tourists' place expectations were usually dated: impressions that required visible landmarks of the past for verification. Boston was not Boston without the Old North Church, since the city's meaning to tourists was very much tied to history book understandings. The West was not the West without evidences of saloons and stage coaches and the other manifestations of western movies. Landmarks rooted in the past could be powerful icons of place. They enabled tourists not only to locate themselves in space, but to locate themselves in time as well. Monuments and markers served where landscapes were altered beyond ready recognition, or lost altogether. Shrines were exaggerated places where markings assumed as much importance as the past that was celebrated. Museums were warehouses for storing relics divorced from their original contexts. Historical places were lived-in landscapes that preserved aspects of context, but which were strongly overlaid by aspects of contemporary life, including the imprints of tourism.

CHAPTER FIFTEEN
CONCLUSION

> The acceptance of the voyage as the true condition of man was a charter to tourism.
>
> Paul Shepard, *Man in the Landscape*

Tourism became a great universal in the early twentieth century. By mid-century the vast majority of Americans and Canadians traveled, if only for short distances. Nearly everyone played at being the tourist, if only for short periods. Tourism provided an important means by which the complex world could be simplified and understood in its interconnectedness. The individual's role in life could be explored in comparison to other people in other places. The tourist trusted what he discovered since his experience was firsthand in a pleasurable social atmosphere unhindered by everyday social bindings. The tourist's view was not always sophisticated. Indeed, too often was it unimaginative and unrewarding, but it was a view he found reliable for it was personally his own. Other ways of knowing, movies, television, newspapers, and even formal education, were potentially deceptive. But traveling for pleasure, with its candid insights into people and places, provided a world view, however incomplete, that could be depended upon.

What tourists actually experienced reflected their own personalities: their desires and fears, strengths and frailties. The individual's intelligence, assertiveness, and amiability, among a myriad of other character traits, dictated travel. People traveled to validate selected place expectations: expectations that fit their own manner of being in the world. As social animals, individuals shared understandings as members of communities variously defined. Being at home in a specific place, working at a specific job, belonging to certain organizations cast one's self-view according to others. Thus group values and expectations influenced what was experienced in travel. Like all behavior, travel was learned. Perhaps the family was most influential in teaching people how to be tourists. Certainly, most touring in early-twentieth-century North America was conducted in family groups.

Touring was an intermittent behavior. Travel could not accrue endlessly since touring became severely routine with over exposure. Rather than sharpening one's view of the world through novelty of action, extensive travel usually dissolved into monotonous repetition, dulling the traveler's interest in places. Travel could not be stored for endless periods. It was a reservoir of experience to be replenished at intervals. As a form of validating the world, travel had to be updated periodically or one's world view became dated. Touring fit into life as a counterpoint to work and everyday forms of recreation as it broke up everyday routines with new rhythms in new places. The pleasure trip was tourism's principal component. In planning, executing, and recollecting trips, the tourist came to grips intellectually with the world around him. Pleasure trips evolved through stages, each stage influencing what the traveler experienced in a given place. What the tourist saw at any one point in time was not only a function of the traveler's personality and social milieu, but of where he stood within the process of trip taking itself.

Tourists traveled not only to relax and play, but to see sights. It was in the seeing of sights that the world was put into perspective and individuals given a sense of social fulfillment through travel. Travel destinations reflected the changing fads and fashions of twentieth-century North American society, but trip destinations, defined in terms of general place-types, remained remarkably constant over time. Nature, region, city, and history were the major themes pursued as measured by the development of contrived tourist attractions. Nature was the great attractor of people seeking spiritual renewal and renewal through physical activity. Seeing how nature operated, even superficially, was an important life perspective. The search for regional differences was primarily a search for cultural identity.

By seeing how different technologies and economies had had various impacts on different physical habitats, by seeing how different religions, languages, and other value systems had had various effects on the organization of life from place to place, the tourist placed his own communities of interest in perspective. Regional peculiarities gave the tourist a sense of reaching out beyond the everyday, enabling him to evaluate his own and other habitats from utilitarian or even aesthetic viewpoints of the picturesque and the romantic. The city was a prime attractor. There society was seen to culminate in civilizing influences. In cities tourists gained access to society's most significant work, social, and cultural displays. Everywhere tourists also searched for history in landscape to anchor life in time.

Recent scholarship has slighted tourism as a form of human behavior. Who travels? Why? When? Where? How? These are questions answered only in their broadest outline. This work has traced in North America the spread of tourism during the early twentieth century from a preoccupation of society's elite to an activity engaged in by nearly all. It has sketched the rationales behind traveling: change of scene, pedagogy, adventure, sociability, social status. It has focused on pleasure trips as recorded in published diaries, journals, and travel books to emphasize modes of travel and the kinds of places visited. Clearly, tourism changed substantially with the coming of the automobile and improved highways. Coupled with increased leisure time, automobiles and highways opened the face of North America to tourism as never before. Automobile travel made tourism the nearly universal behavior it has become.The symbiotic relationship between tourism and automobile technology deserves more attention than it has been given.

Automobiling, as a sport, thrived as a physical and mechanical exercise, placing people in novel environments. It took them off the passenger trains and steamships to play active roles in seeing places. It got them beyond the cities and into nature, and it opened opportunities to experience regional diversity first hand. Thus automobile travel promised to make twentieth-century Americans and Canadians geographically aware as no other peoples had ever been. Driving for pleasure became a force behind highway improvement, although other rationales outwardly dominated the good roads movement. Place encounter was integrally tied to overcoming the difficulties of bad roads, and the difficulties of poor, or nonexistent, hotels, restaurants, and garages. The typical tourist's attention was diverted from landscape to travel logistics. The typical tourist was set to moving as quickly and as easily as possible between destinations. For most tourists, nature, regions, cities, and history were reduced to isolated attractions at destinations separated by landscapes of inattention.

Improved highways encouraged the making of faster and more comfortable automobiles, thus increasing the tourist's range of movement. Long trips of short duration in increasingly standardized highway environments further constricted the tourist's concern with landscape, or, at least, with landscapes beyond the encapsulating highway environment. Automobile camping promised relief. Campers were said to thrive on the democratic auto camps' sociability. The auto camps were said to be the great mixer of social classes and regional origins, but, again, comfort proved the more important impulse with the rise of motels and roadside restaurants to contain and isolate. If travelers by railroad and steamship traveled from hotel to hotel to collect hotel experiences, so travelers by automobile did the same, making liberal use of new, highly standardized highway-oriented facilities.

As highways came to dominate travel landscape, roadsides came to form a new kind of environment in its various commercial manifestations, a new dominant place-type in the North American experience. The commercial strip became the framework for suburban expansion as highways and urbanization became synonymous. Turnpikes and freeways, as express routes, salvaged speed and comfort for long-distance driving. In turn, limited access and traffic separation further isolated the motorist in a self-contained world of metal and concrete. The new roads were divorced even from the roadsides. On the new highways the engineer totally dominated the traveler's experience between destinations. As engineers designed by formula, so too was much travel experience reduced to formula.

As Americans and Canadians opted for a new highway world, there came a breakdown in geographical and environmental awareness. The promise of broadened geographical horizons held out at the beginning of the twentieth century proved an illusion. Place and landscape, as concepts, lost meaning in the rush for increased geographical mobility. The making of new places became standardized in the image of the new mobility. Increasingly, the salvaging of diversity in landscapes became a function of tourism. Diversity was preserved in attractions contrived for tourists, although much of the contrivance followed standard formats. The curiosities of nature were preserved in parks following prescribed rules of place sparing. Regional attractions were stereotyped along lines of historical interest since new landscapes, oriented to highways, were becoming very much alike everywhere in North America. History was contrived through the prescriptions of monuments and museums, and self-conscious historical places.

There was still great diversity in North America, but twentieth-century North Americans seemed less inclined to search for it. Rapid mobility, both geographical and social, reduced peoples' caring about places lived in. Work places derived significance primarily through career opportunity or job security. By and large, Americans and Canadians did not learn to value places as aesthetic displays, as symbols of community consciousness, or as displays instructive of life anchored both in past and present time. They did not see the need to study the subtleties of landscape variation from place to place. They were content with validating place stereotypes propagated in the popular culture of movies, television, and newspapers. They received little if any geography or other environmental education at school. Thus, travelers were ripe for the contrivances of packaged and standardized tourism. Landscapes were rarely confronted critically. They were little appreciated as integral reflections of human adjustment to place, but valued primarily as neutral repositories of locational need.

Nonetheless, travelers of the early twentieth century have much to teach. It was they who led the way, opting as they did for the automobile as the main travel vehicle. They were influenced by their time, but were influencers also. Those who wrote travel books helped set tastes in travel, focusing attention variously on different kinds of attractions, different kinds of touring. Certainly, it behooves today's generation to examine these pioneering travel assumptions, expectations, and experiences. What did early-twentieth-century tourists hope to gain from travel? How, in fact, did they benefit? What kind of travel legacy has derived? Modern tourism remains a significant means by which modern man assesses his world, fitting himself into complex social realities. How can we rise above travel as the superficial validater of popular myths? How can we make tourism perform individually and collectively toward profound cultural ends?

Certainly, we should seek to understand the attractions of tourism. What attracts? Why? What are society's most significant work displays? Its most profound cultural and social displays? How are common places differentiated? What role does chance encounter play? How are places compared? How do people orient themselves in new places and learn locally appropriate behaviors? How do people play the role of tourists? We should seek to understand tourism's role in landscape and place cognition. Travel, as the deliberate encountering of new places, is a logical arena in which to study environmental knowing. What are the predominant icons of landscape used in travel? How do beliefs and attitudes attach? How do tourists discover personality of place?

Early-twentieth-century tourism teaches that there was an art to effective travel. Keeping the mind open to new comprehensions was a skill. At base, the mixing of comprehension and pleasure short of self-indulgence required discipline. Leisure time could be an invitation to intellectual laziness, but the responsible or diligent tourist mixed pleasure with learning to grow and mature. The irresponsible tourist did not grow, but only pleasured, often learning little and keeping prejudices firmly intact. It seems that the coming of the automobile, with mass tourism following in its wake, obscured the values of responsible travel. The automobile encouraged irresponsibility. Certainly, the quest for speed and comfort in travel was overindulged by highway departments, petroleum corporations, and motel and restaurant chains. Travel was encapsulated in comfort. To go and to move comfortably became the order of the day, the typical tourist ignoring much of what could be seen along the way. Touring became easy, perhaps too easy. The effortless adventure diminished diligence in geographical awareness.

Responsible traveling functioned at all stages of trip taking. The diligent traveler weighed options carefully, creating realistic expectations about places rooted in credible information. Itineraries were planned realistically, giving ample time to explore and absorb the essences of places visited. Departure was appropriately timed, the traveler thoroughly prepared both physically and mentally. Outward and homeward stretches were planned for breadth of experience as well as for penetrating, if not profound, glimpses of life at various destinations. The sense of turnabout was anticipated and respected, the trip allowed to run its natural course unforced. Close attention was paid to landscapes en route, and not just to landscapes at obvious destinations. Openmindedness was the watchword as the diligent tourist sought to empathize with new people and new customs encountered. He avoided imposing his own biases on situations. He sought local informants when possible to avoid self-imposed parochialism. He returned home to seriously recollect his experiences, to place his new comprehensions in thoughtful perspective. At each stage of the trip, the responsible tourist demanded full value for his time and money invested.

The diligent tourist did not avoid the obvious world of tourism, but viewed his mode of travel, the service facilities he used, and the sights he saw for what they were. He assessed contrived attractions critically, viewing them as sights with social meaning. He was aware of being a tourist. He played touristic roles, but he kept the perspective of the true student, being always inquisitive and never satisfied with the apparent and the obvious. He was a seeker of back regions by instinct, but a good judge of front regions and their contexts. The diligent tourist set clear objectives for travel beyond rest and relaxation. Travel was treated not so much as a luxury as an opportunity. He was a seeker of novel experiences in order to place in perspective everyday existence. He was a questor of knowledge, even universalities of human condition, which he applied to himself and those around him. Above all, the responsible tourist saw travel as an art that could be enhanced and improved with practice. He recognized style in travel and worked to perfect his own.

NOTES

Chapter One: Introduction

1. Foster R. Dulles, *America Learns to Play: A History of Recreation* (New York: Appleton-Century-Crofts, 1965), pp. 386–89; Max Kaplan, *Leisure in America: A Social Inquiry* (New York: Wiley, 1960), p. 148; C. E. M. Jones, *Diogenes: Or the Future of Leisure* (London: 1928), p. 65.
2. Kaplan, *Leisure in America*, p. 173; Dean MacCannell, *The Tourist: A New Theory of the Leisure Class* (New York: Schocken, 1976), p. 1.
3. Kaplan, *Leisure in America*, p. 211.
4. Clare A. Gunn, *Vacationscape: Designing Tourist Regions* (Austin, Tex.: University of Texas, Bureau of Business Research, 1972), p. 20.
5. John Muir, *Our National Parks* (Boston: Houghton Mifflin, 1903), p. 52; Henry Miller, *The Air-Conditioned Nightmare* (New York: New Directions, 1945), p. 109.
6. For a discussion of tourism's lack of scholarly respect, see Marion Clawson and Jack L. Knetsch, *Outdoor Recreation Research: Some Concepts and Suggested Areas of Study* (Washington, D.C.: Resources for the Future Report no. 43, 1963), p. 251.
7. Edward Relph, *Place and Placelessness* (London: Pion, 1976), p. 83; Erik Cohen, "Who is a Tourist? A Conceptual Clarification," *Sociological Review* 22 (November 1974): 527; Robert Kinney, *The Bachelor in New Orleans* (New Orleans: Riley, 1942), p. 32.
8. See: Yi-Fu Tuan, "Visual Blight: Exercises in Interpretation," in

Visual Blight in America, edited by Peirce F. Lewis, David Lowenthal, and Yi-Fu Tuan (Washington, D.C.: Association of American Geographers, Resource Paper no. 23, 1973), p. 24.

9.   Kaplan, *Leisure in America*, p. 215.

10. Erik Cohen, "A Phenomenology of Tourist Experiences," *Sociology* 13 (May 1979): 192; Daniel J. Boorstin, *The Image: A Guide to Pseudo-Events in America* (New York: Harper Colophon, 1961), p. 77.

11. Kenneth Craik, "Human Responsiveness to Landscape: An Environmental Psychological Perspective," in *Response to Environment*, Student Publications of the School of Design, vol. 18 (Raleigh, N.C.: North Carolina State University, 1969), p. 181.

12. John Steinbeck, *Travels with Charley in Search of America* (New York: Bantam, 1962), p. 4; Kaplan, *Leisure in America*, p. 148, 215; MacCannell, *Tourist*, p. 1; Craik, "Human Responsiveness," p. 181; Cohen, "A Phenomenology," p. 192.

13. See John L. Crompton, "Motivations for Pleasure Vacation," *Annals of Tourism Research* 5 (October–December 1979): 411.

14. Zephine Humphrey, *Green Mountains to Sierras* (New York: Dutton, 1936), p. 32; Steinbeck, *Travels with Charley*, p. 10.

15. Theodore Dreiser, *A Hoosier Holiday* (New York: Lane, 1916), p. 25.

16. Boorstin, *Image*, p. 77; Frederic Van de Water, *The Family Flivvers to Frisco* (New York: Appleton, 1927), p. 9.

17. David M. Steele, *Going Abroad Overland*, (New York: Putnam's, 1917), p. 5; Winifred H. Dixon, *Westward Hoboes* (New York: Scribner's, 1921), p. 3.

18. Christopher D. Morley, *Travels in Philadelphia* (Philadelphia: McKay, 1920), pp. 10–11.

19. Irvin S. Cobb, *Roughing It Deluxe* (New York: Doran, 1914), p. 17. Cobb's title derives from Mark Twain, *Roughing It* (Hartford, Conn.: American, 1903); Emily Post, *By Motor to the Golden Gate* (New York: Appleton, 1916), p. 44.

20. Webb Waldron, *We Explore the Great Lakes* (New York: Century, 1923), p. 323.

21. Beatrice L. Massey, *It Might Have Been Worse* (San Francisco: Wagner, 1920); Miller, *Air-Conditioned Nightmare*, p. 18.

22. Steinbeck, *Travels with Charley*, p. 161; Bernard McEvoy, *From the Great Lakes to the Wide West* (Toronto: Briggs, 1902), p. 121;

Charles J. Finger, *Foot-Loose In the West* (New York: Morrow, 1932), p. 34.

23. Marion Clawson, "Implications of Recreational Needs for Highway Improvements," in *Impacts and Implications of Highway Improvements* (Washington, D.C.: National Academy of Sciences, National Research Council, Highway Research Board, Bulletin 311, 1962), p. 35.

24. See Fred Fischer, "Ten Phases of the Animal Path: Behavior in Familiar Situations," in *Behavior and Environment: The Use of Space by Animals and Men*, edited by Aristide H. Esser (New York: Plenum, 1971), p. 10. Fischer's phases include: 1) Need for change of location; 2) Start integration; 3) First step; 4) Outward stretch; 5) Before the goal; 6) Turnabout; 7) Return stretch; 8) Approach to home; 9) Entering home.

25. Post, *By Motor*, p. 3; Melville Ferguson, *Motor Camping on Western Trails* (New York: Century, 1925), p. 3; Massey, *It Might Have Been Worse*, p. 1; James M. Flagg, *Boulevards All the Way—Maybe* (New York: Doran, 1925), p. 16.

26. Mary C. Bedell, *Modern Gypsies: A 12,000-Mile Motor Camping Trip Encircling the United States* (New York: Brentano's, 1924), p. 12; Post, *By Motor*, pp. 4–7; Massey, *It Might Have Been Worse*, p. 2; Steinbeck, *Travels with Charley*, p. 19.

27. Post, *By Motor*, p. 15; Nathan Asch, *The Road in Search of America* (New York: Norton, 1937), p. 13.

28. Humphrey, *Green Mountains*, p. 26; Post, *By Motor*, p. 16.

29. See Maurice L. Farber, "Some Hypotheses on the Psychology of Travel," *Psychoanalytical Review* 41 (July 1954): 269.

30. Finger, *Foot-Loose*, p. 5.

31. Gunn, *Vacationscape*, p. 141; Massey, *It Might Have Been Worse*, p. 83; Edward Dunn, *Double-Crossing America By Motor* (New York: Putnam's, 1933), p. 203.

32. Steinbeck, *Travels with Charley*, pp. 219, 273; Julian Street, *American Adventures* (New York: Century, 1917), p. 675.

33. Humphrey, *Green Mountains*, p. 253.

34. Clawson and Knetsch, *Outdoor Recreation*, p. 253; Van de Water, *Family Flivver*, p. 8.

35. Morris Longstreth, *The Lake Superior Country* (New York: Century, 1924), p. 181.

36. Sinclair Lewis, *Free Air* (London: Cape, 1933), p. 87.

37. Van de Water, *Family Flivvers*, p. 58; Humphrey, *Green Mountains*, p. 54.
38. Dreiser, *Hoosier Holiday*, p. 72; Dixon, *Westward Hoboes*, p. 89.
39. Steinbeck, *Travels with Charley*, p. 273.
40. Boorstin, *Image*, pp. 92, 116.
41. For examples of stereotype place imagery see John A. Jakle, *Images of the Ohio Valley: A Historical Geography of Travel, 1740 to 1860* (New York: Oxford University Press, 1977).
42. Post, *By Motor*, p. viii.
43. Mark Pepys, *Mine Host, America* (London: Collins, 1937), p. 12.
44. Post, *By Motor*; Earl Pomeroy, *In Search of the Golden West: The Tourist in Western America* (New York: Knopf, 1957), pp. 149, 219–21.
45. W. H. Auden, "Introduction," in Henry James, *The American Scene* (New York: Scribner's, 1946), p. v.
46. Henry S. Canby, "Traveling Intelligently in America," in *Essays of Today (1926–1927)*, edited by Odell Shepard and Robert Hillyer (New York: Century, 1928), p. 169; Mary D. Winn, *The Macadam Trail: Ten Thousand Miles by Motor Coach* (New York: Knopf, 1931), p. 300.
47. Mary E. Hitchcock, *Two Women in the Klondike* (New York: Putnam's, 1899), p. vii.
48. Canby, "Traveling Intelligently," p. 169; Jonathon Daniels, *A Southerner Discovers New England* (New York: Macmillan, 1940), pp. 8–9.
49. Canby, "Traveling Intelligently," p. 170; Dunn, *Double-Crossing*, p. 25.
50. Canby, "Traveling Intelligently," p. 170.

Chapter Two: Tourists in the Landscape

1. MacCannell, *Tourist*, p. 48.
2. Roy C. Buck, "The Ubiquitous Tourist Brochure: Explorations in Its Intended and Unintended Use," *Annals of Tourism Research* 4 (March–April, 1977): 204.
3. MacCannell, *Tourist*, p. 44; Erving Goffman, *Relations in Public: Microstudies of the Public Order* (New York: Basic Books, 1971), p. 62.
4. Anne M. Peck and Enid Johnson, *Roundabout America* (New York: Harper, 1933), p. 16.

5. Effie P. Gladding, *Across the Continent by the Lincoln Highway* (New York: Brentano's, 1915), p. 195; MacCannell, *Tourist,* p. 136.

6. Cobb, *Roughing It Deluxe,* p. 45.

7. MacCannell, p. 84; Boorstin, *The Image,* p. 101; Glimpses of New York (New York: New York Edison, 1911), p. 82; Henry James, *The American Scene* (New York: Scribner's, 1946), p. 384.

8. Erving Goffman, *The Presentation of Self in Everyday Life* (Garden City, N.Y.: Doubleday, 1959), p. 144; MacCannell, *Tourist,* pp. 92–94.

9. Boorstin, *Image,* p. 103; Dixon, *Westward Hoboes,* pp. 175–79.

10. Ruth K. Wood, *The Tourist's California* (New York: Dodd, Mead, 1914), p. 48; A. G. MacDonnell, *A Trip to America* (London: Macmillian, 1935), p. 69; Rupert Hughes, *The Real New York* (London: Smart Set, 1903), p. 280.

11. Eric Cohen, "Rethinking the Sociology of Tourism," *Annals of Tourism Research* 6 (January–March 1979): 26.

12. Flagg, *Boulevards,* p. 47; Asch, *Road,* p. 18.

13. MacCannell, *Tourist,* p. 13; Asch, *Road,* p. 28.

14. MacCannell, *Tourist,* pp. 63–64.

15. Julian Street, *Abroad at Home,* p. 150.

16. Ibid., pp. 92, 95, 100.

17. Ilya Ilf and Eugene Petrov, *Little Golden America* (London: Routledge, 1936), pp. 92, 101.

18. S[tuart] P. B. Mais, *A Modern Columbus* (Philadelphia: Lippincott, 1934), p. 170.

19. Winn, *Macadam Trail,* p. 128.

20. Anthony Jenkinson, *America Came My Way* (London: Barker, 1936), pp. 129–32; Winn, *Macadam Trail,* p. 130.

21. Asch, *Road,* pp. 194, 258; Ernie Pyle, *Home Country* (New York: Sloane, 1947), p. 299.

22. William S. Thomas, *Trails and Tramps in Alaska and New Foundland* (New York: Putnam's 1913), p. 26; Mais, *Modern Columbus,* p. 210; Pepys, *Mine Host, America,* p. 328.

23. Dixon, *Westward Hoboes,* p. 168.

24. Jan Gordon and Cora J. Gordon, *On Wandering Wheels: Through Roadside Camps from Maine to Georgia in an Old Sedan Car* (New York: Dodd, Mead, 1928), pp. 234, 239.

25. Ibid., p. 62; Asch, *The Road,* pp. 63, 79.

26. Cecil Roberts, *And So to America* (London: Hodder and Stoughton, 1946), pp. 185, 192, 195.

27. MacDonnell, *Trip to America*, p. 237; Lewis Gannett, *Sweet Land* (Garden City, N.Y.: Sun Dial Press, 1937), p. 5.

28. Dallas L. Sharp, *The Better Country* (Boston: Houghton Mifflin, 1928), p. 43; Humphrey, *Green Mountains*, p. 59.

29. Pepys, *Mine Host, America*, p. 125; Gordon and Gordon, *Wandering Wheels*, p. 113.

30. Finger, *Foot-Loose in the West*, p. 272; Pyle, *Home Country*, p. 57; Ida Morris, *A Pacific Coast Vacation* (New York: Abbey Press, 1901), p. 129; Rollo W. Brown, *I Travel by Train* (New York: Appleton-Century, 1939), p. 10.

31. Ralph D. Paine, "Discovering America by Motor," *Scribner's* 53 (February 1913): 137; Street, *Abroad at Home*, p. 365.

32. Boorstin, *Image*, pp. 106, 108; Pomeroy, *In Search of the Golden West*, pp. 47–48.

33. Gunn, *Vacationscapes*, p. 114. Gunn draws on Jerome S. Bruner, "Personality Dynamics and the Process of Perceiving," in *Perception*, edited by Robert R. Blake and Glenn V. Ramsey (New York: Ronald Press, 1951), p. 123.

34. Louise C. Hale, *We Discover the Old Dominion* (New York: Dodd, Mead, 1916), pp. 153, 222; Harrison Rhodes, *In Vacation America* (New York: Harper, 1915), p. 33.

35. David Steele, *Going Abroad Overland*, p. 121; Van de Water, *Family Flivvers*, p. 202.

36. Miller, *Air-Conditioned Nightmare*, p. 220; Cobb, *Roughing It Deluxe*, p. 37; Finger, *Foot-Loose in the West*, p. 51.

37. Roberts, *And So to America*, p. 99; Steinbeck, *Travels with Charley*, p. 166.

38. Ilf and Petrov, *Little Golden America*, pp. 287–88.

39. Webb, *We Explore the Great Lakes*, pp. 21, 75.

40. Relph, *Place and Placelessness*, p. 1.

41. Henry V. Poor, *An Artist Sees Alaska* (New York: Viking, 1945), p. 42.

42. E. B. White, *Here Is New York* (New York: Harper, 1949), p. 26; Ilf and Petrov, *Little Golden America*, p. 20; Akira Oto, *A Garioan in the United States* (Tokyo: Hokuseido, 1955), p. 19; George Mikes, *How to Scrape Skies* (London: Wingate, 1949), pp. 13, 61.

43. Pyle, *Home Country*, p. 391; Robert E. L. Farmer, *From Florida to the Far West* (Bartow, Fla.: author, 1936), p. 57.

44. Steele, *Going Abroad Overland*, p. 129.

45. Jonathan Daniels, *A Southerner Discovers the South* (New York: Macmillan, 1938), p. 135; Pyle, *Home Country*, p. 393.

46. Lawrence Durrell, *Spirit of Place: Letters and Essays on Travel*, ed. Allan G. Thomas (New York: Dutton, 1969), p. 158; James, *American Scene*, p. 273; D. H. Lawrence, *Studies in Classic Literature* (London: Heinemann, 1964), p. 6.

47. Street, *Abroad at Home*, p. 18; Canby, "Traveling Intelligently in America," pp. 169, 174.

48. Street, *Abroad at Home*, pp. 66, 139.

49. Miller, *Air-Conditioned Nightmare*, p. 27; Craik, "Human Responsiveness to Landscape," p. 170.

50. David Lowenthal, "The American Scene," *Geographical Review* 58 (1968): 72.

51. Janette Routledge, *How to Tour the United States in Thirty-One Days for $100* (New York: Harian, 1938, pp. 1f; *New York Standard Guide* (New York: Forster and Reynolds, 1917), p. 17.

52. Harry A. MacFadden, *Rambles in the Far West* (Hollidaysburg, Penn.: Standard, 1906), p. 251; Street, *Abroad at Home*, p. 427; J. B. Preistley, *Midnight on the Desert* (New York: Harper, 1937), p. 111.

53. Morse, *Pacific Coast Vacation*, p. 2; [Arthur J. Eddy], *2,000 Miles on an Automobile—By "Chauffeur,"* (Philadelphia: Lippincott, 1902), p. 304; Ernest Peixotto, *Romantic California* (New York: Scribner's, 1910), p. 32.

54. [Eddy], *2,000 Miles on an Automobile*, p. 304.

Chapter Three: Nature as an Attraction

1. Hans Huth, *Nature and the American: Three Centuries of Changing Attitudes* (Lincoln: University of Nebraska Press, 1972), p. 106.

2. Advertisement, *Travel* 13 (July 1908): 435; David M. Steele, *Vacation Journeys East and West* (New York: Putnam's, 1918), pp. 34–35.

3. Rhodes, *In Vacation America*, p. 32.

4. Steele, *Vacation Journeys*, p. 124; Walter Citrine, *My American Diary* (London: Routledge, 1941), p. 223.

5.   Charles E. Funnel, *By the Beautiful Sea: The Rise and High Times of That Great American Resort, Atlantic City* (New York: Knopf, 1975), pp. 5, 44.

6.   Thorstein Veblen, *The Theory of the Leisure Class* (New York: Viking, 1967), p. 35.

7.   See Kaplan, *Leisure in America*, p. 86.

8.   Funnel, *By the Beautiful Sea*, p. 45; George A. Birmingham, *Connaught to Chicago* (London: Nisbet, 1914), p. 89.

9.   Birmingham, *Connaught to Chicago*, p. 85.

10.   Funnel, *By the Beautiful Sea*, pp. 132–40.

11.   Rhodes, *In Vacation America*, pp. 10, 126.

12.   Ibid., p. 116; Cecil Roberts, *Gone Sunward* (London: Hodder and Stoughton, 1936), p. 269.

13.   Street, *American Adventures*, p. 597; John Van Schaick, Jr., *Cruising Cross Country* (Boston: Universalist, 1926), p. 303; Roberts, *Gone Sunwards*, p. 170.

14.   MacFadden, *Rambles*, p. 122; Wood, *Tourist's California*, pp. 310, 315.

15.   Post, *By Motor*, p. 119; *Road Maps and Tour Book of Western North Carolina* (Raleigh: North Carolina Good Roads Association and the State Highway Commission, 1916), p. 34.

16.   G. W. Stevens, *The Land of the Dollar* (Edinburgh: Blackwood, 1897), p. 253.

17.   MacFadden, *Rambles*, pp. 115–17.

18.   Horace Sutton, *Travelers: The American Tourist from Stagecoach to Space Shuttle* (New York: Morrow, 1980), p. 227.

19.   Dreiser, *Hoosier Holiday*, p. 477.

20.   Ibid., p. 479; Hale, *We Discover the Old Dominion*, p. 180; Kenneth L. Roberts, *Sun Hunting* (Indianapolis: Bobbs-Merrill, 1922), p. 23.

21.   [Eddy], *2,000 Miles*, p. 266; Street, *American Adventures*, p. 600.

22.   Edward Bok, "Summers of Our Discontent," *Ladies Home Journal* 18 (May 1901): 16; Van Schaick, *Cruising Cross Country*, p. 137.

23.   Pomeroy, *In Search of the Golden West*, p. 117.

24.   Peter J. Schmitt, *Back to Nature: The Arcadian Myth in Urban America* (New York: Oxford University Press, 1969), p. xvii; Morley, *Travels in Philadelphia*, p. 148.

25. Dreiser, *Hoosier Holiday*, p. 140; William Saroyan, *Short Drive, Sweet Chariot* (New York: Phaedra, 1966), p. 71.

26. Pepys, *Mine Host, America*, p. 194.

27. Steele, *Going Abroad Overland*, p. 121.

28. Finger, *Foot-Loose in the West*, p. 186; C. K. Shepard, *Across America by Motorcycle* (New York: Longmans, Green, 1922), p. 188.

29. Finger, *Foot-Loose in the West*, p. 143; MacFadden, *Rambles*, p. 127; Charles J. Finger, *Adventure under Sapphire Skies* (New York: Morrow, 1931), p. 207.

30. Finger, *Foot-Loose in the West*, p. 144; Lord Kinross, *The Innocents at Home* (New York: Morrow, 1959), p. 155; Dixon, *Westward Hoboes*, p. 221; Hoffman Birney, *Roads to Roam* (Philadelphia: Penn, 1930), p. 59.

31. See Huth, *Nature and the Americans*, p. 102; Roderick Nash, *Wilderness and the American Mind* (New Haven: Yale University Press, 1967), p. 155; Schmitt, *Back to Nature*, pp. 23, 154.

32. F. Fraser Darling and Noel D. Eichhorn, *Man and Nature in the National Parks* (Washington, D.C.: Conservation Foundation, 1967), p. 13.

33. Frank C. Brockman, *Recreational Use of Wild Lands* (New York: McGraw-Hill, 1959), p. 140.

34. Enos A. Mills, *Your National Parks* (Boston: Houghton, Mifflin, 1917), p. 379.

35. Ibid., p. 385.

36. Nash, *Wilderness*, p. 108; John Ise, *Our National Park Policy: A Critical History* (Baltimore: Johns Hopkins University Press, 1961), p. 4.

37. Schmitt, *Back to Nature*, p. 160.

38. Franklin K. Lane, letter to Stephen T. Mather, May 13, 1918, as quoted in *Report of the Department of the Interior, 1918, vol. I* (Washington, D.C.: 1918), p. 110.

39. Brockman, *Recreational Use of Wild Lands*, p. 113.

40. Stephen T. Mather, "Sieur De Monts and Yosemite, The Problem of Our National Parks," *Outlook* 15 (April 25, 1917): 750.

41. [Geroge H. Lorimer], "Selling Scenery," *Saturday Evening Post* 170 (October 11, 1919): 28.

42. Bob R. O'Brien, "The Yellowstone National Park Road System:

Past, Present, and Future," (Ph.D. diss., University of Washington, 1965), p. 8.

43. Ise, *Our National Park Policy*, p. 564.

44. Nash, *Wilderness*, p. 161.

45. Ise, *Our National Park Policy*, pp. 202–3.

46. Schmitt, *Back to Nature*, p. 161.

47. Ibid., p. 163.

48. U.S. National Park Service, *Park Structures and Facilities* (Washington, D.C.: 1935), p. 3.

49. Ise, *Our National Park Policy*, p. 362.

50. Hiram M. Chittenden, *The Yellowstone National Park* (St. Paul: Haynes, 1927), p. 117.

51. F. Everett Brimer, *Autocamping Facts* (Chicago: Outer's Book Co., 1924), p. 7.

52. Ise, *Our National Park Policy*, p. 210.

53. Brimer, *Autocamping Facts*, p. 2.

54. Massey, *It Might Have Been Worse*, p. 91; Thomas Wolfe, *A Western Journal: A Daily Log of the Great Parks Trip, June 20–July 2, 1938*, ed. Edward C. Aswell (Pittsburgh: University of Pittsburgh Press, 1951), p. 46.

55. Massey, *It Might Have Been Worse*, pp. 96–97.

56. Gannett, *Sweet Land*, p. 169.

57. Van de Water, *Family Flivvers*, p. 194; Ferguson, *Motor Camping on Western Trails*, p. 87; Steinbeck, *Travels with Charley*, p. 161.

58. Gladding, *Across the Continent*, p. 99.

59. Ise, *Our National Park Policy*, pp. 58, 71.

60. Ibid., p. 82.

61. Bedell, *Modern Gypsies*, p. 149; Steele, *Going Abroad Overland*, p. 163.

62. Gannett, *Sweet Land*, pp. 160–61.

63. Ise, *Our National Park Policy*, p. 457.

64. Darling and Eichhorn, *Man and Nature*, p. 31.

65. W. A. Clarke, "Automobiling in Yosemite Valley," *Overland Monthly* 40 (July–December 1902): 109.

66. Bedell, *Modern Gypsies*, p. 146.

67. Steele, *Going Abroad Overland*, p. 171; Finger, *Foot-Loose in the West*, p. 221.

68. Ise, *Our National Park Policy*, p. 457.

69.	Steele, *Going Abroad Overland*, p. 38; Cobb, *Roughing It Deluxe*, pp. 38, 42.

70.	Wolfe, *Western Journal*, p. 21; Flagg, *Boulevards*, p. 134; Finger, *Foot-Loose in the West*, p. 122.

71.	Ilf and Petrov, *Little Golden America*, pp. 164–65.

72.	Muir, *Our National Parks*, pp, 1–2; Aldo Leopold, *Sand County Almanac: And Sketches Here and There* (New York: Oxford, 1949).

73.	Aldo Leopold, "The Last Stand of the Wilderness," *American Forests and Forest Life* 31 (October 1925): 601.

74.	Roderick Nash, *The Nervous Generation: American Thought, 1917–1930* (Chicago: Rand McNally, 1970), p. 84; Nash, *Wilderness*, p. 145.

75.	Ibid., p. 200; Ise, *Our National Park Policy*, p. 639.

76.	Roger Todhunter, "Banff and the Canadian National Park Idea," *Landscape* 25 (Autumn 1981): 35.

77.	A. R. Byrne, *Man and Landscape Change in the Banff National Park Area Before 1911*, Department of Geography, National Park Series no. 1, Studies in Land Use and Landscape Change (Calgary: University of Calgary, 1968), pp. 124–26, 137.

78.	McEvoy, *From the Great Lakes*, p. 114; Pyle, *Home Country*, p. 60.

79.	Todhunter, "Banff," p. 39.

80.	Roderick Nash, "Wilderness and Man in North America," in *The Canadian National Parks: Today and Tomorrow*, ed. J. G. Nelson and R. C. Scarce, Department of Geography, National Park Series, Studies in Land Use and Landscape Change (Calgary: University of Calgary, 1968), p. 79; Morris T. Longstreth, *The Lake Superior Country* (New York: Century, 1924), pp. 193, 242.

Chapter Four: Travel by Railroad and Steamship

1.	U.S. Bureau of the Census, *Historical Statistics of the United States: Colonial Times to 1957* (Washington, D.C.: U.S. Government Printing Office, 1961), p. 429; Canada, Ministere Des Chemins De Fer Et Canaux, *Rapport Annuel* (Ottawa: 1901), p. ix.

2.	U.S. Bureau of the Census, *Historical Statistics*, p. 436.

3.	Street, *Abroad at Home*, p. 105.

4.	Birmingham, *Connaught to Chicago*, p. 94; Andre La Fond, *Impressions of America* (Paris: Fondation Strassburger, 1930), p. 35;

Van Schaick, *Cruising Cross Country*, p. 243; Street, *Abroad at Home*, p. 514.

5.   Brown, *I Travel by Train*, p. 9; A. G. MacDonnell, *A Visit to America* (London: MacMillan, 1935), p. 228.

6.   Citrine, *My American Diary*, p. 123; Jenkinson, *America Came My Way*, p. 169; Flagg, *Boulevards*, p. 142.

7.   Brown, *I Travel by Train*, p. 6; McEvoy, *From the Great Lakes*, p. 89; Street, *Abroad at Home*, p. 512.

8.   John T. Faris, *Seeing the Eastern States* (Philadelphia: Lippincott, 1922), p. 74.

9.   Street, *Abroad at Home*, p. 470; Dallas L. Sharp, *The Better Country* (Boston: Houghton Mifflin, 1928), p. 31.

10.   Street, *Abroad at Home*, p. 440; Waldron, *We Explore the Great Lakes*, p. 316.

11.   Street, *Abroad at Home*, p. 17; Brown, *I Travel by Train*, p. 101; Steele, *Going Abroad Overland*, p. 177.

12.   Longstreth, *Lake Superior Country*, p. 51; Jenkinson, *America Came My Way*, p. 172.

13.   Cecil Roberts, *And So to America*, p. 96; McEvoy, *From the Great Lakes to the Wide West*, p. 100.

14.   Birmingham, *Connaught to Chicago*, p. 99.

15.   McEvoy, *From the Great Lakes to the Wide West*, p. 135; Citrine, *My American Diary*, p. 185.

16.   John A. Kouwenhoven, *The Beer Can by the Highway* (Garden City, N.Y.: Doubleday, 1961), p. 14.

17.   Ibid., p. 16; Edward Hungerford, *The Personality of American Cities* (New York: McBride, Nast, 1913), p. 198; Street, *Abroad at Home*, p. 7.

18.   MacDonnell, *Visit to North America*, p. 72; Street, *Abroad at Home*, p. 7.

19.   Christopher Morely, *Travels in Philadelphia*, pp. 49, 249.

20.   Jenkinson, *America Came My Way*, p. 169.

21.   William Saroyan, *Short Drive, Sweet Chariot*, p. 81; McEvoy, *From the Great Lakes*, p. 185.

22.   McEvoy, *From the Great Lakes*, pp. 18–20.

23.   H. Bennett Abdy, *On the Ohio* (New York: Dodd, Mead, 1919), pp. 15, 25.

24.   Hitchcock, *Two Women in the Klondike*, p. 57.

25. McEvoy, *From the Great Lakes*, p. 19; Morris, *Pacific Coast Vacation*, p. 55.

26. John C. Van Dyke, *The New New York* (New York: MacMillan, 1909), p. 28.

27. Ethel Fleming, *New York* (New York: MacMillan, 1929), p. 115; MacFadden, *Rambles*, p. 95.

28. MacFadden, *Rambles*, p. 89; Milton M. Shaw, *Nine Thousand Miles on a Pullman Train* (Philadelphia: Allen, Lane, and Scott, 1898), pp. 87–89.

Chapter Five: Touring by Automobile before World War I

1. U.S. Bureau of the Census, *Historical Statistics to 1957*, p. 91.

2. Foster R. Dulles, *America Learns to Play,1* p. 313.

3. Woodrow Wilson, quoted in Mark Sullivan, *Our Times* (New York: Scribner's, 1923), p. 431.

4. For examples see: Winthrop Scaritt, *Three Men in a Car* (New York: Dutton, 1906); Francis Miltoun, *The Automobilist Abroad* (Boston: Page, 1907); Edith Wharton, *The Motor Flight through France* (New York: Scribner's, 1909); A. T. Wood and B. R. Wood, *Ribbon Roads: A Motor Tour Abroad* (New York: Putnam's, 1910).

5. Horace Sutton, *Travelers*, p. 128.

6. [Eddy], *2,000 Miles on an Automobile*, pp. 9, 40.

7. Thaddeus S. Dayton, "The Motor-Car Vacation: The 'Grand Tour' of To-Day Is Made by Automobiles," *Harper's Weekly* 55 (July 1, 1911): 10; see also Henry B. Joy, "The Traveler and the Automobile," *Outlook* 115 (April 25, 1917): 739.

8. Saroyan, *Short Drive, Sweet Chariot*, p. 111; Warren J. Belasco, *Americans on the Road: From Autocamp to Motel, 1910–1945* (Cambridge: M.I.T. Press, 1979), p. 20.

9. Dreiser, *Hoosier Holiday*, pp. 92–93; Post, *By Motor*, p. 22; Belasco, *Americans on the Road*, p. 24.

10. Belasco, *Americans on the Road*, p. 37.

11. [Eddy], *2,000 Miles on an Automobile*, p. 7.

12. John B. Rae, *The Road and the Car in American Life* (Cambridge: M.I.T. Press, 1971), p. 34.

13. Lincoln Highway Association, *The Lincoln Highway: The Story of*

a Crusade That Made Transportation History (New York: Dodd, Mead, 1935), p. 6.

14. F. E[verett] Brimer, *Motor Campcraft* (New York: MacMillan, 1923), p. 207.

15. Antonio Scarfoglio, *Round the World in a Motor-Car*, trans. J. Parker Heyes (New York: Kennerley, 1909), p. 54.

16. Ibid., p. 92.

17. Alice H. Ramsey, *Veil, Duster, and Tire Iron* (Covina, Cal.: Dahlstrom, 1961); Harriet F. White, *A Woman's World Tour in a Motor* (Philadelphia: Lippincott, 1911), p. 353.

18. John R. Eustis, "The Automobile, the Ideal Vehicle of Travel," *Travel* 14 (January 1909): 178.

19. A. L. Westgard, *Tales of a Pathfinder* (New York: author, 1920), p. 60.

20. Victor Eubank, "Log of an Auto Prairie Schooner," *Sunset* 28 (February 1912): 188.

21. George O. Draper, "A View of the Tour from One Participating," *Horseless Age* 16 (July 26, 1905): 153.

22. Hugo A. Taussig, *Retracing the Pioneers from West to East in an Automobile* (San Francisco: author, 1910), pp. 20, 50–55.

23. Thomas W. Wilby, *A Motor Tour through Canada* (London: Lane, 1914), pp. ix, 169, 196.

24. Advertisement for the Automobile Blue Book Publishing Company in *New York Standard Guide* (New York: Foster and Reynolds, 1917), p. 175.

25. *Tourbook: The Midland Trail* (Grand Junction, Colo.: Midland Trails Log Book Co., 1916), p. 3.

26. Dreiser, *Hoosier Holiday*, p. 201; Wilby, *Motor Tour through Canada*, p. 93; Dixon, *Westward Hoboes*, p. 28; [Eddy], *2,000 Miles on an Automobile*, p. 36.

27. [Eddy], *2,000 Miles on an Automobile*, p. 88.

28. Taussig, *Retracing the Pioneers*, p. 33; Thornton E. Round, *The Good of It All* (Cleveland: Lakeside, 1957), p. 1.

29. Post, *By Motor*, p. 22; Belasco, *Americans on the Road*, p. 34.

30. Wilby, *Motor Tour through Canada*, p. 122.

31. Gladding, *Across the Continent*, p. 136; Post, *By Motor*, p. 82; Paine, "Discovering America by Motor," p. 114.

32. Brimer, *Autocamping Facts*, p. 56; Lincoln Highway Associa-

tion, *The Complete Official Road Guide of the Lincoln Highway* (Detroit: 1916), p. 19; *Tourbook,* p. 3.

33. See Dulles, *History of Recreation,* p. 315; Edith W. Hughes, *Motoring in White from Dakota to Cape Cod* (New York: Knickerbocker Press, 1917), p. 5.

34. Dreiser, *Hoosier Holiday,* p. 69.

35. Lewis, *Free Air,* p. 54.

36. Wood, *The Tourist's California,* p. 50; Gladding, *Across the Continent,* p. 228.

37. Lewis, *Free Air,* p. 31; Gladding, *Across the Continent,* pp. 139–40; Flagg, *Boulevards.*

38. Flagg, *Boulevards,* p. 212; Wilby, *Motor Tour through Canada,* p. 130.

39. Vernon McGill, *Diary of a Motor Journey from Chicago to Los Angeles* (Los Angeles: Grafton, 1922), p. 12; Round, *The Good of It All,* p. xvii; L. L. Whitman, *Across America in a Franklin* (New York: H. H. Franklin Co., [1906]); *Official Timetable* (Omaha: Union Pacific Railroad, February 1, 1909), p. 15.

40. [Eddy], *2,000 Miles on an Automobile,* pp. 62 and 65; Street, *Abroad at Home,* p. 255; Gladding, *Across the Continent,* p. 201.

41. Act. no. 196, *Public Acts of Michigan,* 1905, quoted in Philip P. Mason, "The League of American Wheelmen and the Good Roads Movement, 1880–1905," (Ph.D. diss., University of Michigan, 1957), p. 191; Post, *By Motor,* p. 36; Hyde, "Automobile Club of California," p. 101.

42. Wilby, *Motor Tour through Canada,* p. 79; Piexotto, *Romantic California,* p. 7.

43. Dreiser, *Hoosier Holiday,* pp. 65, 116, 267.

Chapter Six: Highways and Tourism

1. Rae, *Road and the Car,* p. 50.

2. M. C. Urquhart (ed.), *Historical Statistics of Canada* (Cambridge, Ontario: MacMillan, 1965), p. 550.

3. Dulles, *History of Recreation,* p. 320.

4. Wilby, *Motor Tour through Canada,* p. 71.

5. Mason, "The League of American Wheelman," p. 50.

6. Rae, *Road and the Car,* p. 32.

7. Harwood Frost, *The Art of Roadmaking* (New York: McGraw-Hill, 1910), p. 19.
8. Advertisement for the Portland Cement Association, *Outlook* 115 (April 25, 1917): 754; Joy, "The Traveler and the Automobile," 115:752, 754.
9. Rae, *Road and the Car*, p. 32.
10. Lincoln Highway Association, *Lincoln Highway*, pp. 1, 57, 118.
11. Ibid., p. 199.
12. Newton A. Fuessle, "The Lincoln Highway: A National Road," *Travel* 24 (February 1915): 26–27.
13. George R. Chatburn, *Highways and Highway Transportation* (New York: Crowell, 1923), p. 12.
14. Lincoln Highway Association, *Lincoln Highway*, p. 227.
15. Ibid., p. 228; Van de Water, *Family Flivvers*, p. 70.
16. Rae, *Road and the Car*, p. 37.
17. Ibid., pp. 39, 62; Sigrald Johannesson, "Highway Finances and Related Problems," in *Highways in Our National Life*, ed. Jean Labatut and Wheaton J. Lane (Princeton: Princeton University Press, 1950), p. 211.
18. Rae, *Road and the Car*, pp. 74, 188.
19. U.S. Department of Transportation, *Highway Statistics: Summary to 1965* (Washington, D.C.: Government Printing Office, 1965), p. 120.
20. Frederic L. Paxson, "The Highway Movement: 1916–1935," *American Historical Review* 51 (January 1946): 239.
21. Edwin C. Goulet, *The Story of Canadian Roads* (Toronto: University of Toronto Press, 1967), p. 155.
22. Ibid., p. 166.
23. Ibid., p. 156.
24. Ibid., p. 224.
25. Thomas D. Murphy, *Oregon the Picturesque* (Boston: Page, 1917), p. 76; Van de Water, *Family Flivvers*, p. 16.
26. Massey, *It Might Have Been Worse*, p. 66; Dixon, *Westward Hoboes*, pp. 26–29.
27. Wilby, *Motor Tour through Canada*, p. 76; Flagg, *Boulevards*, pp. 99, 188; Gladding, *Across the Continent*, p. 111; Dreiser, *Hoosier Holiday*, p. 111; Van de Water, *Family Flivvers*, p. 118.
28. Gordon and Gordon, *On Wandering Wheels*, pp. 193, 281.
29. [Eddy], *2,000 Miles on an Automobile*, p. 173; U.S. Public Roads

Administration, *Highway Practice in the United States of America* (Washington, D.C.: Government Printing Office, 1949), p. 6.

30. Dreiser, *Hoosier Holiday*, p. 176.

31. Thomas H. MacDonald, "The History and Development of Road Building in the United States," *Transactions, American Society of Civil Engineers* 92 (1928): 1,199.

32. Ferguson, *Motor Camping on Western Trails*, pp. 110, 134.

33. "The Columbia River Highway," *The American City* 14 (January 1916): 2.

34. Chatburn, *Highways and Highway Transportation*, p. 441.

35. Myron M. Stearns, "Notes on Changes in Motoring," *Harper's* 189 (September 1936): 443.

36. Pepys, *Mine Host, America*, p. 81; Ilf and Petrov, *Little Golden America*, p. 64.

37. Irvin S. Cobb, *Some United States* (New York: Doran, 1926), p. 272; Kenneth L. Roberts, "Travels in Billboardia," *Saturday Evening Post* 174 (October 15, 1928): 186.

38. Kinross, *Innocents at Home*, p. 74; Gordon and Gordon, *On Wandering Wheels*, p. 243.

39. See John Robinson, *Highways and Our Environment* (New York: McGraw-Hill, 1971), p. 272.

40. *Roadside Improvement* (Washington, D.C.: American Planning and Civic Association, 1938), p. 5.

41. Gordon Brinley, *Away to Quebec* (New York: Dodd, Mead, 1937), p. 255.

42. Roberts, "Travels in Billboardia," p. 186; Cobb, *Some United States*, p. 290.

43. Robinson, *Highways and Our Environment*, p. 52.

44. Christopher Tunnard and Boris Pushkarev, *Man-Made America: Chaos or Control?* (New Haven: Yale University Press, 1963), p. 162.

45. Robinson, *Highways and Our Environment*, p. 52.

46. J. B. Priestley, *Midnight on the Desert* (New York: Harper, 1937), p. 86; Ilf and Petrov, *Little Golden America*, p. 64.

47. Robinson, *Highways and Our Environment*, p. 48.

48. See Robert A. Caro, *The Power Broker* (New York: Vintage Books, 1975), pp. 6–8.

49. Roberts, *And So to America*, p. 119; Caro, *Power Broker*.

50. Ise, *Our National Park Policy*, p. 421.

51. Spencer Miller, Jr., "History of the Modern Highway in the United States," in Labatut and Lane (eds.), *Highways in Our National Life*, p. 106.

52. MacDonnell, *Visit to America*, p. 27.

53. Rae, *Road and the Car*, p. 125.

54. Tunnard and Pushkarev, *Man-Made America*, p. 165.

55. Daniels, *A Southerner Discovers New England*, p. 14.

56. J. Todd Snow, "The New Road in the United States," *Landscape* 17 (Autumn 1967): 13.

57. Gunn, *Vacationscape*, p. 92.

58. Tunnard and Pushkarev, *Man-Made America*, p. 169.

59. Gordon and Gordon, *On Wandering Wheels*, p. 42.

60. John Nolen and Henry V. Hubbard, Parkways and Land Values (Cambridge: Harvard University Press, 1937), p. 43; John Brooks, *The Landscape of Roads* (London: Architectural Presls, 1960), p. 12; Tunnard and Pushkarev, *Man-Made America*, p. 209.

61. Nolen and Hubbard, *Parkways and Land Values*, p. 113.

62. Upton Sinclair, *Oil!* (New York: Grosset and Dunlap, 1926), p. 5.

63. Tunnard and Pushkarev, *Man-Made America*, p. 179.

64. Paxson, "The Highway Movement, 1916–1935," p. 251.

65. Robinson, *Highways and Our Environment*, p. 192.

66. Wilhelm Miller, "The First Roadside Planting along the Lincoln Highway," *American City* 14 (April 1916): 326; J. M. Bennett, *Roadsides: The Front Yard of the Nation* (Boston: Stratford, 1936), p. 55; Brinley, *Away to Quebec*, p. 33.

67. See Malcolm M. Willey and Stuart A. Rice, "The Agencies of Communication," in *Recent Social Trends in the United States*, (New York: McGraw-Hill, 1933), p. 172; Robinson, *Highways and Our Environment*, p. 10.

68. Cynthia G. Dettlebach, *In the Driver's Seat: The Automobile in American Literature and Popular Culture* (Westport, Conn.: Greenwood Press, 1976), p. 91; Ilf and Petrov, *Little Golden America*, p. 61.

Chapter Seven: Automobile Travel between the World Wars

1. [Eddy], *2,000 Miles on an Automobile*, p. 201; Flagg, *Boulevards*, pp. 28–29.
2. Stearns, "Notes on Changes in Motoring," p. 441.
3. Belasco, *Americans on the Road*, p. 89.
4. See Austin F. Bement, "The Lincoln Highway Tour in 1916," in *The Complete Official Road Guide of the Lincoln Highway* (Detroit: Lincoln Highway Association, 1916), p. 31; Norman S. Hayner, "Auto Camps in the Evergreen Playground," *Social Forces* 9 (December 1930): 256.
5. Tunnard and Puschkarev, *Man-Made America*, p. 172.
6. Van de Water, *Family Flivvers*, pp. 42, 194; Sharp, *Better Country*, p. 44.
7. Pyle, *Home Country*, p. 407.
8. Steinbeck, *Travels with Charley*, p. 23.
9. Pomeroy, *In Search of the Golden West*, p. 210.
10. Wolfe, *A Western Journal*, p. 3.
11. See Belasco, *Americans on the Road*, p. 68.
12. Humphrey, *Green Mountains*, p. 17.
13. Sharp, *Better Country*, p. 193; Gordon and Gordon, *On Wandering Wheels*, p. 17.
14. Van de Water, *Family Flivvers*, p. 144.
15. Ilf and Petrov, *Little Golden America*, p. 64.
16. Gordon and Gordon, *On Wandering Wheels*, p. 141; Birney, *Roads to Roam*, p. 242; Gannett, *Sweet Land*, p. 93.
17. Van de Water, *Family Flivvers*, pp. 101, 165.
18. Mary Bedell, *Modern Gypsies*, p. 77; Guy K. Austin, *Covered Wagon, 10 H.P.* (London: Bles, 1936), p. 90; Bedell, *Modern Gypsies*, p. 172.
19. Elon Jessup, *The Motor Camping Book* (New York: Putnam's, 1921), p. 7.
20. Belasco, *Americans on the Road*, p. 3; J. C. Long and John D. Long, *Motor Camping* (New York: Dodd, Mead, 1923), p. 15; Brimmer, *Motor Campcraft*, p. 1.
21. Jessup, *Motor Camping Book*, p. 7; Belasco, *Americans on the Road*, p. 83; Dixon, *Westward Hoboes*, p. 50.

22. Ferguson, *Motor Camping on Western Trails*, p. 266; Belasco, *Americans on the Road*, p. 71.
23. Van de Water, *Family Flivvers*, pp. 61, 173; Ferguson, *Motor Camping on Western Trails*, p. 233.
24. Jessup, *Motor Camping Book*, p. 5; Van de Water, *Family Flivvers*, p. 203.
25. Van de Water, *Family Flivvers*, pp. 71, 86; Gordon and Gordon, *On Wandering Wheels*, p. 82.
26. See Belasco, *Americans on the Road*, p. 98; Van de Water, *Family Flivvers*, pp. 34, 66; Ferguson, *Motor Camping on Western Trails*, p. 179.
27. Gordon and Gordon, *On Wandering Wheels*, p. 85; Brimmer, *Motor Campcraft*, p. 23; Webb, *We Explore the Great Lakes*, p. 273; Van de Water, *Family Flivvers*, p. 242.
28. Gladding, *Across the Continent*, p. 146; Lorimer, "Selling Scenery," p. 28.
29. Earl C. May, "The Argonauts of the Automobile," *Saturday Evening Post* 197 (August 9, 1924): 89.
30. Elon Jessup, "The Flight of the Tin Can Tourist," *Outlook* 128 (May 18, 1921): 166; Long and Long, *Motor Camping*, p. 2; Brimmer, *Motor Campcraft*, p. 194.
31. Jessup, "Flight of the Tin Can Tourist," p. 167.
32. Pomeroy, *In Search of the Golden West*, p. 147.
33. Roland S. Wallis, "Tourist Camps," *Engineering Extension Service Bulletin* vol. 21, no. 36 (Ames: Iowa State College, February 7, 1923), p. 40.
34. Belasco, *Americans on the Road*, p. 72.
35. Oscar Lewis, "Free Auto Camp Ground," in *Essays of Today (1926–1927)*, ed. Odell Shepard and Robert Hillyer (New York: Century, 1928), p. 119.
36. Long and Long, *Motor Camping*, p. 197.
37. Brimmer, *Motor Campcraft*, p. 196.
38. Long and Long, *Motor Camping*, p. 200.
39. Roberts, *Sun Hunting*, p. 89.
40. Belasco, *Americans on the Road*, pp. 112–15; Van de Water, *Family Flivvers*, p. 109.
41. American Automobile Association, *Official Camping and Campsite Manual* (Washington, D.C.: 1925); American Automobile

Association, *Official AAA Camp Directory* (Washington, D.C.: Government Printing Office, 1928).

42. Gordon Brinley, *Away to the Gaspé* (New York: Dodd, Mead, 1935), p. 71.

43. Van de Water, *Family Flivvers*, p. 55.

44. Roberts, *Sun Hunting*, p. 85; Gordon and Gordon, *On Wandering Wheels*, p. 87.

45. Ferguson, *Motor Camping on Western Trails*, p. 119; Sharp, *Better Country*, p. 123.

46. Pomeroy, *In Search of the Golden West*, p. 207.

47. Donald O. Cowgill, *Mobile Homes: A Study of Trailer Life* (Philadelphia: author, 1941), p. 5; Franklin McCann, "The Growth of the Tourist Court in the United States and Its Relationship to the Urban Development of Albuquerque, New Mexico," *Dennison University Scientific Laboratories Journal* 37 (1942): 52.

48. J. N. Darling, *The Cruise of the Bouncing Betsy: A Trailer Travelogue* (New York: Stokes, 1937), pp. 14, 72, 95.

49. Wallace W. True, "Significant Trends in the Motel Industry," *Appraisal Journal* 27 (April 1959): 229.

50. Van de Water, *Family Flivvers*, p. 223; Ferguson, *Motor Camping on Western Trails*, p. 164; Gordon and Gordon, *On Wandering Wheels*, p. 82.

51. Brimmer, *Autocamping Facts*, p. 2; Hayner, "Auto Camps in the Evergreen Playground," p. 256.

52. John A. Jakle, "Motel by the Roadside: America's Room for the Night," *Journal of Cultural Geography* 1 (Fall–Winter 1980): 34–49.

53. Humphrey, *Green Mountains*, p. 56.

54. U.S. Bureau of the Census, *Census of Business: 1935*, vol. 8, pt. 6, *Tourist Camps* (Washington, D.C.: Government Printing Office, 1937), p. 1; U.S. Bureau of the Census, *Census of Business: 1939, Tourist Courts and Tourist Camps, Preliminary Summary* (Washington, D.C.: Government Printing Office, 1941), p. 1.

55. John A. Jakle, "Roadside Restaurants: The Evolution of Place-Product-Packaging," *Journal of Cultural Geography* 3 (Fall–Winter 1982): 76–93.

56. Ilf and Petrov, *Little Golden America*, p. 27; Saroyan, *Short Drive, Sweet Chariot*, p. 127.

57. Cecil Roberts, *Gone Sunwards*, p. 205.
58. John B. Jackson, "Other Directed Houses," *Landscape* 6 (Winter 1956–57): 31.
59. Ilf and Petrov, *Little Golden America*, p. 32; Sinclair, *Oil!*, p. 16.
60. Dixon, *Westward Hoboes*, p. 48; Gannett, *Sweet Land*, p. 206.
61. John A. Jakle, "The American Gasoline Station, 1920 to 1970," *Journal of American Culture* 1 (Spring 1976): 520–42.
62. Birney, *Roads to Roam*, p. 184; Pepys, *Mine Host, America*, p. 154.
63. Johannesson, "Highway Finances and Related Problems," p. 207.
64. Massey, *It Might Have Been Worse*, p. 145; Paul E. Vernon, *Coast to Coast By Motor* (London: Black, 1930), p. 99; Finger, *Foot-Loose in the West*, p. 285; Routledge, *How to Tour the United States*, p. 27.
65. Julius H. Parmelee and Earl R. Feldman, "The Relation of the Highway to Rail Transportation," in *Highways in our National Life*, ed. Jean Labatut and Wheaton J. Lane (Princeton: Princeton University Press, 1950), p. 238.
66. Julius Weinberger, "Economic Aspects of Recreation," *Harvard Business Review* 15 (Summer 1937): 456.

Chapter Eight: Travel by Bus and Air

1. Rae, *Road and the Car*, p. 97.
2. Horace Sutton, *Travelers*.
3. Lewis R. Freeman, "Exploring America by Motor Bus," *Travel* 35 (May 1930): 55.
4. Parmelee and Feldman, "The Relation of the Highway to Rail Transportation," p. 237.
5. Rae, *Road and the Car*, p. 99.
6. Burton B. Crandall, *The Growth of the Intercity Bus Industry* (Syracuse, N.Y.: author, 1954), pp. 130, 136, 285.
7. Rutledge, *How to Tour the United States*, p. 22.
8. Mary Day Winn, *Macadam Trail*, p. 85; Kinross, *Innocents at Home*, pp. 85–89.
9. Winn, *Macadam Trail*, p. 274; Asch, *Road*, p. 137.
10. Winn, *Macadam Trail*, p. 5.
11. Asch, *Road*, p. 139.
12. Ibid., p. 8; Winn, *Macadam Trail*, p. 14.

13. Winn, *Macadam Trail,* p. 195; Asch, *Road,* p. 8; Freeman, "Exploring America by Motor Bus," p. 27.

14. Asch, *Road,* p. 266; Kinross, *Innocents at Home,* p. 89.

15. Winn, *Macadam Trail,* p. 111.

16. See Pomeroy, *In Search of the Golden West,* p. 29.

17. Henry L. Smith, *Airways: The History of Commercial Aviation in the United States* (New York: Knopf, 1942), pp. 84–87.

18. Carl Solberg, *Conquest of the Skies: A History of Commercial Aviation in America* (Boston: Little, Brown, 1979), p. 32.

19. Smith, *Airways,* pp. 106, 113.

20. Advertisement in *Travel* 53 (August 1929): 43.

21. James Reddig as quoted in Solberg, *Conquest of the Skies,* p. 107.

22. Smith, *Airways,* p. 157.

23. Kenneth Hudson, *Air Travel: A Social History* (Totowa, N.J.: Rownan and Littlefield, 1972), p. 31.

24. Solberg, *Conquest of the Skies,* p. 110.

25. Sutton, *Travelers,* p. 159.

26. Hudson, *Air Travel,* p. 46.

27. Bernard De Voto, "The Easy Chair: Transcontinental Flight," *Harper's* 205 (July 1952): 48; Pepys, *Mine Host, America,* p. 320.

28. President's Research Committee on Social Trends, *Recent Social Trends in the United States* (New York: McGraw–Hill, 1934), p. xxvi.

29. Advertisement in *Travel* 72 (October 1938): 43.

30. Peck and Johnson, *Roundabout America,* p. 1.

31. Pepys, *Mine Host, America,* pp. 345–52.

32. De Voto, "Easy Chair," p. 48; Citrine, *My American Diary,* p. 160; De Voto, "Easy Chair," p. 48.

33. Pepys, *Mine Host, America,* p. 321.

34. Hudson, *Air Travel,* p. 46.

35. Pepys, *Mine Host, America,* p. 323; De Voto, "Easy Chair," p. 50.

36. Citrine, *My American Diary,* p. 161; Pepys, *Mine Host, America,* pp. 346, 410.

37. Solberg, *Conquest of the Skies,* p. 115.

38. Ibid., p. 221.

39. Smith, *Airways,* p. 345.

40. Solberg, *Conquest of the Skies.*

41. Van Schaick, *Cruising Cross Country,* p. 23.

42.   Solberg, *Conquest of the Skies.*
43.   Hudson, *Air Travel,* p. 164.
44.   Solberg, *Conquest of the Skies.*
45.   A. D. Rathbone, III, "America's Airports of the Future," *Travel* 85 (September 1945): 25.
46.   Pepys, *Mine Host America,* p. 320.
47.   De Voto, "Easy Chair," p. 47.
48.   Pepys, *Mine Host, America,* p. 353.

Chapter Nine: The Automobile and Tourism after World War II

1.   Kaplan, *Leisure in America,* p. 3.
2.   U.S. Department of Commerce, *Survey of Current Business, 1949* (Washington, D.C.: 1949), as reported in *The Vacation Travel Market of the United States: A Nationwide Survey, No. 1* (Philadelphia: Curtis, 1950), pp. 17, 19.
3.   U.S. Bureau of the Census, *1963 Census of Transportation* (Washington, D.C.: 1963), as reported in Elridge Lovelace, "The Automobile and Recreation," *Traffic Quarterly* 20 (October 1966): 531.
4.   John B. Lansing and Ernest Lilienstein, *The Travel Market 1955: A Report to the Travel Research Association* (Ann Arbor: University of Michigan Survey Research Center, Institute for Social Research, 1963), pp. 5–9; Victor H. Lanning, *The Wisconsin Tourist* (Madison: University of Wisconsin Bureau of Research and Services and Bureau of Community Development, 1950), p. 13.
5.   *Vacation Travel Market,* p. 27; U.S. Bureau of Public Roads, *Highways and Economic and Social Changes* (Washington, D.C.: Government Printing Office, 1964), p. 158; *Vacation Travel Market,* p. 35; Kaplan, *Leisure in America,* p. 212; Lansing and Lilienstein, *Travel Market 1955,* p. 5.
6.   Lansing and Lilienstein, *Travel Market 1955,* p. 20; U.S. Bureau of the Census, *Travel Survey—1957* (Washington, D.C.: 1958) as reported in L. J. Crampton, *Tourist Travel Trends* (Boulder: University of Colorado Bureau of Business Research, 1961), p. 20.
7.   *Michigan Tourist Survey* (East Lansing: Michigan State College, Bureau of Business Research, Research Report no. 7, 1953), p. 6;

L. J. Crampton and F. W. Ellinghaus, *1953 Colorado Statewide Summer Tourist Survey* (Boulder: University of Colorado Bureau of Business Research, 1953), p. 40.

8. U.S. Department of Commerce, *Survey of Current Business* (Washington, D.C.: Government Printing Office, 1949), as reported in *Vacation Travel Market*, p. 7.

9. U.S. National Park Service, *U.S. Travel: A Digest* (Washington, D.C.: Government Printing Office, 1949), p. 3.

10. H. H. Chadwick, *Vermont's Tourist Business: A Study Covering Ten Years, 1934–1943* (Montpelier: Vermont Department of Natural Resources, 1944), p. 3.

11. For an example, see George F. Deasy and Phyllis R. Griess, "Impact of a Tourist Facility on Its Hinterland," *Annals, Association of American Geographers* 56 (June 1966): 290–306.

12. Lanning, *Wisconsin Tourist*, p. 4; J. Ellis Voss, *Summer Resort: An Ecological Analysis of a Satellite Community* (Philadelphia: author, 1941), p. 1; *Vacation Travel Market*, p. 27; American Automobile Association, *Profile of the American Tourist* (Washington, D.C.: 1962), p. 18.

13. Eva Mueller and Gerald Gunn, *The Demand for Outdoor Recreation* (Ann Arbor: University of Michigan Institute of Social Research, 1961), p. 192.

14. Gunn, *Vacationscape*, p. 76.

15. *Vacation Travel Market*, p. 23.

16. Miller, "History of the Modern Highway," p. 107.

17. Edwin C. Goulet, *Story of Canadian Roads*, p. 193.

18. Steinbeck, *Travels with Charley*, p. 89.

19. John Jerome, *The Death of the Automobile: The Fatal Effect of the Golden Era, 1955–1970* (New York: Norton, 1972).

20. William Saroyan, *Short Drive, Sweet Chariot*, p. 127; Steinbeck, *Travels with Charley*, p. 94.

21. John Updike, *Rabbit Run* (New York: Knopf, 1960), p. 30.

22. Relph, *Place and Placelessness*, pp. ii, 93.

23. Asa Briggs, "The Sense of Place," in *The Fitness of Man's Environment: Smithsonian Annual II* (New York: Harper Colophon, 1968), p. 95.

24. Sinclair, *Oil!*, p. 18; Street, *American Adventures*, p. 89.

25. Relph, *Place and Placelessness*, p. 136.

26. Briggs, "Sense of Place," pp. 90–91.
27. Tunnard and Pushkarev, *Man-Made America*, p. 159; Finger, *Adventure under Sapphire Skies*, p. 25.
28. Belasco, *American on the Road*, p.170; *Profile of the American Tourist*, p. 13; *Vacation Travel Market*, pp. 43–45; Crampton and Ellinghaus, *1953 Colorado Statewide Summer Tourist Survey*, p. 35; *Michigan Tourist Survey*, p. 3.
29. Steinbeck, *Travels with Charley*, pp. 47, 182.
30. Jakle, "Motel by the Roadside," 1:43.
31. Jakle, "Roadside Restaurants," 3:76–93.
32. Kinross, *Innocents at Home*, p. 193; Steinbeck, *Travels with Charley*, pp. 90–91, 140.
33. Jack Kerouac, *On the Road* (New York: Viking, 1955); Vladimir Nabokov, *Lolita* (New York: Olympia Press, 1955), p. 160; See Dettlebach, *In the Driver's Seat*, p. 35.

Chapter Ten: The Region as an Attraction

1. Daniels, *A Southerner Discovers the South*, p. 334.
2. Kinross, *Innocents at Home*, p. 125; Ilf and Petrov, *Little Golden America*, p. 68.
3. Thomas Benton, "America's Yesterday: In the Ozark Mountains of Arkansas—Life and Customs on a Forgotten Frontier," *Travel* 63 (July 1934): 8–11.
4. Ibid.; Steinbeck, *Travels with Charley*, p. 106.
5. James, *The American Scene*, p. 50; Dixon, *Westward Hoboes*, p. 61; Kinross, *Innocents at Home*, p. 125; Steinbeck, *Travels with Charley*, p. 79.
6. [Eddy], *2,000 Miles on an Automobile*, p. 311.
7. Wilby, *Motor Tour through Canada*, p. 31; Pepys, *Mine Host, America*, p. 97.
8. Wilby, *Motor Tour through Canada*, p. 60; Harry A. Franck, "The France across Our Border," *Travel* 75 (May 1940): 15.
9. Wilby, *Motor Tour through Canada*, pp. 61–62; Daniels, *A Southerner Discovers New England*, p. 299.
10. Wilby, *Motor Tour through Canada*, p. 62.
11. Advertisement in *Travel* 47 (July 1926): 5; Brinley, *Away to Quebec*, p. 35.
12. Brown, *I Travel by Train*, p. 156; Humphrey, *Green Mountains*, p. 21; Gordon and Gordon, *On Wandering Wheels*, p. 135.

13. Cobb, *Some United States*, p. 287.
14. Clifton Johnson, *Highways and Byways from the St. Lawrence to Virginia* (New York: MacMillan, 1913), p. 157; Cobb, *Some United States*, p. 289.
15. Daniels, *A Southerner Discovers New England*, pp. 15, 61; Clara W. Whiteside, *Touring New England* (Philadelphia: Penn, 1926), p. 4; James, *American Scene*, p. 39.
16. James, *American Scene*, p. 14; Daniels, *A Southerner Discovers New England*, pp. 38, 380.
17. Daniels, *A Southerner Discovers New England*, p. 50; Cobb, *Some United States*, pp. 18–20.
18. Steele, *Vacation Journeys East and West*, p. 189; Dreiser, *Hoosier Holiday*, p. 266.
19. Dreiser, *Hoosier Holiday*, p. 335.
20. Sharp, *Better Country*, pp. 57, 62.
21. De Voto, "Easy Chair," 205:48; Pepys, *Mine Host, America*, p. 135.
22. Dreiser, *Hoosier Holiday*, p. 152; Kouwenhoven, *Beer Can*, p. 14.
23. Steinbeck, *Travels with Charley*, pp. 105–6.
24. Daniels, *A Southerner Discovers New England*, p. 1; Winn, *Macadam Trail*, p. 195.
25. Daniels, *A Southerner Discovers the South*, pp. 46, 338; Gordon and Gordon, *On Wandering Wheels*, p. 242.
26. Hale, *We Discover the Old Dominion*, p. 66; Hungerford, *Personality of American Cities*, p. 136.
27. Johnson, *Highways and Byways*, p. 330; Oto, *A Garioan in the United States*, p. 69.
28. Citrine, *My American Diary*, p. 28; Birmingham, *Connaught to Chicago*, pp. 133–35.
29. Gordon and Gordon, *On Wandering Wheels*, pp. 249–50, 262; Hungerford, *Personality of American Cities*, p. 140.
30. Steinbeck, *Travels with Charley*, p. 255.
31. Humphrey, *Green Mountains*, p. 43; Winn, *Macadam Trail*, p. 196.
32. Johnson, *Highways and Byways*, p. 334; Daniels, *A Southerner Discovers the South*, p. 143.
33. Cobb, *Some United States*, p. 328; Gordon and Gordon, *On Wandering Wheels*, p. 271.
34. Daniels, *A Southerner Discovers the South*, pp. 36, 75.

35. Roberts, *Sun Hunting*, p. 81; Roberts, *Gone Sunwards*, pp. 103, 127.
36. Roberts, *Gone Sunwards*, pp. 129–33; Roberts, *And So to America*, p. 66.
37. Street, *American Adventures*, p. 200.
38. Van Schaick, *Cruising Cross Country*, p. 292; Roberts, *Gone Sunwards*, p. 314.
39. Hervert C. Lanks, *Highway to Alaska* (New York: Appleton, 1944), pp. 8–9, 63, 75.
40. Poor, *An Artist Sees Alaska*, p. 43.
41. Ibid., p. 252; Hitchcock, *Two Women in the Klondike*, p. 22.
42. Thomas, *Trails and Tramps in Alaska and New Foundland*, p. 21; Poor, *An Artist Sees Alaska*, p. 268.
43. Poor, *An Artist Sees Alaska*, p. 48.
44. Ibid., pp. 241–43.
45. Ibid., p. 247.
46. Pyle, *Home Country*, p. 183.

Chapter Eleven: The American West as a Region

1. Street, *Abroad at Home*, p. 372; Van de Water, *Family Flivvers*, pp. 100, 151; Gannett, *Sweet Land*, pp. 49–50.
2. Steele, *Vacation Journeys East and West*, p. 189; Stuart Martin, "An Englishman's First Impressions of the West," *Travel* 24 (December 1914): 30; Margaret Follett and Wilson Follett, "In Search of the Real America," *Travel* 65 (June 1935): 55; Gannett, *Sweet Land*, p. 24.
3. Steele, *Vacation Journeys East and West*, p. 189; Street, *Abroad at Home*, p. 511; Lord Dunraven, *Past Times and Pastimes*, 2 vols. (London: Hodder and Stoughton, 1922), 1:72.
4. Peck and Johnson, *Roundabout America*, p. 92; Jack D. Rittenhouse, *A Guide Book to Highway 66* (Los Angeles: author, 1946), pp. 32, 78; Massey, *It Might Have Been Worse*, p. 52; Flagg, *Boulevards*, p. 79.
5. Steinbeck, *Travels with Charley*, p. 153; Dixon, *Westward Hoboes*, p. 367; Street, *Abroad at Home*, p. 513; Flagg, *Boulevards*, p. 191.
6. Cobb, *Some United States*, p. 196; Priestley, *Midnight on the Desert*, p. 91; Ernest Peixotto, *Our Hispanic Southwest* (New York: Scribner's, 1916), p. 196.

7.   Post, *By Motor*, p. 113; Wilby, *Motor Tour through Canada*, p. 169; Humphrey, *Green Mountains*, p. 52.

8.   Post, *By Motor*, p. 114; Sharp, *Better Country*, p. 129; Wolfe, *Western Journal*, p. 64.

9.   Priestley, *Midnight on the Desert*, p. 84; Dixon, *Westward Hoboes*, p. 244.

10. Dunn, *Double-Crossing America*, p. 123; Caroline Poole, *A Modern Prairie Schooner on the Transcontinental Trail: The Story of a Motor Trip* (San Francisco: Nash, 1919), p. 42; Massey, *It Might Have Been Worse*, p. 118; Humphrey, *Green Mountains*, p. 98.

11. Birney, *Roads to Roam*, p. 104; Priestley, *Midnight on the Desert*, p. 3; Gladding, *Across the Continent*, p. 130; Dixon, *Westward Hoboes*, p. 68; Ferguson, *Motor Camping on Western Trails*, p. 271; Pyle, *Home Country*, p. 291.

12. Cobb, *Some United States*, p. 352.

13. Flagg, *Boulevards*, p. 99; Massey, *It Might Have Been Worse*, p. 73.

14. Poole, *Modern Prairie Schooner*, pp. 40–41; McGill, *Diary of a Motor Journey*, p. 69; Winn, *Macadam Trail*, p. 186.

15. Dunn, *Double-Crossing America*, p. 187; Ferguson, *Motor Camping on Western Trails*, p. 69.

16. MacFadden, *Rambles*, pp. 21–22.

17. See Pomeroy, *In Search of the Golden West*, p. 176.

18. Herbert Carolan, *Motor Tales and Travels In and Out of California* (New York: Putnam's, 1936), p. 51.

19. Street, *Abroad at Home*, pp. 292–94; Gladding, *Across the Continent*, p. 202; Massey, *It Might Have Been Worse*, p. 45; Peck and Johnson, *Roundabout America*, p. 106.

20. Jenkinson, *America Came My Way*, p. 121; Cobb, *Some United States*, pp. 187–89; Priestley, *Midnight on the Desert*, p. 101.

21. Advertisement for Harveycar Motor Cruises in *Travel* 50 (February 1928); Charles F. Saunders, "The Pueblo Indians," *Travel* 16 (February 1911): 151; Gannett, *Sweet Land*, p. 66.

22. Priestley, *Midnight on the Desert*, pp. 64–65.

23. Birney, *Roads to Roam*, p. 258; Ferguson, *Motor Camping on Western Trails*, pp. 274, 282.

24. Post, *By Motor to the Golden Gate*, pp. 161–62.

25. Pomeroy, *In Search of the Golden West*, p. 32.

26. Dixon, *Westward Hoboes*, p. 35; Dunn, *Double-Crossing America*, p. 86; Peixotto, *Romantic California*, p. 3.

27. Poole, *A Modern Prairie Schooner*, p. 36; Dixon, *Westward Hoboes*, p. 149.
28. Austin, *Covered Wagon*, pp. 67, 75.
29. Peck and Johnson, *Roundabout America*, p. 115.
30. Flagg, *Boulevards*, p. 202; White, *A Woman's World Tour in a Motor*, p. 311; Poole, *Modern Prairie Schooner*, p. 37.
31. McEvoy, *From the Great Lakes*, p. 105; Flagg, *Boulevards*, p. 46; Massey, *It Might Have Been Worse*, p. 72.
32. Van Schaick, *Cruising Cross Country*, p. 43; Austin, *Covered Wagon*, p. 114.
33. Gladding, *Across the Continent*, p. 26; Post, *By Motor*, p. 213; Sharp, *Better Country*, p. 235.
34. Advertisement for the Southern Pacific Railroad in *Travel* 13 (November 1907): p. 94; Gannett, *Sweet Land*, p. 127; Wood, *Tourist's California*, pp. 26, 29.
35. Dixon, *Westward Hoboes*, p. 4; Rhodes, *In Vacation America*, p. 5; Austin, *Covered Wagon*, p. 114; Thomas D. Murphy, *On Sunset Highways* (Boston: Page, 1921), p. 3.
36. Van Schaick, *Cruising Cross Country*, p. 106.
37. A. G. MacDonnell, *Visit to America* (London: MacMillan, 1935), p. 232; Steinbeck, *Travels with Charley*, pp. 230–31.
38. Wolfe, *Western Journal*, pp. 33, 39; Pyle, *Home Country*, p. 108.
39. Priestley, *Midnight on the Desert*, p. 109; Steele, *Going Abroad Overland*, p. 55; Winn, *Macadam Trail*, p. 71; Birney, *Roads to Roam*, p. 142.
40. Pomeroy, *In Search of the Golden West*, p. 188.

Chapter Twelve: The Tourist in the the City

1. In the United States in 1900, 40 percent of the population lived in cities, but in 1960 some 67 percent were urban residents. In Canada in 1901, 37 percent of the people lived in urban places, but 66 percent in 1956. See U.S. Bureau of the Census, *Historical Statistics of the United States, Colonial Times To 1970*, pt. 1 (Washington, D.C.: Government Printing Office, 1975), p. 11; M. C. Urquhart and K. A. H. Buckley (eds.), *Historical Statistics of Canada* (Toronto: MacMillan, 1965), p. 14.
2. Gunn, *Vacationscapes*, p. 87.
3. Morely, *Travels in Philadelphia*, p. 87.
4. Street, *Abroad at Home*, p. 379.

5. McEvoy, *From the Great Lakes*, p. 70.
6. Kinross, *Innocents at Home*, pp. 6–9; Jenkinson, *America Came My Way*, p. 7.
7. Van Dyke, *The New New York*, pp. 32–39.
8. Street, *American Adventures*, pp. 5, 69; Webb, *We Explore the Great Lakes*, p. 185.
9. Webb, *We Explore the Great Lakes*, p. 190; Jenkinson, *America Came My Way*, p. 98.
10. Street, *Abroad at Home*, pp. 184, 285; Priestley, *Midnight on the Desert*, p. 92.
11. Webb, *We Explore the Great Lakes*, p. 52.
12. Birmingham, *Connaught to Chicago*, pp. 78, 113; Ilf and Petrov, *Little Golden America*, pp. 29–30.
13. Hungerford, *Personality of American Cities*, pp. 109–12; Brinley, *Away to the Gaspé*, p. 45.
14. Advertisement for the Royal Blue Line Motor Tours in *New York Standard Guide* (New York: Foster and Reynolds, 1917), p. 145; Advertisement for Captain John P. Roberts, in *New York Standard Guide* (New York: Foster and Reynolds, 1917), p. 147.
15. James, *American Scene*, p. 1; Street, *Abroad at Home*, p. 193.
16. MacFadden, *Rambles*, p. 188.
17. Gannett, *Sweet Land*, p. 18; Jenkinson, *America Came My Way*, pp. 66, 68, 70.
18. Kinross, *Innocents at Home*, pp. 30–32.
19. Post, *By Motor*, pp. 52, 94; Cobb, *Some United States*, p. 38.
20. Dreiser, *Hoosier Holiday*, p. 398.
21. Finger, *Foot-Loose in the West*, pp. 185–86.
22. Paul Morand, *New York* (New York: Holt, 1930), p. 162; Ilf and Petrov, *Little Golden America*, p. 19.
23. Belasco, *Americans on the Road*, p. 57.
24. Rufus Jarman, *A Bed for the Night* (New York: Harper and Row, 1952), p. 27.
25. Post, *By Motor*, p. 49; Wilby, *Motor Tour through Canada*, p. 2.
26. Citrine, *My American Diary*, p. 22; Post, *By Motor*, p. 96.
27. Rhodes, *In Vacation America*, p. 127; Steinbeck, *Travels with Charley*, pp. 117–18.
28. Saroyan, *Short Drive, Sweet Chariot*, p. 11.
29. Norman S. Hayner, *Hotel Life* (College Park, Mar.: McGrath, 1969), p. 158.

30. Howard E. Morgan, *The Motel Industry in the United States: Small Business In Transition* (Tucson: University of Arizona Bureau of Business Research, 1964), p. 15.

31. *Glimpses of New York* (New York: New York Edison, 1911), p. 65.

32. Hungerford, *Personality of American Cities*, p. 50; Morand, *New York*, pp. 59, 167.

33. Wood, *Tourist's California*, p. 48; Peixotto, *Our Hispanic Southwest*, p. 15; Kinney, *Bachelor*, p. 41.

34. Sutton, *Travelers*, p. 132; Morand, *New York*, pp. 174–75; La Fond, *Impressions of America*, p. 13.

35. Morand, *New York*, p. 269; MacDonnell, *Visit to America*, pp. 62–64.

36. Samuel P. Wilson, *Chicago by Gaslight* ([Chicago]: author, c.1910), p. 121; Asch, *Road*, p. 53.

Chapter Thirteen: The Metropolis as an Attraction

1. See Kevin Lynch, *The Image of the City* (Cambridge: M.I.T. Press and Harvard University Press, 1960); Anselm L. Strauss, *Images of the American City* (New Brunswick, N.J.: Transaction, 1976); John A. Jakle, "Images of Place: Symbolism and the Middle Western Metropolis," in *The Metropolitan Midwest*, ed. Clyde Patton and Barry Checkoway (Urbana: University of Illinois Press, 1983).

2. Street, *American Adventures*, p. 627.

3. Harry Carr, *Los Angeles: City of Dreams* (New York: Grosset and Dunlap, 1935), p. 233; Street, *Abroad at Home*, p. 202.

4. Dreiser, *Hoosier Holiday*, p. 61; Kouwenhoven, *Beer Can*, p. 43.

5. See Wayne Attoe, *Skylines: Understanding and Molding Urban Silhouettes* (Chichester, United Kingdom: Wiley, 1981), p. xi.

6. James, *American Scene*, p. 76; Van Dyke, *The New New York*, p. 6.

7. Will Irwin, *Highlights of Manhattan* (New York: Century, 1927), p. 14; Charles Whibley, *American Sketches* (Edinburgh: Blackwood, 1908), pp. 14–15.

8. Mais, *Modern Columbus*, p. 291; Pepys, *Mine Host, America*, p. 82.

9. Brown, *I Travel by Train*, p. 292.

10. Morand, *New York*, pp. 53, 56.

11. Hulbert Footner, *New York, City of Cities* (Philadelphia: Lippincott, 1937), pp. 13–16.

12. Ilf and Petrov, *Little Golden America*, p. 21; Kinross, *Innocents at Home*, pp. 10–11.

13. Lynch, *Image of the City*, p. 49.

14. Scarfoglio, *Round the World in a Motor-Car*, p. 67.

15. Kinross, *Innocents at Home*, pp. 5, 9.

16. Faris, *Seeing the Eastern States*, p. 119; MacDonnell, *Visit to America*, p. 45.

17. Hughes, *The Real New York*, p. 91; Morand, *New York*, pp. 186, 191.

18. Morand, *New York*, pp. 143–44.

19. MacDonnell, *Visit to America*, p. 42.

20. Carr, *Los Angeles: City of Dreams*, p. 251.

21. Morand, *New York*, pp. 48, 145; Fleming, *New York*, p. 12.

22. Waldron, *We Explore the Great Lakes*, p. 181.

23. Van Dyke, *The New New York*, p. 7; Roberts, *And So to America*, p. 47; Birmingham, *Connaught to Chicago*, p. 68.

24. Street, *American Adventures*, pp. 90–92.

25. Street, *Abroad at Home*, p. 49.

26. Kinross, *Innocents at Home*, p. 165; Daniels, *A Southerner Discovers the South*, p. 291.

27. Hungerford, *Personality of American Cities*, p. 190; Street, *Abroad at Home*, p. 36.

28. Steele, *Vacation Journeys East and West*, p. 188; Ilf and Petrov, *Little Golden America*, p. 108; Mais, *Modern Columbus*, p. 242.

29. Theodore Dreiser, *The Color of a Great City* (New York: Boni and Liveright, 1923), pp. 3, 156.

30. Asch, *Road*, pp. 10–11.

31. LaFond, *Impressions of America*, p. 118.

32. Konrad Bercovici, *Around the World in New York* (New York: Appleton-Century, 1938); James, *American Scene*, pp. 131–33; Dreiser, *Color of a Great City*, p. 112.

33. Morand, *New York*, pp. 268, 270; Bercovici, *Around the World in New York*, p. 211.

34. MacFadden, *Rambles*, pp. 155–57.

35. Hungerford, *Personality of American Cities*, pp. 79–80.

36. Ibid., pp. 181, 230.

37. Kinross, *Innocents at Home*, p. 53; Priestley, *Midnight on the Desert*, p. 117.

38. Steinbeck, *Travels with Charley*, p. 181; Gordon and Gordon, *On Wandering Wheels*, p. 319.

39. Morand, *New York*, pp. 307, 313; Post, *By Motor*, p. 238; Miller, *Air-Conditioned Nightmare*, p. 284.

40. James, *American Scene*, pp. 111–12; Helen W. Henderson, *A Loiterer in New York* (New York: Doran, 1917), pp. 188–89.

41. Kinross, *Innocents at Home*, p. 53; Vernon H. Bailey and Arthur B. Maurice, *Magical City: Intimate Sketches of New York* (New York: Scribner's, 1935), p. 13.

Chapter Fourteen: History as an Attraction

1. David Lowenthal, "The American Way of History," *Columbia University Forum* 9 (Summer 1966): 27.

2. Van Dyke, *The New New York*, pp. 133, 139, 144.

3. James, *American Scene*, p. 268; Mais, p. 271.

4. Cobb, *Roughing It Deluxe*, pp. 141–42.

5. Morely, *Travels in Philadelphia*, p. 178.

6. David Lowenthal, "Past Time, Present Place: Landscape and Memory," *Geographical Review* 65 (January 1975): 24; Agnes Rothery, *New Roads in Old Virginia* (Boston: Houghton, Mifflin, 1929), p. 17.

7. Frank B. Kelley, *Historical Guide to the City of New York* (New York: Stokes, 1913); Henderson, *Loiterer*, p. 74.

8. Daniels, *A Southerner Discovers New England*, p. 120; Johnson, *Highways and Byways*, pp. 326–27.

9. Whiteside, *Touring New England*, p. 234; [Eddy], *2,000 Miles on an Automobile*, p. 191.

10. Hale, *We Discover the Old Dominion*, pp. 63, 66, 104; Ilf and Petrov, *Little Golden America*, p. 117.

11. MacDonnell, *Visit to America*, p. 60; Wolfe, *Western Journal*, p. 38.

12. Daniels, *A Southerner Discovers New England*, p. 113; Winn, *Macadam Trail*, p. 248; Hughes, *Motoring in White*, p. 40; Ilf and Petrov, *Little Golden America*, p. 122.

13. Daniels, *A Southerner Discovers New England*, p. 117.

14. Lowenthal, "American Way of History," pp. 31–32; Roberts, *And So To America*, p. 423.

15. Street, *American Adventures*, p. 63; Kinross, *Innocents at Home*, pp. 61–62.

16. [Eddy], *2,000 Miles on an Automobile*, p. 258; Whiteside, *Touring New England*, p. 227.

17. Ilf and Petrov, *Little Golden America*, pp. 97–98.

18. Charles B. Hosmer, Jr., *Preservation Comes of Age: From Williamsburg to the National Trust, 1926–1949* (Charlottesville: University of Virginia Press, 1981), p. 75.

19. Peck and Johnson, *Roundabout America*, p. 21; Daniels, *A Southerner Discovers the South*, p. 19; William O. Stevens, *Old Williamsburg and Her Neighbors* (New York: Dodd, Mead, 1938), p. 49; Daniels, *A Southerner Discovers the South*, pp. 14–15; Kinross, *Innocents at Home*, p. 75; Kenneth Chorley as quoted in Freeman Tilden, *The State Parks: Their Meaning in American Life* (New York: Knopf, 1962), p. 25.

20. Whibley, *American Sketches*, p. 33; Cobb, *Some United States*, p. 371.

21. Hosmer, *Preservation Comes of Age*, pp. 292, 328.

22. Daniels, *A Southerner Discovers the South*, p. 328.

23. Ibid., pp. 19–142.

24. Flagg, *Boulevards*, p. 106; Pyle, *Home Country*, p. 78; Lewis Gannett, *Sweet Land*, p. 51.

25. MacDonnell, *Visit to America*, p. 156; Finger, *Adventure under Sapphire Skies*, p. 114.

BIBLIOGRAPHY

Abdy, H. Bennett. *On the Ohio*. New York: Dodd, Mead, 1919.

Agg, Thomas R. *American Rural Highways*. New York: McGraw-Hill, 1920.

American Association of State Highway Officials. *The History and Accomplishments of Twenty-Five Years of Federal Aid for Highways*. Washington, D.C.: 1944.

American Automobile Association. *The Chosen Millions*. Washington, D.C.: 1963.

———. *Official AAA Camp Directory*. Washington, D.C.: 1928.

———. *Official Camping and Campsite Manual*. Washington, D.C.: 1925.

———. *Profile of the American Tourist*. Washington, D.C.: 1962.

Amory, Cleveland. *The Last Resorts*. New York: Harper, 1952.

Ansted, Harry B. "The Auto-Camp Community." *Journal of Applied Sociology* 9 (1924): 136–42.

Asch, Nathan. *The Road in Search of America*. New York: Norton, 1937.

Attoe, Wayne. *Skylines: Understanding and Molding Urban Silhouettes*. Chichester, United Kingdom: Wiley, 1981.

Auden, W. H. "Introduction" in Henry James, *The American Scene*. New York: Scribner's, 1946. Pp. v–xxiii.

Austin, Guy K. *Covered Wagon, 10 H.P.* London: Bles, 1936.

The Automobile Road Book with Descriptions of Highways. Chicago: Rand, McNally, 1924.

Ayers, Raymond F. "Travel and Sports on Tires." *Travel* 14 (March 1909): 265–67.

Bailey, Vernon H., and Arthur B. Maurice. *Magical City: Intimate Sketches of New York*. New York: Scribner's, 1935.

Baird, David M. *Nature's Heritage: Canada's National Parks*. Scarborough, Ont.: Prentice-Hall, 1967.

Barry, Griffin. "America's Buses are Going Places." *Travel* 74 (November 1939): 33–36, 49.

Bedell, Mary C. *Modern Gypsies: A 12,000-Mile Motor Camping Trip Encircling the United States*. New York: Bretano's, 1924.

Belasco, Warren J. *Americans on the Road: From Autocamp to Motel, 1910–1945*. Cambridge, Mass.: M.I.T. Press, 1979.

Bennett, Jesse M. *Roadside Development*. New York: MacMillan, 1929.

———. *Roadsides: The Front Yard of the Nation*. Boston: Stratford, 1936.

Benton, Thomas. "America's Yesterday: In the Ozark Mountains of Arkansas—Life and Customs on a Forgotten Frontier," *Travel* 63 (July 1934): 7–11, 45–46.

Bercovici, Konrad. *Around the World in New York*. New York: Appleton-Century, 1938.

Birmingham, George A. *Connaught to Chicago*. London: Nisbet, 1914.

Birney, Hoffman. *Roads to Roam*. Philadelphia: Penn, 1930.

Bishop, H. O. "The National Park-to-Park Highway." *Outdoors Pictorial* 2 (July 1925).

Blake, Peter. *God's Own Junkyard*. New York: Holt, Rinehart and Winston, 1964.

Bok, Edward. "Summers of Our Discontent." *Ladies Home Journal* 18 (May 1901): 16.

Boorstin, Daniel J. *The Image: A Guide to Pseudo-Events in America*. New York: Harper Colophon, 1961.

Bossemeyer, James L. "Travel: American Mobility." *Annals of the American Academy of Political and Social Science* 313 (September 1957): 113–16.

Breese, Frank. "How to Stay Youthful at Fifty: The NPN Story." *National Petroleum News* 51 (February 1959).

Briggs, Asa. "The Sense of Place." In *The Fitness of Man's Environment: Smithsonian Annual II*. New York: Harper Colophon, 1968. Pp. 79–97.

Brimmer, F. Everett. *Autocamping Facts*. Chicago: Outer's Book Co., 1924.

———. *Motor Campcraft*. New York: MacMillan, 1923.

Brinley, Gordon. *Away to Cape Breton*. New York: Dodd, Mead, 1937.

———. *Away to the Gaspé*. New York: Dodd, Mead, 1935.

————. *Away to Quebec*. New York: Dodd, Mead, 1937.

Brockman, Frank C. *Recreational Use of Wild Lands*. New York: McGraw-Hill, 1959.

Brooks, John. *The Landscape of Roads*. London: Architectural Press, 1960.

Brooks, Paul. *Roadless Area*. New York: Knopf, 1964.

Brown, Cecil K. *The State Highway System of North Carolina: Its Evolution and Present Status*. Chapel Hill: University of North Carolina Press, 1931.

Brown, Rollo W. *I Travel by Train*. New York: Appleton-Century, 1939.

Buck, Roy C. "The Ubiquitous Tourist Brochure: Explorations in Its Intended and Unintended Use." *Annals of Tourism Research* 4 (April–June, 1977): 195–207.

————. "Toward a Synthesis on Tourism Theory." *Annals of Tourism Research* 5 (January–March, 1978): 110–11.

Burch, William R., Jr. "The Play World of Camping: Research into the Social Meaning of Outdoor Recreation." *American Journal of Sociology* 70 (March 1965): 604–12.

Byrne, Anthony R. *Man and Landscape Change in the Banff National Park Area before 1911*. Calgary: University of Calgary Department of Geography, National Park Series no. 1, Studies in Land Use and Landscape Change, 1968.

Canada, Ministere Des Chemins De Fer Et Canaux. *Rapport Annuel*. Ottawa: 1901.

Canby, Henry S. "Traveling Intelligently in America." In *Essays of Today (1926–1927)*, edited by Odell Shepard and Robert Hillyer. New York: Century, 1928. Pp. 166–79.

Carnes, Cecil. *You Must See Canada*. Chicago: Ziff-Davis, 1949.

Carolan, Herbert. *Motor Tales and Travels In and Out of California*. New York: Putnam's, 1936.

Carpenter, Edwin H., Jr., and Cora F. Carpenter. *Driving from the Mississippi River to the Pacific Coast Fifty Years Ago*. South Pasadena, Cal.: privately printed, 1967.

Carr, Harry. *Los Angeles: City of Dreams*. New York: Grosset and Dunlap, 1935.

Catton, William, and Lennart Berggren. "Intervening Opportunities and National Park Visitation Rates." *Pacific Sociological Review* 7 (1964): 66–73.

Chadwick, H. H. *Vermont's Tourist Business: A Study Covering Ten Years, 1934–1943*. Montpelier: Vermont Department of Natural Resources, 1944).

Chatburn, George R. *Highways and Highway Transportation*. New York: Crowell, 1923.

Chittenden, Hiram M. *The Yellowstone National Park*. St. Paul: Haynes, 1927.

Citrine, Walter. *My American Diary*. London: Routledge, 1941.

Clarke, Alfred. "The Use of Leisure and Its Relation to Levels of Occupational Prestige." *American Sociological Review* 21 (June 1956): 301–7.

Clarke, W. A. "Automobiling in the Yosemite Valley." *Overland Monthly* 40 (July–December 1902): 104–10.

Clawson, Marion. *The Crisis in Outdoor Recreation*. Washington, D.C.: Resources for the Future, 1959.

———. *How Much Leisure, Now and in the Future?* Washington, D.C.: Resources for the Future, 1964.

———. "Implications of Recreational Needs for Highway Improvements." *Impacts and Implications of Highway Improvements*. Washington, D.C.: National Academy of Sciences, National Research Council, Highway Research Board, Bulletin 311, 1962. Pp. 31–38.

Clawson, Marion, and Jack L. Knetsch. *Outdoor Recreation Research: Some Concepts and Suggested Areas of Study*. Washington, D.C.: Resources for the Future, Report no. 43, 1963.

Clay, Grady. *Close-Up: How to Read the American City*. New York: Praeger, 1973.

Cobb, Irvin S. *Roughing It Deluxe*. New York: Doran, 1914.

———. *Some United States*. New York: Doran, 1926.

Cohen, Erik. "A Phenomenology of Tourist Experiences." *Sociology* 13 (May 1979): 179–201.

———. "Rethinking the Sociology of Tourism." *Annals of Tourism Research* 6 (January–March 1979): 18–35.

———. "Who is a Tourist? A Conceptual Clarification." *Sociological Review* 22 (November 1974): 527–55.

"Columbia River Highway." *The American City* 14 (January 1916): 1–3.

Colwell, M. Worth. "Motoring through the Mountains: A Climb over the Chestnut, Laurel, and Allegheny Ridges." *Travel* 13 (August 1908): 507–9.

Coon, Horace. *100 Vacations Costing from $50 to $500.* New York: Doubleday, Doran, 1939.

Cooper, Courtney R. *Go North, Young Man.* Boston: Little, Brown, 1929.

Cowgill, Donald O. *Mobile Homes: A Study of Trailer Life.* Philadelphia: author, 1941.

Craik, Kenneth. "Human Responsiveness to Landscape: An Environmental Psychological Perspective." In *Response to Environment.* Raleigh, N.C.: North Carolina State University, Student Publications of the School of Design, vol. 18, 1969. Pp. 170–93.

Crampton, L. J. (ed.). *Tourist Travel Trends.* Boulder: University of Colorado Bureau of Business Research, 1961.

Crampton, L. J., and F. W. Ellinghaus. *1953 Colorado Statewide Summer Tourist Survey.* Boulder: University of Colorado Bureau of Business Research, 1953.

Cramton, Louis C. *Early History of Yellowstone National Park and Its Relation to National Park Policies.* Washington, D.C.: U.S. National Park Service, 1932.

Crandall, Burton B. *The Growth of the Intercity Bus Industry.* Syracuse, N.Y.: author, 1954.

Crompton, John L. "Motivations for Pleasure Vacations." *Annals of Tourism Research* 5 (October–December 1979): 408–24.

Dahl, J. O. *Selling Public Hospitality.* New York: Harper, 1929.

Daniels, Jonathon. *A Southerner Discovers New England.* New York: MacMillan, 1940.

———. *A Southerner Discovers the South.* New York: MacMillan, 1938.

Dann, Graham M. S. "Anomie, Ego-Enhancement, and Tourism." *Annals of Tourism Research* 4 (March–April 1977): 184–94.

Darling, F. Fraser, and Noel D. Eichhorn. *Man and Nature in the National Parks.* Washington, D.C.: Conservation Foundation, 1967.

Darling, J. N. *The Cruise of the Bouncing Betsy: A Trailer Travelogue.* New York: Stokes, 1937.

Dayton, Thaddeus S. "The Motor-Car Vacation: The 'Grand Tour' of To-Day Is Made by Automobiles." *Harper's* 55 (July 1, 1911): 10.

Deasy, George F., and Phyllis R. Griess. "Impact of a Tourist Facility on Its Hinterland." *Annals, Association of American Geographers* 56 (June 1966): 290–306.

Demars, Standford E. "The Triumph of Tradition: A Study of Tourism in Yosemite National Park, California." Ph.D. diss., University of Oregon, 1970.

Dettelbach, Cynthia G. *In the Driver's Seat: The Automobile in American Literature and Popular Culture.* Westport, Conn.: Greenwood Press, 1976.

De Voto, Bernard. "The Easy Chair: Transcontinental Flight." *Harper's* 205 (July 1952): 47–50.

Dixon, Winifred H. *Westward Hoboes.* New York: Scribner's, 1921.

Draper, George O. "A View of the Tour from One Participating." *Horseless Age* 16 (July 26, 1905).

Dreiser, Theodore. *The Color of a Great City.* New York: Boni and Liveright, 1923.

———. *A Hoosier Holiday.* New York: Lane, 1916.

Dulles, Foster R. *America Learns to Play: A History of Recreation.* New York: Appleton-Century-Crofts, 1965.

Dunn, Edward D. *Double-Crossing America by Motor.* New York: Putnam's, 1933.

Dunraven, Lord. *Past Times and Pastimes.* 2 vols. London: Hodder and Stoughton, 1922.

Durrell, Lawrence. *Spirit of Place: Letters and Essays on Travel.* Edited by Alan G. Thomas. New York: Dutton, 1969.

Eckbo, Garrett. "The Landscape of Tourism." *Landscape* 18 (Spring–Summer 1969): 29–31.

[Eddy, Arthur J.]. *2,000 Miles on an Automobile—By "Chauffeur."* Philadelphia: Lippincott, 1902.

Eiselin, Elizabeth. "Tourist Industry of a Modern Highway: U.S. 16 in South Dakota." *Economic Geography* 21 (April 1945): 221–30.

Ekirch, Arthur, Jr. *Man and Nature in America.* Lincoln: University of Nebraska Press, 1963.

Eubank, Victor. "Log of an Auto Prairie Schooner." *Sunset* 28 (February 1912): 188–95.

Eustis, John R. "The Automobile, the Ideal Vehicle of Travel." *Travel* 14 (January 1909): 175–79.

Farber, Maurice L. "Some Hypotheses on the Psychology of Travel." *Psychoanalytical Review* 41 (July 1954): 267–71.

Faris, John T. *Roaming American Highways.* New York: Farrar and Rinehart, 1931.

———. *Seeing the Eastern States.* Philadelphia: Lippincott, 1922.

———. *Seeing the Middle West.* Philadelphia: Lippincott, 1923.

Farmer, Robert E. L. *From Florida to the Far West.* Bartow, Fla.: author, 1936.

Ferguson, Melville. *Motor Camping on Western Trails.* New York: Century, 1925.

Fieguth, Wolfgang. "Historical Geography and the Concept of the Authentic Past as a Regional Resource." *Ontario Geography* 1 (January 1967): 55–59.

Finger, Charles, J. *Adventure under Sapphire Skies.* New York: Morrow, 1931.

———. *Foot-Loose in the West.* New York: Morrow, 1932.

Fischer, Fred. "Ten Phases of the Animal Path: Behavior in Familiar Situations," in *Behavior and Environment: The Use of Space by Animals and Men.* Edited by Aristide H. Esser. New York: Plenum, 1971: 9–21.

Flagg, James. *Boulevards All the Way—Maybe.* New York: Doran, 1925.

Fleming, Ethel. *New York.* New York: MacMillan, 1929.

Flink, James J. *The Car Culture.* Cambridge, Mass.: M.I.T. Press, 1975.

Fitzsimmons, Allan K. "The Automobile and the Roads of Yosemite Valley." *California Geographer* 11 (1970): 43–50.

Follett, Margaret, and Wilson Follett. "In Search of the Real America." *Travel* 65 (June 1935): 9–14, 55–56.

Footner, Hulbert. *New York, City of Cities.* Philadelphia: Lippincott, 1937.

Foscue, Edwin, J., and Louis Q. Quam. *Estes Park: Resort in the Rockies.* American Resort series no. 3. Dallas: Southern Methodist University Press, 1949.

Franck, Harry A. "The France across Our Border." *Travel* 75 (May 1940): 15–17, 43.

Freeman, Lewis R. "Exploring America by Motor Bus." *Travel* 35 (May 1930): 25–28, 55–57.

Frost, Harwood. *The Art of Roadmaking.* New York: McGraw-Hill, 1910.

Fuessle, Newton A. "The Lincoln Highway: A National Road." *Travel* 24 (February 1915): 26–29; (March 1915): 30–33, 57; (April 1915): 30–33.

Funnel, Charles E. *By the Beautiful Sea: The Rise and High Times of That Great American Resort, Atlantic City.* New York: Knopf, 1975.

Gannett, Lewis. *Sweet Land.* Garden City, N.Y.: Sun Dial Press, 1937.

Garrett, Edmund. *Romance and Reality of the Puritan Coast.* Boston: Little, Brown, 1897.

Geddes, Norman B. *Magic Motorways*. New York: Random House, 1940.

Gibson, William H. *Highways and Byways: Or Saunterings in New England*. New York: Harper, 1903.

Gladding, Effie P. *Across the Continent by the Lincoln Highway*. New York: Bretano's, 1915.

Glimpses of New York. New York: New York Edison, 1911.

Goffman, Erving. *The Presentation of Self in Everyday Life*. Garden City, N.Y.: Doubleday, 1959.

————. *Relations in Public: Microstudies of the Public Order*. New York: Basic Books, 1971.

Gordon, Jan, and Cora J. Gordon. *On Wandering Wheels: Through Roadside Camps from Maine to Georgia in an Old Sedan Car*. New York: Dodd, Mead, 1928.

Goulet, Edwin. *The Story of Canadian Roads*. Toronto: University of Toronto Press, 1967.

Greene, Frederick S., et al. *The Billboard: A Blot on Nature and a Parasite on Public Improvements*. New York: Moore, 1939.

Gubbels, Jac L. *American Highways and Roadsides*. Boston: Houghton, Mifflin, 1938.

Gunn, Clare A. *Vacationscape: Designing Tourist Regions*. Austin, Tex.: University of Texas Bureau of Business Research, 1972.

Hale, Louise C. *We Discover the Old Dominion*. New York: Dodd, Mead, 1916.

Hanes, J. Carter, and Charles H. Connors (eds.). *Landscape Design and Its Relation to the Modern Highway*. New Brunswick: Rutgers University, College of Engineering, 1953.

Harding, Horace W. *The Kansas Tourist Survey, 1952*. Lawrence: University of Kansas Bureau of Business Research, 1953.

Havighurst, Robert J., and Kenneth Feigenbaum. "Leisure and Life Style." *American Journal of Sociology* 54 (January 1959): 396–405.

Hawkins, C. A. "Automobile Endurance." *Overland Monthly* 40 (July–December 1902): 111–14.

Hayner, Norman S. "Auto Camps in the Evergreen Playground." *Social Forces* 9 (December 1930): 256–66.

————. *Hotel Life*. College Park, Mar.: McGrath, 1969.

Henderson, Helen W. *A Loiterer in New York*. Doran, 1917.

Hendrick, Paul. *Vacation Travel Business in New Hampshire*. [Concord]: New Hampshire Division of Economic Development, 1962.

352

Hewes, Laurence I. *American Highway Practice*. New York: Wiley, 1942.

Hills, Theodore L., and Jan Lundgren. "The Impact of Tourism in the Caribbean: A Methodological Study." *Annals of Tourism Research* 4 (May–September 1977): 248–67.

Hitchcock, Mary E. *Two Women in the Klondike*. New York: Putnam's, 1899.

Hosmer, Charles B., Jr. *Preservation Comes of Age: From Williamsburg to the National Trust, 1926–1949*. Charlottesville: University of Virginia Press, 1981.

Hudson, Kenneth. *Air Travel: A Social History*. Totowa, N.J.: Rownan and Littlefield, 1973.

Hughes, Edith W. *Motoring in White from Dakota to Cape Cod*. New York: Knickerbocker Press, 1917.

Hughes, Rupert. *The Real New York*. London: Smart Set, 1903.

Hulme, Katherine C. *How's the Road?* San Francisco: author, 1928.

Humphreys, J. R. *The Lost Towns and Roads of America*. Garden City, N.Y.: Doubleday, 1961.

Humphrey, Zephine. *Green Mountains to Sierras*. New York: Dutton, 1936.

Hungerford, Edward. *The Personality of American Cities*. New York: McBride, Nast, 1913.

Huth, Hans. *Nature and the American: Three Centuries of Changing Attitudes*. Lincoln: University of Nebraska Press, 1972.

Hyde, F. A. "Automobile Club of California." *Overland Monthly* 40 (July–December 1902): 97–103.

Ilf, Ilya, and Eugene Petrov. *Little Golden America*. London: Routledge, 1936.

Irwin, Will. *Highlights of Manhatten*. New York: Century, 1927.

Ise, John. *Our National Park Policy: A Critical History*. Baltimore: Johns Hopkins University Press, 1961.

Jackson, John B. "Other-Directed Houses." *Landscape* 6 (Winter 1956–57): 29–35.

———. "The Stranger's Path." *Landscape* 7 (Spring–Summer 1957): 11–15.

Jakle, John A. "The American Gasoline State, 1920–1970." *Journal of American Culture* 1 (Spring 1976): 520–42.

———. *The American Small Town: Twentieth-Century Place Images*. Hamden, Conn.: Archon, 1982.

———. *Images of the Ohio Valley: A Historical Geography of Travel, 1740 to*

1860. New York: Oxford University Press, 1977.

———. "Images of Place: Symbolism and the Middle Western Metropolis." In *The Metropolitan Midwest*. Edited by Clyde Patton and Barry Checkoway. Urbana: University of Illinois Press, 1983.

———. "Motel by the Roadside: America's Room for the Night." *Journal of Cultural Geography* 1 (Fall–Winter 1980): 34–49.

———. "Roadside Restaurants: The Evolution of Place-Product-Packaging." *Journal of Cultural Geography*. Forthcoming.

James, Henry. *The American Scene*. New York: Scribner's, 1946.

Jarman, Rufus. *A Bed for the Night*. New York: Harper and Row, 1952.

Jenkinson, Anthony. *America Came My Way*. London: Barker, 1936.

Jerome, John. *The Death of the Automobile: The Fatal Effect of the Golden Era, 1955–1970*. New York: Norton, 1972.

Jessup, Elon. "The Flight of the Tin Can Tourist." *Outlook* 128 (May 18, 1921): 166–67.

———. *The Motor Camping Book*. New York: Putnam's, 1921.

Johannesson, Sigrald. "Highway Finances and Related Problems." In *Highways in Our National Life*. Edited by Jean Labatut and Wheaton J. Lane. Princeton: Princeton University Press, 1950.

Johnson, Clifton. *Highways and Byways from the St. Lawrence to Virginia*. New York: MacMillan, 1913.

———. *Highways and Byways of California with Excursion into Arizona, Oregon, Washington, Nevada, Idaho*. New York: MacMillan, 1915.

———. *Highways and Byways of the Old South*. New York: MacMillan, 1904.

Jones, C. E. M. *Diogenes: Or the Future of Leisure*. London: 1928.

Joy, Henry B. *National Highways and Country Roads*. New York: National Institute of Efficiency, Monographs of Efficiency no. 3, 1917.

———. "The Traveler and the Automobile." *Outlook* 115 (April 25, 1917): 739–42.

Kaplan, Max. *Leisure in America: A Social Inquiry*. New York: Wiley, 1960.

Kates, Robert. "The Pursuit of Beauty in the Environment." *Landscape* 16 (Fall–Winter, 1966–67): 21–4.

Kelley, Frank B. *Historical Guide to the City of New York*. New York: Stokes, 1913.

Kendrick, Baynard H. *Florida Trails to Turnpikes, 1914–1964*. Gainesville: University of Florida Press, 1964.

Kerouac, Jack. *On the Road*. New York: Viking, 1955.

Kinney, Robert. *The Bachelor in New Orleans*. New Orleans: Riley, 1942.

Kinross, Lord. *The Innocents at Home*. New York: Morrow, 1959.

Kouwenhoven, John A. *The Beer Can by the Highway*. Garden City, N.Y.: Doubleday, 1961.

Krarup, Marcus C. "From Coast to Coast in an Automobile." *World's Work* 8 (May 1904): 4,740–54.

Labatut, Jean, and Wheaton J. Lane (eds.). *Highways in Our National Life: A Symposium*. Princeton: Princeton University Press, 1950.

Laber, Gene. "Determinants of International Travel between Canada and the United States." *Geographical Analysis* 1 (October 1969): 329–36.

La Fond, Andre. *Impressions of America*. Paris: Fondation Strassburger, 1930.

Lane, Franklin K. Letter to Stephen T. Mather, May 13, 1918. As quoted in *Report of the Department of the Interior 1918*, vol. 1. Washington, D.C.: 1918.

Lanning, Victor H. *The Wisconson Tourist*. Madison: University of Wisconsin Bureau of Business Research and Services and Bureau of Community Development, 1950.

Lansing, John B., and Ernest Lilienstein. *The Travel Market: 1955: A Report to the Travel Research Association*. Ann Arbor: University of Michigan Survey Research Center, Institute for Social Research, 1963.

Larimore, Emma P. *Our Corner Book: From Maine to Mexico, from Canada to Cuba*. Nashville, Tenn.: author, 1912.

Lawrence, D. H. *Studies in Classic Literature*. London: Heinemann, 1964.

Leacock, Stephen. "On the Art of Taking of a Vacation." *Outlook* 128 (May 25, 1921): 161–62.

Leopold, Aldo. "The Last Stand of the Wilderness." *American Forest and Forest Life* 31 (October 1925).

———. "The Wilderness and Its Place in Forest Recreational Policy." *Journal of Forestry* 19 (November 1921): 718–21.

Leopold, Luna B. "Landscape Esthetics." *Natural History* 7 (October 1969): 36–45.

Lewis, David M., and Wesley P. Newton. *Delta: The History of an Airline*. Athens: University of Georgia Press, 1979.

Lewis, Oscar. "Free Auto Camp Ground." In *Essays of Today (1926–*

27). Edited by Odell Shepard and Robert Hillyer. New York: Century, 1928. Pp. 117–23.

Lewis, Peirce F., David Lowenthal, and Yi-Fu Tuan. *Visual Blight in America*. Washington, D.C.: Association of American Geographers, Resource Paper no. 23, 1973.

Lewis, Sinclair. *Free Air*. London: Cape, 1933.

Lincoln Highway Association. *The Complete Official Road Guide of the Lincoln Highway*. Detroit: 1916.

———. *The Lincoln Highway Association: Its Eighth Year of Progress, 1921*. Detroit: 1922.

———. *The Lincoln Highway: The Story of a Crusade that Made Transportation History*. New York: Dodd, Mead, 1935.

Linton, D. "The Assessment of Scenery as a Natural Resource." *Scottish Geographical Magazine* 84 (1968): 219–38.

London, Jack. *The Road*. New York: MacMillan, 1907.

Long, J. C., and John D. Long. *Motor Camping*. New York: Dodd, Mead, 1923.

Longstreth, Morris. *The Lake Superior Country*. New York: Century, 1924.

[Lorimer, George H.]. "Selling Scenery." *Saturday Evening Post* 165 (October 11, 1919): 28.

Lovelace, Elridge. "The Automobile and Recreation." *Traffic Quarterly* 20 (October 1966): 525–40.

Lowenthal, David. "America as Beauty." *Geographical Review* 56 (April 1966): 115–18.

———. "The American Scene." *Geographical Review* 58 (January 1968): 61–88.

———. "The American Way of History." *Columbia University Forum* 9 (Summer 1966): 27–32.

———. "Not Every Prospect Pleases: What is Our Criterion for Scenic Beauty?" *Landscape* 12 (Winter 1962–1963): 19–23.

———. "Past Time, Present Place: Landscape and Memory." *Geographical Review* 65 (January 1975): 1–36.

Lucas, Robert C. "Wilderness Perception and Use." *Natural Resources Journal* 3 (January 1964): 394–411.

Lundberg, Donald E. "Why Tourists Travel." *The Cornell Hotel and Restaurant Administration Quarterly* 11 (February 1971): 75–81.

Lundgren, Jan. "Tourism in Quebec." *Revue de Geographie de Montreal* 20 (1966): 59–73.

Lynch, Kevin. *The Image of the City*. Cambridge: M.I.T. Press, 1960.

———. *Managing the Sense of a Region*. Cambridge: M.I.T. Press, 1976.

———. *What Time Is This Place?* Cambridge: M.I.T. Press, 1972.

McCann, Franklin. "The Growth of the Tourist Court in the United States and Its Relationship to the Urban Development of Albuquerque, New Mexico." *Denison University Science Laboratories Journal* 37 (1942): 51–66.

MacCannell, Dean. *The Tourist: A New Theory of the Leisure Class*. New York: Schoken, 1976.

MacDonald, Thomas H. "History of the Development of Road Building in the United States." *Transactions, American Society of Civil Engineers* 92 (1928): 1181–206.

MacDonnell, A. G. *A Visit to America* (London: MacMillan, 1935).

McEvoy, Bernard. *From the Great Lakes to the Wide West*. Toronto: Briggs, 1902.

MacFadden, Henry A. *Rambles in the Far West*. Hollidaysburg, Penn.: Standard, 1906.

McGill, Vernon. *Diary of a Motor Journey from Chicago to Los Angeles*. Los Angeles: Grafton, 1922.

Mais, S[tuart] P. B. *A Modern Columbus*. Philadelphia: Lippincott, 1934.

Martin, Stuart. "An Englishman's First Impressions of the West." *Travel* 24 (December 1914): 30–33.

Mason, Philip P. *A History of American Roads*. Chicago: Rand McNally, 1967.

———. "The League of American Wheelmen and the Good Roads Movement, 1880–1905." Ph.D. diss., University of Michigan, 1957.

Massey, Beatrice L. *It Might Have Been Worse*. San Francisco: Wagner, 1920.

Mather, Stephen T. "Sieur De Monts and Yosemite, The Problem of Our National Parks." *Outlook* 15 (April 25, 1917): 750–51.

May, Earl C. "The Argonauts of the Automobile." *Saturday Evening Post* 170 (August 9, 1924): 25, 89.

———. "Highways and Waterways in Florida." *Travel* 62 (January 1939): 12–16, 50.

Mead, Margaret. "Outdoor Recreation in the Context of Emerging American Cultural Values: Background Considerations." *Trends in American Living and Outdoor Recreation*. Washington, D.C.: ORRRC Study Report 22, 1962. Pp. 2–25.

357

Meinig, D. W. (ed.). *The Interpretation of Ordinary Landscapes*. New York: Oxford University Press, 1979.

Meyersohn, Rolf. "The Sociology of Leisure in the United States." *Journal of Leisure Research* (Winter 1969): 53–68.

Michigan Tourist Survey. East Lansing: Michigan State College Bureau of Business Research, Report no. 7, 1953.

Miller, Henry. *The Air-Conditioned Nightmare*. New York: New Directions, 1945.

Miller, Spencer, Jr. "History of the Modern History in the United States." In *Highways in Our National Life: A Symposium*. Edited by Jean Labatut and Wheaton J. Lane. Princeton: Princeton University Press, 1950.

Miller, Wilhelm. "The First Roadside Planting along the Lincoln Highway." *American City* 14 (April 1916): 326.

Mills, Charles M. *Vacations for Industrial Workers*. New York: Ronald, 1927.

Mills, Enos A. *Your National Parks*. Boston: Houghton, Mifflin, 1917.

Miltoun, Francis. *The Automobilist Abroad*. Boston: Page, 1907.

Mikes, George. *How to Scrape Skies*. London: Wingate, 1949.

Morand, Paul. *New York*. New York: Holt, 1930.

Morgan, Howard E. *The Motel Industry in the United States: Small Business in Transition*. Tucson: University of Arizona Bureau of Business Research, 1964.

Morley, Christopher D. *Travels in Philadelphia*. Philadelphia: McKay, 1920.

Morris, Ida. *A Pacific Coast Vacation*. New York: Abbey Press, 1901.

Moss, W. T. "Some Human Aspects of Camping." *American Forests* 70 (1964): 24–25, 45–46.

Mueller, Eva, and Gerald Gunn. *The Demand for Outdoor Recreation*. Ann Arbor: University of Michigan Institute of Social Research, 1961.

Muir, John. *Our National Parks*. Boston: Houghton, Mifflin, 1903.

Murphy, Thomas D. *On Sunset Highways*. Boston: Page, 1921.

———. *Oregon the Picturesque*. Boston: Page, 1917.

Nabokov, Vladimir. *Lolita*. New York: Olympia Press, 1955.

Nairn, Ian. *The American Landscape*. New York: Random House, 1965.

Nash, Roderick. *The Nervous Generation: American Thought, 1917–1930*. Chicago: Rand McNally, 1970.

———. *Wilderness and the American Mind.* New Haven: Yale University Press, 1967.

———. "Wilderness and Man in North America." *The Canadian National Parks: Today and Tomorrow.* Edited by J. G. Nelson and R. C. Scarce. (Calgary: University of Calgary Department of Geography, National Park Series, Studies in Land Use and Landscape Change, 1968): 66–93.

National Highways Association. *National Highways and Good Roads.* Washington, D.C.: 1913.

National Research Council, Highway Research Board. *Roadsides: Their Use and Protection.* Washington, D.C.: 1954.

Nelson, J. G., and A. R. Byrne. "Man as an Instrument of Landscape Change: Fire, Floods and National Parks in the Bow Valley, Alberta." *Geographical Review* 56 (July 1966): 226–38.

Newby, Peter T. "Literature and the Fashioning of Tourist Taste." In *Humanistic Geography and Literature: Essays on the Experience of Place.* Edited by Douglas C. Pocock. London: Helm, 1981. Pp. 130–41.

New York Standard Guide. New York: Forster and Reynolds, 1917.

Nolen, John, and Henry V. Hubbard. *Parkways and Land Values.* Cambridge: Harvard University Press, 1937.

O'Brien, Bob R. "The Future Road System of Yellowstone National Park." *Annals, Association of American Geographers* 56 (September 1966): 385–407.

———. "The Yellowstone National Park Road System: Past, Present, and Future." Ph.D. diss., University of Washington, 1965.

O'Rourke, Barry. "Travel in the Recreational Experience: A Literature Review." *Journal of Leisure Research* 6 (Spring 1974): 140–56.

Oto, Akira. *A Garioan in the United States.* Tokyo: Hokuseido, 1955.

Paine, Ralph D. "Discovering America by Motor." *Scribner's* 53 (February 1913): 137–48.

Parmelee, Julius H., and Earl R. Feldman. "The Relation of the Highway to Rail Transportation." In *Highways in Our National Life: A Symposium.* Edited by Jean Labatut and Wheaton J. Lane. Princeton: Princeton University Press, 1950.

Paxson, Frederic L. "The Highway Movement: 1916–1935." *American Historical Review* 51 (January 1946): 236–53.

Pearce, W. "Establishment of National Parks in the Rockies." *Alberta Historical Review* 10 (1962): 9.

Peck, Anne M., and Enid Johnson. *Roundabout America*. New York: Harper, 1933.

Peixotto, Ernest. *Our Hispanic Southwest*. New York: Scribner's, 1916.

——. *Romantic California*. New York: Scribner's, 1910.

Pepys, Mark. *Mine Host, America*. London: Collins, 1937.

Pomeroy, Earl. *In Search of the Golden West: The Tourist in Western America*. New York: Knopf, 1957.

Poole, Caroline B. *A Modern Prairie Schooner on the Transcontinental Trail: The Story of a Motor Trip*. San Francisco: Nash, 1919.

Poole, Marjorie L. "Tin Can Tourists Terrifying California." *Literary Digest* (May 16, 1925): 73–76.

Poor, Henry V. *An Artist Sees Alaska*. New York: Viking, 1945.

Post, Emily. *By Motor to the Golden Gate*. New York: Appleton, 1916.

President's Research Committee on Social Trends. *Recent Social Trends in the United States*. New York: McGraw-Hill, 1934.

Priestley, J. B. *Midnight on the Desert*. New York: Harper, 1937.

Pritchett, Victor S. *The Offensive Traveler*. New York: Knopf, 1964.

Pushkarev, Boris. "Esthetic Criteria in Freeway Design." *Proceedings, Highway Research Board* 41 (1962): 89–108.

——. "The Esthetics of Freeway Design." *Landscape* 10 (Winter 1960–61): 7–15.

Pyle, Ernie. *Home Country*. New York: Sloane, 1947.

Rae, John B. *The Road and the Car in American Life*. Cambridge: M.I.T. Press, 1971.

Rajala, Clifford A. "'A National Tourist Attraction Combined with a Regional Outdoor Recreation Resource: A Case Study of the Coulee Dam National Recreation Area." Ph.D. diss., University of Michigan, 1966.

Ramsey, Alice H. *Veil, Duster, and Tire Iron*. Covina, Cal.: Dahlstrom, 1961.

Rathbone, A. D., III. "America's Airports of the Future." *Travel* 85 (September 1945): 25–28, 32.

Recreational Resources of Federal Lands. Washington, D.C.: National Conference on Outdoor Recreation, 1928.

Relph, Edward. *Place and Placelessness*. London: Pion, 1976.

Rhodes, Harrison. *In Vacation America*. New York: Harper, 1915.

Rickard, Michael J. *Across the Continent with the Soakems*. New York: author, 1906.

Ritchie, J. R. Brent, and Michael Zins. "Culture as Determinant of the Attractiveness of a Tourism Region." *Annals of Tourism Research* 5 (April–June 1978): 252–67.

Rittenberg, Caroline. *Motor West*. New York: Vinal, 1926.

Rittenhouse, Jack D. *A Guide Book to Highway 66*. Los Angeles: author, 1946.

Road Maps and Tourbook of Western North Carolina. Raleigh: North Carolina Good Roads Association and State Highway Commission, 1916.

Roberts, Cecil. *And So To America*. London: Hodder and Stoughton, 1946.

———. *Gone Sunwards*. London: Hodder and Stoughton, 1936.

Roberts, John M., et al. "The Small Highway Business on U.S. 30 in Nebraska." *Economic Geography* 32 (April 1956): 139–52.

Roberts, Kenneth L. *Sun Hunting*. Indianapolis: Bobbs-Merrill, 1922.

———. "Travels in Billboardia." *Saturday Evening Post* 174 (October 15, 1928): 24–25, 186, 189–90.

Robinson, John. *Highways and Our Environment*. New York: McGraw-Hill, 1971.

Rose, Albert C. "The Highway from the Railroad to the Automobile." In *Highways in Our National Life*. Edited by Jean Labatut and Wheaton J. Lane. Princeton: Princeton University Press, 1950.

Rothery, Agnes. *New Roads in Old Virginia*. Boston: Houghton, Mifflin, 1929.

Round, Thornton E. *The Good of It all*. Cleveland: Lakeside, 1957.

Routledge, Janette. *How to Tour the United States in Thirty-One Days for One Hundred Dollars*. New York: Harian, 1938.

Sabin, Gula. *California by Motor*. Milwaukee: author, 1926.

Saroyan, William. *Short Drive, Sweet Chariot*. New York: Phaedra, 1966.

Saunders, Charles F. "The Pueblo Indians." *Travel* 16 (February 1911): 151–54.

———. *Under the Sky in California*. New York: McBride, Nast, 1913.

Scarce, R. C. "Banff Townsite: The Historical Geography of a National Park Community." Master's thesis, University of Calgary, 1967.

Scarfoglio, Antonio. *Round the World in a Motor-Car*. Translated by J.

Parker Heyes. New York: Kennerly, 1909.

Scaritt, Winthrop. *Three Men in a Car*. New York: Dutton, 1906.

Schmitt, Peter J. *Back to Nature: The Arcadian Myth in Urban America*. New York: Oxford University Press, 1969.

Shackleton, Robert. *The Book of Chicago*. Philadelphia: Penn, 1920.

Shankland, Robert. *Steve Mather of the National Parks*. New York: Knopf, 1951.

Sharp, Dallas L. *The Better Country*. Boston: Houghton Mifflin, 1928.

Shaw, Milton M. *Nine Thousand Miles on a Pullman Train*. Philadelphia: Allen, Lane, and Scott, 1898.

Shepard, C. K. *Across America by Motor Cycle*. London: Longmans, Green, 1922.

Shepard, Paul, Jr. "The Cross Valley Syndrome." *Landscape* 10 (Autumn 1961): 4–8.

———. *Man in the Landscape: A Historic View of the Esthetics of Nature*. New York: Knopf, 1967.

———. "The Nature of Tourism." *Landscape* 5 (Summer 1955): 29–33.

Simonson, Wilber H. *Roadside Improvement*. Washington, D.C.: Bureau of Public Roads, 1934.

Sinclair Upton, *Oil!* New York: Grossett and Dunlap, 1926.

Smith, Henry J. *Chicago: A Portrait*. New York: Century, 1931.

Smith, Henry L. *Airways: The History of Commercial Aviation in the United States*. New York: Knopf, 1942.

Smith, Michael A., and Louis Turner. "Some Aspects of the Sociology of Tourism." *Society and Leisure* 5 (1973): 55–69.

Snow, J. Todd. "The New Road in the United States." *Landscape* 17 (Autumn 1967): 13–16.

Solberg, Carl. *Conquest of the Skies: A History of Commercial Aviation in America*. Boston: Little, Brown, 1979.

Stansfield, Charles A. "The Development of New Jersey Seashore Resorts." *Echoes of History* 5 (August 1975): 46–50.

Stearns, Myron M. "Notes on Changes in Motoring." *Harper's* 189 (September 1936): 441–44.

Steele, David M. *Going Abroad Overland*. New York: Putnam's, 1917.

———. *Vacation Journeys East and West*. New York: Putnam's, 1918.

Steinbeck, John. *Travels with Charley in Search of America*. New York: Bantam, 1962.

———. *The Wayward Bus*. New York: Viking, 1947.

Stevens, G. W. *The Land of the Dollar*. Edinburgh: Blackwood, 1897.

Stevens, William O. *Old Williamsburg and Her Neighbors*. New York: Dodd, Mead, 1938.

Stimson, Henry L. *My Vacations*. N.p.: author, 1949.

Stockett, Maria L. *America: First, Fast, and Furious*. Baltimore: Norman-Remington, 1930.

Strauss, Anselm L. *Images of the American City*. New Brunswick, N.J.: Transactions, 1976.

Street, Julian. *Abroad at Home*. New York: Century, 1914.

———. *American Adventures*. New York: Century, 1917.

Sullivan, Mark. *Our Times*. New York: Scribner's, 1923.

Sutton, Horace. *Travelers: The American Tourist from Stagecoach to Space Shuttle*. New York: Morrow, 1980.

Swanson, Ernst W. *Travel and the National Parks: An Economic Study*. Raleigh: North Carolina State University, 1969.

Taussig, Hugo A. *Retracing the Pioneers from West to East in an Automobile*. San Francisco: author, 1910.

Theroux, Paul. *The Old Patagonian Express: By Train through the Americas*. Boston: Houghton, Mifflin, 1979.

Thomas, Lawrence C. "Leisure Pursuits by Socio-economic Strata." *Journal of Educational Sociology* 29 (May 1956): 367–77.

Thomas, William S. *Trails and Tramps in Alaska and New Foundland*. New York: Putnam's, 1913.

Tilden, Freeman. *The National Parks: What They Mean to You and Me*. New York: Knopf, 1951.

———. *The State Parks: Their Meaning in American Life*. New York: Knopf, 1962.

Tobin, Gary A. "The Bicycle Boom of the 1890s: The Development of Private Transportation and the Birth of the Modern Tourist." *Journal of Popular Culture* 8 (Spring 1974): 838–49.

Todhunter, Roger. "Banff and the Canadian National Park Idea." *Landscape* 25 (Autumn 1981): 33–39.

Tombaugh, Larry (ed.). "Tourism and Mobility." *Landscape* 11 (Spring 1962): entire issue.

Tourbook: The Midland Trail. Grand Junction, Colo.: Midland Trails Logbook Co., 1916.

True, Wallace W. "Significant Trends in the Motel Industry." *Appraisal Journal* 27 (April 1959): 229.

Truettner, William H., and Robin Bolton-Smith. *National Parks and the American Landscape.* Washington, D.C.: Smithsonian Institution Press, 1972.

Tuan, Yi-Fu. "Visual Blight: Exercises in Interpretation." In *Visual Blight in America.* Edited by Pierce F. Lewis, David Lowenthal, and Yi-Fu Tuan. Washington, D.C.: Association of American Geographers, Resource Paper no. 23, 1973. Pp. 23–27.

Tunnard, Christopher, and Boris Pushkarev. *Man-Made America: Chaos or Control?* New Haven: Yale University Press, 1963.

Tyler, Poyntz. *American Highways Today.* New York: Wilson, 1957.

Ullman, Edward L. "Amenities as a Factor in Regional Growth." *Geographical Review* 44 (April 1954): 119–32.

Updike, John. *Rabbitt Run.* New York: Knopf, 1960.

U.S. Bureau of the Census. *Census of Business: 1935,* vol. 8, pt. 6, *Tourist Camps.* Washington, D.C.: 1937.

———. *Census of Business: 1939, Tourist Courts and Tourist Camps, Preliminary Summary.* Washington, D.C.: 1941.

———. *Historical Statistics to 1970.* Washington, D.C.: 1975.

———. *Historical Statistics of the United States: Colonial Times to 1970.* Washington, D.C.: 1961.

U.S. Bureau of Public Roads. *Highways and Economic and Social Changes.* Washington, D.C.: Government Printing Office, 1964.

U.S. Civilian Conservation Corps. *The Civilian Conservation Corps and Public Recreation.* Washington, D.C.: 1941.

U.S. Department of Interior. *Report of the Department of the Interior, 1919.* Washington, D.C.: 1919.

U.S. Department of Transportation. *Highway Statistics: Summary to 1965.* Washington, D.C.: Government Printing Office, 1965.

U.S. National Park Service. *The Economics of Public Recreation: An Economic Study of the Monetary Evaluation of Recreation in the National Parks.* Washington, D.C.: 1949.

———. *Park Road Standards.* Washington, D.C.: 1968.

———. *Park Structures and Facilities.* Washington, D.C.: 1935.

———. *Portfolio of Representative Structures Designed by Landscape Division, National Park Service.* Washington, D.C.: 1933.

U.S. Public Roads Administration. *Highway Practice in the United States.* Washington, D.C.: 1949.

———. *U.S. Travel: A Digest.* Washington, D.C.: 1949.

Urquhart, M. C., and K. A. H. Buckley (eds.). *Historical Statistics of Canada*. Cambridge, Ont.: MacMillan, 1965.

Vacation Travel Market of the United States: A Nationwide Survey, no. 1. Philadelphia: Curtis, 1950.

Vance, James. "California and the Search for the Ideal." *Annals, Association of American Geographers* 65 (June 1972): 185–210.

Van de Water, Frederic F. *The Family Flivvers to Frisco*. New York: Appleton, 1927.

Van Doren, Carlton S. *America's Park and Recreation Heritage: A Chronology*. Washington, D.C.: Bureau of Outdoor Recreation, 1975.

Van Dyke, John C. *The New New York*. New York: MacMillan, 1909.

Van Schaick, John, Jr. *Cruising Cross Country*. Boston: Universalist, 1926.

Veblen, Thorstein. *The Theory of the Leisure Class*. New York: Viking, 1967.

Venturi, Robert, Denise S. Brown, and Steven Izenour. *Learning from Las Vegas*. Cambridge, Mass.: M.I.T. Press, 1972.

Vernon, Paul E. *Coast to Coast by Motor*. London: Black, 1930.

Vincent, Stillman P. *Tourist Courts and Cabin Camps in Kansas*. Lawrence: University of Kansas School of Business, Kansas Studies in Business no. 23, 1948.

Voss, J. Ellis. *Summer Resort: An Ecological Analysis of a Satellite Community*. Philadelphia: author, 1941.

Waldron, Webb. *We Explore the Great Lakes*. New York: Century, 1923.

Wallis, Roland S. "Tourist Camps." *Engineering Extension Service Bulletin*. Ames: Iowa State College, vol. 21, no. 36 (February 7, 1923).

Waters, S. R. "The American Tourist." *Annals, American Academy of Political and Social Sciences* 46 (1966): 109–18.

Waugh, Robert E. *The American Traveler: More Darkness Than Light?* Austin: University of Texas Bureau of Business Research, 1962.

Weeden, Jeannie L. *Rhode Island to California by Motor*. Santa Barbara, Cal.: Pacific Coast, 1917.

Weinberger, Julius. "Economic Aspects of Recreation." *Harvard Business Review* 15 (Summer 1937): 448–63.

Westbrook, Margaret. *Highway Travelers: 68 Days on Southern Highways*. Los Angeles: Suttonhouse, 1939.

Westgard, A. L. *Tales of a Pathfinder*. New York: author, 1920.

————. *Through the Land of Yesterday: Our Glorious Southwest.* New York: author, 1915.

Wharton, Edith. *The Motor Flight through France.* New York: Scribner's, 1909.

Whibly, Charles. *American Sketches.* Edinburgh: Blackwood, 1908.

Whitaker, Samuel N. *Across the Continent in a Ford.* Grand Rapids, Mich.: Dean-Hicks, 1915.

White, Arthur S. *Palaces of the People: A Social History of Commercial Hospitality.* New York: Taplinger, 1970.

White, E. B. *Here is New York.* New York: Harper, 1949.

White, Harriet F. *A Woman's Tour in a Motor.* Philadelphia: Lippincott, 1911.

White, Rueul. "Social Class Differences in the Uses of Leisure." *American Journal of Sociology* 61 (September 1955): 145–50.

Whiteside, Clara W. *Touring New England.* Philadelphia: Penn, 1926.

Whyte, William Foote. "The Social Structure of the Restaurant." *American Journal of Sociology* 54 (January 1949): 302–10.

Wilby, Thomas W. *A Motor Tour through Canada.* London: Lane, 1914.

Willey, Day A. "Long Distance Runs by Automobile." *Travel* 14 (May 1909): 355–58.

Willey, Malcolm M., and Stuart A. Rice. "The Agencies of Communication." In *Recent Social Trends in the United States.* New York: McGraw-Hill, 1933.

Williamson, Ada C. *Touring New England.* Philadelphia: Penn, 1926.

Wilson, Samuel P. *Chicago by Gaslight.* [Chicago]: author, c. 1910.

Wilson, William B. *From the Hudson to the Ohio.* Philadelphia: Kensington, 1902.

Winn, Mary D. *The Macadam Trail: Ten Thousand Miles by Motor Coach.* New York: Knopf, 1931.

Wolfe, Ray I. "Recreational Travel: The New Migration." *Canadian Geographer* 10 (January 1966): 1–14.

————. "Summer Cottages in Ontario." *Economic Geography* 27 (January 1951): 10–32.

Wolfe, Thomas. *A Western Journal: A Daily Log of the Great Parks Trip, June 20–July 2, 1938.* Edited by Edward C. Aswell. Pittsburgh: University of Pittsburgh Press, 1951.

Wood, A. T., and B. R. Wood. *Ribbon Roads: A Motor Tour Abroad.* New York: Putnam's, 1910.

Wood, Ruth K. *The Tourist's California*. New York: Dodd, Mead, 1914.

——. *The Tourist's Maritime Provinces*. New York: Dodd, Mead, 1915.

Woody, Thomas. "Leisure in the Light of History." *Annals, American Academy of Political and Social Science* 113 (September 1957): 4–10.

INDEX

Butte, Mont., 33, 262

Calgary, Alb., 109, 239
Camden, N.J., 139
Camping, 11, 16, 69, 72–73, 76–
    77, 146, 152–63, 170, 187,
    304
Canada Highways Act of 1919,
    127
Canadian Pacific Railroad, 81, 90,
    96, 128, 239
Canandaigua, N.Y., 111
Canby, Henry, 19–20, 47
Cape May, N.J., 56
Carlsbad Caverns National Park,
    66
Caro, Robert, 138
Carroll, Charles, 294
Catskill Mountains, 63
Chance encounters, 36–39, 52,
    103, 306
Chapin, Roy, 105, 126
Charleston, S.C., 172, 214–15,
    263, 283, 298
Charleston, W.Va., 122
Charlottesville, Va., 115, 288
Chattanooga, Tenn., 125
Chester, Daniel, 290
Cheyenne, Wyo., 106, 228
Chicago, Burlington, and Quincy
    Railroad, 172
Chicago, Ill., 31, 36, 48–49, 85,
    91–92, 111, 117, 125, 175–
    76, 183, 188, 217, 226–27,
    249–50, 252–54, 258, 260,
    268–69, 272, 276–77, 278,
    282
Chorley, Kenneth, 297

Cincinnati, Ohio, 35
Cities, xii, 92, 193, 206, 243, 245–
    85, 302–4; approach to,
    91–95, 98–99, 246–48;
    bird's-eye views, 263,
    266–68, 284; central busi-
    ness districts, 272, 275;
    skylines, 98, 206, 248,
    263–66, 284, 287; sub-
    urbs, 207, 241, 281–82, 304
Citrine, Walter, 215, 258
City planning, 194
Civilian Conservation Corps, 72
Claremont, Calif., 240
Clawson, Marion, 10, 14
Cleveland, Ohio, 31, 36, 105, 111–
    12, 117, 131, 169, 276, 278
Climate, 10, 53, 187, 209, 218, 236,
    240–41
Cobb, Irvin, 8, 26, 41, 78–79, 135–
    36, 206, 209–10, 217, 228,
    231, 234, 255, 288, 297
Coeur d'Alene, Idaho, 158
Cohen, Eric, 3–5, 29
Collingwood, Ont., 94
Colonial Air Transport, 176–77
Colorado Springs, Colo., 49, 60
Columbia River Highway, 109,
    133
Columbus, Miss., 89
Concord, Mass., 290–92
Council for National Defense, 126
Conservation movement, 53, 68–
    70, 80–81, 83
Continental Trailways, 172
Craik, Kenneth, 5, 48
Crater Lake National Park, 70
Credit cards, 102